STILL
THE BEST
CONGRESS
MONEY
CAN BUY

STILL
THE BEST
CONGRESS
MONEY
CAN BUY

Philip M. Stern

REGNERY GATEWAY
WASHINGTON, D. C.

Library of Congress Cataloging-in-Publication Data

Stern, Philip M.
    Still the best Congress money can buy / Philip M. Stern.—Rev. ed.
      p. cm.
    Rev. ed. of: The best Congress money can buy. 1st ed. © 1988.
    Includes bibliographical references and index.
    ISBN 0-89526-527-3 (paper : alk. paper) : $12.95 (est.)
    1. Political action committees—United States. 2. Lobbying—United States. 3. Conflict of interests—United States. 4. United States. Congress. I. Stern, Philip M. Best Congress money can buy. II. Title.
JK1991.S734   1992
324'.4'0973—dc20
                                                92-8540
                                                 CIP

Published in the United States by
Regnery Gateway
1130 17th Street, NW
Washington, DC 20036

Distributed to the trade by
National Book Network
4720-A Boston Way
Lanham, MD 20706

Printed on acid free paper

Manufactured in the United States of America

10 9 8 7 6 5 4 3 2 1

This book is dedicated to my grandchildren who are (in order of appearance):

Margaret Nozuka
Jonathan Stern
Sandy Nozuka
George Nozuka
Philip Nozuka
Justin Nozuka
Ryan Stern
Henry Nozuka
and new baby Stern

ACKNOWLEDGMENTS

DISCERNING READERS WILL have little difficulty observing that these acknowledgments are written against a background of failing health.

First, thanks are due to my research assistant, Carrie Laughlin, to whom fell the responsibility of rooting out and checking the accuracy of the myriad facts in the book, as well as the painstaking task of preparing the source notes confirming each fact.

Her meticulousness, patience and thoroughness were all models of behavior.

Next, I owe unbounded gratitude to Anne A. Plaster, affectionately known to me over, lo, these ten years of our association, colleagueship and affectionate friendship as "Mz. P." She has been in all respects my faithful friend and right arm. I don't know what I would do without her. If there were an Olympic event in conscientious worrying of the best kind, I have no doubt that "Mz. P." would win the gold.

Next, I am grateful to the staff of the West End Branch of the District of Columbia Public Library, where I spent countless hours seeking refuge from the distraction of the telephone. Each member of that staff showed me such extraordinary kindness that each one deserves mention by name: Barbara Kubinski, Reynaldo Aparicio, Betsy Fowler, James Hudson, Nellie Salas and Stephanie Anderson.

Where are the words to express my appreciation for my debt to Susan Popkin Willens? I don't find them coming easily to the surface. All I can say is that few people have been as blessed as I in having a life-mate as exceptionally gifted, supporting and loving as

Susan. I have been fortunate indeed to be a part of her life, albeit briefly.

One of her prime attributes and gifts are her skills as a teacher. My father, although not a religious man, believed that each person has an afterlife, palpable and measurable, consisting of all those he or she touched, for better or worse, during his or her lifetime and who lived on afterwards. Measured in those terms, Susan Willens is going to have an enviably rich afterlife, in the myriad students she has taught during her career.

I am one of the beneficiaries of her teaching gifts, just as I have been a beneficiary of her gift for love, affection and support.

And how do I acknowledge sufficiently my debt to my friend, helper, and teammate Jorge? What would I do without him and his patience? I wish I could count the number of steps up which he has pulled me and my wheelchair to gain access to one semi-unattainable place after another.

And then there is Elizabeth, who has responded to my outrageously frequent and often inconsistent nocturnal requests for help with patience often approaching sainthood.

Much of the information emanated from the Center for Responsive Politics, headed by the excellent Ellen Miller and her fine staff, especially those number-crunching geniuses, Larry Makinson and Joshua Goldstein.

Instantaneous statistics were obtained from the National Library on Money & Politics, ably staffed by Ann Driscoll and Matthew Costello.

Finally, this book and I owe an enormous debt of gratitude to my journalist-hero, Brooks Jackson, who formerly covered the campaign finance "beat" for the *Wall Street Journal*. Invariably knowledgeable and enterprising, yet skeptical to the end.

CONTENTS

FOREWORD

By Senator William Proxmire

Senator Proxmire's comments were written after a review of this book's predecessor, The Best Congress Money Can Buy, *published in 1987 by Pantheon Books.*

SPECIAL INTERESTS ARE buying your national government. They're paying millions for it. And they're getting billions of dollars of rip-offs in return. In *The Best Congress Money Can Buy*, Philip Stern dramatically proves this thesis.

For instance, Stern reports that through its various political action committees (PACs), American Telephone and Telegraph (AT&T) contributed nearly $1.4 million to congressional candidates between 1979 and 1986. Congress paid AT&T off with tax savings totaling $12 billion. So—as Stern figures—AT&T's PAC contributions earned a return of 867,145%!

But, as Stern writes, AT&T was not alone. Using the same kind of calculations, General Electric got a 673,759% return for their PAC investment. And Sears enjoyed a 510,581% pay off. Of course all those multibillion dollar payoffs came out of your pocket and the pockets of the other American taxpayers.

A few years ago the Director of the Realtors Political Action Committee in a moment of frankness, told a *Wall Street Journal* reporter: "When I make a contribution from my PAC, I buy legislation." Dwell on the significance of that statement for a minute. This is precisely what PAC contributions do. Why do PACs exist? They exist to permit legalized bribery. The special interests who offer the contribution from a PAC intend it as a bribe, that is to "buy legislation." Congressional candidates who accept the contribution understand the intention and one way or another, they consistently deliver.

The pay-off may be as obvious and overt as a floor vote in favor of the contributor's desired tax loophole or appropriation. Or it may be subtle. The pay-off may come in a floor speech not delivered. It may take the form of a bill pigeonholed in subcommittee by a PAC bribe-receiving chairman, or by an amendment not offered by an opponent of the PAC's over-all interests.

The bribe may silence a contributor's opponent in the private party caucus from which the media is excluded. Unlike floor sessions, these party caucuses are heavily attended, and attendance makes the difference. Generally one caucus speech is worth ten floor speeches. Members can be frank. Nothing is recorded. The press and public don't hear a word. Or the pay-off can come in a private conversation with four or five key colleagues in the privacy of the cloak room. When voting is heavy and steady on the floor, these informal conferences are where a great deal of influence is exerted with no public knowledge.

So the member of Congress receiving the PAC bribe may take no overt action that is ever reported. But the bribe pay-off takes place. The bribing PAC official knows it. The bribed member of Congress knows it. But you as a member of the public never know it.

This book explodes the illusion that most of the big campaign contributions go to lawmakers who believe in the donor's principles. The big contributions are far more often becoming a transparent bribe—as in the case of gifts to lawmakers who don't even have an opponent! And it's a bribe that consistently wins a pay-off.

How else explain the fact that $8 out of $9 contributed by the fastest growing source of campaign money—corporate PACs—have gone to incumbents and most of it to Democratic incumbents? Does anyone really believe these hard headed business PAC managers favor the Democrats' espousing of taxation based on ability to pay? Do these PAC directors really want to help members of Congress who put environmental protection ahead of low-cost business operation? Are these big business PAC directors pushing contributions to committee chairmen who put consumer protection ahead of their own corporation profits because they want to reduce their corporation's profits?

Of course not. The answer is that the business PACs have the big money. The liberal Democrats occupy the power positions in Congress and most of them enjoy a virtually sure ride to re-election. So the bribe goes to the sure winner regardless of the member's record or philosophy. The pay-off comes when the members of Congress use their power to make just a "little" change in the tax law. That "little" change may save the corporation contributing through its PAC a hundred million dollars, or even a billion dollars or more. A slight modification of wording in an environmental protection bill frequently saves the contributing corporation a thousand dollars or more for every dollar contributed.

Not only does Stern tell of PAC contributions to candidates who have no opponent, he also describes contributions by the *same* PAC to both opposing candidates in a close race. He writes of contributions to one candidate during a campaign, and if that candidate suffers a surprising loss, there's a switch: an after-the-election contribution to the winner.

The Best Congress Money Can Buy also makes solid recommendations for correcting this deplorable situation. Stern strongly recommends public financing of campaigns, as we already have for Presidential elections. Public financing is essential to provide the basis for effectively limiting both the amount spent in the campaign and sharply reducing the size of personal campaign contributions as well as PAC contributions.

Stern's appendices are by themselves well worth the price of this book and then some. Do you wonder how your own senators and your own congressman stack up in receiving political action committee money? In appendices A & B Stern lists the amount of PAC contributions to every incumbent member of Congress, House or Senate, in their last four elections. These appendices include: the contributions received from PACs, the left over cash received in total, and each member's "conflict of interest" receipts.

Appendix C is another eye opener. It tells the dollar contributions of the 100 largest political action committees.

Philip Stern has done more to expose corruption in American politics than anyone including Lincoln Steffens. *The Best Congress Money Can Buy* comes after previous Stern blockbusters including *The Great Treasury Raid*, *The Shame of a Nation* and *The Rape of the Taxpayer*.

If you can read only one, this book is it.

FOREWORD

By Senator Barry Goldwater

WHEN MR. STERN interviewed me for the hardback edition of this book, I told him that my first statewide race for the U.S. Senate in 1952 had cost $45,000. At the time we talked, I estimated that if I wanted to run again in 1986, I would have to raise at least $3 million—sixty times what it cost me in 1952. Even taking account of inflation and the rise in the state's population since 1952, the cost of campaigning has skyrocketed since I first ran.

That fact alone, I am convinced, is producing ruinous effects on American lawmakers and their capacity to legislate in the national interest.

Just think what the soaring cost of campaigning means.

First, it means that politicians are constantly preoccupied—maybe obsessed is the right word—with raising money. It wasn't that way forty years ago. Then, United States Senators didn't have to worry about fundraising until a year or two before their next elections. That is, during the first four or five years of their terms, they could devote more or less full time and attention to their legislative duties. No longer. Virtually the day after senators are elected, they must start scrambling to raise money for their next race, even though that is a full six years away. I am all too painfully aware of that: I am constantly bombarded by newly-elected senators to participate in one or another fundraising event.

That obsession with money causes elected officials to spend more time raising money than attending to their public duties. By fostering the growth of special-interest groups, each with its particular interest, the money-obsession distracts legislators from their one pre-eminent duty: to serve the *national* interest. Who ever dreamed that the Oral and Maxillofacial Surgeons would have its own political action committee? Even the sugar industry is divided into such sub-interest groups as the crystal sugar growers, the Florida sugar cane growers, and the Great Lakes sugar beet growers. Believe it or not, the Smokeless Tobacco Council has its own PAC!

Lawmakers tend to become paralyzed with the fear of alienating this or that interest group, lest those groups withhold sorely needed dollars. Senators and representatives, faced incessantly with the need to raise ever more funds to fuel their campaigns, can scarcely avoid weighing their every decision against the question, "How will this affect my fundraising prospects?" rather than "How will this affect the national interest?" I don't blame the candidates for that; I blame the system that permits limitless escalation of campaign costs and spending.

The task of raising millions of dollars also discourages able and public-spirited men and women from running for public office. To cite but two examples: former Senator Eagleton of Missouri told Mr. Stern that he decided, after his 1980 race, that he would never again subject himself to what he called "tin-cupping it" across the nation. And in Florida, former Governor Reuben Askew withdrew from the Senate race—even though he was the unquestioned front-runner at the time—because of the fundraising burden he would have to carry. Again, I don't blame such people. Asking people for money is a demeaning, totally unrewarding task. But the nation pays dearly if able and experienced people who would make fine senators or representatives refrain from public office because they have to raise so much money. The Founding Fathers would frown in their graves if they saw us rationing candidacies sheerly on the basis of money: who has—or can raise—the millions necessary to run for office.

Democracy suffers in another way: when candidates must spend the bulk of their time raising money—especially when they have to go outside their home states or districts to do it—that takes away from the time they can spend talking with, and listening to, the voters of their states or districts.

All these problems are laid out clearly in this thought-provoking book. You don't have to agree with all Mr. Stern's solutions—and I disagree with many of them—to conclude that the sheer cost of running for office is having a corrosive effect not only on American politics but on the quality of American government, and that something must be done to liberate candidates from their dependence on special-interest money.

Intro ?

A CAUTIONARY SCENARIO

THROUGHOUT THIS BOOK you will read of campaign contributions or other favors by interested parties to lawmakers that may or may not affect their official conduct.

As you will see, almost invariably these gifts are accompanied by denials on the lawmakers' part that the contribution or favor had any effect whatever on their subsequent actions.

Each time such a denial appears in this book, reference is made to this page and its imaginary scenario,* so that readers can appraise the credibility of the lawmaker's disclaimer:

The scene: Yankee Stadium. The setting: the seventh, and deciding, game of the World Series. On this game hangs the world championship.

The pitcher completes his warm-up, then walks to the plate and does something that stuns the over 57,000 people who fill every seat of the stadium. In plain view of all 57,000, he reaches into his pocket and proceeds, methodically, to count out, and place into the umpire's outstretched palm, one hundred crisp new hundred-dollar bills— $10,000 in all.

This done, he walks back to the mound. The umpire pockets the $10,000, takes his position behind the plate, and says, "Play ball."

For a few instants, the fans sit in unbelieving silence. Then the stadium erupts. With ten thousand dollars of the pitcher's money tucked away in his pocket, is it *conceivable* that the umpire's judgment

---

* For which I am indebted to former Democratic Senator William Proxmire of Wisconsin.

xix

will be totally unaffected by the pitcher's money and that he will be able to be objective in calling the pitches that emanate from that pitcher's arm?

None of the fans on hand that day believes so. So strong is their disbelief that they throw everything they can lay their hands on at the umpire—and at the pitcher who gave the money. Then, in protest, they empty the stands. The game is postponed.

Later, in a massively attended press conference the umpire emphatically denies that his judgment has been in any way affected by the pitcher's gift. But, in all the land, not a reporter or a newspaper—nor, for that matter, a single baseball fan—can be found that believes him.

PREFACE

THIS BOOK—OR, at any rate, my passion about the importance of money in politics—dates back to the mid-Fifties. A friend called and asked me to attend a meeting to raise money for a liberal Democratic member of the Senate Commerce Committee. As it developed, at the last minute, I couldn't attend the fundraising meeting, and a few days later, I called my friend to apologize. "Oh, that's all right," he said, "X agreed to raise money from the airlines and Y said he would take care of the truckers and Z promised to cover the highway people. So I think we're all set."

I suppose I was naive, but I couldn't believe what I was hearing. Here was a senator I had considered highly principled *soliciting money from the very interest groups he was supposed to be regulating!* If that was the way this liberal Democrat got his money, I wondered how much money more business-minded and less punctilious senators must be getting from those same interest groups. A hell of a way to run a country, I thought.

And that's how this book, and its predecessor, began.

In ensuing years, that incident stuck in my mind, and the subject of campaign finance reform continued to preoccupy me. In 1962, I wrote a cover article in *Harper's Magazine* proposing a plan for government financing of federal election campaigns, much like the one enacted for presidential campaigns twelve years later, and similar to the proposal for "citizen financing" of all federal election campaigns set forth in Chapter 11 of this book.

From 1973 to 1987, I engaged my energies in various reform activities. In 1973, as the Watergate revelations began to unfold and congressional interest in the campaign finance reform bubbled up, I founded the Center for Public Financing of Campaigns, a lobbying and coalition-building organization that played a significant part in the enactment of the presidential public-financing provisions of the 1974 campaign-reform law. Eleven years later, I started Citizens Against PACs, a bipartisan citizens' group that published prominent advertisements in hometown newspapers setting forth the PAC record of the local representatives.

Early in 1987, I set aside my other reform activities to research and write *The Best Congress Money Can Buy*, which was published by Pantheon in mid-1988. I was prompted to do so in part by this striking fact: fewer than one-third of the American people even understood what a political action committee was, much less appreciated the danger the PACs posed for representative democracy.

Some—especially members of Congress—may think that this book's title and that of its predecessor (which originated with Will Rogers) unfairly portrays the U.S. Congress. Most members, they will say, are unwilling to let campaign contributions influence their conduct, and only a few are venal. (Venal or not, it is notable that when the Center for Responsive Politics, a Washington research group, interviewed members of Congress in 1987, fully one-fifth acknowledged that political contributions affected their votes on legislation.) One political scientist implored me not to use this title, arguing that it would only add to the already growing cynicism about politicians and about Congress.

But it is the facts in this book, each one meticulously documented (see the lengthy source notes at the end of the book) that give rise to inferences of impropriety. All too often, the public record shows that Senator X or Representative Y received a campaign contribution or honorarium from Interest Group A and then did (or had already done) as Group A desired. Or Lawmaker X or Y, a member of, say, a banking committee or a defense-related committee, received favors from banking interests or defense contractors. If senators and representatives resent the implications of impropriety that those facts invite, let those lawmakers change the current campaign finance laws so as to prohibit such conflicts of interest.

This book deals only with the problems of financing congressional campaigns; the matter of paying for presidential campaigns is mentioned only tangentially, for several reasons. For one thing, Congress has already enacted public funding of presidential campaigns. The benefits of that reform have been, in large part, undone by the "soft money" loophole, discussed in Chapter 10. Second, contributions by political action committees play a miniscule part in presidential campaigns. PAC money comprised 1.4 percent of the total spent in the 1988 presidential election.

Moreover, even though presidential primary candidates must still raise millions of dollars of private money, the very enormity of their campaign budgets limits the influence that any individual gift can buy. In presidential campaigns, a $1,000 contribution is so commonplace that the recipient is likely to be unaware of it. By contrast, a $1,000 contribution in a House campaign is vastly more conspicuous and therefore stands a much better chance of gaining the candidate's attention and appreciation.

So it is in the congressional arena—the subject of this book—that the need for reform is most urgent.

Many opponents of campaign finance reform argue that there is no need for a wholesale outlawing of PACs as long as the PACs have to disclose how much they are giving to whom. The best hope, say these observers, lies in bringing campaign finance out into the sunshine.

Well, obviously those who argue thus have never tried to write a book about campaign finance—for often, in the course of researching this book, I have been struck by how difficult it is to get at the truth of who gave what to whom in hopes of what.

For example, here's a simple question: how much in campaign contributions have PACs of the leading Wall Street brokerage firms given the senators on the banking committee (which regulates Wall Street) over the six years of their present terms? That *ought* to be fairly simple to discover, since the Federal Election Commission maintains all the data on PAC contributions on computers. But for a time, due to "budgetary constraints," the PAC information was available on computer only back through 1983. To get information prior to that, you had to go in person to the FEC and copy the information from microfilm records—at best a monumental chore.

Even with complete PAC data, you have rooted out only a part of the picture. For example, as described in Chapter 8, certain Wall Street firms were singularly successful in mobilizing their executives to make *individual* contributions to the likes of New York Republican Senator Alfonse D'Amato, especially when he chaired the banking subcommittee most concerned with securities regulation. By law, candidates are required to report the employer or the occupation of their large donors, but all too often, that information is missing from their reports. Getting the full truth, then, requires combing through each of the thousands of names on senators' contributions list over the six years of their term.

Moreover, until recently, you still lacked an important piece of the puzzle: the honoraria that interest groups paid lawmakers as speaking fees (or merely for dropping in briefly on a Washington breakfast). Because senators and representatives could legally pocket these speaking fees, more and more interest groups found the honorarium, recently barred by both Senate and House rules, a more effective (and often a cheaper) way of getting a lawmaker's attention than a campaign contribution, which could only be put in the legislator's campaign treasury, rather than in her or his bank account. The trouble is, information about who paid how much in honoraria to whom was only tardily available, and was no where computerized. To ascertain the data about honoraria received by U.S. senators, you had to journey to Capitol Hill and copy out the information by hand, senator by senator, year by year. Try getting *that* information on the leading Wall Street firms for all the senators on the banking committee for the past six years!

In these pages, I sometimes (as in Chapters 3 and 7) bemoan congressional victories by small interest groups such as the dairy farmers or the auto dealers over far more numerous groups such as auto buyers and dairy consumers. Lest the reader conclude that I am an absolute majoritarian, I am not. I recognize—and deplore—tyrannies of the majority (as when an inflamed majority brought about the internment of the Japanese-Americans at the outset of World War II). I also favor government assistance to the poor and the handicapped, even though those groups constitute only a tiny minority of the voting population whose causes would be defeated on any congressional vote that followed strict one-person-one-vote lines. What I object to is the use of *money*—especially money aggregated by political action committees in a manner not available to inchoate groups like consumers and the poor—to magnify the political influence of small groups, thereby distorting representative democracy.

In recent years, I have become increasingly troubled about the way modern candidates allow themselves to be merchandised like detergent or beer, taking their cues from marketing experts (that is, sophisticated pollsters), media consultants, and political mercenaries who, far from being homegrown, often direct an Iowa candidate's campaign strategy from behind a distant desk in Washington, Boston or New York. Many who share my concern about the merchandising of candidates point the finger at the mounting piles of money available to run campaigns. Why, then, is this not a campaign finance problem? Why, in view of my own concerns, is it not explicitly discussed in this book?

Tempted though I have often been to vent my disquiet in these pages, about the use of high-tech politics (especially the 30-second TV spot) to oversimplify and/or distort issues, I have concluded that the problem of technology and the problem of money are two separate topics. That is, even if candidates got all of their money from heaven (or from the U.S. Treasury, as the citizen funding I propose in Chapter 11), rather than from special-interest groups, they could still spend it on pollsters and media consultants and professional campaign managers, and there would be nothing to stop them from using that money to buy distorted TV commercials.

As others have pointed out, the problem does not lie in the *amount* of money spent on politics (about as much as Americans spend on soft drinks in eight days). The problem lies with the *source* of the money, and the extent to which campaign money comes from people and groups with axes to grind.

In the course of conducting the interviews of current and former members of Congress that constitute Chapter 5, I was struck by the contrast between two interviews that, by chance, fell on the same day, April 21, 1987.

During the morning, I talked with former Senator Thomas Eagleton of Missouri, who said that immediately after his 1980 campaign, during which he was obliged to "tin-cup it"—"begging for money literally from Maine to Hawaii"—he resolved not to subject himself to that demeaning experience again. Therefore, he observed, his final six years in the Senate were years of freedom, of not having to weigh each substantive decision against the background of past obligations or future gain or loss. "When Mr. X came in to see me," he said, "I didn't have to put money on the scale, and say, 'How does this factor out in fundraising?'"

Just a few hours later, I spoke with Democratic Senator Kent Conrad of North Dakota. Conrad had been elected only a few months earlier. He would not face the voters again for another six years. Yet when I asked him whether he had started raising money for that 1992 campaign, he replied, "Absolutely."

What a contrast, I thought, between Senator Eagleton's six years of freedom from the money chase to Senator Conrad's prospective enslavement to pursuing every campaign dollar. I do not intend any disparagement of Senator Conrad's character. On the contrary, he appears to have demonstrated unusual independence in the conduct of the public offices he held before coming to the Senate. Yet by his own acknowledgment that he had already begun his quest for re-election funds, it was clear that fundraising would seldom be far from his thoughts.

If that were the case, that should not be. Senator Conrad deserves better. So does the country. That is why I believe so passionately in providing House and Senate candidates with an alternative of "disinterested" money, via expanding the existing citizen funding of presidential elections to cover congressional campaigns, as proposed in Chapter 11.

The central theme of this book is that money determines far too many factors in American politics today.

Far too often, money determines who shall run for office.

Much too often, money is a preoccupation (or an obsession) in the minds of candidates and lawmakers.

Yet that prime determinant, money, is a poor tool of democracy, for money is indifferent to truth and to justice, since it is, essentially, unjustly distributed.

The late U.S. Appellate Court Judge J. Skelly Wright, who wrote eloquently on the subject of campaign finance reform, as on other topics, quoted Anatole France who once observed that, "The law, in its majestic equality, permits the rich as well as the poor to sleep under bridges, to beg in the streets and steal bread."

Judge Wright continues, "A latter-day Anatole France might well write, after observing American election campaigns, 'The law, in its majestic equality, allows the poor as well as the rich to form political action committees, to purchase the most sophisticated polling, media and direct mail techniques and to drown out each other's voices by overwhelming expenditures in political campaigns.'"

"Financial inequities," concludes Judge Wright, "pose a pervasive and growing threat to the principle of 'one person, one vote' and undermine the political proposition to which this nation is dedicated—that all men are created equal."

STILL
THE BEST
CONGRESS
MONEY
CAN BUY

 *Chapter One*

THE CAMPAIGN MONEY CRISIS

CONSIDER THESE TWO statements:

> We cannot turn our democracy over to an aristocracy of money. Yet year by year we are insidiously chopping away at the ability of any citizen to enter the political arena regardless of his or her economic status or ability to raise money.

> Unlimited campaign spending eats at the heart of the democratic process.
> It feeds the growth of special-interest groups created solely to channel money into political campaigns.
> It creates the impression that every candidate is bought and owned by the biggest givers.
> And it causes the elected officials to devote more time to raising money than to their public duties.

Neither of those speakers is the kind of person you would expect to hear bemoaning an "aristocracy of money" or excoriating "special interest" groups.

The first, Senator Robert C. Byrd of West Virginia, is a centrist Democrat; the second, former Senator Barry Goldwater of Arizona, is the one-time standard-bearer of conservative Republicans and one of the few who, as recently as 1985, favored a repeal of the widely accepted law providing public funding of presidential elections.

The two represent opposing political parties and sharply differing political philosophies.

But they have two things in common: both have witnessed the impact of money on Congress and the political process from the inside. And both now see an urgent need for campaign finance reform.

Their accord on this point is one measure of the crisis in the way America pays for its congressional election campaigns.

America pays a terrible price for the present method of paying for election campaigns. Among the principal costs:

- The American ideal of candidacy for public office being open to all citizens regardless of wealth or station is negated. Instead, candidacy is confined by *money*—limited to those who have it or can raise it.
- Competition for congressional seats—especially in the House—has been all but eliminated, as incumbents outraise and outspend challengers nearly four to one and, on average, over 97 percent of House members who seek re-election win.
- "Carpet bagging" has returned to the American political scene, in the sense that many members of Congress (again, especially in the House) get a majority of their political funds, not from their constituents, but from outsiders who are not even allowed to vote for them on election day.
- Legalized corruption is woven into Congress. Flagrant conflicts of interest, prohibited in both the judicial and the executive branch, are not only legal, but are commonplace on Capitol Hill.
- The basic constitutional concept of one-person/one vote has been substantially eroded as money enables small but well-organized and well-financed groups to carry the day over groups far more numerous but far less endowed and cohesive (see, for

example, how 200,000 dairy farmers carried the day over, and imposed colossal costs on, tens of millions of dairy consumers [p. 171]).

- The spectrum of views offered to the voters becomes ever narrower, as the candidates and their respective political parties owe their financial allegiance to the same narrow group of funders. That would be a plausible explanation for the increasingly dismal voter turnout, since it would be reasonable if, as a result of this "tweedle-dum, tweedle-dee" similarity between parties' and the candidates' platforms, the voters adopted a "why-should-I-care?" attitude and stayed away from the polls.

- The time and attention of lawmakers and candidates are ever more consumed by the demeaning task of raising money (primarily from out-of-state "fat-cats") rather than with attending to legislative duties or meeting and listening to their own voters.

- And all these costs mount progressively as candidates and their advisers, growingly fearful of being outspent, engage in "arms races," ratcheting up the amounts they raise and spend.

The result may be summed up thus: *money-power has replaced people-power as the driving force in American politics and the determinant of electoral victory.*

The "special interest groups created solely to channel money into political campaigns," to which Senator Goldwater referred, are many and they span the economic and social spectrum: labor unions, corporations, trade associations such as the realtors and the American Medical Association, and even the dairy farmers. They also include groups not ordinarily thought of as "special interest," such as environmental and pro-peace groups.

These interest groups exert their financial and political muscle in two ways: contributions from political action committees, or PACs, and gifts from *individuals* connected with the interest group in some fashion: typically executives or employees of companies in the affected industry, or members of the affected trade association.

Recently, public attention has been focused mainly on PACs.*
This attention is understandable for two reasons: first, PACs pour
tens of millions of dollars into the campaign coffers of federal
candidates; second, Federal records make it easier to identify the
interest group connected with each PAC.

But, increasingly, as you will see, interest groups have been
exercising their clout via gifts from well-heeled members of their
organization—i.e., doctors or dentists or realtors. Often—all too
often, say critics of the existing political system—these individual
contributors are spouses—*or even minor children*—of, say, a company executive, raising the suspicion that the money for these
family members' contributions really comes from the executives
themselves. For example, skeptics raise an eyebrow when they spot
a $1,000 contribution from someone who lists herself as "house-
wife" on government reporting forms. (For example, Mrs. Vernon
Clark, the wife of former billboard trade association executive
Vernon Clark, contributed the impressive total of over $17,000 to
lawmakers in the 1990 cycle.)

Neither factions nor special-interest money are new to American
politics. In *Federalist No.10*, James Madison warned of the dangers
of factionalism. From William McKinley's 1896 election, financed
largely by special assessments on corporations, to Richard Nixon's
1972 campaign, to which corporations made illegal contributions,
business interests have sought to use their financial might to sway
elections. Beginning in the 1930's, organized labor began efforts to
offset business influence.

But suddenly, in the last two decades, three new developments
have converged on the American political scene:

First, *new legal limits on rich givers* ($1,000 per election, per
candidate, $25,000 per year to all federal candidates combined)
mean that office-seekers can no longer finance their campaigns by

---

* The history and nature of the PACs and their methods of operation are described more
fully in the next chapter.

turning to a few wealthy givers such as insurance mogul W. Clement Stone, who contributed $2.1 million to Richard Nixon's 1972 campaign, but must look elsewhere to raise their money.

Second, *soaring campaign costs* result from *the advent of high-tech political campaigns*, with their expensive polls, well-paid consultants, costly direct-mail—and, above all, hugely expensive television, the indispensable political communicator that devours all the dollars politicians will feed it.

So campaign costs have shot up alarmingly. For example, in 1978, the major-party candidates for the U.S. Senate in South Dakota spent a total of $602,000. Just eight years later, the figure was up more than elevenfold to $6,777,000. Between 1976 and 1990, the cost of an average House campaign rose nearly fivefold, the average Senate campaign over sixfold (see Chapter 2). Today, a U.S. senator must, on average raise $12,405 a week, every week, *during his or her entire six-year term*.

As a result, politicians are increasingly obsessed with money. Their preoccupation was compounded in 1976, when the Supreme Court banned compulsory ceilings on campaign spending. Thus, even "safe" candidates, ever fearful of being outspent, are never free of the money-raising fixation.

With politicians desperate for more and more money, enters now a third force: *the political action committees*. PACs have the perfect answer for satisfying candidates' hunger by *aggregating* money and using their funds, often unsolicited, in amounts, and to numbers of candidates, in a manner far beyond the reach of individual citizens.

This power to pool political money makes the PACs particularly enticing to politicians in frantic search of short-cuts. The PACs, proffering gifts of $5,000 (and even $10,000 to candidates who have both a primary and a general election contest), offer tempting paths of least resistance.

The PACs' allure is the prime cause of a disturbing trend: representatives and senators are becoming more and more indebted to outside special-interest PACs. Thus, lawmakers obligate them-

---

* Statistics detailing this upward trend appear in Chapter 2.

selves, morally at least, to accord favored treatment to those PACs' lobbyists, even though those lobbyists are not permitted to vote in their elections. In 1990, for 236 representatives—over half the U.S. House—more than 50 percent of their campaign funds came from outside political action committees rather than from their own constituents. (Detailed information on which lawmakers are thus obligated to PACs for their funds appear in appendices A and B.) Many lawmakers got 60 or 80 percent of their funds in this manner.

The U.S. Constitution calls them "representatives." But when lawmakers are obligated to outsiders for 60 percent or 80 percent of their campaign funds, whom do they *really* represent? For example, when, over a six-year period, a representative like Banking Committee member Stephen L. Neal, a North Carolina Democrat, accepts over a third of a million dollars from banking interests, is he the representative of his North Carolina congressional district? Or is he the representative of the banking industry?

The capacity to aggregate money, the crucial *new* element the PACs have introduced, endows interest groups with two new and important powers:

First, it enables them to magnify their group's political influence without relationship to the numbers of their members or the merits of their arguments.

Second, it allows the group to impose huge costs on the rest of the public. For example, every time you buy milk or butter at the supermarket, you are a victim of artificially high prices resulting from a single measure approved by Congress. In September, 1985, the U.S. House of Representatives voted on an issue—the dairy subsidy—that squarely pitted the interests of tens of millions of dairy *consumers* against those of, at most, 200,000 dairy *farmers*. On a strict one-person-one-vote reckoning—that is, if each person counted equally in each representative's political calculation—the tens of millions of consumers and taxpayers should have decisively defeated those 200,000 farmers in that House vote. But that was not the result. Instead, the dairy farmers prevailed by a margin of 78 votes.

Something, apparently, had thwarted one-person-one-vote democracy. The raw evidence suggests that at least a *part* of that something was money—$12 million collected by three huge dairy cooperatives and distributed, over eight years, to hundreds of representatives—not just rural legislators but big-city representatives, *some of whom do not have a single dairy cow in their districts.* * Of those who received $30,000 or more, all voted with the dairy lobby in 1985; of those who received $2,500 to $10,000, 60 percent did; of those receiving nothing, only 23 percent did (see table on page 166).

Many PAC defenders argue that with more than 4,000 countervailing PACs, the special interests tend to balance each other out. But is that really the case?

Consider, for example, the line-up of forces as the House of Representatives prepared to vote that September afternoon. On one side stood the dairy farmers, comparatively few in number, but each with a significant stake in the outcome of that vote, well organized through their cooperatives, and with a highly effective means of collecting, pooling and distributing political money (described in more detail on page 171).

On the other side were tens of millions of consumers and taxpayers, large in number but each with a comparatively tiny stake in the dairy subsidy. More important, *they have no means of communicating with one another or for collecting and pooling money to give to politicians.*

The thwarting of the one-person-one-vote principle is illustrated in an even more dramatic fashion on the issue of a cut in the capital gains tax rate. Sixty percent of the savings from this tax cut would benefit the top one percent of the population. Who can doubt that if lawmakers cast their legislative votes on a strict one-person-one-vote calculation, the capital gains tax cut would be resoundingly defeated? But with political money in the picture, the calculus changes. According to a *Washington Post* report, many Democratic

---

* For example, in the years 1979 through 1986, a leading recipient of dairy lobby contributions was Rep. Martin Frost of Dallas, who has, at most, three dairy *farmers* in his district—compared to some 527,000 dairy *consumers*.

lawmakers told House Majority Leader Dick Gephardt that they could not oppose the tax cut "because it would anger their financial backers." One party leader told the *Post* that a number of Democrats had put it even more cynically, saying, "*I get elected by voters, [but] I get financed by contributors.* (Emphasis added.) Voters don't care about this. Contributors do."

Kansas Republican Senator Robert Dole summed up the unevenness of many congressional battles. "You might get a different result if there were a 'Poor-PAC' " on Capitol Hill.

But there *is* no Poor-PAC. There is no Consumer PAC.

Nor is there a PAC representing the interests of the average taxpayer. Most large corporations and other special-interest organizations have a Washington lobbyist or a PAC or both. But other more inchoate groups, such as dairy consumers, the poor, or average taxpayers, have no PAC and no paid lobbyist to plead for, say, lower dairy prices or tax fairness.

Consider, for example, this anomaly: the U.S. tax law obliges tens of millions of taxpayers to pay 10 to 30 percent of their incomes to the Internal Revenue Service every April. By contrast, in one or more of the years 1982 through 1985, 130 large corporations—including General Electric, the nation's sixth largest—contrived, through adroit use of tax loopholes enacted by Congress, to not pay a penny of tax on their billions of dollars of profits.*

This produced an irony, which Illinois Democratic Senator Paul Simon summed up when he declared, "The astonishing result is that the janitor at General Electric pays more taxes than GE."

But the plight of the GE janitor, who has no PAC, is lost sight of in the Washington influence-peddling game, which is increasingly winked at and laughed about by influence-buyers and sellers alike.

For example, the GE janitor did not loom large in the minds of the several hundred people—mainly lobbyists—who each paid $500 in June, 1985 to pay tribute to Illinois' Dan Rostenkowski, the Democratic chairman of the committee that handles all tax legislation, the House Ways and Means Committee.

---

* This taxlessness was achieved prior to the enactment of the Tax Reform Act of 1986, which closed many corporate tax loopholes and reduced the number of tax-free corporations from 130 to 7.

The main speaker was the then Speaker, Tip O'Neill. He beamed over the audience. "Danny," he said, "this is really marvelous. All this for just a little piece of legislation—which might or might not get to the [House] floor."

The crowd roared with laughter.

Why were they laughing? They knew that this fund-raising party was not about "just a little piece of legislation." It was about the most sweeping tax-loophole-closing measure in memory—the Reagan tax reform program, unveiled only months earlier. Tens of billions of dollars were at stake.

The lobbyists in the audience also knew that Dan Rostenkowski needed campaign money about as much as the Sultan of Brunei needs scholarship money for his children's schooling. Rostenkowski was and is a political fixture in his north Chicago congressional district, typically winning by a four-to-one margin.

So everyone—the Speaker, Rostenkowski, those in the audience—everyone knew what this fund-raiser was *really* about. It was about buying insurance, to be sure to get and stay on the good side of the King. In blunter terms, it was buying access to a crucial ear for that critical few seconds in the legislative process when that access might mean success or failure for a lobbyist.

Those in the audience might have suspected that Congressman Rostenkowski, being both a prodigious fund-raiser and a sure-fire winner who need spend very little on his campaigns, had built up an immense campaign surplus which he may be able to transfer to his own bank account when he leaves Congress, provided he does so prior to January 1, 1993—to act, in effect, as his personal pension fund. At the time of that 1985 fundraising party, Rostenkowski had ended his previous campaign with $593,000 left over in his campaign treasury, the fourth highest in the U.S. House. As of December 31, 1989,* it had climbed to $1.052 million.

Moreover, in 1990, Rostenkowski was by far the House's leading

---

* The actual cutoff date under the most recent law is November 30, 1989. But the government issues no official statistics on representatives' surpluses as of that date.

recipient of honoraria, or speaking fees, which at the time could have been a more effective device for winning a lawmaker's appreciation than a campaign contribution. Unlike campaign gifts, honoraria could be pocketed by the lawmakers themselves. Thus, such fees were a perfectly legal, and sometimes even a tax-deductible, way of lining a legislator's pocket. But in 1990, the last year honoraria were legal for House members, Congressman Rostenkowski permitted corporations and other interest groups to ingratiate themselves to him to the tune of $310,000. That record-high figure made him far and away the leading recipient of honoraria that year. (The second-ranking congressman, New York Democrat John J. LaFalce, received only $93,350 in speaking fees.)

Despite the patent conflicts of interest involved—in accepting campaign contributions and other favors from groups with a huge stake in his official decisions, in Rostenkowski's accumulating an immense surplus that he may be able to transfer to his own bank account when he leaves Congress, in his formation of a personal PAC to expand his own powers in Congress, in his acceptance of nearly $310,000 in speaking fees, much of it from interest-groups—all of this was, at the time, entirely legal and within House ethical rules—and junkets, "leadership" PACs and other favors remain so.

In November 1989, the House banned honoraria, effective January 1, 1991 (in exchange for a $35,000 pay raise). The Senate followed suit in July 1991.

Lacking, however, was a ban on expense-paid trips for members of Congress—often to posh resorts—sponsored by interest groups that had a vested interest in particular legislative matters pending before Congress. Those are discussed in detail in Chapter 9.

At the time of the O'Neill-Rostenkowski money-raising event, there was some grumbling among the lobbyists about how, even in that nonelection year, the "going rate" for Ways and Means fund-raisers had doubled or even quadrupled since the Reagan Treasury Department unveiled its sweeping reform proposals.

Yet, with all the grumbling, the *Wall Street Journal*'s Brooks Jackson reported that "lobbyists say privately that with billions of dollars at stake . . . they can't afford" to turn down a member's request for a contribution.

So the money poured in to Ways and Means members: from insurance companies, from military contractors, from drug companies, and even from horse breeders, each group eager to protect its own pet tax loophole.

Compared with two years earlier, when there was no tax reform proposal before the committee, the Reagan program had spurred striking increases in PAC giving, even to the most safely ensconced members of Ways and Means. For example, PAC money flowing to Florida Congressman Sam Gibbons, a consistent three-to-one winner in his Tampa district, jumped *two-hundred-fold*—from $750 in the first half of 1983 to over $156,000 in the same period in 1985.

PAC statistics of that kind shrink from the dramatic to mere common sense in light of the immense amounts at stake. Viewed in that manner, PAC contributions can be looked upon as the cheapest investment most interest groups could make.

For example, because of the tax loopholes enacted by Congress over the years, a single company (AT&T) was able to earn nearly $25 billion in profits from 1982 through 1985 without paying one penny of taxes—in fact, the government actually paid AT&T $635 million in tax rebates. The company's tax savings totaled more that $12 billion.

AT&T has had a number of PACs. In the years 1979 through 1986, those PACs contributed nearly $1.4 million to congressional candidates, mainly incumbent representatives and senators. So an officer or director of AT&T might calculate that on the $12.1 billion tax savings alone, the nearly $1.4 million given by the company PAC netted a return of 867,145 percent.

Using similar reasoning, directors of General Electric (then another lightly taxed company) might likely have concluded that their company's PAC was producing a 673,759 percent rate of return; Sears Roebuck's directors might gloat over the firm's 510,581 percent return, and so forth.

Obviously there is not a direct cause-and-effect relationship between these companies' PAC contributions and their tax savings, and those rate-of-return calculations are not rigorous. The point is that with stakes so immense and PAC contributions so comparatively tiny, it requires only a grain of success to make the PAC gifts pay off astronomically. To turn the coin over, most PACs can afford to expand their total contributions almost indefinitely before they hit the point of diminishing returns.

Some campaign reformers argue that the public has been misled into focusing its attention primarily, if not exclusively, on the political action committees (PACs). Such people contend this has diverted the public attention away from another growing source of influence: large *individual* contributors, the wealthy few able to contribute $200 or more to politicians' campaigns.

In the 1990 congressional elections, for example, those large donors gave $164.2 million directly to candidates—*more than the total amount contributed by PACs*! Add to that the nearly $72 million those same contributors gave to PACs, which in turn contributed to candidates, you come up with the impressive total of more than $236 million from the $200-and-over givers.

But the overall totals disguise the significance—and ominousness—of individual examples. For example, in the 1990 elections, some fifty pro-Israel PACs combined to contribute just over $4 million to federal candidates (compared with $914,000 contributed by PACs who are opposing gun control and $747,000 from PACs on both sides of the abortion issue). But even the $4 million pro-Israel PAC contributions far understates the case: a September, 1991 study by the Center for Responsive Politics, a non-partisan Washington research group, found an additional $3.5 million in direct contributions to candidates from individuals who had given to pro-Israel PACs, and could fairly, therefore, be assumed to have pro-Israel sympathies. The imbalance between pro-Israel individual vs. PAC contributions is most dramatic in the case of individual senatorial candidates, as follows:

	PRO-ISRAEL CONTRIBUTIONS	
Candidate	From PACS	From Individuals
John Kerry (D-MA)	$ 250	$121,945
Bill Bradley (D-NJ)	$ 29,500	$124,082
Arlen Specter (R-PA)	$ 15,000	$ 96,300
Carl Levin (D-MI)	$214,300	$348,773

Among some 1990 House candidates, comparisons are as follows:

	PRO-ISRAEL CONTRIBUTIONS	
Candidate	From PACS	From Individuals
Mel Levine (D-CA)	$ 18,179	$ 71,600
Sidney R. Yates (D-IL)	$ 24,450	$ 50,800

This phenomenon of individual contributions outweighing those of like-minded PACs is by no means confined to pro-Israel proponents. Examples:

- Senator Bob Dole has received far more money from the individuals associated with the commodities industry and Dow Chemical than from the PACs of either interest.
- Individuals associated with an assortment of Wall Street firms contributed over four times as much to New York Republican Senator Alfonse D'Amato's campaign as did their PACs.
- A similar situation occurred between D'Amato and the brokerage firm Drexel Burnham Lambert.
- Even the $3,400 contributed to Rep. John Miller by the Arctic Alaska Company was overshadowed by individual gifts totaling $10,000 from individuals associated with the corporation.

Some reformers argue that the political influence problem presented by these individual givers is more serious than even those figures suggest—mainly because the donors' legislative interests are far more difficult to detect in the case of individual contributors as compared with the contributions of PACs. For example, no matter how innocently a political action committee may be named (e.g., The Society for Good Government), the law requires the

PAC to identify clearly the corporation or interest group with which it is connected (e.g., General Electric, the United Auto Workers, etc.). Moreover, the Federal Election Commission computerizes the PACs' contributions, so that if a reporter or indignant citizen is curious about the hypothetical political largess of, say, the General Motors' PAC, which has lobbied against increased auto fuel efficiency, the FEC could, with the push of a button, disgorge a printout of all the legislators who had received contributions from General Motors' PAC. But it is more difficult to ascertain the identities of individual contributors affiliated with General Motors.

It is also a formidable task to correlate the individual givers to pro-Israel PACs with personal contributions from those contributors to the candidacy of, say, a Bill Bradley or a John Kerry.

But it is still more difficult to identify the legislative or other interests of an individual contributor. Technically, the law requires candidates for Congress to identify the occupation or employer of every individual contributor of $200 or more. In fact, that law is largely observed technically, if at all. In the 1990 elections, for example, thirty-one percent of such contributions carried either no disclosure at all or what amounts to a worthless disclosure (e.g., "executive," "retired," or "housewife"). In fact, "housewives" are the most frequently reported occupation on FEC candidate reports. Not only are those housewives numerous; they also appear to be flourishing: in 1990, "housewives" made contributions totaling $14 million in amounts of $200 or more.

The extent to which the financial or legislative interests of these large contributors are disguised may be summed up thus: in the 1990 elections, $62 million—two-fifths of the amount given to candidates by PACs—was given to candidates by large contributors without any indication (or with "worthless indications") of the identity of the contributor.*

The PAC-vs.-individual-contributor disguise may be even more insidious than those examples indicate. Consider the example of

---

* Despite this massive $62 million breech of the law in one election year alone—totaling a quarter of a *billion* dollars since the election law was first enacted in the early 1970s—the Federal Election Commission has only prosecuted a handful of violations.

the $80,000 fundraising party held in Washington, D.C. by the cable television industry on behalf of Colorado's Democratic Senator Timothy Wirth, who would play a pivotal role in helping block passage of a measure, vigorously opposed by the cable industry to regulate cable television. If eight industry PACs had each given Senator Wirth $10,000 (the legal ceiling if Wirth faced both a primary and a general election), the source of the money would have been quite clear. Instead, a cluster of cable television executives who may or may not have been clearly identified with the industry gathered at a reception. The net effect, from Senator Wirth's point of view was the same: an $80,000 addition to his campaign treasury.* But from the point of view of public disclosure, the result was different as night and day.

The so-called "influence industry"—lawyers, lobbyists, public relations firms—poses another peculiar problem of concealment of interests. When, for example, an attorney in one of Washington's mega-law firms doing business on a variety of legislative fronts for a variety of clients, makes a contribution to a given legislator, the probability is he or she is not doing so on behalf of a single client but, rather, to assure access for him/herself (and/or other members of his or her firm) with that given lawmaker whenever it may be needed, no matter what the cause or who the client.

In all, the "influence industry" contributed $28 million in the 1990 elections—$19 million directly to candidates and an additional $9 million to parties and PACs who, in turn, passed the money on to candidates.

"Fat cat" giving has a peculiarly undemocratic element. For example, in the 1990 elections, one-tenth of one percent of the voting age population accounted for forty-six percent of the total money raised by congressional candidates. One-*twentieth* of one percent of the voting age population accounted for all the large donor money received by winning Senate candidates that year.

---

* A Wirth aide denied any connection between the contributions and Wirth's opposition to the re-regulation legislation opposed by the industry. (See Baseball Scenario, on page xix.)

That concentration was, to be sure, written into the very election laws themselves in the early '70s when an individual was allowed to give $1,000 per candidate per election—a sum out of reach for all but the very wealthiest citizens. But the disparity does not end there. The very rich have contrived to magnify their power in several ways.

First of all, many of them violate the legal limits outright—typically with impunity. For example, a *Los Angeles Times* study found that in 1988, corporate raider Harold C. Simmons gave nearly $60,000 to candidates all over the country, more than twice his $25,000 over-all limit. This patent infraction went unpunished by the Federal Election Commission which, according to an FEC spokesman, has "no legal authority to fine anyone." However, it can try to negotiate civil fines of up to $5,000 for unwitting violations and $10,000 for willful violations. The *Los Angeles Times* was unable to unearth a single penalty approaching a fraction of those limits.

But the Simmonses of this world need not violate the letter of the law: they can achieve the same purpose by inducing other family members—including minor children—to contribute to many of the same candidates they do.

For example, the following table lists contributions made by members of the Harold Simmons family (*including three daughters, still in college*) as unearthed by the *Los Angeles Times*:

	1987	1988	1989
Harold C.	$24,660	$ 59,958	$22,250
Annette (wife)		10,750	5,000
Andrea (daughter)	5,000	16,000	
Lisa (daughter)	10,000	14,000	5,000
Scheryle (daughter)	10,000	17,000	
Serena (daughter)		4,000	5,000
Douglas (brother)		4,800	
G. Reuben (brother)		8,375	
Mrs. G. Reuben		2,000	
TOTAL	$49,600	$136,883	$37,250

That the members of the Simmons family gave to a similar list of candidates was no accident. Simmons' lawyer acknowledged that

Simmons, his wife and daughters discuss their contributions before making them.

Perhaps an even more striking example of family giving is that of the Keenan family, which made gifts to Arkansas Democratic Representative John Paul Hammerschmidt, in the name of two family *trusts*!

All told, family giving amounts to a striking amount of money. A Citizen Action study of the 1990 elections reckoned it added up to $30.6 million.

Topping the list of politically generous families in 1990 was the wine-making family of Ernest and Julio Gallo, which gave a total of $294,100, including $20,000 to one candidate on a single day.

These "fat-cat" contributors also inject what some might term a "carpetbagger" element into congressional politics. In 1990, congressional candidates in fourteen states received more money from out-of-state large donors than from in-state. An all-too-typical undemocratic phenomenon is the rush of candidates racing from Los Angeles to New York to Chicago to Houston, rattling their tin cups before the well-heeled, rather than spending their time meeting with, and listening to, their *own* constituents.

When undertaken by candidates for primary nominations, this quest for out-of-state funds is sometimes referred to as "the cocktail party primary." Thus, if a cocktail-hour gathering in, say, New York is a flop, the candidate is likely to return to his/her home state convinced that he or she will not be able to raise the necessary funds, and may decide not to undertake the race. In such instances, well-heeled New York East Siders have become, in effect, gate-keepers for, say, Idaho elections. One wonders whether the Founders intended any such "cocktail party primaries."

On occasion, the self-interest of moneyed contributors are comparatively easy to identify. Take, for example, the contributions of corporate buy-out specialists Harold C. Simmons, Henry Kravis and Ronald O. Perelman. Clearly, those individuals (and their family members who joined them in giving to lawmakers) had an interest in blocking legislation to curb corporate takeovers. According to an outstanding piece of investigative reporting by Sara Fritz and Dwight Morris of the *Los Angeles Times*, "Over the past three years, the Simmons, Kravis and Perelman families *each* made more than $250,000 in political contributions, most of them to [President] Bush and members of Congress who were in a position to play a key role in killing any corporate take-over legislation." (Emphasis added.)

For example, in the House, Simmons gave contributions of between $500 and $1,000 to the men with the most control over the legislation: Michigan Democrat John Dingell, Chairman of the House Energy and Commerce Committee; Massachusetts Democrat Edward J. Markey, Chairman of the House committee with direct responsibility for the financial markets, and three other members of the Commerce Committee. Although Markey's committee held extensive hearings during 1989, it failed to draft any legislation.

Similarly, in the Senate, Simmons and Kravis gave contributions of $1,000 to $2,000 to many members of the Senate Banking and Finance Committee. In addition, of course, to these comparatively paltry contributions to members of Congress, these individuals made colossal "soft-money" gifts to the national and state parties for so-called "party building activities"—such as voter registration and get-out-the-vote activities.*

Kravis made a $100,000 "soft-money" contribution to "Team 100," a program run out of Republican National Committee headquarters in 1988 by Bush's chief fund-raiser, Robert A. Mosbacher, later named Secretary of Commerce. Corporate raider Perelman, on the other hand, was more even handed in his "soft-money" giving: he gave $100,000 each to the Bush and Dukakis camps.

More typically, though, these large donors are far less celebrated than the Kravises, the Perelmans and the Simmonses, and their real interests are known only to a few who follow the ins and outs of the legislative affairs of a particular industry in meticulous detail. Who, for example, would know that Arthur Cameron (who gave the impressive total of $45,300 to members of Congress from 1985 to 1990) is an attorney for a major billboard-owning company, which is subject to strict congressional regulation? Only a

---

* For more on the "soft-money" loophole, see Chapter 10.

person like Edward McMahon, who closely follows billboard regulation legislation on behalf of Scenic America, would be able to pick Cameron's name out of a long list of otherwise indistinguishable contributors.

The primary lesson to be drawn from the growing phenomenon of contributions by large *individual* donors is this: in assessing the extent to which a given lawmaker receives his or her contributions from special interests, it makes little or no difference whether the dollars come from a PAC or an executive of that PAC's company or from a lawyer, lobbyist or public relations consultant employed by the company. The problem is: how to unearth and identify the contributor. On this score, great improvements need to be made in the provisions—and, particularly, the *enforcement*—of the disclosure laws.

Combine the soaring costs of campaigns with a politician's constant anxieties about being outspent, and mix in the almost infinite capacity of the interest groups to feed the politicians' appetites for money, and you have the perfect recipe for a Congress beset by money fever and prey to corrupt influence. Even the staunchest apologists for the conduct of the "Keating Five" assailed this money-raising system.

Virtually all Senate candidates echo former Congressman Mike Barnes' statement (see Chapter 5) that 80 to 90 percent of their time and attention is spent in raising money rather than meeting with the voters. It's the rare Washington evening that passes with fewer than three congressional fund-raisers; often there are six or more. The U.S. Senate even suspends roll-call voting during the cocktail hour, the favored time for money-raising, so that senators are free to forage for money without fear of missing a vote. PAC managers and lobbyists drift from one lawmaker's party to another, making their appearance, making sure they're seen and given credit, then moving on to the next event, having achieved their objective: to be sure they are recognized as having paid the requisite dues when the favor-seekers are lined up ten deep in the corridors and lawmakers have only so many precious minutes to parcel out.

We would all be shocked, of course, if those lobbyists-in-the-corridors behaved like a patron in a chic, in-demand restaurant who shook the hand of the maitre d' while pressing a large amount of cash into his palm. In Congress, though, the system is more sophisticated: the money has changed hands well in advance, through a campaign contribution at one of those six-an-evening fundraisers.

Former Senator William Proxmire of Wisconsin has an even more vivid analogy drawn from the world of baseball which I have rewritten (see page xix). He asks us to imagine a World Series baseball game in which the pitcher walks up to the plate umpire before the game begins, pulls a wad of $100 bills from his pocket and proceeds to hand the umpire 100 of them—$10,000 in all—which the umpire jams into his pocket and goes about his business of calling balls and strikes. Would anyone—the fans, the media, the other team—imagine he could possibly do so fairly? Surely not.

The analogy applies aptly, says Senator Proxmire, to members of legislative committees who have received campaign contributions from interest groups or individual donors with a stake—often an immense stake—in their decisions as committee members. "Yes," says Senator Proxmire, "the [legislative] game is fixed. [That] is why you as a consumer and a taxpayer don't have a chance."

Such a practice entails a flagrant conflict of interest that is forbidden by law to members of the executive and judicial branches of the government. Yet, as we will see repeatedly throughout this book, it is an every-day occurrence in the Congress.

Increasingly, lobbyists privately tell tales of extortion tactics utilized by members of Congress, as lawmakers have come to *expect* campaign contributions in return for a favor, or even for an appointment to see them. In recent years, one Washington law firm after another has been obliged to form a PAC of its own, to kick into the campaigns of lawmakers important to its clients. As recounted in Chapter 4, sometimes the extortion is brazen. More often, though, it is far more subtle, almost taken for granted by both sides. As Jerald terHorst, former Director of National Public Affairs for the Ford Motor Company, put it, "If a congressman or senator comes to you as a loyal supporter, and says, 'I'd like to have your support again this year,' what do you say, 'Get lost'?"

It would be difficult to imagine anything more destructive of traditional democratic ideals than the current campaign finance system. The existing system fails in in three major respects:

First, it destroys the notion that candidacy for federal office is open to all comers, regardless of their wealth or station in life.

Second, far from giving the electorate the opportunity to "throw the bums out," it has created a permanent Congress. The U.S. House of Representatives, in particular, resembles the British House of Lords in the permanence of its make-up.

Finally, the inevitable political money chase (exacerbated by the importance of the thirty-second TV spot as *the* message carrier in modern American politics) is the enemy of face-to-face contact between candidate and voter and, more important, any serious discussion of the important issues of the day.

The story of Wisconsin's Ed Garvey graphically illustrates all three points.

Garvey was raised in a small Wisconsin town by parents who taught him that this was a great country because it wasn't just for the rich. Everyone with an education, they said, had an equal chance to succeed.

Moreover, in the Wisconsin politics that he knew, the standard political gathering consisted of breakfast at a local hotel at five dollars a plate. The five dollars went to pay for the breakfast. "If anyone had invited my father to a hundred-dollar-a-plate dinner," Garvey recalls, "he would have asked, 'What in the world could they serve for that amount of money?'"

Wisconsin's Senator William Proxmire, in particular, had made it a tradition to run his campaigns for next to no money. So, in

Garvey's experience, election campaigns were based on ideas and personal contact. Any candidate who didn't get around to the small towns didn't have much of a chance.

Garvey was no newcomer to politics. He had been a student body president, and had lived in Washington, D.C. for thirteen years. A union leader (executive director of the National Football League Players Association), Garvey was well known among national labor leaders.

So, he was excited when a group gathered in 1986 to discuss the possibility of his running against the incumbent Republican Senator, Bob Kasten, who opposed everything that Garvey stood for.

While he was considering running, he talked with an old-time farmer who grew out of the old tradition of Wisconsin's progressive senator, Bob LaFollette. The farmer told Garvey that the most important thing he could do as a candidate was to educate the voters. "Like Bob LaFollette," the farmer told him, "you should judge your campaign on how you teach, not on the number of votes you get."

So, with this ideal in mind, Garvey journeyed to Washington in search of expertise in the craft of politics—and, more important, in quest of money. He found, to his dismay, that the political consultants—even those who professed to agree wholeheartedly with his politics—didn't care about his political viewpoint. "The only thing that mattered, they said, was how much money I could raise. One consultant, an old friend, put it this way: 'Your job is to raise money. I want you to spend seventy-five percent of your time raising money and the rest of the time on the campaign.' " When Garvey protested that in his state they didn't run expensive campaigns, he was dismissed with the riposte, "Every first-time candidate says that."

Despite a basic conflict with his campaign manager and media consultant (they wanted him to spend at least five hours a day raising money; he wanted to visit every senior citizen center and union hall he could), he embarked on the campaign.

One of his first and major disillusionments was that major sources of money he had counted on evaporated before his very eyes.

He had been a labor leader for thirteen years and had hoped for substantial labor union support. But he found that labor unions rarely get involved in primary campaigns. Even when a state branch breaks tradition and endorses a primary candidate, that is not binding on the national union, which hands out the money.

Likewise the women's groups: even though, unlike the Republican incumbent, he had been staunchly on their side and had been endorsed by the state chapter of the National Organization of Women (NOW). (The national NOW had no money for him.)

So he had no recourse but to spend his days making long distance calls, asking strangers in distant states for money. In general, he found that they, like the campaign consultants, cared far less about his positions on the issues than about his standing in the polls—that is, his chances of winning: "Out-of-state people who give to candidates for the House and Senate want a good investment, not a long-shot." Most of them told him to call back after he won the primary.

And the political action committees? "The PACs pride themselves on 'smart giving', and it just isn't smart to give to a candidate challenging an incumbent in a primary fight."

In spite of all these obstacles, Garvey won the 1986 Democratic primary.

He quickly found himself vastly out-gunned financially by incumbent Senator Robert Kasten, who ultimately raised $3.2 million. Having won the primary, Garvey managed to scratch together enough to pay for a small staff, direct-mail, posters, yard signs—all the makings of a successful grass-roots campaign decades ago. But this was the television age and soon, thirty-second television spots by Garvey's opponent began reaching every voter in the state two, three, five, ten times a day. Kasten's name became a household word. "Suddenly," observed Garvey, "he was a celebrity, recognized on the streets. He was Vanna White, Pat Sajak, Oprah, Donahue."

But Garvey didn't have the money for paid TV time. His sole remedy: free media time. Garvey was sure he could out-perform his opponent in televised debates and news conferences, and could persuade the voters with his positions on the issues. But, he says, Kasten wouldn't debate; wouldn't hold news conferences;

wouldn't attend candidate forums; wouldn't talk about the issues. So, the "free media door" was largely closed to Garvey.

Kasten's TV advantage hit Garvey like a cold wind after he had spent three hours on a chilly Sunday shaking hands outside a Green Bay Packers football game. After those three hours, Garvey had shaken two thousand or, at most, three thousand hands. Afterward, Garvey crossed the street to a local emporium to relax. And what did he see? Yet more of his opponent's TV commercials.

> "I realized that if I could have shaken the hands of all 53,000 people entering Lambeau Field that day, I wouldn't have reached a tenth of the people watching that commercial at that moment. I did some quick arithmetic on my pocket calculator: if I averaged 2,000 hand-shakes a day—a practical impossibility, what with fund-raising trips and calls—it would take me 1,600 days to reach the 3.2 million potential voters in Wisconsin. One television spot could reach them all in a day—not once but over and over again."

But those TV messages can only be purchased one way: for cold, hard cash in advance. No credit. And cash, in turn, inevitably involves the political money-chase.

Ultimately, Garvey lost that 1986 election by 51,610 votes. Kasten's two and a half to one financial advantage ($3.2 million to Garvey's $1.3 million) was a key factor.

Compared with the average candidate for the House of Representatives, Ed Garvey was fortunate.

For one thing, he was running for the United States Senate—which in itself made his race more important in the eyes of many contributors than the vast majority of House races. He was also better known nationally than the average House candidate—particularly among national labor leaders. Thus, from the outset he had far more advantages than the typical House candidate.

So imagine you were the *average* House challenger running against an incumbent.

Even before the campaign begins—that is, even before either of you raises a dime—your incumbent opponent is likely to start off with a large surplus in his or her campaign treasury, left over from the last campaign. Those House incumbent surpluses have grown steadily over the last few elections. In 1986, they totaled $44 million. By the end of the 1990 elections, the total had nearly doubled—to $80 million. A hundred House members emerged from that campaign with over $250,000 in each of their campaign treasuries.*

In the campaign itself, if you are the average challenger, you will, on average, be outspent three-and-a-half to one by your incumbent opponent.

Political action committees? Forget it. The PACs are out to "bet smart"—that is, to place their bets on powerful incumbents whose favor and attention they may need in the future, even where those incumbents do not necessarily share their philosophies. (This will be set forth in more detail in Chapter 2.) In the 1990 House elections, for example, in races where the incumbents sought re-election, the PACs gave ninety-two percent to the incumbent, and only eight percent to challengers.

All of these dollar advantages fail to take into account the non-financial leverage enjoyed by incumbents: massive use of free mailing privileges (paid for by the taxpayers) to mail out glowing reports about themselves to their constituents over the entire course of their terms in office; inherent advantages in gaining free media attention (such as ribbon-cutting and award-granting ceremonies); the rendering of personal service to countless constituents twelve months a year; the use of taxpayer-paid computers to do highly targeted mailings to their voters; and, by no means least, the use of their taxpayer-paid congressional staffs to do what amounts, essentially, to campaign work.

One candidate who was not even running against an incumbent but, instead, for an open seat in 1990 was Steve Sovern, formerly a sign manufacturer in Cedar Rapids, Iowa. In March 1990, Sovern

---

* In early 1991, Chuck Alston, an enterprising journalist for *Congressional Quarterly*, reported that many members of Congress had sufficient leftover surpluses in their campaign treasuries to buy added incumbent protection. They gave contributions to key members of state legislatures who would be critical in deciding where the 1992 reapportionment lines would be drawn in new congressional districts.

attended a workshop put on in Washington by the Democratic Congressional Campaign Committee (DCCC). On hand were some seventy Democratic candidates for Congress from all over the country. Among the political "wisdom" the aspirants heard was the following:

> *From Marty Stone, a DCCC staff member*: "Money drives this town."

> *From Congressman Peter Hoagland, a Nebraska Democrat*: "Raising campaign money from Washington PACs is much easier than from individuals, because it's a business relationship."

Sovern wondered just what kind of business relationship Hoagland had in mind, having learned from his twenty-five years in business that such a relationship was an exchange of money or some other consideration for products or services of value. DCCC staffer Stone clarified this concept: "These people [the PAC agents in attendance] are paid to give you money. You have to *do* certain things, but they *want* to give you money." (Emphasis theirs.)

From PAC manager George Gould, of the Letter Carriers Union (explaining why so little money goes to challengers—and how PAC giving has less to do with ideology than with access to power): "I don't give my people's money to those I think are going to lose, so you have to convince me you're going to win." Gould continued, "When you take PAC money, you are saying you are their friend."

Sovern was one of two candidates on hand who had a policy of refusing PAC money, having worked since 1980 on a campaign reform agenda. His anti-PAC stance was discouraged by Congressman Hoagland who cautioned restraint: "Don't let zeal for reform influence you. Process challenges just don't work." Hoagland had spent $180,000 of his own money on his own campaign and said that "the ultimate test of your own commitment is how much of your own money you are willing to put into your own campaign. If you aren't willing to use your own money, you ought to think about [doing] something else." He added that winning would be "permanent career change: You'll be here as long as you want."

On the second day of the workshop, there occurred what Sovern calls a "mating dance" brunch between candidates and PACs, with candidates wearing blue name tags and PAC representatives wearing red.

Gould also warned against relying on volunteers from home districts, saying that while they might be needed to "walk the streets" near election day, "in the first phases, they'll be no help. They can't do polling, radio, direct mail or TV." (At that very time, Sovern had lined up numerous volunteers to help in his campaign.)

Finally, candidate Sovern could stand it no longer. He stood and gave an emotional entreaty to candidates and panelists alike against the kind of politics that had been preached during this workshop. He said it ought to be the Democrats who took the lead in returning politics to a participatory process involving folks back home.

There followed an uncomfortable moment of silence that was broken when PAC director Gould said, "Well, I guess we don't have to worry about contributing to *that* campaign!" Shortly thereafter, Sovern reports, his campaign was cut from the DCCC mailing list and the DCCC materials. Thereafter, those materials went only to Sovern's primary opponent, who was making his third run for the House and had been the third highest PAC-funded challenger in the nation during his prior election effort. When Sovern called his opponent on election night to concede, the phone was answered by a DCCC staff member.

But let your optimism run free and imagine that, despite all these advantages enjoyed by the incumbents, you have built up an inspired group of followers who have joined you in knocking on doors, holding coffee klatches, posting yard signs and bumper stickers and the like. Miraculously, the polls show you have begun to draw nearly even with your opponent, and show signs of pulling ahead. It is mid-October. The last three crucial weeks of the campaign remain. Will you be able to sustain your momentum?

That is where the most crushing statistic (taken from the October 17, 1990 FEC reports) comes into play: in the average House race, your incumbent opponent (assuming he or she is the average) still had $224,319 in his or her campaign treasury—enough to saturate the airwaves in those final, crucial weeks.

And how much is in your campaign bank account? Again, if you are the average challenger, you had the grand total of $8,664—barely enough to pay your campaign staff and stagger to the finish line—without a single TV commercial.

In 1990, in 371 House races—ninety percent of the total—the incumbents were either totally unopposed, financially unopposed (their opponents raised less than $25,000), or the races were financially uncompetitive (the incumbents outspent their challengers by more that two to one).

Given all this, it's surprising that anyone has the courage to run against an incumbent for the U.S. House. For in the last three elections, an average of more than ninety-seven percent of House incumbents who sought reelection have emerged victorious. Fewer than three percent of challengers won.

As former President Ronald Reagan observed, the Soviet Politburo was, during his tenure as President, a more competitive institution than the U.S. House of Representatives!

It was not so long ago when voters were able to draw sharp distinctions between the policies of the Democrats and the Republicans. Within memory, the Democratic Party represented itself as the party of populist-liberals like Thomas Jefferson and Andrew Jackson, annually revered in "Jefferson-Jackson Day" dinners with a maximum ticket price of $100.

As campaign costs have soared, the Democratic Party has turned more and more to the well-heeled for their funds. The $100 dinner has been replaced by black-tie dinners where the ticket price is $1,500 per plate. Tickets are bought not only by the leaders of industry but of labor as well.

Another striking example of Democratic appeal to moneyed contributors is "The Speaker's Club" of the Democratic Congressional Campaign Committee. In 1984, then-Speaker O'Neill and then-Representative Tony Coelho, the chairman of that committee, dispatched a letter to wealthy Democratic contributors inviting them to join the Club, which they described as "an elite organization of national leaders." The club's allure: "A wealth of opportunities for its club members to meet members of Congress. . . A private dinner at the home of a Committee Chairman, a round of golf with the Speaker, a briefing by the House leadership, or cocktails with the Democratic members of the [tax-writing] Ways and Means Committee." The price tag: $5,000 *per year* for an individual member or, as a group member, $15,000 *per year* in PAC funds—hardly sums affordable by the disciples of Jefferson and Jackson.

Harvard professor Robert B. Reich has written in the *New York Times* that

"The Democrats . . . lost their identity [as the champion of the little fellow] not because Americans became more respectful of wealth and power or more convinced trickle-down economics would actually work (polls show widespread opposition to capital gains breaks for the rich), *but because Democrats became dependent on the rich to finance their campaigns. . .* (emphasis added) It is difficult to represent the little fellow when the big fellow pays the tab. The problem is not corruption. The inhibition is more subtle. . . . *Democrats have come to sound like Republicans because they rely on the same funders to make the same contacts as the GOP.*" (Emphasis added.)

While there are no statistics to document the proposition, it would be reasonable to suppose that the increasing similarity between policies proposed by the two parties and their candidates contributes to the recent downturn in voter turnout.

More and more, the current campaign finance system runs counter to a sense of fairness and traditional concepts of representative democracy. If we imagine the entrances to congressional offices as turnstiles, most of us would like to believe that all citizens have *roughly* equal access through those turnstiles.

But who gets to go through the turnstiles? More importantly: *how does that question get decided?*

The central theme of this book is that under the present system, *that question is decided altogether too much on the basis of money.* That is why the PACs are so unfair. With their capacity to pool money, they almost certainly have the power to command congressional attention far more than ordinary, unorganized citizens, only about one tenth of whom contribute any amount of money to political candidates. That fact in itself enlarges politicians' dependence on, and the influence of, the wealthy individual contributors, (and their families) who each may legally give politicians an attention-getting gift of up to $1,000 per election.

Most voters can't afford to contribute $250, much less $1,000, to a politician's campaign. But for most PACs, $250 is a routine contribution given to *many* candidates; a $1,000 contribution is commonplace; and a $5,000 contribution to *the* strategically positioned senator or representative is entirely feasible.

As noted earlier, lawmakers are indebted to outside interest groups for their campaign money to a growing—and disturbing—degree. Thus, the PACs and their lobbyists are often able to push their way in through the turnstile ahead of a lawmaker's own constituents, even though they do not live, vote, or pay taxes in the lawmaker's state or district. To the extent that this happens, the influence of local voters is diluted—a set-back for the gains in voter influence achieved by the civil rights movement of the sixties.

This book is about how money and other favors affect congressional decision-making: money as campaign contributions, formerly money in the form of honoraria, posh trips, and contributions to lawmakers' own PACs and to their charitable foundations.

It is about how even the most idealistic members of Congress quickly get caught up by money fever.

This book is about how the aggregation of money through the PACs and wealthy individuals is distorting representative government in America.

It is about how the PACs and their money have enabled numerically small groups—the auto dealers, the dairy farmers, and the billboard industry, for example—to prevail in Congress and, often, to impose huge costs on the majority of the population.

It is about how outside PACs lavish money on powerful lawmakers—even the most politically secure who don't need the funds—while shunning far needier challengers.

It is about how, as a result, the PACs help entrench sitting representatives and senators and deprive the public of new personalities and new ideas.

It is about how PACs help institutionalize the practice of congressional foxes guarding the chicken coops, as lawmakers routinely accept large campaign contributions, honoraria and other favors from interest groups with an immense stake in their official acts.

It is about how legislators often choose their committee assignments by seeking out the "PAC heavens"—committees that deal with major legislative controversies and hence are magnets for PAC contributions.

It is about how the line between a campaign contribution and a bribe is only, as one former senator put it, "a hair's breadth"—and how PACs and rich "interested" givers make it difficult for even the most upstanding lawmakers to be sure which side of the line they're on.

It is about how the present system of financing American political campaigns costs consumers and taxpayers tens of billions of dollars every year.

It is about how loopholes in the election laws still permit interest groups and well-heeled individuals to give unlimited political gifts, often in secret, despite the ostensible limits and the disclosure requirements of the seventies that most people believe were cures to the worst abuses.

And it offers a plan by which America can extricate itself from the mess the campaign finance laws and the PACs have produced.

The crisis in the way we now finance our congressional election campaigns can be summarized in two concise facts:

First: Campaigns have become so expensive that the average United States senator must raise more than $12,000 a week *every week during his or her entire six-year Senate term.*

Second: Under the current system, even the most idealistic senator has no alternative for achieving that task other than to solicit and accept massive contributions from special-interest groups.

The result is this: In the first six months of 1989 (a non-election year), thirty-two U. S. senators raised over $6.7 million in campaign funds. Of that sum, nearly a million dollars came from outside special-interest PACs.

These thirty-two are not a random sampling of senators. *Each of them had just been elected only months earlier.*

All thirty-two would not face the electorate again until 1994—*five years hence*! Yet here they were already, shaking the money tree for all they were worth!

 *Chapter Two*

A PAC PRIMER

Wᴴᴬᵀ, ᴾᴿᴱᶜᴵˢᴱᴸʸ, *ɪѕ* a political action committee, or PAC? How did PACs come about? How do they work? How were political campaigns paid for before there were PACs?

In brief, a political action committee is a device through which like-minded people (members of labor unions, professional or trade groups or employees of a corporation) can elect to make political contributions, rather than giving their money directly to candidates of their choice. The PACs then pool that money and hand it out to federal candidates in large amounts ($1,000, $2,000, up to a ceiling of $10,000 per election if there is both a primary and a general election) to tens, or even hundreds, of House and Senate candidates—a feat far beyond the reach of any individual contributor, even a Rockefeller.

PACs are simple in operation and clear in objective.

It is this capacity to pool, or aggregate, individual contributions that makes the PACs a new phenomenon in American politics.

Federal election laws place an annual $25,000 ceiling on the gifts an individual may make to all federal candidates in any election. By contrast, *there is no legal limit on the total amount a PAC can give.* In the 1990 congressional elections, twenty-one PACs each handed out more than a million dollars to candidates for the U.S. House and

Senate, and four PACs—the National Association of Realtors, the American Medical Association, the National Education Association and Teamsters Union—each dispensed over $2 million. The No. 1 PAC, the Realtors, dispensed over $3 million to candidates in 1990 (see Appendix C).

Most PACs have a simple objective: to gain influence with—or, at the least, favored access to—representatives and senators.

That influence-buying motive is often strikingly (some would say shockingly) transparent. For example, the PACs have shoveled money at New York Democratic Representative Charles Rangel even though since 1972 he has won, on the average, 96.7 percent of the vote in his Harlem district. Apparently, then, he doesn't need to collect or spend a dime to be reelected. Yet his PAC receipts tripled in four years (1980–84). But even that trebling was not enough for the PACs. In the ensuing two years, their contributions to this unbeatable congressman increased by half again, so that in 1986, Congressman Rangel received a third of a million dollars—two-thirds of his total contributions—from PACs. They appeared indifferent that their gifts helped the congressman emerge from his 1986 campaign with a cash surplus of over a quarter of a million dollars, *which, at the time, he was legally entitled to take with him upon leaving Congress.**

The average citizen, with limited funds to give politicians and expecting nothing special in return, would not dream of contributing so much as a dime to a sure-shot winner like Charles Rangel. Why, then, did the PACs continue to boost their contributions to him?

Simple. Number 1: Congressman Rangel was and is the fourth-ranking Democrat on the House Ways and Means Committee, which writes all the tax laws, in which the change of a single sentence can mean tens (or even hundreds) of millions in the tax paid by a given company or industry. Number 2: In 1985, the Reagan Administration proposed the most sweeping tax reform in

---

* Since that time the law has been changed—so that only House members elected prior to 1980 may take only their campaign surpluses as of November 30, 1989, and then only if they leave Congress prior to January 1, 1993.

recent history. For industry after industry, multi-billion dollar tax loopholes seemed in jeopardy. Thus, favored access to Congressman Rangel's ear might have been worth many times the third of a million dollars the PACs gave him for his 1986 "campaign." Cheap at twice (or three times) the price.

The political action committees expose the nakedness of their influence-buying in another way: the manner in which they lopsidedly favor incumbents and spurn challengers. If you were to give a sum of money to each of a hundred randomly chosen citizens and ask that they use it to contribute to candidates in fifty congressional races, you might expect them to divide their gifts fairly evenly between challengers and incumbents—no more than, say 60–40 either way—if only because the country is fairly evenly divided as to political party preference. You would expect such an even split, that is, assuming that those hundred citizens had no axes to grind, that they expected nothing for themselves in return for their contributions.

But the PACs *do* have an axe to grind. They *do* expect something in return for the support they give candidates—namely, influence, or at least preferred access to the powerful. Hence, in 1990, in House races where the sitting lawmakers sought re-election the PACs did not split their contributions 50–50 or 60–40. *Instead, they gave 92 percent of their contributions to incumbents, only 8 percent to challengers.* Can virtually all incumbents be that worthy, and the challengers so universally unmeritorious? Did the PACs give more to House chairmen of leading committees than to the average representative—15 percent more, on average—because those chairmen are fifteen percent more intelligent and decent than the others?

Consider this striking statistic: in 1990 House races, the PACs gave slightly over $13 million to seventy-nine incumbents unopposed in general election. By contrast, they gave less than half that amount to 331 challengers running for the House! Additionally, PACs gave $26.4 million to House incumbents who had won by more than three to one in their previous two elections.

There is another malign consequence of PAC favoritism for incumbents: it crushes the American ideal that political office should be open to all citizens, regardless of their wealth or station in society. Suppose, for example, that Abraham Lincoln were alive today and aspired to a seat in the House in a congressional district represented by a powerful committee chairman. Chances are that, whatever his personal merits or the quality of his ideas, most PACs and, for that matter, most individual givers* would greet candidate Lincoln with, at best, polite snickers and send him away empty-handed. Since Lincoln's committee-chairman opponent could raise almost unlimited funds from special-interest groups, Lincoln's candidacy would be snuffed out, purely for want of *money*. What a price to pay! What a way to ration candidacies!

The giving tactics of PACs as a whole leave little doubt that their prime motive is to buy influence or access. They give millions to candidates *who had no opponent* and hence no need for the money; and they give to candidates who are shoo-ins for re-election.

PACs sometimes contribute to opposing candidates in the same contest. They may contribute to candidates whose philosophies they don't share (see page 56). And, at times, *after* the election, when they find they have backed a loser, some PACs unabashedly switch and give to the new winner, the candidate they had previously tried to defeat!

---

* At this juncture an author's confession is in order. In early 1990, I received a letter from a candidate aspiring for the seat now occupied by Dan Rostenkowski, Chairman of the tax-writing House Ways and Means Committee, and then sitting on a surplus in his campaign treasury of $1,114,068. Even though I knew I shouldn't take this attitude, I couldn't help myself. I put the letter in my "deferred action file," thinking to myself, oh, well, this fellow doesn't have a prayer against Rostenkowski. No matter how much he raises, Rostenkowski has an unlimited capacity to raise more. Besides, Rostenkowski has won three-to-one in the last four elections.

I threw the appeal letter away, unanswered, reasoning that this fellow, no matter what his qualifications or merits, doesn't have a prayer of beating Rostenkowski with over $1 million in his campaign treasury carried over from his 1988 campaign and who could, moreover, raise additional infinite sums from interest groups willing to give to him as Chairman of the House Ways and Means Committee.

Here endeth my confession. But if I, believing as I do about the existing campaign finance system, am willing to toss that candidate's appeal in the wastebasket for those reasons, think of the reactions of others less reform-minded than I.

On occasion, the PACs post-election "awakening" takes dramatic proportions. For example, in 1988, political newcomer Republican Craig James, running against long-entrenched Florida Representative Bill Chappell, Jr., received only $7,295 from PACs, a tiny fraction of the $421,450 which the PACs showered on Chappell.

However, after James' surprise victory over Chappell, the PACs provided James with over $200,000 in contributions for his 1990 campaign.

Recent political giving by General Electric's PAC has also included examples of these last two practices (see pages 55 to 58). Doubtless, many of those who gave to GE's PAC would not condone such opportunistic tactics. Too late: they have surrendered control over their money to less fastidious PAC managers.

PAC defenders publicly minimize how much political action committees influence Congress. Judging from their behavior though, the PACs disagree, for every year, they give more and more in congressional races. In fact PAC giving is, in Wall Street parlance, very much a "growth industry." Over the years 1974–90, their campaign contributions to congressional candidates grew, on average, at the rate of 40 percent every *election* (not adjusted for inflation). Evidently, the PACs have no doubt they're getting their money's worth.

In the congressional influence-peddling game, it takes two to tango and, on occasion the sellers are as brazen as the buyers. For example, in January, 1987, when the Democrats regained control of the Senate, Texas Senator Lloyd Bentsen ascended to the chairmanship of the Senate Finance Committee, which, like the House Ways and Means Committee, handles tax legislation. Bentsen lost little time in inviting lobbyists to a series of intimate breakfast meetings with him. The price of a seat at the Bentsen breakfast table: a $10,000 campaign contribution. Even at that price, lobbyists eagerly subscribed to the breakfast series. Then the story of Bentsen's naked influence-peddling broke in the *Washington Post*. The report provoked editorial indignation on the part of those unaware that Bentsen's predecessor, Oregon Republican Bob Pack-wood, had held similar breakfast meetings at $5,000 a ticket. The editorial outcry prompted Bentsen to cancel his breakfast series, refund the money already given him, and admit he had made a "doozy" of a mistake.

Most PACs make no bones that their aim is to further *their own group's* special interests. The director of the American Trucking Association's PAC put it bluntly: "We'll buy a ticket to anyone's fund-raising event, *as long as he didn't vote the wrong way on trucking issues.*" (Emphasis added.)

That "me-first" attitude is also reflected in the way interest groups balkanize Congress, carefully cultivating their special provinces. The nation's defense contractors, whose PAC contributions increased thirty-two percent between 1988 and 1990, focused their contributions on members of the defense-related committees of Congress (the Armed Services and Defense Appropriations panels). Although those representatives and senators comprised only 18 percent of the entire Congress, they received 38 percent of the defense industry's 1990 PAC gifts. On the House side, members of defense committees make up fourteen percent of the House, but received fifty-one percent of the 1989 honoraria, or speaking fees, that defense firms paid to members of Congress when Congressional rules permitted such fees.*

Today, it seems as if every organized group has a PAC: from the Tri-State Albanian-American Club to the Oral and Maxillofacial Surgeons. The dairy farmers and realtors each have large PACs; so do most major labor unions, as do defense contractors, the beer wholesalers (who at one time nicknamed their PAC SIXPAC), peace groups, and a growing number of pro-Israel organizations.

PACs fall into six principal categories: those formed by labor unions; by corporations; by trade associations and professions, such

---

* In 1989, the House outlawed the receipt of honoraria by its members. In 1991, the Senate passed a similar prohibition for U.S. senators in its version of a campaign reform bill.

as the automobile dealers or the doctors; and by cooperatives, such as the dairy co-ops mentioned above. A fifth category consists of the "ideological" PACs—such as those pursuing peace, environmental, or across-the-board liberal or conservative agendas.

A sixth group consists of the "leadership" PACs formed, in general, by legislators seeking to enlarge their influence with their colleagues. They do so by persuading groups to contribute to their own "leadership" PACs, the proceeds of which they then distribute to key colleagues, thereby creating indebtednesses and enlarging the donors' influence. Such "leadership" PACs are typically formed by presidential candidates (such as Senator Robert Dole, of Kansas) or by congressional leaders (such as House Speaker Thomas Foley or Ways and Means Chairman Dan Rostenkowski).

An example of the use of a "leadership" PAC to expand a Senator's influence is Louisiana Senator J. Bennett Johnston's "Pelican PAC," which, during the 1988 election cycle, collected $391,980, $118,502 of which came from the energy industry, including natural gas, oil, coal and nuclear companies. The PAC distributed $202,154 to congressional candidates during the 1988 cycle. In 1991, the Pelican PAC bestowed $5,000 contributions on four key Energy Committee members as well as Commerce Committee chair Ernest Hollings of South Carolina, at a time Senator Johnston was launching an intensive campaign to bring his omnibus energy bill to the Senate floor.

By and large, PACs may, by law, solicit only their group's members, employees and shareholders, which the PACs typically do once a year. Occasionally, PACs employ an efficient collection mechanism—the checkoff. Under that system, contributions are routinely subtracted from members' paychecks or, in the case of the dairy cooperatives, from farmers' monthly milk checks. The $3,309,000 amassed by the three large dairy co-ops from their 47,500 members in the 1984 elections attests to the efficacy of this collection device.

A random-sample study conducted by University of Virginia political scientist Larry J. Sabato in 1981 and 1982 found that typically one-quarter to one-third of the eligible contributors actually gave to their PAC. The overall average contribution for the two-year election cycle was $100, ranging from an average gift of $160 for corporate PACs and $81 for trade association PACs down to $14 for labor PACs.

PACs almost always decide which candidate gets how much in a more or less undemocratic manner. Contributors are rarely asked how their donations should be spent, if only for the practical reason that the rapidly changing events of an election year ensure the impracticality of such contributor participation. Whatever the reasons, those who give their money through PACs essentially turn over control of their money to a very few people. Professor Sabato found that in three-quarters of the PACs he surveyed, the decision was made by a small PAC board or committee.

The PACs' lack of consultation with their contributors is, in a way, a rebuttal of the frequently heard notion that the political action committees serve to increase citizen participation in politics. Few statistics support that contention. More important, as University of Minnesota political scientist Frank Sorauf has observed, a citizen's contribution to a PAC is "one of the least active forms of political activity"; it "requires little time or immediate involvement; in a sense, it buys political mercenaries [and] frees the contributor from the need to be personally active in the campaign."

The criteria for selecting the favored candidates vary somewhat, but basically all the PACs follow the same bottom-line reasoning: what will best advance the interests of their group and its members? Two things flow naturally from that line of reasoning. First, over the years more and more PACs have come to give the bulk of their money to incumbent members of Congress—those in power, and in a position to help or hurt interest groups—and to spurn challengers. The PACs' unbalanced kindness to incumbents has increased steadily since the PAC explosion began in 1974. But between 1982 and 1990, the share PACs gave to incumbents leapt by thirteen percentage points, far more than in any previous eight-year period. In 1990, in House races where the incumbent sought re-election (i.e., leaving aside "open seats") PACs as whole gave more than 92 percent of their money to sitting members of

Congress. Less than 8 percent went to challengers. That imbalance, in turn, helped House incumbents outspend challengers more than 3.5 to one, and almost certainly contributed heavily to the remarkable statistic that over the prior three elections, an average of 97 percent of House incumbents who sought re-election won.*

Second, not only do the PACs favor incumbents over challengers, they typically concentrate their gifts on the members of the congressional committees that most affect them. In 1990, for example, the PACs of banks and other financial institutions favored members of the House and Senate banking committees with campaign contributions totaling more than $3.5 million. This constituted forty-three percent of their total contributions that year, even though those lawmakers made up only fourteen percent of the members of Congress.

The respective categories of PACs differ in the degree of their pro-incumbent favoritism, especially in contests for the House. In those 1990 House races where incumbents sought re-election, the business-affiliated PACs—those formed by corporations and trade associations—gave roughly 95 percent of their funds to incumbents, and only 5 percent to challengers. Corporate PACs led the pro-incumbent pack in 1990, giving 96 percent of their gifts to present officeholders. In 1990, labor PACs gave 86 percent to incumbents in House contests where incumbents sought to succeed themselves; "ideological" PACs about 88 percent. Both figures represented a significant increase over four years earlier, when labor gave incumbents just under seventy percent of their funds and "ideological" PACs about 72 percent.

This pro-incumbent proclivity on the PACs' part is easily explainable not only by the incumbents' superior power to help or hurt interest groups but by the fact that they are odds-on favorites to retain their seats, especially in the U.S. House. As former Senator Thomas Eagleton, of Missouri, put it, "A PAC contribution is an

---

* Political historians will caution that this 97 percent figure must be kept in perspective. They will argue—correctly—that the *non-financial* advantages of incumbency are such that only three times since 1958 has the percentage of incumbent reelection fallen below 90 percent—and then only barely. Since 1958, it has never fallen below 87 percent.

investment. Find me anyone on Wall Street who will give you a 97 percent chance your investment is going to pay off."

The increasing prominence the PACs, and, in particular, their "targeting" of particular committees have introduced into modern American politics two phenomena that distort traditional concepts of representative democracy.

First, they have re-introduced "carpetbagging" into American politics, for the first time since Reconstruction. That is, to the extent candidates and lawmakers derive their funds from PACs, they are receiving their money from entities *outside* their state or district, essentially, from people *who are not allowed to vote for them on election day.**

The second distortion of democracy is the new meaning with which this new found money-built connection between interest groups and legislative committees has altered the word "constituency." Constituents used to be citizens within a candidate's district or state who where entitled to *vote* for him or her. Voters. That was all. Today, PACs have introduced a new definition: members of Congress now represent: first, their voters, and second, (what may be more important to them) their *legislative* or *economic* constituencies as well—who may or may not be (probably are *not*) part of their voting constituency. For example: the members of the Armed Services Committees and Defense Appropriations Subcommittees have as their natural economic "constituents" the defense contrac-

---

* I consider all PACs to be "outside" PACs unless (a) the decision as to how the PAC's money is distributed is made *within the state or district* of the particular candidate or lawmaker; or (b) unless the PAC's procedures provide for donors from a given district or state to earmark their funds for the local candidate.

Many PACs and PAC defenders dispute this line of reasoning, arguing that in instances where a given PAC represents a company that has large plants and many employees in, say, the Fourth District of North Carolina, it is wrong to label that company's PAC an "outside" PAC. I maintain, however, that if that PAC is headquartered in, say, Pittsburgh, and if the decisions as to how that PAC's money is distributed nationwide are made there rather than in North Carolina, it is wrong to say that those decisions are made with the interests of the people of the Fourth District of North Carolina primarily in mind, no matter how many plants or employees that company may have in that district.

tors. Similarly, members of the Telecommunications Subcommittees of the House and Senate have, as their legislative and economic "constituents," broadcasters, telephone companies, the cable industry, and others affected by government regulation of communications.

It's an ugly, undemocratic new concept.

How much influence do the PACs *really* have? Do they actually sway votes? Do they even win preferential access for their lobbyists?

As noted, defenders of the PACs argue that PAC donations have a minimal influence on the outcome of legislation. Lawmakers themselves—the recipients of the PACs' largess—indignantly protest that the PACs' influence is virtually nil. The typical refrain is, "I spent $500,000 on my last campaign. It's absolutely preposterous to suggest I would I would sell my vote for $1,000—or even $5,000—just one percent of my campaign budget!"*

There are several counter-arguments: the first—and most self-evidently powerful—is the raw evidence of the steady increases in PAC donations to candidates which have risen, on average, forty percent annually since 1974. Evidently, the PACs think they are getting something for their money. After all, they are not charities. Here are the statistics:

Year	Number of PACs	PAC Gifts to Congressional Candidates
1974	608	$12.5 million
1978	1,653	$35.2 million
1982	3,371	$83.6 million
1986	4,157	$135.2 million
1990	4,681	$150.5 million

Second, many legislators acknowledge that money influences their votes. In a 1987 survey of twenty-seven senators and eighty-seven House members, the non-partisan Center for Responsive

---

* See Baseball Scenario on page xix.

Politics found that twenty percent of surveyed members told the interviewers that political contributions have affected their votes. An additional thirty percent were "not sure."*

Third, there are examples of how contributions influence members of Congress:

- Former Republican Senator Rudy Boschwitz, of Minnesota, after receiving $30,000 from the manufacturers of pesticides, pushed an amendment on behalf of the Chemical Specialties Manufacturers Association (CSMA) to block states from writing regulations stiffer than federal requirements. Prior to its consideration by the Senate Agriculture Committee, the Boschwitz amendment was "widely referred to" as the "CSMA" amendment, according to *The Nation*.
- Republican Senator Orrin Hatch, of Utah, received $30,000 from company officials and PACs of the major Health Industry Manufacturers Association (HIMA) members (Eli Lilly, Bristol-Myers and Pfizer) for his 1988 campaign. After receiving those contributions, Hatch successfully blocked a measure intended to better regulate such items as pacemakers, incubators and X-ray machines.

A more dramatic example is that of a massive campaign by the privately owned utilities to postpone repayment of $19 billion collected from consumers.

Over a period of years utilities collected money from consumers as a reserve from which to pay federal income taxes. But the 1986 tax reform act lowered the corporate tax rate from forty-six to thirty-four percent, thus reducing the utilities' taxes by $19 billion, a savings the companies owed consumers. (The utilities owed the typical residential customer around $100.)

---

* In addition, two-thirds of the senators and eighty-seven percent of their staff members said that raising money affected the time they spent on legislative work. Forty-three percent of members participating in the survey said that PACs had a "largely or somewhat negative" influence on the political process. *Not a single one of the 115 staff members surveyed said that PACs had a positive impact* (Emphasis mine).

But how quickly should the utilities be required to repay consumers? Ordinarily that question would be left up to state regulators, but in 1986 Congress passed a special provision allowing the refunds in all states to be paid out over as long as a thirty-year period.

The following year, North Dakota Democrat Byron Dorgan introduced a bill calling for a faster refund of the $19 billion. Initially, forty-eight other Democrats and nine Republicans were signed as co-sponsors.

Immediately the utilities responded by stepping up their political contributions. During 1987, 1988, and 1989, PACs sponsored by utilities and their trade associations gave over $5 million to sitting House members. $510,000 of that went to members of the tax-writing House Ways and Means Committee, through which Dorgan's bill had to pass.

The utilities' honoraria increased as well, totaling $446,000 in the years 1987 and 1988.

Slowly, supporters of the Dorgan bill changed their minds. Some examples:

- Missouri Democrat Richard Gephardt, an original co-sponsor of the Dorgan bill, withdrew his co-sponsorship after the utilities donated over $46,000 to his 1988 campaign.
- South Carolina Democrat Butler Derrick switched his position on the Dorgan bill after the utility industry lavished him with trips, honoraria and campaign contributions. Derrick told the *Wall Street Journal* that the money and trips had "nothing to do with [his decision not to renew co-sponsorship of the Dorgan bill]."*
- Eight of the nine representatives who formally repudiated the Dorgan bill after co-sponsoring it received campaign donations from utility PACs averaging $13,000 each.

* * *

---

* See Baseball Scenario on page xix.

The original Dorgan bill died without a vote in the House Ways and Means Committee at the end of 1988.

As mentioned, the unique characteristic of the PACs is their ability to aggregate the gifts of many individual donors. The leverage thus gained is compounded when the aggregators themselves begin to aggregate—that is, when the PACs begin to run in packs.

A powerful example of this is the coalition of business PACs that have, since 1983, gathered together to limit the rights of plaintiffs in lawsuits over allegedly defective products in so-called "product-liability claims." (That is, to place ceilings on the damages such plaintiffs can win in defective-product lawsuits.)

That business coalition, made up primarily of chemical, auto and pharmaceutical manufacturers as well as insurance companies, has, since 1983, contributed over two million dollars to members of the Senate Commerce Committee (which handles liability legislation).

A bill limiting product-liability has been introduced in each new Congress since 1983. Most recently, such a bill was approved by the Senate Commerce Committee in May 1990. Six members of that panel, all of whom voted for the bill, received more than twelve percent of their PAC money in their most recent reelection campaigns from interests lobbying for the measure. For example, Texas Senator Lloyd Bentsen, Missouri's John Danforth, Wisconsin's Robert Kasten and Alaska's Ted Stevens each received over $150,000 from the product-liability coalition—and sided with the coalition on the product-liability bill. Washington's Republican Senator Slade Gorton received more than $200,000 from product-liability PACs for his Senate races in 1986 and 1988.

The principal organized opposition to the product-liability measure came from the American Trial Lawyers Association (ATLA), but this was a case of a mouse fighting an elephant. Compared to the two million dollars contributed by the business PACs pushing the legislation, the lawyers' combined contributions totaled $81,000. In Senator Gorton's case, the product-liability coalition's two hundred thousand dollars far outweighed the trial lawyers' five thousand dollar gift (which Gorton also accepted). At this writing

(January, 1992), the bill is dormant in the House and awaits further action on the Senate floor.

PAC proponents strenuously debate the question: how much influence do PACs really have? Do their contributions actually buy lawmakers' *votes*?

Former Wisconsin Senator William Proxmire, a legislator with thirty-one years experience, says the influence need not be that direct. He has written of the various subtle ways money can influence a legislator's behavior:

> It [the influence of a campaign contribution] may not come in a vote. It may come in a speech not delivered. The PAC payoff may come in a colleague not influenced. It may come in a calling off of a meeting that otherwise would result in advancing legislation. It may come in a minor change in one paragraph in a 240-page bill. It may come in a witness not invited to testify before a committee. It may come in hiring a key staff member for a committee who is sympathetic to the PAC. Or it may come in laying off or transferring a staff member who is unsympathetic to a PAC.

The modern political action committee, a relatively recent phenomenon in American politics, was first introduced by organized labor. That fact is ironic, since in recent years, contributions by business-minded PACs (those formed by corporations, trade associations and professional groups) have far outstripped those of labor PACs. By 1990, the business PACs had outspent their labor counterparts by three to one.

The first modern PAC, organized to collect and pool *voluntary* political contributions, was established in 1943 by the Congress of Industrial Organizations, the CIO, and in the 1944 election, the CIO-PAC raised more than $1.2 million.

It was not until the early sixties that business groups began to adopt the idea. In 1962, the American Medical Association formed

AMPAC, followed, a year later, by the National Association of Manufacturers' Business-Industry Political Action Committee (BIPAC).

Before the days of PACs, campaigns for the House were inexpensive and could be largely financed by contributions from political parties and by fundraising barbecues and chicken dinners and somewhat larger contributions from businessmen. House Ways and Means Chairman Dan Rostenkowski recalls paying for his first House campaign in 1958 largely out of his own pocket. Back then, though, the price tag was only $25,000, a tiny fraction of the average cost of winning a modern House campaign ($407,556).

Presidential campaigns, involving a different magnitude of money, were financed in considerable part by business. In the 1896 presidential campaign, for example, assessments against corporations imposed by Republican National Chairman Mark Hanna filled William McKinley's campaign coffers. The revelation that McKinley's successor, Theodore Roosevelt, had received a secret $50,000 contribution from a New York life-insurance company in the 1904 election ignited national headlines, and prompted Congress, in 1907, to prohibit direct corporate contributions to federal campaigns.

But neither the 1907 law nor a subsequent law passed in 1925 materially changed business' methods of steering money to federal candidates—either by "laundering" the funds through petty cash funds, professional fees; by "bonuses" to compensate executives for their political contributions; or simply through that least traceable means: cash. Russell Hemenway, who now directs a liberal PAC, the National Committee for an Effective Congress, remembers Oklahoma's Democratic Senator Robert Kerr distributing the largess of the oil industry to lawmakers "in plain envelopes, always in cash." Lloyd Hackler, a former Lyndon Johnson aide, once said that "under the old system, I bagged a lot of money, everybody did."

In 1971, amid widespread uneasiness about such under-the-table tactics, Congress enacted a new election law containing three important new features. The first tightened the loophole-ridden reporting-and-disclosure requirements for political gifts. The second laid the basis for government financing of presidential election campaigns by permitting taxpayers, in filling out their income tax forms, to earmark a dollar (two dollars for a married couple) for that purpose. Third, and the most important for the formation and growth of political action committees, the law explicitly permitted both corporations and labor unions to tap their respective treasuries to pay the expenses of soliciting PAC contributions and administering PACs. That feature proved to be the critical springboard for PAC growth, because it opened up the enormous corporate and union treasuries to finance the PACs' often-considerable administrative costs. Political scientist Herbert Alexander, a PAC expert, estimated that in the 1988 election, PACs spent $150 million on administrative expenses.

In view of the way business PACs have outdistanced those of labor, it is ironic that the unions, in 1971, pushed Congress to approve the tapping of corporate as well as union treasuries to run political action committees. At the time, labor leaders were convinced that the formation of business PACs would be limited by the prohibition against political involvement by those with government contracts. Union leaders believed that obstacle would surely bar most large corporations from starting PACs. Three years later, though, in 1974, Congress removed even that barrier to corporate PAC development—again, paradoxically, with labor's assent. By then, unions had secured federal job training contracts which they felt would be endangered as long as the prohibition against mixing politics with government contracts remained in force.* David Cohen, then a lobbyist for Common Cause, the group most actively opposing the PAC legislation, recalls that, ironically, labor lobbyists roamed Capitol Hill, pressing for an end to that prohibition—unaware, he says, that their business counterparts were secretly pursuing the same goal.

Cohen says he foresaw the superior capacity of corporations to raise PAC money and warned labor leaders of the dangers that lay ahead for them. His admonition has surely been borne out. By 1978

---

* That same 1974 law contained other important reform features essentially unrelated to PAC growth, principally ceilings on political contributions by individuals. That had the indirect effect of increasing candidates' reliance on PACs.

(the earliest year for which comparative figures are available), business-related PACs gave congressional candidates twice as much money as labor PACs. By 1990, the margin had grown to three to one.

The 1974 law set off a PAC explosion. In the next sixteen years, the number of PACs was to grow from 608 to more than 4,600 (although a significant number of those are currently inactive), and PAC contributions to congressional candidates rose from $12.5 million to nearly $150.5 million.*

As television became the undisputed number-one way of selling candidates, campaign costs rose meteorically. Barbecues and chicken dinners mixed with gifts from a few wealthy donors became a hopelessly inadequate means of financing House and Senate campaigns. Candidates, especially incumbent representatives and senators, found that the PACs—able and, at times, only too eager to make large contributions—were by far the easiest source of money. A study by the late Richard P. Conlon, the able director of the Democratic Study Group in Congress, found that between 1974 and 1984 there was a marked decline in small contributions in congressional campaigns. Conlon found that the under-$100 gifts fell from 38 to 23 percent of receipts in Senate campaigns and from 46 to only 15 percent of receipts in House campaigns. So lawmakers, especially members of the House, became more and more dependent on PACs. As noted, between 1974 and 1990, the percentage of House members dependent on special-interest PACs for roughly a third of their money grew from 28 percent to 85 percent (see table on page 54).

A sharply growing number of lawmakers began to receive more than half their funds from political action committees. Still more

---

* As with all campaign-finance dollar figures in this book, these are unadjusted for inflation, since it is difficult to make such an adjustment precisely and fairly. The consumer price index, the traditional inflation adjuster, which rose 122 percent from 1974 to 1986, the period this book is most concerned with, is of limited value because campaign costs are made up of narrow and specialized components, such as TV rates, polling costs, consultants' fees, and the like, which often bear no relation to normal consumer costs such as food, housing and entertainment.

disturbing, by 1990, nearly one-third of the representatives got *sixty* percent of their campaign money from PACs headquartered outside their districts.

Many, however, view these statistics as a symptom of a deeper cause—the soaring costs of running a modern campaign—portrayed in the following table:

**AVERAGE COST OF A
WINNING CAMPAIGN FOR**

Year	U.S. House	U.S. Senate
1978	$126,900	$1,208,600
1982	$236,000	$2,066,308
1986	$355,000	$3,099,554
1990	$407,556	$3,870,621

In the eyes of these observers these escalating campaign costs fuel candidates' hunger—indeed, desperation—to raise more and more money. That, in turn, makes them likely prey for the political action committees sponsored by special-interest groups.

Thus, in the past decade, more and more members of the House have fallen into deep dependency on outside special-interest PACs. In 1990, 236 representatives received at least half their campaign funds from PACs, and 137—over one-third of the House—got at least sixty percent.

The following table shows dramatically the rise in dependency on outside PACs:

Year	Number of House winners taking at least half of their campaign funds from PACs
1978	63
1980	85
1982	94
1984	164
1986	185
1988	210
1990	236

The increase in the number of House members who depend on PACs for 30 percent of their campaign money tells the tale even more dramatically:

Year	Percentage of House winners taking more than 30 percent of their funds from PACs
1974	28%
1978	55%
1982	69%
1986	82%
1990	85%

Thus, to me, those statistics say this: nearly nine-tenths of the U.S. representatives are "hooked" on special-interest PAC money—in the sense that they are dependent on PACs for a third of their campaign funds, and therefore feel they can't survive, politically, without the PACs.

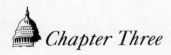 *Chapter Three*

THE BUYERS OF INFLUENCE

IMAGINE THAT YOU unexpectedly inherited some money from a distant aunt and decided to contribute your windfall to candidates for the U.S. House and Senate. Can you imagine—

- contributing to a candidate who had no opponent and hence did not need your money to win re-election?
- contributing to a candidate who disagreed with you on the issues you consider most important?
- giving to both opposing candidates in a given election?
- contributing to one candidate *before* the election and then, if your candidate lost, switching and giving to his or her opponent *after* the election?

If your answer to those questions is "No," you reason differently from most political action committees. At any rate, your logic would differ from General Electric's PAC when it handed out money in 1990 to House and Senate candidates.

For example, you would not consider giving to an unopposed or a sure-to-win candidate who doesn't need your money. But in the 1990 election, the GE PAC gave money to nineteen House candidates who faced *no* opponent, and to another seventy who had won by at least three-to-one margins in their last two elections, and hence could be predicted to coast to easy victories. Those eighty-nine candidates hardly needed GE's money to win re-election. *

Moreover, just as candidates' political philosophy counts heavily with most contributors, you would expect a candidate's pro- or anti-business attitude to be a major concern of General Electric, America's sixth largest industrial corporation. Surprise. In 1990, GE's PAC managers appeared singularly indifferent to candidates' attitudes toward business, as measured by the approval rating given lawmakers' congressional voting records by the U. S. Chamber of Commerce. For example, in the 1990 Michigan U. S. Senate race, the GE PAC gave $4,200 to Democrat *incumbent* Carl Levin (1988 Chamber of Commerce approval rating: 21 percent) and only $1,000 to the Republican challenger, Congressman Bill Schuette, whose prior voting record in the House had received a 93 percent Chamber approval rating in 1988.

As to betting on both horses in a single election or making a post-election switch, in 1990, GE's PAC managers had no scruples about contributing to opposing candidates in eight Senate elections in 1990, and in two instances in 1986, one in the Senate and one in the House, when their preelection "horse" lost, the General Electric PAC directors found some extra money, after the votes had been counted, to give to the candidate they had previously tried to defeat.

The GE PAC is a not untypical of how the 4,000-plus PACs extant in 1990 spent their money. For example, in 1990 PACs as a whole gave slightly over $13 million to House candidates who had no major-party opponent, and $26.4 million to House candidates who had won their previous two elections by margins of at least three to one.

Moreover, two studies by Common Cause unearthed at least 494 instances in which PACs gave to both opposing candidates in 1986 Senate elections, in addition to 150 postelection switches. Thirty-

---

* The research on the General Electric PAC's giving pattern was conducted in connection with a shareholder's suit against GE, in which the author of this book is plaintiff.

nine of these occurred in the state of North Dakota, where Democrat Kent Conrad upset the Republican incumbent, Senator Mark Andrews. Example: after the election, the American Bankers Association, which had made the maximum contribution of $10,000 to Andrews before the election, turned around and gave the same amount to Senator-elect Conrad.

Likewise, the Marine Engineers Union, displaying a mystifying interest in the landlocked state of North Dakota, at first bestowed $6,500 on Andrews and then, after Andrews lost, gave a $5,000 gift to Andrews' victorious opponent.

The General Electric PAC, which had spent $2,000 trying to defeat Conrad, now came to his aid with a $1,000 contribution.

The title of the Common Cause study sums it up: "If at First You Don't Succeed, Give, Give Again."*

Surveying the facts about political action committee giving leads to this conclusion:

> If the PACs had deliberately set out to convince the public that they are unabashed and unprincipled purchasers of influence, they could not have done a better job than to leave behind them the damning trail of evidence—the contributions to unopposed and "shoo-in" candidates; the betting on both horses; the postelection switch-giving when their horse lost.

But it is in their overwhelming favoritism for incumbents that the PACs have furnished the most persuasive evidence of influence-buying motives.

Consider again the example of the General Electric PAC. In 1990, out of 224 House contests in which the incumbent sought reelection, GE backed the incumbent in 221 cases (including 19 in which the incumbent had no opponent.) That is, GE selected the

---

* A subsequent Common Cause study of 1988 Senate elections uncovered a similar pattern of post-election switches to surprise winners in Montana, Connecticut, Nevada and Nebraska.

incumbent *98.7 percent of the time*. Aside from three instances where GE backed both opposing candidates, in only 3 of 224 contests—1.3 percent—did the GE PAC managers find the challenger preferable to the incumbent. It was as if someone from On High had issued instructions: "Never mind candidates' party affiliation, their attitudes toward big business, or their need for campaign funds. Whatever you do, *support the incumbent.*"

That apparent edict certainly applied to GE PAC giving in the 1990 Senate contests. Not once in twenty-eight Senate races in which the GE PAC gave and the incumbent sought reelection did the PAC forsake the incumbent, although in seven contests, it gave to both incumbent *and* challenger. Even there, GE was more generous to the incumbent.

GE's penchant for supporting incumbents is characteristic of PACs as a whole—particularly in races for the U. S. House. A 1987 Common Cause analysis revealed that one-third of all PACs gave at least 80 percent of their money to incumbents in the 1986 elections. Moreover, as previously noted, in contests where incumbents were seeking reelection in 1990, PACs overall gave more than 92 percent of their money to them. Only 8 percent went to challengers. PACs formed by corporations like incumbents the best. Also as noted, in 1990, corporate PACs as a whole gave 96 percent of their money to those already in office.

In considerable part as a result of that PAC imbalance, 1990 House incumbents outspent challengers more than three and a half to one. And in considerable part as a consequence of *that*, of incumbents seeking reelection, fully 96 percent won. Only four percent of challengers managed to upset sitting representatives.

Clearly, then, PACs' pattern of political giving differs sharply from that of most ordinary citizens. To the average $5 or $10 contributor, the PACs' giving patterns must seem illogical and thoroughly unprincipled.

The main difference between average citizens and PACs lies in their motivations for contributing. Most small donors contribute to candidates not because they expect anything for themselves in return for their money, but because they want to help them win. That is, private citizens, especially small givers, typically make political contributions because they want to influence the outcome of the election.

Most PACs also care about influence, but it's *post*-election influence they want. That is, they give because they want to maximize their chances of access to an officeholder who has the power to help them, and to have that access at the moment they need help.

Usually, when they make a contribution, most PACs don't know precisely what they want or when they may want it. But they assume that they will want a lawmaker's attention on some future occasion. When that moment arrives, they want to be as sure as possible of being able to make their case directly to the pivotal representatives and senators *in person*, and not to some junior assistant. Moreover, when the legislative machinery shifts into high gear, especially in the closing hours before Congress adjourns for the year, the time to see the lawmaker is *now*. Tomorrow—or even three hours from now—won't do. By then the vote may be over, and it will be too late.

Thus, when it comes to making political contributions, the difference between the motives of the typical citizen-contributor and a PAC can be summed up this way:

> The average citizen is mainly interested in influencing the outcome of an election.

> A PAC is less interested in the influence it has on an election outcome than in the influence it buys with the winner *after the ballots have been counted*.

That summary explains the PACs' apparently irrational behavior toward Democratic Congressman John Dingell, of Michigan.

Few ordinary citizens would give a dime to Dingell no matter how much they agree with his voting record. Why? Because he doesn't need the money to win. Dingell is a solid fixture in his Michigan district: he has never won by less than two to one; typically he wins by *three* to one. Yet, although he didn't need to spend a dollar to win reelection in 1990, that didn't discourage the PACs from loading $625,727 into his 1990 campaign coffers.

How does one explain this illogical PAC behavior? Why did they heap so much money on a lawmaker who so clearly didn't need a penny of it for his re-election campaign?

If you're in tune with PACs' reasoning, the explanation is perfectly obvious. Congressman Dingell is Chairman of the House Energy and Commerce Committee, which governs the fate of all bills of interest to the immense (and politically influential) oil and gas, securities, public utilities, automobile and chemical industries.

Not only does Congressman Dingell chair this potent panel; he has the reputation for doing so with an iron hand. Thus, a nod or shake of his head could make a difference of millions of dollars to one industry or another. Therefore, throwing a few thousand dollars Dingell's way—enough so he would be hard pressed to refuse an audience to a PAC's lobbyist—could be cheap at twice the price.*

Under this logic, repeated throughout the Congress, PACs have consistently given the lion's share of their money to incumbents—particularly in House races. But, as noted above, from 1982 to 1990, the PACs' pro-incumbent partiality took a marked leap. In those 1982 House elections in which the incumbent sought reelection, the PACs gave just under four-fifths of their money to incumbents, By 1990, the figure had risen to ninety-two percent.

That increase coincided with an equally marked rise in the percentage of incumbents who were successful at the polls. In 1990, incumbents who sought reelection had a 96 percent success rate, a jump of more than 5.4 percentage points over 1982.

Year	Percent of PAC money going to incumbents seeking reelection	Percent of House incumbents reelected
1974	n.a.	87.7%
1978	71.8%	93.7%
1982	78.9%	90.6%
1986	87.9%	98.0%
1990	92.0%	96.0%

---

* This reasoning parallels the logic, set forth in Chapter 2, behind the heavy PAC giving to securely ensconced Harlem Congressman Charles Rangel.

It would unduly oversimplify matters to claim that the PACs' favoritism for incumbents is solely responsible for their electoral success. A multitude of other factors come into play: the inherent advantages of incumbency and pro-incumbent redistricting, to mention just two. Nonetheless, the "bottom line" fact bears repeating (and reflection):

> In 1990, only three percent of the challengers for the U. S. House of Representatives were successful. Over 97 percent of the incumbents emerged victorious.

Brooks Jackson of the *Wall Street Journal* has suggested that we are witnessing a phenomenon—or is it an institution?—that the Founding Fathers never envisaged: the *congressman-for-life*.

Given most PACs' pre-eminent desire to buy influence or access, their pro-incumbent bias is perfectly natural.

Natural, perhaps. But good for the country and its political system? I believe not. The PAC support of incumbents has three malign consequences:

First, it tends to freeze out congressional candidates of experience, ability and idealism—solely for one reason: money.

Consider this freeze-frame snapshot of the electoral picture in contests for the U.S. House of Representatives as of October 17, 1990, less than one month before election day. The incumbents' treasuries had an average balance of $224,319. The *challengers'* campaign bank balances, by contrast, were, on average, $8,664—barely enough to pay staff and buy a few bumper stickers, but surely not sufficient to buy even one second's time on television during those final crucial weeks of the campaign.

Is it really good for the country to ration candidacies on the basis of how much money candidates possess or can raise—particularly when the incumbents have the unique advantage of being able to collect massive amounts of money from outside special-interest groups?

Again, suppose that a new Abe Lincoln were born in Congressman Dingell's district or a new Martin Luther King, Jr. in Congressman Charles Rangel's Harlem district (see Chapter 2). What chance would a second King or Lincoln have of successfully competing with Rangel or Dingell and their immense, virtually limitless campaign war chests?

Former Senator Barry Goldwater put it this way:

"What are we doing? Are we saying that . . . only the people who have influential friends who have money can be in the Senate? We're excluding a lot of young people that I think would make damn good additions to this body [the Senate] by not giving them access to money. . ."

Second, to the extent that the PACs' pro-incumbent favoritism reduces challenge, it narrows the spectrum of public discourse, and offers the voters less choice.

Third and worst of all, the PACs' preference for incumbents protects sitting officeholders from serious challenge even though their conduct in office may be seriously defective. Incumbency carries enough other inherent advantages, even without the political action committees. PAC favoritism compounds the imbalance.

As noted in Chapter 1, the modern campaign finance system has introduced a new meaning to the word "constituent"—one that the Founding Fathers doubtless did not foresee.

Most of the PACs—at least those representing business interests—and many of the large individual donors are linked to one interest group or another: banking, or oil, or chemicals, or the defense industry. Usually, a given industry's activities are supervised by one or two special congressional committees: banking legislation is dealt with by the banking committees, whose members take on special importance to banks and other financial institutions. The energy committees and their members hold special powers over the oil, gas and chemical industries; members of the telecommunications subcommittees are of special interest to telephone companies, the broadcasters and others. Each industry, therefore, has its own lawmaker "constituents"—those select few representatives and senators pivotal to its future. Conversely, the members of those committees come to regard those interest-group contributors as their "constituents."

United Technologies Corporation PAC actually used the word "constituent" in soliciting new PAC contributions. "We *have* strengthened our relationships with our 'constituent' senators and congressmen. One or more of us on the PAC Steering Committee have developed a personal relationship with each incumbent to whom we have given campaign contributions." (Emphasis theirs.)

Perhaps United Technologies did not intend to imply any proprietorship over its "constituent" members of Congress. Yet it is undeniable, given the financial power of many companies and industries, that they have the capacity to heap money and other favors on those lawmakers most important to them.

We have already noted in Chapter 2 the behavior of the defense-industry contractors, who concentrated 38 percent of their 1990 contributions on the eighteen percent of Congress sitting on defense-related committees of the House and Senate, and fifty-one percent of their 1989 honoraria on the 14 percent of the lawmakers who make up the defense-related committees of the House. Narrowing the lens to the top defense contractor, General Dynamics, you find that the firm's PAC carefully gave to every single member of the House Defense Appropriations Subcommittee (the committee that actually votes the military money), and to fifty-one of the fifty-four members of the House Armed Services Committee.

Naturally, as a "constituent" committee member rises in seniority and power, the pocketbooks of defense contractors open up correspondingly. For example, as will be observed in Chapter 4, since 1985, Alabama Representative William Dickinson, the ranking Republican member of the House Armed Services Committee, received more than $227,090 in campaign contributions from the leading defense contractors. In that same period, leading defense firms have lavished over more than $388,332 on Pennsylvania Democratic Congressman John Murtha, who presides over the House Defense Appropriations Subcommittee. Even more striking, in the short period of nineteen months, defense contractor PACs gave $134,582 to Virginia Republican Senator John Warner, ranking Republican member of the Senate Armed Services Committee.

Congressmen Dickinson and Murtha are supposed to be the public's representatives in dealing with these colossal defense firms, dealing with them fairly but toughly to protect against excessive profits or cost overruns. But with thousands of dollars from defense firms going into the campaign coffers of these two, how can the taxpayers be sure they are fulfilling their duties dispassionately? Indeed, isn't that possibility as dubious as that of the plate umpire calling balls and strikes impartially after receiving $10,000 from the pitcher? (See Baseball Scenario on page xix.)

Another example of a lawmaker carefully cosseted by those he regulated: Republican Senator Alfonse D'Amato of New York and the 1981–86 contributions he received from executives of sundry Wall Street firms. In the years 1981 through 1986, while the Republicans controlled the Senate, Senator D'Amato exercised critical control over many of these firms in his capacity as chairman of the Senate Securities Subcommittee. During those years—D'Amato's freshman term in the Senate—the PACs of twelve Wall Street firms gave Senator D'Amato a total of $78,200. But during that same period, *executives* of seventeen Wall Street firms gave the Senator a grand total of $360,780—nearly five times the amount given him by PACs. As you will see in Chapter 8, Senator D'Amato was a *very* good friend to the securities industry.

Paul Houston of the *Los Angeles Times* graphically summed up the new meaning of interest-group "constituents" this way: "In a city where money is the grade-A milk of political nutrition, the PACs and other large contributors have become political milkmen, each with a route to congressional customers who are accustomed to timely deliveries of cash for their campaigns or personal use. And the lobbyists in turn are close at hand when the time comes for important legislative decisions to be made."

Political action committees, then, are the principal but not the only means by which interest groups give to politicians. As in the case of Senator D'Amato, money from companies' and industries' PACs is on occasion far outweighed by personal contributions made by their executives and employees.

For example, the reports submitted to the Federal Election Commission by Senate Republican Leader Robert Dole for 1985–86 show a $1,000 campaign contribution to Dole's Senate reelection committee by Dow Chemical's PAC. Since contributions from PACs and contributions from individuals appear on separate FEC forms, Dole's PAC reports do not disclose the $16,000 in personal contributions by Dow executives *all on the same day*. Nor do those PAC records show that twenty-six executives of USX (formerly U.S. Steel) had such regard for Senator Dole that they contributed a total of $8,750 to the Senator just five days before Christmas, 1985.

Wealthy individuals and families strew campaign gifts among legislators occasionally in search of specific special favors. The political generosity of Ernest and Julio Gallo, who bottle one-fourth of the wine sold in the United States, seems to have played a role in the approval by the House Ways and Means Committee of a special tax provision that came to be called "the Gallo amendment." According to the *Wall Street Journal*, over an eight-year period, the Gallos contributed a grand total of $325,000 to parties and candidates, divided about equally between Democrats and Republicans.*

The Gallo amendment permitted the Gallo brothers to pass roughly $80 million to their grandchildren without paying a 33

---

* A 1991 Citizen Action study revealed the Gallo family as tops among family givers, with a total of $294,100—$20,000 of that to California Democratic Senator Alan Cranston on a single day.

percent estate tax. That would make the amendment worth nearly $27 million in tax savings to the Gallo brothers or their heirs.*

Among other political gifts that helped the Gallo brothers' special tax provision through Congress were $13,000 in campaign contributions to their own representative at the time, California Democrat Tony Coelho, plus $31,750 to the Democratic Congressional Campaign Committee, which Coelho chaired at the time. The *Wall Street Journal* reported that Coelho, then a powerful member of the House Democratic leadership, said he "checked with Congressman Edgar Jenkins [of Georgia, the amendment's sponsor] several times on the progress of the amendment." For a congressman as busy as Coelho, that was an unusual display of energy and interest. (Federal records show no Gallo contributions to Rep. Jenkins.)

In order to clear all the congressional hurdles, the "Gallo amendment" had to pass through the Senate Finance Committee, of which Senator Robert Dole was the ranking Republican member. In 1986, the two Gallo brothers and their wives made the maximum legal contribution to Senator Dole's PAC. If Dole had not formed his own PAC, the maximum the Gallos could have given was $1,000 per person, or a total of $4,000 for the brothers and their spouses. But Dole *had* established his own PAC to which individuals can legally contribute $5,000 per person, rather than $1,000. Accordingly, the Gallo brothers and their wives could (and did) quintuple their expression of regard for Senator Dole; each gave $5,000, for a more conspicuous total of $20,000.†

In 1980, the Washington law firm of Verner, Lipfert, Bernard, McPherson & Hand did not have a PAC. Nor did the Omaha based legal colossus, Kutak, Rock & Campbell.

Today, both have PACs, which give significant amounts of money to the election campaigns of representatives and senators. So do many other law firms, as the following table shows.

---

* The provision would also have applied to other wealthy persons with lots of grandchildren, but they are few in number. The Gallos appear to have been the instigators of "the Gallo amendment."

† The Gallo Amendment ultimately passed and was signed into law.

PAC DONATIONS

Firm Name	Home Base	1980	1990
Akin, Gump, Hauer & Feld	Dallas	$47,025	$259,602
Verner, Lipfert, Bernard, McPherson & Hand	Washington	——	$115,975
Jones, Day, Reavis & Pogue	Cleveland	$ 2,000	$104,212
Dickstein, Shapiro & Morin	Washington	$15,825	$104,275
Kutak, Rock & Campbell	Omaha	——	$ 63,800
Vinson, Elkins, Searls, Connally & Smith	Houston	$56,175	$ 94,666

All of these firms have Washington offices and clients whose problems call for special attention from Congress or the executive branch. Among the most important services those law firms can offer such clients is access to just the right senator or representative.

Increasingly, as observed in Chapter 4, a campaign contribution is the most effective—and, on occasion, the necessary—means of gaining that entree. Many law firms argue that forming a PAC is the fairest way of apportioning the distasteful access-buying burden among the firm's partners. It's unfair, they maintain, for the entire cost of buying tickets to the incessant fund-raisers to be borne solely by those attorneys in the firm who "work the Hill."

The PAC has another advantage: it is the cheapest way of gaining entree for *all* members of the firm. A former junior associate in the Washington "legislative department" of the Texas-based firm of Akin, Gump, Hauer & Feld, which includes former Democratic National Chairman (and newly-appointed U.S. Ambassador to the Soviet Union) Robert Strauss, described how that works:

> Sometimes it fell to me to make the rounds of all those three- or four-an-evening fundraisers that are held every damned night, it seems, on Capitol Hill. I'd go with an Akin Gump check in my pocket representing the firm. At the door, I'd present the check and make damned sure it was properly noted.
>
> Then I'd make sure to introduce myself to the guest of honor, pronouncing the words, "Akin Gump" loud and clear, to make sure it registered that the firm was here and had done its bit.

Then I'd go around the room carefully searching out all the staff members, and do the same thing: "Hi, I'm from Akin Gump." It was the firm *name* that would register, not my face. That way, whenever *anyone* from the firm would call the congressman or senator or anyone from the staff and say "Akin Gump," it would register. "Oh, yeah. I remember Akin Gump was at the fund-raiser."

After that, I'd slip out the back, and go on to the next party and do the same thing—maybe three or four times in an evening. It worked like a charm.

This attorney emphasizes that Akin Gump was by no means unique. On the contrary, he says, his own party-going pattern was standard operating procedure for law firms in the PAC business—so much so that he could expect to bump into the same lawyer-lobbyists at party after party on the same evening.

As congressional expectations of contributions from lobbyists grow, law firms with Washington branches are, one by one, setting up their own PACs. In 1987, Arnold & Porter, one of the most prestigious of Washington law firms, formed a PAC. Observers wondered how long the starchiest and most traditional Washington law firm, Covington & Burling, can hold out. (As of January, 1992, Covington & Burling was still PAC-free.)

The net effect of the mounting torrents of political gifts from "interested" groups, rich individuals and families, from the PACs, from the executives and employees of companies and industries and, finally, from growing numbers of law firms—is to further widen the power gap between the monied and the unmonied, between the organized and the unorganized.

The interest groups' amalgamation of political money has another effect: to enable small but highly organized groups to use money to win the day in Congress, *and to impose huge costs on the rest of the population*. After all the scandals of the past few years, does *anyone* believe the "civics class" view of Congress?

The two groups that carried the day in Congress in the following case studies do not boast millions or even hundreds of thousands of members like, say, the AFL-CIO, the U.S. Chamber of Commerce, or a nationwide environmental or peace organization. The first group, the used-car dealers, numbers about 27,000. The second—the billboard industry—is made up of only a few hundred companies, dominated by fewer than a dozen firms.

At the ballot box, then, both groups combined account for a minuscule number of votes.

Moreover, neither enjoys the widespread public appeal of organizations like the Red Cross or the Boy Scouts. Indeed, with many consumers, used-car dealers are as popular as bill collectors. And few families spend their Saturday afternoons in search of the best buy in a billboard.

Nonetheless, these two groups succeeded in getting their way with Congress. The used-car dealers even carried the day by margins of two-to-one.

Whatever they lacked in people-power, both groups more than compensated for in their adroit use of money-power.

1. The Used-Car Dealers and the "Lemon Law"

In the late 1970s, the Federal Trade Commission began to formulate an administrative ruling, nicknamed the "lemon law," to require used-car dealers to reveal to their customers *any* defects they *know* of in the cars they offer for sale.

Such a rule sets up the following political equation: on one side, millions of used-car buyers, many of whom had bought "lemons," stood to benefit enormously. On the other side, a comparative handful of dealers feared both the possible expense entailed with disclosure and repairs of defects, and the potential loss of sales. So the dealers strenuously opposed the lemon law.

Millions of buyers versus a few thousand dealers. On a strictly one-person-one-vote basis—that is, with lawmakers making a simple ballot-box calculation—the few dealers would seem to face an impossible task trying to convince a majority of Congress that millions of buyers were wrong.

Nonetheless, when in 1980 Congress passed a bill permitting a congressional veto of FTC rules like the lemon law, the used-car dealers went to work.

Their principal instrument was the political action committee that had been formed in 1972 by the National Automobile Dealers Association, or NADA. After a slow start, the NADA PAC grew explosively. In 1972, it dispensed a paltry $9,950. By 1976, though, its collections had swelled to over $368,000, which it distributed in gifts of memorable size among 270 candidates—half the entire Congress.

Four years later, after Congress acquired the veto power over FTC rules, the auto dealers really stepped on the gas. NADA's PAC contributions in 1980 virtually tripled from 1976, breaking the million-dollar mark. Throughout 1981 and 1982, as Congress read-ied itself to vote on the lemon-law veto, the NADA continued to put forth further campaign contributions.

Here is a typical sequence of events, involving Republican Rep. Mickey Edwards of Oklahoma City:

- *August 19, 1981*: Congressman Edwards receives $2,500 cam-paign contribution from the NADA PAC, even though it's not an election year.
- *Sept. 22, 1981*: Congressman Edwards signs up as cosponsor of resolution killing the FTC used-car rule, as strongly favored by NADA.
- *Oct. 19, 1981:* Congressman Edwards receives additional $200 campaign contribution from the NADA PAC.
- *May 26, 1982:* Congressman Edwards votes for a resolution killing the FTC used-car rule.
- *Sept. 30, 1982:* Congressman Edwards receives an added $2,000 contribution from NADA PAC—bringing the total he had received from that PAC since 1979 to $8,100.

Did those contributions buy Representative Edwards' vote? He insists that with his generally conservative anti-government philosophy, he would have voted that way with or without the campaign gifts.*

---

* See Baseball Scenario page xix.

Perhaps so. But to focus on Rep. Edwards alone is to miss the central question: Did the NADA PAC contributions influence the vote of the House as a whole? Here's the statistical evidence:

Of those receiving this amount from the NADA PAC in 1979 through 1982 . . .	. . . this percent voted against the lemon law in 1982
More than $4,000	90.2%
1,000 to $3,000	88.3%
$1 to $1,000	68.0%
Zero	34.2%*

University of Virginia professor Larry J. Sabato, a leading student of political action committees, concluded that the NADA contributions substantially affected and attracted the votes of members of Congress "who were decidedly more liberal or conservative than NADA."

A few thousand car *dealers* prevailed over millions of car *buyers* in both houses by greater than two-to-one margins—first in the Senate, 69–27, and then in the House, 286–133. Apparently something had gotten in the way of strict one-person-one-vote democracy. The figures above suggest that at least part of that something was money, in the form of auto-dealer campaign contributions.

In the succeeding congressional elections of 1982, NADA continued to reward its friends. Of the 251 House members who voted with the auto dealers on the lemon-law veto and who ran for reelection, 89 percent received NADA campaign contributions averaging $2,300. By contrast, only 22 percent of the representatives

* Some defenders of PACs, such as University of California professor Herbert Alexander maintain that such mathematical correlations are overly simplistic, failing to take account of such factors as party loyalty, the member's personal philosophy, regional and constituent differences. He would be correct if my argument was that money is the *sole* determinant of members' votes. I do not so argue. But would Alexander contend that money plays *no* role? So this is not an all-or-nothing argument; it's a question of *how much* political money affects lawmakers' behavior.

who voted against the dealers got NADA money, with contributions averaging less than half as great.

Author Elizabeth Drew asked one congressman why the House had voted as it did on the lemon law. His answer: "Of course it was money. Why else would they vote for used-car dealers?"

2. The Billboard Industry and Regulation of Billboards on Federal Highways

Compared with the car dealers, the billboard industry had an infinitely smaller chance of winning the U.S. Congress—at least in theory. After all, there are 27,000 car dealers; there are at least a few of them in every congressional district; and they sell a product that a great many people need and want.

Not so the billboard industry. It consists of a few hundred companies, ten of which dominate the industry. Aside from a certain number of small businesses, especially hotels and restaurants in rural areas, who feel they need outdoor signs to direct travelers to them, billboards are hardly a popular consumer item.

Yet, while the billboard industry's problem was seemingly greater, the industry succeeded far more than the car dealers in working its will with the U. S. Congress.

The billboard industry's need to deal with the Congress began in 1965, when the new Highway Beautification Act sought to limit billboards along federally funded highways.

At the time it was passed, in 1965, the new law was widely acclaimed. It seemed to offer real hope for controlling billboard blight. Two decades later, though, the results hardly measured up to initial promises. The taxpayers had laid out nearly a quarter of a billion dollars for the removal of some billboards; yet far more had sprung up in their place. The precise number is not known (no national figures exist); but in 1983, when data *was* gathered, the taxpayers had paid for the removal of 2,235 signs, but 13,522 new signs had been erected.

Moreover, under industry pressure, the limits on the signs' size and height were relaxed. The twin result: billboard company income swelled enormously; and the new and larger roadside signs became even worse polluters of the landscape.

By 1982, so completely had the industry turned the Highway Beautification Act to its benefit that Vermont's Senator Robert Stafford, one of the most tenacious of the billboard reformers, bitterly observed the law would be more aptly labeled the Billboard Compensation and Protection Act, and sought to repeal the 1965 law. Ironically, only the billboard industry sought to retain it.

Many believe that the industry's thwarting of the Beautification Act began with the original law itself. It now appears that in 1965, the industry hoodwinked Congress into writing a law that relaxed rather than tightened billboard regulation and made the control process vastly more costly than before.

The background is this: prior to 1965, billboard regulation had been largely a municipal affair. When cities used local ordinances to order billboards removed, signs could be removed without any expenditure of taxpayers' funds. The courts had consistently approved compensating the owners by allowing the signs to remain up during a grace period, with the revenues earned during the grace period serving as proper compensation. After all, the courts reasoned, the signs derived their value solely because of the traffic on the public roads, which had been built at taxpayer expense.

Enter, in 1965, Lady Bird Johnson, the First Lady, pressing for *federal* billboard control. Everyone expected the industry to dig in its heels and fight. But much to the surprise and delight of the bill's sponsors, the industry agreed that "billboards have no place in the scenic areas of our highways."

But when the dust had cleared, it turned out that, while publicly pledging support, industry lobbyists had persuaded Congress to toss aside five decades of court decisions approving the grace-period method of paying billboard owners for the removal of their signs, and requiring that signs removed pursuant to the new federal law be compensated for exclusively in cash—to come out of taxpayers' pockets.

What's more, under the new legislation, in selecting which signs were to be removed and paid for, the government had to choose from a list volunteered by the billboard owners. In practice, the owners typically offered their least desirable signs, often obsolete signs that they had scheduled for demolition anyway. Most galling of all, billboard owners could—and did—use the taxpayers' cash to build new and bigger signs, *often on a nearby stretch of that same road.*

Apparently, even that wasn't enough for the industry. In 1978, the billboard lobby persuaded Congress to make the law twice as sweet for the sign owners—and twice as expensive for the taxpayers. The new law stripped states and cities of much of their power to use the grace-period formula for removing signs under *local* ordinances. Henceforth, if a city wanted to order the removal of *any sign visible from a federal highway*, it would have to compensate the owner in cash, even if the removal was strictly pursuant to a local ordinance and had nothing to do with federal law.

In that single stroke, the billboard industry added about 38,000 signs to the number eligible for cash compensation estimated at a third of a billion dollars. This was in addition to the $427 million already due the industry for billboards covered under the 1965 law. With federal expenditures on billboard removal reduced to an annual rate of $2 million a year (in 1984), that new sum added to $427 million already due the industry meant that the last billboard wouldn't be torn down until at least the year 2367.

Perhaps most offensive, from the beginning, the industry exploited gaping loopholes in the 1965 law, later made more serious by state regulations. The most flagrant: the "unzoned commercial zone" loophole. Under that provision, a stretch of country road previously barred to billboards could be transformed into an approved billboard zone simply by painting the pretext of a sign, MIKE'S WELDING SHOP, on an empty shack overgrown with weeds, or terming a single long-unused gasoline pump as a filling station. The U.S. Department of Transportation issued a report replete with photographs of those and other similar actual examples. In 1985, the General Accounting Office found that in the year ending in mid–1983, just such pretenses made possible the erection of 4,712 billboards. That was twice as many signs as the government paid to tear down that same year.

Compared with the auto dealers, the billboard industry is a midget. The industry's sales are but one-twentieth as great as auto sales, and its 1990 PAC contributions to congressional candidates amounted to a puny $91,850, compared with over $1,288,600 from the car dealers' PAC.

How, then, has this bantam industry worked its magic on Congress over the years?

Answer: by aiming its favors like a rifle, rather than scattering them, shotgun style, over the entire Congress, as the car dealers could afford to do.

The billboard industry was able to adopt this narrow-target strategy because billboard legislation is consistently embedded as a few clauses in immense and complex highway bills handled by the Public Works and Transportation Committees. Thus, billboard questions seldom come to name-by-name roll-call votes, especially in the House. Consequently, on billboard matters, most lawmakers are content to follow the lead of their respective public works committees that oversee highway and billboard legislation.

Thus, unlike the auto dealers, the billboard industry did not have to woo all 535 lawmakers. In general, all it took was to win and maintain influence with the chairmen and a few pivotal members of the public works committees—and, not incidentally, key committee staff members.

It is therefore instructive to focus a microscope on the variety of favors the industry lavished on the late James J. Howard, a representative from the state of New Jersey and long-time chairman of the House Public Works Committee, which controls all billboard legislation.

First there were industry PAC contributions to Congressman Howard's campaigns. In his last five elections, those totaled

$15,250—enough to get any legislator's attention, if not to win his or her sympathies.

But the industry's PACs are comparatively tiny, and their contributions to Congressman Howard were supplemented—indeed, far overshadowed—by gifts from *individuals* connected with the billboard industry, principally executives and employees and, on occasion, their wives. For example, in the 1986 election alone, Congressman Howard received over $40,000 from such individuals.

The billboard industry, being small and unusually close-knit, is peculiarly well positioned to orchestrate contributions from company executives, and this the industry has done with conspicuous success. The role model has been Vernon Clark, now a consulting lobbyist, but for years the president of the Outdoor Advertising Association of America (OAAA), the umbrella trade association for most billboard concerns, and the industry's chief lobbyist in Washington. Clark and his wife, Elaine, have been extraordinarily generous political givers. In the 1990 congressional elections, for example, the pair contributed a total of $54,775 to candidates for Congress.

The couple were particularly open-handed with Chairman Howard. In the four elections prior to his death in March, 1988, they contributed $9,650 to his campaigns.

The billboard industry's closeness to, and influence with Chairman Howard probably had more to do with the industry's unswerving hospitality to Congressman and Mrs. Howard at their annual convention in balmy Palm Springs, California. These conventions consistently took place in January, when cold in the nation's Capital can often be piercing. In some years, the OAAA's hospitality was extensive. According to Sheila Kaplan, writing in *Common Cause* magazine in 1985, billboard interests picked up the tab for Congressman and Mrs. Howard to attend the OAAA festivities for six nights in 1985. That year, Congressman Howard was able not only to soak up a California tan, but to pick up $4,000 in speaking fees (then permissible under House rules)—$2,000 from individual billboard companies, and $2,000 from the Tobacco Institute, which consistently meshes its annual meetings with those of OAAA. (The tobacco industry, of course, is a leading user of billboards.)

These visits had two-way benefits: for the Howards, they meant several days in the California sunshine. For the industry they provided several days for billboard executives to make their names and faces known to the Chairman, on a first-name basis, and to share with him the problems of the outdoor-sign industry in a relaxed and friendly atmosphere impossible to duplicate in Washington.

The billboard industry was also adroit enough to extend Palm Springs hospitality to key congressional staff aides, who often play a pivotal role in shaping not only legislation but their bosses' views as well. According to the *National Journal*, at least fifteen Senate and House aides participated in the OAAA Palm Springs festivities in January, 1986. The *Journal* reported that "the aides were offered an honorarium—in some cases $1,000—air travel and a hotel room for several nights; the association paid the air fare for a least one participant's wife." Among the staff members attending the OAAA convention: Kevin Gottlieb, then executive assistant to Michigan Senator Donald W. Riegle (Gottlieb now heads the Washington lobbying office of the OAAA); Roy F. Greenaway, administrative assistant to California's Alan Cranston, and David M. Strauss, administrative assistant to North Dakota Senator Quentin Burdick, sometime Chairman of the Senate committee that deals with billboard legislation. All three senators are Democrats. A year later, when the roll was called in the Senate on a billboard reform proposal, all three of those senators—Riegle, Cranston and Burdick—who are ordinarily environmentally minded, sided with the industry and against the strongly expressed views of the most activist environmental groups.

The *National Journal* adds that these invitations to congressional staffers to conferences at vacation spots is a regular practice of the billboard industry. The *Journal* quoted one Senate aide who has attended other conferences held by the outdoor advertisers "in locales such as Orlando and Lake Tahoe, Nevada. 'It happens all the time to get invitations for events like this,' [the aide] said. 'That's the way the system works.'"

For the OAAA, "the system works" extraordinarily well, judging from the group's remarkable success, in 1982, in getting Chairman Howard to propose, and the entire Public Works Committee of the U. S. House of Representatives to approve, a sweeping change in the billboard law. The OAAA's case could hardly have been harmed by the $20,500 in honoraria to members of the Committee during the prior four years.

The committee's action was exceptional in that the wording in the provision adopted by voice vote and without debate was virtually identical to that proposed by the industry, even down to the definition of "free coffee" in a provision exempting signs offering "free coffee" to travelers by nonprofit groups.

While the provision did not survive, *Washington Post* reporter Howard Kurtz termed the phenomenon of "a bill passing through the congressional maze almost exactly as it was written by an industry group" a "lobbyist's dream."

Following Chairman Howard's 1988 death, the billboard industry continued its generosity to key members of the panel that deals with billboard-control legislation. For example, in the 1988 and 1990 elections, industry PACs and individuals bestowed over $63,000 in campaign contributions on Pennsylvania Representative Bud Shuster, the second ranking Republican on that committee. Moreover, in the three years, 1987 through 1989, industry honoraria to Shuster totaled $12,850 and billboard companies treated him to round-trip visits to Palm Beach, Los Angeles and Fort Myers.

In 1986, for one fleeting moment, the billboard lobby's grip on Congress appeared in jeopardy. Under the leadership of former Vermont Republican Senator Robert T. Stafford, a veteran in the billboard-reform fight, the Senate Public Works Committee passed a reform proposal by a surprising 11–4 margin. But the highway bill, of which the billboard reform was a part, never passed the full Congress.

When Congress returned to the subject in January 1987, the Senate had shifted to Democratic control. Stafford's chairmanship of Senate Public Works had been taken by North Dakota's Quentin Burdick, a long-time billboard industry ally. But the Committee had three newly-elected Democratic senators who all had sufficiently good records on environmental issues to receive the endorsements, in their 1986 Senate races, of both the Sierra Club and the League of Conservation Voters, an environmental activist group with its own PAC. The three were Robert Graham, former governor of Florida, and former Democratic Representatives Harry Reid of Nevada and Barbara Mikulski of Maryland.

Billboard reformers had hopes of their support when the reform measure came up again. But when the committee roll was called on January 21, all three sided with the billboard lobby. The 11–4 vote of 1986 had evaporated. The new reform proposal lost—by an 8–8 tie vote. If any of the three had voted for the reform, it would have cleared the committee.

Senator Graham's staff members are said to have been at a loss to explain why their boss voted with the billboard industry that day. Thirteen days later, after his vote stirred up an angry tempest in his home state of Florida, he reversed his stance in the full Senate.

The other two new committee members, Senators Mikulski and Reid were beneficiaries of another technique by which the tiny billboard industry magnifies its influence: underwriting fundraising parties for candidates. That technique assures that, in the mind of the beneficiary, the industry gets credit for the entire amount raised at the industry-hosted party, rather than for a mere thousand dollars or two of catering expenses.

For example, on February 10, 1986, the OAAA PAC paid $1,545 to B&B Caterers to cater a Washington fundraising party for Maryland senatorial candidate Barbara Mikulski. While Mikulski's campaign reports don't show precisely how much that particular function party raised and her office declines to discuss the matter, fundraising experts guess that the take was in the thousands of dollars.

In the case of Nevada's new Senator Reid, on October 2, the

OAAA had laid out $552.94 to the Pisces Club in Washington's fashionable Georgetown, as an "in-kind contribution" to Reid's senatorial campaign—presumably to pay part of the expenses of a fundraising party for Reid.

On February 3, 1987, during debate on the highway bill, Stafford brought up his reform proposal for a vote by the full Senate. While the reform's fate was uncertain, there was one Senator whose vote the Stafford forces felt sure they could count on: Brock Adams, the newly elected Democratic Senator from Washington State. There were three reasons to believe Adams would vote with Senator Stafford: his is an environmentally conscious state; his predecessor, Slade Gorton, had been a reform leader; and, most of all, in 1978, as Secretary of Transportation in the Carter Administration, Adams had, in writing, vigorously supported the core of the Stafford proposal.

But, in 1987, when his name was called, Adams cast his vote against the Stafford reform.

Federal Election Commission records show that in Adams' 1986 senatorial campaign, the billboard industry favored him with $12,000 in contributions, principally from billboard executives, owners, and other persons connected with the outdoor-sign industry.

The billboard industry's use of honoraria demonstrates the potency of speaking fees, when they were still permitted under Congressional rules.

For its size, the billboard industry undoubtedly lavished more money on members of Congress in the way of speaking fees and honoraria than any other industry group. In 1985, for example, the total honoraria paid to members of Congress by this comparative runt of an industry ranked third, surpassed by only two others: the defense contractors (annual sales to the government alone: $163 billion—one hundred fifty times the billboard industry's total sales of $1.2 billion), the other the tobacco industry (annual sales: $34 billion).

A 1979 fund-raising appeal by the Roadside Business Association, a trade association of highway advertisers, explains why. The

RBA entreated its members to contribute to a special fund to pay speaking fees because, said the letter, the honorarium "approach" is more effective than a campaign contribution in bringing "the member [of Congress] closer and more personal [sic] to all RBA members." The appeal concluded, "This is the end of the pitch! You all know how the game is played in Washington. Need I say more?"

Edward McMahon, a former Georgetown University law professor now director of Scenic America, is not surprised by the success of the billboard industry in manipulating Congress and thwarting federal regulation. These achievements, McMahon says, grow out of decades of practice in fighting billboard controls at the municipal level. McMahon feels the industry's skill has a simple explanation. He regards billboards as polluters of the scenic environment. But, he says, the billboard industry is different from other polluters, such as chemicals or steel. In those industries, McMahon observes, the pollution is the *by-product* of making something society wants or needs (chemicals, say, or steel). But in the case of billboards, the pollution *is* the product, and to regulate it is to threaten the very lifeblood of the industry.

Therefore, he concludes, the industry trains its personnel to think of thwarting (McMahon calls it "subverting") public regulatory efforts as an *integral* part of their jobs.

To illustrate his point, McMahon produces the syllabus for a "Corporate Development Seminar" conducted in June, 1982 by the Naegele Outdoor Advertising Company, the nation's sixth-largest billboard firm. "Ordinarily," McMahon says, "you'd expect a 'corporate development' seminar to be devoted to sales and marketing. But almost none of this agenda had to do with that. Almost the entire program was devoted to 'strategy' in blocking a billboard ordinance in a city council."

McMahon says, "Look at these items in the 'Job Description—Corporate Development Department': '1. Amending Ordinances . . . Political Contributions . . . know Local Politicians.'

"And here is an entire section on offering 'public service' billboards to promote the mayor's favorite charity. See how it carefully notes that "The Mayor (being a politician) will recognize the value of being able to get credit for favors to various civic-minded persons [who are] generally the same persons that vote and that are active at election time."

As an example of the selective use of these "public-service" billboards, McMahon cites a giant sign placed in West Des Moines by the Naegele company while it was locked in a court fight with the city over a billboard ordinance. The sign carried the legend, "A Shriner never stands so tall as when he stoops to help a crippled child." The city's attorney, in a letter to the city council, questioned whether it was "accidental" that the judge deciding the Naegele billboard case "is both a Shriner and a resident of West Des Moines."

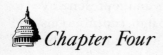 *Chapter Four*

THE SELLERS OF INFLUENCE

ON MAY 11, 1976, a disciplinary action was brought against Justice Frank Vaccaro of the New York Supreme Court for alleged acts of judicial misconduct committed when Vaccaro was a lower-court judge—namely:

- staying, with his wife, at a hotel for a weekend as the guest of a friend's law firm.
- presiding in a handful of cases (out of thousands he heard) involving a law partner of his own law clerk.
- presiding over a small-claims case in which his long-time friend was defendant. The amount at issue: $106.81.

Other than the value of that hotel room, no one had given the judge so much as a dollar. Moreover, the judges ruling on his case were at pains to point out that there was no evidence that any injustice had occurred or that he had given anyone preferred treatment.

Nonetheless, they said, Justice Vaccaro's behavior did *technically* violate the canons of judicial ethics and did "convey the *impression* of impropriety." (Emphasis added.) Their sentence: *Six months suspension, without pay.*

As the Vaccaro case makes clear, because the public expects

judges' decisions to be based as much as possible on merit, it is unthinkable for a federal judge to accept money (or the slightest of favors) from a defendant or a plaintiff—or *anyone* with a stake in that judge's decisions.

It is *not* unthinkable, though, for senators and representatives to do just that. They routinely accept campaign contributions and other favors from interest groups that have hundreds of millions of dollars—sometimes even *billions*—riding on their decisions.

And no one blinks an eye.

William L. Dickinson and John Dingell sit, in effect, as judges. Indeed, they possess powers far greater than any judge—the power to impose immense burdens on, or grant colossal favors to, parties who appear before them.

Dingell, a Democratic representative from Michigan, is the chairman of the House Energy and Commerce Committee. That committee wields enormous powers over a wide variety of massive (and politically active) industries, among them: the oil and gas industry; the securities industry; railroads; public utilities; broadcasting; health and medicine; and radio and TV networks and stations. All those industries have colossal stakes in the actions of Dingell's committee over which he reportedly presides with an iron hand.

The public has a right to expect Congressman Dingell's decisions, like Judge Vaccaro's, to be based as much as possible on merit—in any event untainted by considerations of financial rewards. And yet, in the past three elections, the PACs of industries subject to his committee's jurisdiction contributed $614,655 to his lopsided electoral victories.

Alabama's Dickinson is the highest-ranking Republican on the House Armed Services Committee—a principal judge, in effect, over matters of multi-billion-dollar importance to the nation's defense contractors.

Since 1985, Representative Dickinson has accepted $227,090 in campaign contributions from defense contractors who have enormous stakes in his decisions over their fates.

Both Dingell and Dickinson not only vote on matters critically affecting their benefactors, but as senior members of their respective panels, play leading roles in shaping their committees' decisions.

Neither Dingell nor Dickinson has ever been suspended—not even for one day—for two reasons: first, nothing they did was illegal—or even contrary to Congress' own rules.

Second, Dickinson and Dingell are all too typical of members of Congress. All but a handful of legislators customarily—and unhesitatingly—accept campaign money from groups over whom their committees have jurisdiction. Suspend Dickinson and Dingell and you'd have to discipline ninety-plus percent of their colleagues. Then who would pass the laws?

For the few representatives who come from closely contested districts and win or lose by narrow margins, accepting campaign contributions from parties affected by their congressional votes is at least understandable. For them, eking out every last dollar can be a matter of political life or death.

But most representatives are safely ensconced in their congressional seats. An example is Ronnie G. Flippo, a Democrat from Florence, Alabama, who represented that state's Fifth Congressional District until, in 1990, he chose to run for governor rather than for re-election to the House.

Before he left Congress, Representative Flippo had become a PAC favorite. Between 1978 and 1988, his PAC receipts rose over thirteenfold from $33,000 to $445,960.

This dramatic rise in PAC gifts was not prompted by his need for campaign money. On the contrary: in his last five elections, Congressman Flippo did not face serious opposition in any primary contest, and received, on average, over 83 percent of the vote in the general elections.

Why would outside PACs heap money on such an invincible congressman? Was it out of interest in the welfare of the people of the Fifth District of Alabama? No; the PACs' generosity was, more probably, wholly unrelated to Alabama, but very much related to Congressman Flippo's powerful seat on the House Ways and Means

Committee (the panel that handles tax legislation) and, in particular, to the fact that that committee considered, in 1985 and 1986, a sweeping tax-loophole-closing program proposed by the Reagan Administration, one that could, result, in effect, in billions of dollars of tax increases for many industries.

Since Congressman Flippo constantly won re-election without having to spend much money, the question arises: What happened to all the money the PACs contributed? Answer: it built up into a huge surplus. Here is the way Congressman Flippo's campaign-fund bank balance grew at the end of each successive election:

1978:	$ 35,315
1980:	$126,279
1982:	$139,348
1984:	$338,016
1986:	$603,947
1988:	$810,958

Representative Flippo had several options for that $810,958. One was to transfer the entire amount to his own bank account upon leaving Congress. Flippo enjoyed that remarkable privilege because the House conferred that "golden parachute" benefit on its members.*

Thus, when an interest group made a politically unnecessary campaign contribution to a lawmaker like Representative Flippo, the money served two purposes. First, it bought the legislator's sympathetic attention and, potentially at least, it served as the lawmaker's personal pension fund. Second, it provided the member with a cash reserve that would tend to scare off would-be challengers.

While no retiring House members have thus far helped themselves to the whole amount of their campaign surplus, several have transferred substantial sums. According to a 1991 study by the

---

* In 1979, the privilege was limited to representatives who came to office before January 8, 1980. That limitation didn't affect Congressman Flippo, who 'vas first elected in 1976. Still later, in 1989, the House further trimmed this emolument, confining it to representatives who leave Congress before January, 1993.

Center for Public Integrity, seventy-three "former members of Congress" transferred a total of $6.4 million to their own bank accounts when they retired between 1979 and 1991. Topping the list: the $604,000 of surplus campaign funds conveyed to the survivors of the late Republican Congressman John J. Duncan of Tennessee; and Missouri Republican Gene Taylor, who conveyed nearly $345,000 to his personal use, and gave an additional $52,811 to the Gene Taylor Library and Museum. Washington Representative Al Swift told *Congressional Quarterly*, "I know of a couple of members who have told me flatly, 'This is my retirement account.' "

Even after these private pension funds were trimmed back severely, the large cash balances remaining in lawmakers' campaign accounts continued to be a growing phenomenon in the House. At the end of the 1990 elections, congressional campaign surpluses totaled $72 million, a twenty-two percent rise in just four years. In 1976, only three representatives had leftover funds greater than $100,000. A decade and a half later, fifty percent of the House did. The election-by-election figures are as follows:

Election cycle ending	Numbers of Reps. with campaign surpluses over $100,000
1976	3
1978	6
1980	24
1982	59
1984	120
1986	174
1988	206
1990	219

A few lawmakers are candid about using their campaign balances to scare off would-be challengers. For example, in 1984, Republican Congressman Henson Moore of Louisiana was challenged about $467,000 he had left over in his campaign treasury. In response, he complained that this amount was not too high, but too low—too low, that is, to discourage opposition. It is well known, he said, that a contested House campaign costs $600,000.*

Incumbent senators, too, sometimes end their campaigns with mammoth surpluses, especially when, having exploited their incumbency to raise huge sums, they coast through to victory against a weak opponent. For example, Republican Senator Phil Gramm of Texas ended his 1990 senatorial campaign with over $4 million in his campaign treasury, highest among senators elected that year. But neither that growing treasury, nor a 300–1 financial advantage over his opponent, Hugh Parmer, stopped Gramm from holding a Washington breakfast fund-raiser at $1,000 a ticket in September, 1990. Democrat Sam Nunn, of Georgia, had the second highest campaign surplus with over $1.5 million even though he was unopposed in the general election.

Few prospective opponents will relish taking on an incumbent senator like Gramm with over $4 million in the bank. But in the future, Gramm's surplus is bound to be larger than that. In 1991, five years before his next Senate election, the far-sighted Gramm set up a 1996 Senate re-election fund.

Even when senators don't end their campaigns with large surpluses, they can exploit the power of their incumbency over the course of their six-year term to build up a forbidding campaign treasury. A dramatic example was New York Republican Senator Alfonse D'Amato. During his first term in the Senate, D'Amato never stopped shaking the money tree. By the end of 1981, the very first year after his surprise election to the Senate, his campaign bank balance approached a quarter of a million dollars. With unceasing fundraising effort, the coffers grew steadily. At each year's end, his campaign bank balances stood as follows:

---

* Ironically, Congressman Moore may have been hoist on his own petard. In 1984, Moore is said to have been dissuaded from making a U.S. Senate race against the incumbent, Democratic Senator Bennett Johnston, in part because of the early war chest Johnston had amassed.

Two years later, though, Moore demonstrated another prime utility of a campaign surplus accumulated primarily by virtue of his incumbency. He used the $726,000 in his House campaign treasury at the end of 1984 as a springboard for his own unsuccessful Senate campaign to fill the Senate seat left vacant by the retirement of Senator Russell B. Long.

1982: $ 430,574
1983: $1,383,418
1984: $2,037,486
1985: $4,190,268

On January 1 of an election year, many senators—and virtually all challengers—have not even begun to raise serious money. But here was Alfonse D'Amato, entering *his* election year sitting on a bank balance of more than $4 million!

"Without his pockets" (as used to be said about J. P. Morgan), D'Amato was not a formidable candidate—judging by the conventional political racing forms, at least. He was a first-term Republican Senator in a state where registered Democrats outnumber Republicans by three to two. In 1980, he had won a slender victory in an unusual three-way race.

But with $4 million-plus in his campaign treasury, Alfonse D'Amato appeared formidable. As 1986 rolled on, two prominent Democratic candidates stepped up to the hurdle of a Senate race, only to balk at the last minute. The logical candidate was former Congresswoman Elizabeth Holtzman, who had come within 81,000 votes of defeating D'Amato six years earlier. She, too, backed away, citing D'Amato's large warchest as a major reason.

Finally, late in the game, two relatively unknown Democrats entered the race. There was John Dyson, a multimillionaire who spent $6 million—most of it his own money—in his primary race. He was opposed—and narrowly defeated—by former Nader-raider activist Mark Green. Green was the only Senate candidate in the United States to forswear PAC gifts. Hence he had to run both his primary and general-election campaigns on a shoestring and was outspent heavily in both contests. D'Amato won handily in November.

Alfonse D'Amato vividly illustrates a growing phenomenon that has lobbyists and interest-group givers grumbling: incumbents' use of their power to demand (some say extort) contributions from those who want their help.

For example, from 1981 to 1986, while the Republicans controlled the Senate, D'Amato occupied a strategic position as chairman of the Senate Banking Subcommittee on Securities. As such, he was the key player shaping legislation of vital concern to the stocks-and-bonds industry. During his first five and a half years in office, at his encouragement, PACs and executives of seventeen Wall Street firms contributed half a million dollars to his re-election campaign. *The Wall Street Journal* reported that Senator D'Amato was not "bashful about asking for donations." According to the *Journal*, the forcefulness of the D'Amato fundraising tactics in the securities industry produced grumblings on Wall Street. "Nothing is enough," said one top Wall Street lobbyist. "It's continuous pressure. If you don't contribute, they don't return your phone calls."

That is a complaint heard with increasing frequency in the Washington lobbying community. A leading PAC champion, Richard Armstrong, who heads the Public Affairs Council (a group of Washington corporate public-affairs officers), has publicly charged lawmakers with "extortion." Representatives and senators, he says, "are very heavy-handed."

Heavy-handed is a precise way of describing the tactics employed by former South Dakota Republican Senator James Abdnor in hitting up Washington lobbyists and PAC managers to buy $1,500 tickets to a fundraising dinner at which President Reagan was to be the star attraction. Abdnor sent the invitation around by messenger, with a reply card giving the invitee three choices: to make a $5,000 PAC contribution; to buy one or more tickets; or to say "No, our PAC does not wish to support the salute to Jim Abdnor featuring President Reagan." What angered many PAC managers was Abdnor's instruction to the messenger not to leave the invitee's office without a response of some kind.

One lobbyist (who asked not to be identified) tells of a legislator chastising him and his confreres for failing to come through with campaign contributions when he had done them "a favor" earlier. He told the group that this time, they would have to produce the support *in advance* if they expected his help on a key vote coming up.

Another lobbyist (who also requested anonymity) reports requesting an appointment with a U.S. senator from one of the senator's junior aides. The lobbyist was referred upward to the senator's administrative assistant, who consulted a list of campaign contributors. "We've only got you down for $500," he said. "That's not enough."

Yet another lawyer-lobbyist recounts that when he and his partners declined an invitation to an "expensive" fundraiser for a senator to whom they had already contributed generously, the lobbyist was soon favored with a personal call from the senator himself, reminding the lobbyist how his door had always been open to the lobbyist, and how receptive he had always been to the lobbyist's requests. "The terrible thing," this lobbyist told me, "was that even though my partners and I had given as much as we thought we should, we still gave more. After a 'hint' like that senator gave us, what could we do?"

Occasionally a member of Congress openly acknowledges the price tag for obtaining a personal audience. One such is Wisconsin Democratic Congressman Les Aspin, the controversial Democrat who in 1985 leaped over several seniority hurdles to be elevated unexpectedly to the chairmanship of the potent House Armed Services Committee. Aspin told a newspaper in his district that the defense contractors know they have to contribute "if they want to talk to the chairman." Not surprisingly, after Aspin ascended to the chairmanship, the campaign contributions he received from the PACs of defense contractors in the first ten *months* were nearly 50 percent above the total for the previous six *years*.

On occasion, the influence-buying game is played without a word being spoken or an arm twisted. It is just understood that *everyone* wants to be on the good side of those who occupy the seats of the mighty.

In November, 1985, for example, after Speaker Tip O'Neill had announced his intention to retire and Texas Congressman Jim Wright announced his candidacy to succeed him, Wright held what he called a "Cowtown Jamboree" in his hometown of Fort Worth.

No serious candidate had yet emerged to oppose Wright for the speakership, and yet the turnout at the jamboree was enormous. Wright said later that the "overwhelming bulk" of the $1.3 million he raised that year, nearly half of it from PACs, was raised at that single event.

On its face, the success of the jamboree had an especially curious aspect. Congressman Wright had, only a year earlier, won re-election without opposition.

Why, then, did Wright need the million dollars? Answer: he planned to put part of it into a PAC of his own, from which he would dispense financial aid to the re-election campaigns of Democratic colleagues who would choose the next speaker. In the 1986 elections, Wright's PAC handed out $392,000 to 141 Democratic members. Let would-be challengers for the Speakership trump *that* card.

Thus, in part, does Congress choose the person two heartbeats away from the presidency—the Speaker of the House of Representatives.

At a lesser level, some representatives have found it helpful to form and use their own personal PACs in order to win a subcommittee chairmanship.

Case in point: a PAC bearing the intriguing name of the "24th Congressional District of California PAC." What in the world is *that* PAC? Who are its beneficiaries—and on what basis does it select them?

As the *Almanac of Federal PACs* gently put it, the 24th District PAC makes its gifts "in consultation with" Representative Henry Waxman, a Democrat who happens to represent California's 24th District in the U. S. House. Since Congressman Waxman consistently wins re-election by two-to-one margins, he can afford to devote his fundraising powers to the cause of his PAC. He then donates the proceeds to the campaigns of certain select colleagues. The *PAC Almanac* notes that some $24,000 of Waxman PAC money was channeled to Democratic members of House Energy Committee (on which Congressman Waxman sits), whose votes determine the chairmanship of the committee and its subcommittees. And that, the *Almanac* continues, "may have played a role in Waxman's 1979 [upset] election as chairman of the committee's Health and Environment Subcommittee . . . over a more senior panel member," former Democratic Congressman Richardson Preyer of North Carolina.

Even the most reform-minded lawmakers succumb to the temptation to form a so-called "leadership" PAC of their own as a means of expanding their power within the Congress.

Consider the example of Illinois Democrat Paul Simon, elected to the U.S. Senate in November 1984, after a campaign that required raising $4.6 million. Although he detests the PAC system, he felt he had no choice but to accept $908,000 from special-interest PACs in his 1984 Senate race. Moreover, although his trademark as a U.S. representative had been in-person communication with his constituents, as a Senate candidate Simon had found himself obliged to take precious days from campaigning in Illinois and spend them on fundraising forays to New York, California, Texas and other states in search of contributions from the rich. After the campaign, he said of the crushing and incessant fundraising burden he had just felt obliged to bear: "I hated every minute of it."

Obliged to bear. In the context of a multi-million-dollar Senate campaign (Simon's opponent, Republican Senator Charles Percy, spent $5.3 million), that word seems appropriate. Simon's acceptance of $908,000 from special-interest political action committees can be looked upon as an involuntary act, and once in office, he lost no time in introducing legislation to provide full public funding of Senate general elections, as a means of offering candidates such as himself an alternative to the experience he had so hated.

But with another six years before his next senatorial race, one would think he would welcome a respite from the constant preoccupation with money.

Yet in early 1985, just a few months after his expensive election campaign, Paul Simon formed his own PAC, The Democracy Fund. He did it, he said, "to have a liberal influence in upcoming House and Senate elections—to be a player." The formation of his own PAC would keep Paul Simon on the fund-raising treadmill.

And that was a *voluntary* act on his part.*

At the opposite end of the political-security spectrum from the Wrights and the Waxmans are those first-term representatives and senators who have personally loaned their campaigns large sums and mortgaged their family's future to finance their costly campaigns. Those lawmakers are peculiarly vulnerable to offers of interest-group contributions that will reduce their personal debt.

For example, in his successful 1982 campaign to unseat Republican Senator Harrison Schmitt in New Mexico, the Democratic challenger—Jeff Bingaman, an attractive young liberal with independent means—personally loaned over $790,000 to his campaign.

During the election campaign, the American Medical Association's PAC (AMPAC) contributed $7,500 to Senator Schmitt. But when Bingaman defeated Schmitt, on December 29, 1982—after the votes had been counted and it was too late to affect the outcome of the election—AMPAC made a $10,000 contribution to Bingaman, the very man AMPAC had just tried to defeat.

Later, when Citizens Against PACs, a citizens group cochaired by the author of this book, questioned Bingaman's acceptance of the AMA's post-election-switch-gift, Bingaman was stung. He insisted that the AMA's gift would not sway his votes in Congress,† which would be dictated by the best interests of all the people of his state.

The citizens group suggested that there was a convincing way of dispelling all questions on that score: return the AMA's contribution.

---

* On December 31, 1986, after the Democrats regained control of the Senate, Simon's PAC ceased raising and dispensing money because, a spokesman said, "The PAC had served its purpose."

† See the Baseball Scenario on page xix.

Senator Bingaman's reply: *"I can't afford to."*

According to figures reported to the Federal Election Commission, in the 1990 elections, New Hampshire Republican Representative Bill Zeliff loaned his campaign $345,500. That is the equivalent of nearly three years' congressional salary for Zeliff. Freshmen Congressmen John Boehner, of Ohio; Dick Nichols, of Kansas; John Reed, of Rhode Island; and Charles Taylor, of North Carolina each made personal loans to their campaigns of more than the $125,000 they will be paid in their first year as representatives. The combined debt of the incoming class of freshman totaled nearly $3.1 million.

To list these new lawmakers is not to disparage them. If anything, it is to question an electoral system that can put so heavy a price tag on candidacy and election, thus making even the most high-minded of candidates prey to campaign contributions from special-interest groups and adding to the pressure on interest groups to make post-election contributions to candidates who have loaned substantial sums to their own campaign.

Campaign finance reformers on both sides of the aisle wax indignant about the ethical question raised by the practice of candidates lending their own campaigns substantial sums, in which event their post-election fund-raising efforts end up not in their campaign treasuries but in their own pockets.

A conspicuous example of this was North Carolina Democratic Senator Terry Sanford's lending his own campaign the astonishing sum of $1.1 million—a large contributing factor to his winning his 1986 Senate race. He raised the $1.1 million—roughly half of his net worth—partly by mortgaging some farm land he owned. Sanford explains that he found it necessary to lend his own campaign so much money by a special circumstance: the sudden and unexpected suicide, in June, 1986 of Senator John East, which found Sanford suddenly facing, as an opponent, former Republican Congressman James T. Broyhill, a wealthy and well-financed candidate. Broyhill, appointed to fill East's Senate term, lent his campaign $550,000, and raised $1 million more than Sanford "by tapping sources from his years as a top Energy and Commerce Committee member," according to *Congressional Quarterly*.

Since the 1986 race, Sanford has repaid himself $947,000 plus interest "with donations from an array of lobbyists, business and trade groups, unions, corporate bigwigs and bankers," according to an article by *Congressional Quarterly*'s enterprising reporter, Phil Kuntz. Altogether, since his 1986 election, he has raised a total of $2.2 million, almost half of which he has used to pay himself back. Meanwhile, the Senate was repeatedly trying to outlaw this practice. There is very little that campaign finance leaders on the respective sides of the aisle agree on, but the unethical nature of loan repayment practices is one of them. Kentucky's Republican Senator Mitch McConnell has long railed against what he terms "the unethical practice of shaking down special interests after an election to repay personal campaign debt. In effect what you are doing is raising special interest money and putting it right into your pocket."

McConnell's Democratic counterpart, Oklahoma Senator David L. Boren, agrees. When donations are used to pay back personal debt, Boren says they are "paying a direct benefit not to a campaign fund but to a person—yourself—and the lobbyist may be under more pressure to cough up." Sanford himself, fails to see the ethical questionability of this practice. "I would appreciate knowing what you think the ethical considerations are," he says, "because I don't see any, and I fancy myself as being very sensitive to ethical considerations." (Ironically, Sanford is the new chairman of the Senate Ethics Committee.) Sanford insists he did not vote to prohibit the practice that he has engaged in since his 1986 campaign. He is wrong about that. Both the Senate reform bills that he supported and voted for contained prohibitions against the practice.

Prior to election day, Sanford had attracted $442,000 from PACs. By the end of the year—not two months later—that total had jumped nearly fifty percent, to $647,000. Banking, insurance and finance PACs were the "biggest Johnny-come-lately donors," more than tripling their pre-election total of $28,000 to $91,350.

During the succeeding election cycle, Sanford's total PAC donations rose to $850,000, nearly half of which came from banking, finance and insurance companies—*whose affairs fall directly under the aegis of the Senate Banking Committee, to which Sanford was appointed a member.*

An equally disturbing aspect of the practice of candidates lending high-stake money to their own campaigns is the eagerness of interest groups to help them pay off those loans. A vivid illustration: freshman Congressman Gary Franks, of Connecticut, had been on the House Armed Services Committee a brief twelve days when a Capitol Hill fundraising event was announced to help him retire his $68,900 campaign debt. The party was sponsored by the lobbyists for four of the leading defense contractors: Northrop, Lockheed, General Dynamics and Textron. Their invitation letter, obtained by Peter Overby, a staff writer for *Common Cause* magazine, told of their high expectations for Franks. Excerpts: "With a large number of contractors in the Northeast, located in and around [Franks'] district, it is paramount that the defense industry is vigorously supported and represented. We feel he [Franks] will add an essential new dimension to this committee and we welcome him *as a valuable ally*." (Emphasis added.) And then the "pitch": "A $500 donation made payable to 'Franks for Congress' would be greatly appreciated. We hope to see you there."

As Senator Bingaman's observation indicated, often the candidate has a highly personal stake in the loans they make to their own campaigns: they mortgage their houses and/or sign pledges to the bank. Thus the pressures are intense for them to raise the money for debt retirement—adding to the temptation to accept money from interest groups.

Political science courses traditionally teach that representatives and senators choose their committee assignments according to what committees will best serve their constituents (e.g. a farm-state senator choosing the agriculture committee) or will win them prestigious headlines or speaking engagements (foreign affairs and armed services committees, for example).

The growth of the PACs has introduced an important new factor: the likelihood of attracting campaign contributions from affected interest groups. Today, lawmakers are likely to clamor for membership on committees that are magnets for PAC dollars, even though that choice promises no headlines and is wholly unrelated to their constituents' needs.

Former Democratic Congressman Robert Kastenmeier of Wisconsin, for example, remembers a time when representatives had to be virtually dragooned into serving on the Civil Liberties, Courts, and Administration of Justice Subcommittee of House Judiciary. Then one year, Kastenmeier noted a curious change: members were inexplicably eager to serve on that subcommittee. Had there been a sudden, renewed interest in civil liberties? Kastenmeier wondered. On reflection, he noted a much more practical reason for the change. The subcommittee had jurisdiction over so-called intellectual property—patents and copyrights and the like—and suddenly two lucrative battles had cropped up in that area of the law. One was the desire of the pharmaceutical industry to prolong drug patent protection, supposedly to make up for the lengthy Food and Drug Administration trial-and-approval period for new drugs. The second was a fierce, high-stakes battle between the motion-picture and video-recorder industries about the right to record movies on home television sets. On both issues the stakes were high and the parties well financed and politically sophisticated—the perfect recipe for attracting PAC money.

So conscious are lawmakers of the money factor that some committees have come to be known as "PAC heavens"—such as the banking and energy committees, which supervise well-heeled and savvy banking, financial, oil and chemicals industries.

But the committees that write the tax laws (House Ways and Means and Senate Finance) are at the apex of the PAC heavens. California Democrat Robert Matsui has observed that being on Ways and Means (as he is) means the difference between taking in $70,000 and a mere $25,000 at a Washington fund-raising event.

The sudden PAC popularity of a new member of Ways and Means can be truly dramatic. Former Democratic Representative Kent Hance of Texas quadrupled his PAC intake (from $32,000 to $142,000) the election after he joined the committee. Similarly, the

PAC gifts to Arkansas Democratic Congressman Beryl Anthony jumped from $28,000 to $165,000 after he won a prized Ways and Means seat.

Such is the power of a seat on Ways and Means that it enabled an obscure New Jersey Democratic congressman named Frank J. Guarini to conduct what might be termed a poor man's Lloyd Bentsen breakfast series. As we saw, Senate Finance Committee chairman Bentsen charged lobbyists $10,000 a ticket—before embarrassing headlines caused him to cancel his breakfast meetings. Guarini was only able to command $1,000 per ticket.

Congressman Guarini is not among Congress' Hundred Neediest Cases, either in campaign funds or in votes. In 1982, for example, he raised and spent $170,000 and won three to one. Nonetheless, he apparently felt he wasn't raising enough money. In particular, he wasn't raising enough from PACs. In 1984, the figure went up to $237,000.

So, according to an account by *Los Angeles Times* reporter Paul Houston, Guarini decided to initiate a series of small, quiet breakfasts, to which he would invite select groups' lobbyists, one industry at a time. His reasoning: the intimate settings would appeal to lobbyists because "you can discuss in depth the issues pertinent to a particular industry instead of mixing ten different issues" at a larger meeting. For example, at one breakfast, twenty-seven lobbyists from the insurance industry paid $1,000 each to eat scrambled eggs, sausages and kiwi fruit with Congressman Guarini. Presumably the $1,000 not only gained them admission to the breakfast, but improved their chances of getting Congressman Guarini's attention should the need arise in the future. If that breakfast served to increase even in the smallest degree Congressman Guarini's sympathy for the multi-billion-dollar tax preferences the insurance industry enjoys, the $1,000 price of admission was cheap indeed.

* * *

As noted earlier, another member of House Ways and Means, former Congressman Flippo, from Alabama, needed to hold no breakfast to attract PAC funds. (Remember, Congressman Flippo habitually won reelection by four to one margins, and thus hardly needed contributions to wage his reelection campaigns.)

It is difficult to imagine that many of the PAC contributions to Congressman Flippo's campaigns were prompted by an interest in the welfare of his Alabama district. The twenty-six closely printed pages listing the PAC contributions to Congressman Flippo's 1986 campaign raise question after question.

- How many members did the National Venture Capital Association of Washington, D.C. have in Congressman Flippo's district? And, if the answer is none or almost none, what would have led that association to give $6,000 of unneeded money to Flippo's 1986 election?
- Why would five giant New York banks (Citicorp, Chemical, Chase Manhattan, Manufacturers Hanover and Morgan) give a total of $5,500 to a small-town congressman from Alabama whose reelection was a foregone conclusion? Why, for that matter, should the American Bankers Association and other financial trade associations around the country contribute nearly $20,000? (To that particular question, there is a plausible answer. On October 15, 1985, Congressman Flippo proposed that the Ways and Means Committee vote to open even wider a long-standing tax loophole that the Reagan Administration had suggested closing entirely. The Flippo amendment, which passed that day by a vote of 17 to 14 but was later killed, would have meant $7.6 *billion* in tax benefits to the banking industry. If Representative Flippo had had his way, that would have meant $7.6 billion that the rest of the taxpayers—including the taxpayers in his district—would have had to make up for in one way or another.)
- What connection, if any, did the Chicago Board of Trade and the Chicago Mercantile Exchange have with Alabama's Fifth District that prompted each of those groups to contribute

$1,000 to Representative Flippo's 1986 campaign? (Coincidentally, traders on both those Chicago commodity exchanges had tax problems that would give them a natural interest in a member of the Ways and Means Committee.)

- Why, although little if any beet or cane sugar is grown in Flippo's district, would two national sugar associations each contribute $1,500 to his campaign? Was it to insure his continued support of a sugar subsidy that obliges American consumers—including the 151,000 families in his district—to pay more for sugar than if that price were governed by the free market?

- The following national groups made sizable 1986 contributions: the American Medical Association ($10,000), the American Dental Association ($4,000), the American Academy of Ophthamology ($1,000) and the American Podiatry Association ($500). Was the legislation they favored in the best interests of the people of the Fifth District of Alabama?

- Others that contributed were: the American Yarn Spinners Association of Gastonia, North Carolina, and the American Horse Council's Committee on Legislation and Taxation of Washington, D.C. (which called itself COLT, and was interested in preserving the tax preferences long enjoyed by horse owners). Then there were the following law firms, each of which maintains a Washington office, with registered lobbyists: Dow, Lohnes & Albertson, Washington ($3,000); Vinson & Elkins, Houston ($1,500); Akin, Gump, Strauss, Hauer & Feld, of Dallas ($1,000); and Jones, Day, Reavis & Pogue, Cleveland ($500). And let's not overlook the National Beer Wholesalers Association ($2,000) and the National Wine and Spirit Wholesalers ($2,000)

The voters of the Fifth District of Alabama had good reason to ask: *From* whom did their representative get his campaign money? *To* whom was he indebted? Whom did he really represent? The people of his district—or those outsiders?

For Ronnie Flippo, the answers, for the 1986 election, were:

- Nearly two-thirds (65.5 percent) of his money came from outside special-interest PACs.
- An added 10.4 percent came from individual contributors who reside outside his district. Over half of that money came from people who do not even live in Alabama.

Thus, in 1986, more than three-fourths of Congressman Flippo's campaign funds came from groups or people who don't live, vote or pay taxes in his district—in fact, *people who are not even permitted to vote for him on election day.*

Some do not find that fact unduly disturbing because, they contend, Congress is a *national* legislature. Representatives and senators have a broader responsibility than representing their constituents, these observers argue, and if lawmakers base their votes in Congress solely on the parochial interests of their respective districts or states, the national interest suffers.

Congress is, indisputably, a national legislature. But is that fact relevant to the PAC money on which lawmakers are increasingly dependent? Are most political action committees really concerned with the *national* interest, or with the interests of their particular group? The bankers' and trial lawyers' PACs exist first and foremost to promote the interests of bankers and trial lawyers. That's why their members contribute to the PAC. So to the extent that is true, lawmakers' dependence on PAC money detracts from, rather than adds to, Congress' role as a truly national legislature.

In that same vein, many members of Congress object strenuously to characterizing PACs as "outside" special interest groups. They argue that the PAC of a company that has a local plant, or of a union with members in their district, cannot fairly be called an outside group. My position on this point, and my reasons for arguing that almost all PACs deserve to be called "outside PACs" even when they have a substantial employment within a given state or district, has already been stated. (See page 44.)

* * *

High as was the proportion of Congressman Flippo's 1986 funds coming from outside PACs (65.5 percent), it was far from the highest in the House. Surpassing Flippo by far was California Democrat Augustus Hawkins, who received 92 percent of his funds from PACs. Pennsylvania Democrat William Coyne ranked No. 2, with 91 percent.

Perhaps most distressing is the universality with which the influence-peddling practices described here—especially the conflicts of interest—have come to be accepted by lawmakers.

For example, Paul Houston reported in the *Los Angeles Times* that, as of August 1984, members of the House Banking Committee had received (and accepted) a total of $57,750 from the American Bankers Association's PAC. In 1983 alone, they had also accepted a total of $18,000 in speaking fees from the ABA, as well as travel and lodging to such vacation spots as Hawaii, site of the ABA's 1983 annual convention. Houston observed, "A decade ago . . . revelations of such payments might have mortified the [banking committee] legislators. Today, the committee's embarrassment of riches seems to embarrass virtually no one."

Appallingly, the "PAC habit" is quickly adopted—by even the most idealistic lawmakers. Take, for example, Bruce Morrison, a liberal Democratic congressman from New Haven until 1990, when he ran, unsuccessfully, for governor of Connecticut. Elected in 1982 by a scant 1,700 votes, the thirty-eight-year-old Morrison came to Washington with the reputation of a reformer. As director of the New Haven Legal Services office, he was motivated to run for Congress in 1981 by President Reagan's effort to halt the entire Legal Services program. According to the political almanac *Politics in America*, the professional "pols" looked on Morrison as an idealistic political novice, and reacted skeptically to his candidacy. But he assembled a devoted organization of social-service workers, community activists, and union members, and won the Democratic nomination over the local Democratic organization's choice. Then, even more surprising, he went on to defeat the popular Republican Congressman, Lawrence DeNardis.

As challenger to a sitting Republican congressman, Morrison had certainly not been the darling of the PACs. Business PACs, in particular, did not provide a dollar of his 1982 PAC money.

Despite his idealistic beginnings, once in Washington, Morrison quickly adopted the fund-raising tactics of the most traditional of legislators. He won a seat on the House Banking Committee. Suddenly, his prowess at raising campaign contributions from business interests soared. In July 1984, he voted for a measure to erect a legal fence to separate the activities of banks and their non-bank rivals. The *Los Angeles Times* reported that only days later, he was on the phone to some of the bill's beneficiaries (Merrill Lynch and J.C. Penney, for example), urging them to buy a ticket to a New York fundraising party. Some of the invitees considered Morrison's tactics heavy-handed and "gauche," but the phone calls worked. By mid–1984, he had taken in $7,000 from PACs interested in banking legislation. By the time of the 1984 election, Morrison's receipts from bank PACs had risen to nearly $21,000.

Didn't the new reformist congressman see anything amiss in his raising campaign funds from groups that had a clear interest in his conduct as a Banking Committee member? His answer—after less than two years in the House: That's "standard practice."

As a result of being an incumbent rather than a challenger and of his willingness to adopt the "standard practice" of fundraising, Morrison's PAC contributions quintupled—from $70,000 (as a 1982 *challenger*) to over $361,000 (as a 1984 *incumbent*). In addition, he raised half a million dollars of non-PAC money.

And so, in a repeat of the 1982 battle, spending more than $900,000, he defeated former Congressman DeNardis by 14,000 votes, and went on, two years later, to win again with 70 percent of the vote.

Whatever else might be said about Morrison's "standard practice," it worked.

Before finding fault with Bruce Morrison rather than with the current system of paying for congressional campaigns, put yourself in Morrison's shoes. With the help of a lot of idealistic people's hard work, you've clawed your way to a seat in Congress. You think it likely that ex-Congressman DeNardis is going to try to win back his seat. You also assume that he will be well bankrolled—from PACs in general and business PACs in particular. (DeNardis did, in fact, spend half a million dollars on his 1984 campaign.)

All around you, you see your colleagues in Congress using the power of their incumbency to rake in money.

Given those realities, what do you do? You have two choices: either play the game, or tie your hands by rejecting interest-group money.

The second choice amounts to unilateral disarmament.

There's another part to your mental calculation. Picture yourself receiving a PAC check for, say, $5,000. There's a fair chance the contribution came in without your asking for it. You sit there, looking at the check, and thinking, "Now how much would it take to raise this amount of money in small gifts? Let's see . . . this check is for $5,000—that's the equivalent of two hundred $25 gifts. Think of the trouble, the work—and the expense—involved in getting two hundred people to give $25! Getting it door-to-door would require ten canvassers five evenings each—and if you had to pay the canvassers $5 an hour, that would double the time it would take to net $5,000. And getting that much from direct-mail solicitations would involve enormous printing and mailing expenses . . . Here, on the other hand, is this PAC check for $5,000. It's unsolicited: I didn't have to lift a finger to get it."

The more you look at that check, and the more you think about the alternatives, the sweeter that PAC money looks to you.

Bruce Morrison is by no means unique. There are many members of Congress just like Morrison—champions of the "public interest" movement, who came to Congress through the efforts of environmentalists or peace activists—who become inured to "the system," the "standard practice" of taking PAC money, and lots of it. Either they don't perceive conflicts of interest or the conflicts don't seem to inhibit them much.

Two such are former Republican Congresswoman Claudine

Schneider of Rhode Island (who left the House in 1990 for an unsuccessful bid for the U.S. Senate) and Democratic Congresswoman Barbara Boxer from Marin County, California. They have virtually identical election histories: each won narrowly the first time she was elected to the House, and since then, has won by increasingly lopsided margins. In 1984, for example, each received 68 percent of the vote—helped along by substantial amounts of PAC money. Two years later, however, despite their two-to-one victories, each accepted large PAC gifts—about $165,000—and each piled up even larger victory margins (72 and 74 percent, respectively), outspending their opponents five to one and twenty-seven to one, respectively.

Why does Barbara Boxer, a lifelong reformer, accept all that PAC money despite comfortable election margins? "I play the game by the rules. I don't have any problem taking PAC money if it's legal. I want a hefty war chest to be ready for a serious challenge." Congresswoman Boxer, who sits on the Armed Services Committee accepts money from defense contractors, although she refuses money from the top ten defense firms.

Claudine Schneider actively sought out the interest groups that are affected by the committees on which she served. For example, she spent time with her fundraising staff thinking of high-tech companies that might be interested in the work she was doing as a member of the Science and Technology Committee.

And why not? As Bruce Morrison said, it's all "standard practice."

The present system of financing congressional campaigns poses two core problems for idealistic representatives like Bruce Morrison, Claudine Schneider, and Barbara Boxer. First, campaigns are expensive and getting more so (and they must bear in mind, constantly, there are no limits on what an opponent can spend). Second, and more important, until and unless Congress broadens the existing system of government funding of presidential general elections to cover congressional campaigns, public-spirited congressional candidates will have no alternatives for raising the enormous sums required—other than to accept money from special-interest groups.

The results—and malign consequences—of this unfortunate system are set forth in the following three case studies:

Case Study 1: Robert J. Dole

Senator Robert J. Dole of Kansas has no illusions about what political action committees expect when they contribute to a candidate. He has said it himself: "When these political action committees give money, they expect something in return other than good government."

Yet Dole is well known as a leading favorite of the PACs. According to Federal Election Commission statistics, from 1972 to the end of 1990, he received $3,693,709 from special-interest PACs.

The PACs contributed over $1 million toward Dole's 1986 reelection campaign. He didn't need the money. Long in advance, that contest was expected to be a charade, since no important challengers came forward.* In fact, Senator Dole raised so much and spent so little that he emerged with a $2 million reserve in his campaign treasury—nearly *three times* as much as any other senator facing reelection that year.

So why, if he didn't need the money, and if he knew that the PACs expected something in return for their money, did Senator Dole raise and accept the PACs' million dollars?

Even more intriguing: in light of what he himself has said about political action committees, why did Dole start a PAC of his own, thereby providing yet another channel for PACs and other influence-seekers to contribute money and expect something from him "other than good government"?

Finally, why did Dole open the door to inferences of improper influence-seeking by establishing a charitable foundation to which

---

* Dole's Democratic senatorial opponent in 1986 was Guy MacDonald, a political unknown who didn't believe in raising or spending large amounts of campaign money. (He apparently raised less than $5,000, for he failed to file a report with the Federal Election Commission.)

large corporations and wealthy people could (and did) make enormous, attention-getting gifts?

The following is the story of the multiple channels that Robert J. Dole made available to those doing business with the U.S. Government—channels that at the very least created the opportunity for those groups to attract Dole's sympathetic attention. It is also the story of the special favors that Senator Dole reportedly did for some of them.

Robert Dole's money-raising success is entirely to be expected. There are many good reasons why people doing business with, or receiving favors from, the U.S. Government should want to be on the good side of this particular senator.

For openers, as a senior Republican member of the Agriculture Committee, he can be helpful to farmers and large agribusiness interests.

Second, as the senior Republican on the Finance Committee, he could offer crucial assistance to anyone desiring (or hoping to protect) a tax loophole worth hundreds of millions or even billions of dollars. Most important, from 1980 to 1984, with the Republicans in control of the Senate, Dole was the Senate Majority Leader, and therefore influential across the legislative spectrum.

And then . . . in 1985 and 1986 (the period this chapter concentrates on) there was a real possibility that Robert J. Dole just might be the next president of the United States.

And so it's not surprising that, even though Dole didn't need the money for his reelection campaign, the following interest groups across the economic spectrum gave at least $5,000 toward the election of this shoo-in senator: the American Medical Association, the Associated General Contractors of America, the National Association of Homebuilders, the American Bankers Association, E. F. Hutton, Chrysler, auto dealers selling imported cars—and six PACs from the sugar and sweetener industry, to which, as will be recounted shortly, Senator Dole gave special help. In all, the PACs gave $1 million toward Dole's 1986 reelection. But even that was surpassed by gifts from *individuals*, which totaled $1.3 million.

Another way to get Senator Dole's attention was by making contributions to Campaign America, a personal PAC established in 1978 partly to help the campaigns of other Republican candidates for Congress, but more to finance the springboard for Dole's own presidential aspirations. Campaign America had a shaky start, but after Dole became Senate Republican Leader, it blossomed. In 1985 and 1986 alone, PACs contributed $500,000 while well-heeled individuals kicked in gifts totaling an added $2.5 million.

Once again, individual gifts to Campaign America outstripped PAC contributions. Take the commodity industry, for example. In 1983–84, PACs from that industry gave Campaign America $21,000. But individuals connected with the industry contributed $49,500. Their generosity may or may not be related to the fact that in 1984, Senator Dole, in a complete reversal of his previous position, was instrumental in conferring a multi-million-dollar tax blessing on 333 commodity traders. More about that later in this chapter and in Chapter 8.

Some of these individual givers seemed happy to take advantage of the higher ceiling on personal gifts to PACs—$5,000, rather than the $1,000-per-donor-per-election on contributions directly to candidates. Among those were Ernest and Julio Gallo, the celebrated California winemakers, whose generosity we have encountered in Chapter 3. Apparently their enthusiasm for Senator Dole was shared by their wives, for, as previously noted, each of the four contributed $5,000 to Campaign America, for a tidy and conspicuous total of $20,000 in the 1986 cycle. In 1989 and 1990, Campaign America received $65,000 from the Gallos. This was over and above the $18,000 the Gallos gave the Dole senatorial campaign in those same years.

From many donors' viewpoint, however, a more advantageous way of attracting Robert Dole's attention has been by contributing to the Dole Foundation, a charitable foundation dedicated primarily to helping the handicapped.

Giving to a foundation like Dole's is preferable to a political gift in a number of respects. For one thing, corporations, barred since 1907 from contributing to federal campaigns, may give freely to politically-connected charitable foundations such as Dole's. AT&T, for example, whose rates are subject to federal regulation, made memorable gifts totaling $100,000 to the Dole Foundation. Atlantic Richfield, IBM, and the R.J. Reynolds Tobacco Company (prior to its merger with Nabisco Brands) each contributed $25,000.

Second, gifts to a charitable foundation such as the Dole Foundation are tax deductible. Since deductible gifts reduce the taxes of the donor—for example, at the then applicable tax rates, AT&T's $100,000 gift saved that company $46,000 in taxes. Thus, part of the burden is shifted to other taxpayers who are unable to fend off the higher tax load.

Third, gifts to foundations are not limited in size, as are political contributions.

Finally, unlike political gifts, contributions to foundations may be made in secret, even though they are connected with political figures. For example, former New York Republican Representative Jack Kemp, who later became Secretary of Housing and Urban Development, repeatedly refused to disclose the list of donors to the Fund for an American Renaissance, the charitable foundation he founded and controlled. (Finally, in late summer 1986, he released the data.) The Dole Foundation does not pursue such a policy of secrecy; on the contrary, it willingly released its full list of contributors. In doing so, the foundation's president, Jackie Strange, emphasized the nonpolitical nature of the foundation, that there is "absolutely no interference with the foundation's operation." Moreover, while Congressman Kemp's foundation paid the expenses of publishing Kemp's speeches and other writings as well as paying the travel expenses of Kemp and his aides on a fact-finding trip, the Dole Foundation's outlays have been confined to grants to conventional charities unrelated to the Senator's political activities.

Nonetheless, the Dole Foundation is undeniably a means by which donors can attract the sympathetic attention of the Senate

Republican leader, who serves as the Foundation's chairman. In the year ending June 30, 1986, major companies and two individuals gave the Dole Foundation slightly over $1 million. Various industries and economic interest groups, many of which are regulated by the government or receive federal subsidies, are prominent on the list of contributors. For example, life-insurance companies and oil firms, both of which enjoy major tax preferences, gave a total of $136,000; pharmaceutical companies, subject to strict federal regulation, gave $45,000; tobacco firms (beneficiaries of a federal subsidy, and the objects of Senator Dole's special help) gave $40,000.

In his financial disclosure reports to the Senate, Dole lists himself as chairman of the Dole Foundation. Presumably, then, he is aware of all these acts of generosity. Presumably, too, he has a warm place in his heart for those who have furthered his charitable enthusiasm for helping the handicapped.

Beyond contributing to Dole's Senate and presidential campaigns and to his foundation, interest-groups and companies once could favor Senator Dole with honoraria or speaking fees (before those were barred by Senate rules), embellished, perhaps, with a comfortable ride on a company jet—as when an R.J. Reynolds jet flew Dole to Winston-Salem, where he picked up a $2,000 honorarium or speaking fee (which he gave to charity), and then carried the Senator on to Ft. Lauderdale.

For Dole, the top honoraria recipient in the Senate for five of the six years from 1980 through 1986—speaking fees for 1978 through 1986 brought in $825,266. According to the *Kansas City Star* and Senate financial disclosure reports, he kept $395,967 of this and gave the balance to charity, as required by Senate rules.

Even with these charitable gifts, however, the fact remains that through 1986 (when speaking fees were still permitted under Senate rules), Senator Dole accepted honoraria from seventy-eight groups whose PACs also contributed to the Dole political entities, the Dole Foundation, or both.

*　*　*

The Dole-for-Senate Committee. Campaign America. The Dole Foundation. Honoraria. Corporate jet trips.

Surveying that array of possibilities of gaining the attention of the Senate Republican Leader (and possible future president), an interest group may ask itself, "Why choose just one?" In fact, many have found it just too hard to choose. In the period 1985 through mid–1987, when Dole's pursuit of the presidency was at or near its peak, several pursued more than one avenue provided by Dole. And in many cases, employees of the donating group made further individual donations, just to make sure the Senator noticed.

FUNDS GIVEN TO SENATOR DOLE
FROM 1985 TO MID-1987

By	Dole for Senate	Campaign America	Dole Found.	Honoraria
Mass. Mutual Life Ins. Co.	$ 5,500	$ 5,000	$10,000	$ 5,000
Merrill Lynch	$ 2,000	$ 1,000	$ 5,000	$ 2,000
Merrill Lynch Employees	$ 4,000			
Ford Motor Co.	$ 1,000		$20,000	
Ford Employees	$12,000			
Marriott Company	$ 2,000		$20,000	$ 2,000
Marriott Employees		$ 4,000		
5 Tobacco Companies	$13,400		$40,000	$ 2,000
Tobacco Employees	$ 1,000	$ 5,000		
Insurance Industry	$86,000	$ 3,500	$30,500	$15,000
Insurance Employees	$ 1,000	$26,000		
8 Sugar & Sweetener PACs	$40,000	$ 7,000	$25,000	
Sugar-industry Employees	$ 5,000			

In pursuing multiple channels to Robert Dole's attention, gratitude, and friendship, none has been more resourceful than the multi-billion-dollar food processing firm of Archer-Daniels-Midland (ADM) and its charismatic principal stockholder, Dwayne Andreas.

ADM and the Andreas family have been extraordinarily generous to the Dole political conglomerate. The ADM PAC provided $15,500 to the Dole for Senate campaign and to Campaign America from 1978 through mid–1985. The ADM Foundation has given a total of $160,000 to the Dole Foundation. Over a seven-and-a-half-year period, Andreas himself donated $5,000 and Andreas family members have contributed a total of $16,500 to Dole political committees. Dole received $4,000 as fees for two speeches ($2,000 from ADM and $2,000 from ADM's Foundation), which Dole gave to charity. And Dole's Senate disclosure report for 1983 reveals three Dole trips on ADM corporate planes.

Moreover, in 1982 the Doles bought a three-room apartment in an oceanfront cooperative building in Bal Harbour, Florida, of which Dwayne Andreas is chairman, secretary, treasurer, and major stockholder. According to a *New York Times Magazine* article, in November 1987, the Doles received, at the least, "preferential treatment from Mr. Andreas" in having access to the shares and, arguably, a price break on the apartment; a similar apartment in a less desirable location in the same building sold for $190,000 three months before the Doles bought theirs for $150,000.

Finally, starting in 1984, ADM, with Mobil Oil, sponsored "Face-Off," a three-minute daily radio debate carried on 160 Mutual Broadcasting Network stations featuring Dole and Senator Edward M. Kennedy. Michael Fumento, who wrote a major investigative article on ADM's political activities for *National Review*, calculates that ADM had, through "Face-Off," provided Dole—as well as Kennedy—$195,000 of free radio exposure through 1986.

Altogether, then, one could say that Robert Dole is indebted to ADM and the Andreas family for a total of at least $261,000.

One could also say that he owes a debt of gratitude—

- to political action committees for the $3,693,709 they have given his senatorial campaigns since 1972.
- to wealthy donors, many of them affiliated with companies or industries vitally affected by U.S. government actions, for the

$1,300,000 they gave his senatorial committee and the
$2,500,000 they gave to his own PAC, Campaign America,
during 1985 and 1986.
- to the companies and industries that have given him over
$800,000 in speaking fees, even though he gave slightly more
than half of that sum to charity.
- to the companies and rich people who gave over $1 million to
the Dole Foundation in the twelve months ending mid–1986.

With so much money from so many interest groups on Robert Dole's
political debit books, it is only natural that reports surface, from
time to time, about actions that he has taken to further the interests
of one or another group that has helped him. Here are a few:

• **Reportedly aiding passage of a high sugar subsidy—an
indirect help to ADM and other producers of corn-sweet-
eners:** In 1981, and again in 1985, Congress enacted a program to
support the price of domestically produced sugar far above the
world market (see Chapter 7). That opened the way for sugar to be
undercut by sellers of a lower-priced corn sweetener, produced by
ADM at great profit (21.5 percent compared with 6 percent for flour
milling). The higher the price of domestic sugar, the greater the
price at which a corn sweetener could undercut sugar and the
greater ADM's sweetener profits.

One way to keep sugar prices artificially high is to choke off
imports of foreign sugar. That trade restriction worried free-trade
advocates such as Republican Congressmen Philip Crane of Illinois
and former member Bill Frenzel of Minnesota, who were members
of the House-Senate conference committee on the 1985 farm bill.
Crane and Frenzel proposed, and understood they had agreement
on, a provision supported by the Reagan Administration that had
the effect of easing the sugar trade restrictions.

But, according to an article by Sheila Kaplan in the May/June
1986 *Common Cause* magazine, when the sugar portions of the farm
bill were printed by the Government Printing Office and returned
to Congress to be voted on by the House and Senate, the

Frenzel-Crane provision was missing. Crane and Frenzel, incredulous and incensed, demanded to know what had happened. Reporter Kaplan quotes Harris Jordan, a Crane aide, as saying the deletion of their provision had been caused by "a very senior senator from Kansas." (According to Kaplan, a Dole spokesman denied "the Senator went anywhere near the Printing Office," but acknowledged that "Dole's staff read the substitute [Frenzel-Crane] provision and rejected it.") Crane aide Jordan recalls congressional staff members and sugar lobbyists who were following the bill at the time telling him that the excision of the Frenzel-Crane provision was known among them to be "ADM's deal."

In September of 1990, at the culmination of a major budget battle, the *Wall Street Journal* reported that Dole (while publicly parading as a big deficit cutter) privately had been pressing for "a half billion a year tax break, with the biggest benefit going to a single company [Archer-Daniels-Midland] with close ties to him."

The *Journal* stated that Dole has "argued forcefully behind closed doors" to extend tax incentives that prop up the fledging ethanol-fuels industry. About seventy percent of the nation's ethanol is produced by the Archer-Daniels-Midland Company.

Referring to $160,000 in ADM contributions to the Dole Foundation, a 1990 *Wall Street Journal* editorial quoted John Ford, of the American Corn Growers Association, as saying that "the corn industry, the politics of it, is controlled by one man [Andreas], and Bob Dole is his gofer on [Capitol] Hill."

The *Journal* also said that Dole's advocacy of continuing the revenue-losing subsidy had drawn criticism of Dole, even from members of his own political party who questioned whether this was properly includable in a deficit-*cutting* plan.

Finally, the *Journal* reported that the budget-cutting talks were not the first time Dole had pressed for extending the tax loopholes for ADM and the ethanol industry. "Over the past year or so, [Dole] has delayed at least two trade bills trying to gain leverage for the extensions."

• **Promoting a tobacco subsidy:** Although only minuscule amounts of tobacco are grown in Senator Dole's home state, David Corn reported in *The Nation* magazine that in the fall of 1985,

Senator Dole pushed hard in the Senate Finance Committee to rescue a tobacco-subsidy program that Republican Senator Jesse Helms, from the tobacco state of North Carolina, had failed to get approved by the Agriculture Committee, which Helms chaired. Dole attempted the rescue operation by tying the subsidy to a cigarette-tax measure under consideration by the Finance Committee panel. Reporter Corn says the tobacco cause was so important to Dole that committee chair Packwood delayed taking up the cigarette tax until Dole could be present.

The Helms-Dole plan called in part for selling government-owned tobacco to cigarette manufacturers at up to a 90 percent discount, a move opposed by the Reagan Administration. Budget Director James Miller estimated that aspect of the plan would cost the taxpayers over $1 billion.

Why would a Kansas senator expend so much energy on behalf of a crop almost nonexistent in his state? A spokesman explained that Dole supported farm commodities whether or not produced in Kansas. Reporter Corn lists other possible reasons, among them his appreciation for Senator Helms' support in Dole's 1984 election as Senate Republican Leader, and Dole's desire to help tobacco-state Republican senators in the 1986 elections. But there is an additional fact to be considered: the generosity of the tobacco industry in contributing to various parts of the Dole political conglomerate. Federal Election Commission records show that in 1985 and 1986, the Big Five tobacco companies contributed a total of $13,400 to Senator Dole's reelection campaign. Three of them (Philip Morris, R. J. Reynolds and U. S. Tobacco) contributed a total of $40,000 to the Dole Foundation, and tobacco firms from 1982–1986 gave the Senator $6,000 in honoraria.

In addition, one tobacco firm, U.S. Tobacco, also furnished Dole its plush executive jet for a 1987 weekend campaign trip to Iowa. U.S. Tobacco only charged the Dole campaign $7,272, less than 40 percent of the $19,000 required to charter an equivalent jet. Said a U.S. Tobacco spokesman: "When a congressman or senator asks for this kind of help, it gives us the opportunity to help them in a unique way. We've known Senator Dole for many years and have admired his work."

• **Tax help for 333 Chicago commodity traders:** In 1984, Senator Dole, in a 180-degree about-face, came to the rescue of 333 wealthy Chicago commodity traders who were embroiled in a controversy with the Internal Revenue Service over their questionable use of a special tax loophole (see Chapter 8). Two years earlier, in 1982, Dole had chided Senate Democrats for helping these very commodity traders, who had been politically generous to the Democrats. Moreover, as reported in *Common Cause* magazine, Dole had gone to the trouble of writing the IRS, taking the opposite stance from the one he was now adopting in 1984. But that inconsistency did not inhibit Dole, during a late night House-Senate conference-committee session on the 1984 tax bill, from abruptly reversing himself and approving a proposal that would let the traders off the hook with the IRS. Dole's reversal-of-opinion was worth at least $300 million for the traders, an average of $866,000 apiece.

Federal Election Commission records show that in the preceding two years, individuals and PACs in the commodity industry contributed $70,500 to Campaign America, six times what they had given two years earlier.

• **Promoting subsidies and tariffs on gasohol, of which ADM is a major producer.** ADM is the nation's largest producer of the grain alcohol that goes into "gasohol," a nine-to-one mixture of gasoline and alcohol. Gasohol came into vogue during the oil shortages of the late seventies. It has always received enormous federal subsidies, estimated by the Federal Highway Administration at nearly half a billion dollars in 1986 alone.

According to Michael Fumento's article in *National Review*, Senator Dole sponsored a major tax concession for gasohol in 1978, and has sponsored at least twenty-three other bills to promote gasohol.

In 1980, despite the government subsidies, American gasohol was undersold by Brazil, and Dwayne Andreas pushed for a tariff against Brazilian gasohol. Late that year, Robert Dole introduced such a tariff as an amendment to a complicated revenue bill and, according to Fumento, "rammed [it] through the Senate Finance Committee and the full Senate without debate."

Four years later, Dole was part of a successful effort to persuade the U.S. Customs Service to tighten up on imports of Brazilian gasohol, an effort in which he was joined by several other senators, the Corn Growers Association, the secretary of agriculture—and Archer-Daniels-Midland.

Both in 1980 and 1984, Dole responded to criticisms about his help to a large campaign contributor such as Andreas by saying no one needed to bribe him to support farmers and to protect them against a "flood" of imported Brazilian alcohol. In response to questions from *Washington Post* reporter Michael Isikoff, Dole said, "Our primary goal was not to help any one company. I'm a farm-state senator, and our interest was in finding an outlet for some farm commodities." But Fumento points out that while the "nobody-here-but-just-this-farm-senator" argument is plausible, it has its weaknesses. For example, a given increase in demand for corn to produce gasohol may raise *corn* prices two to four cents a bushel. But Fumento says that the resulting by-products cut *soybean* prices twelve to thirteen cents per hundredweight. In total cash value, the two crops are almost equal in Kansas. Moreover, energetically pushing an increase in tariffs against Brazil is a tricky business for a Kansas senator, given that Kansas's biggest crop is wheat and that Brazil is the world's fifth largest importer of wheat. Not only does an anti-Brazil tariff invite retaliation; it also deprives Brazil of the dollars it needs to buy American wheat.

Item: Manifold generosity to Dole by the Archer-Daniels-Midland Company and its principal stockholder, Dwayne Andreas, followed by special Dole favors for ADM.

Item: Generous contributions by the tobacco industry to Dole causes, after Dole had energetically pushed a tobacco subsidy, even though virtually no tobacco is grown in his home state.

Item: Increased campaign contributions to Dole causes by Chicago commodity traders, followed by a Dole flip-flop on a tax problem many traders were having with the IRS, resulting in a multi-million-dollar tax benefit to the traders.

Was Senator Dole prompted to take any of those actions because of the contributions of his benefactors? The public cannot be sure.

That's not good for the public or fair to Senator Dole. But the inferences are there.

To the extent implications of impropriety exist, Senator Dole can only blame the campaign finance *system* under which he and all other lawmakers must now function. The inferences are built into the election laws under which senators and representatives routinely and legally accept large amounts of money from strangers who have immense amounts at stake in those lawmakers' conduct. Senator Dole has created opportunities for the offering and receiving of such "conflict of interest" contributions as imaginatively as any member of Congress. And he continues to do so. In early 1987, he formed a new Dole-for-Senate committee, and began accepting contributions for his next Senate race, in 1992.

If Senator Dole objects to the implications of impropriety, he has two alternatives:

First, let him cease actively seeking (indeed, let him decline to accept) money tainted with conflicts of interest; or

Second, let him use his position of national power to change the system so as to give candidates and lawmakers an alternative to accepting money and other favors that inevitably give rise to inferences of impropriety.

In the latter respect, Senator Dole has been inconsistent. After insisting in 1985 that the campaign-finance system "cries for reform," in August, 1986, he voted *against* a bipartisan PAC limitation cosponsored by Senators David Boren and Barry Goldwater, which nonetheless passed the Senate, 69–30. Moreover, in January, 1987, when Senators Boren and Byrd introduced a new and more comprehensive reform bill, Senator Dole said, "I do not believe there will be any effort to stall any such legislation." Yet Dole voted seven successive times *against* breaking a filibuster that was delaying a senate vote on the Byrd-Boren reform bill.

So if Senator Dole wishes to avoid criticism of his campaign-finance activities, he would do well to bring his actions more in line with his cries for reform.

*   *   *

Case Study 2: Glenn M. Anderson

Robert J. Dole is a nationally known figure. But who is Glenn M. Anderson?

Here are a few clues.

Representative Anderson, a California congressman, is known in Corvallis, Oregon, where the CH2M Hill Company thought well enough of him to contribute $1,650 toward his 1988 and 1990 reelection campaigns.

Representative Anderson is also known in Morristown, New Jersey. The Allied Signal company there sent him campaign contributions totaling $550 in 1988 and 1990.

He's known, too, in Baton Rouge, Louisiana, where the Lamar Corporation contributed $1,000 to his 1990 campaign.

It would be difficult to guess, from those scattered clues, that Glenn Anderson is a representative from San Pedro, California. But why is California's Glenn Anderson known, and apparently highly regarded, by communities as distant from his Southern California district as Corvallis, Oregon, Morristown, New Jersey and Baton Rouge, Louisiana? Why do firms so far from the Los Angeles coastline care who represents the Thirty-second District of California?

Here are some further clues to Congressman Anderson's identity:

- in 1988 and 1990 he received campaign contributions totaling $15,500 from American, Eastern, TWA, Delta, and five other airlines.
- He also received $4,350 from the American Bus Association, $1,900 in contributions from Greyhound Lines—and $250 from Trailways.
- He got $7,600 in campaign contributions from the American Trucking Association; $4,000 in contributions from Yellow Freight System, Inc., a trucking firm located in Shawnee Mission, Kansas, plus a total of $19,600 from seven other trucking firms.
- He also received $20,000 from the Teamsters Union.

• In addition, over the two election cycles, he also received $16,950 from United Parcel Service, and $10,000 from Federal Express.

No more clues. Democratic Congressman Glenn M. Anderson was, when those contributions were made, from 1988 to 1990, Chairman of the House Public Works and Transportation Committee.

That committee is responsible for legislation spanning a number of multi-million-dollar economic activities, including—

• The building and maintenance of federal highways and bridges;
• the construction of all federal buildings;
• the dredging of rivers and harbors and inland waterways;
• the regulation of bus, airline and inland-waterway transportation; and
• the regulation of billboards on federal highways.

The committee's decisions on those subjects vitally affect the prosperity of companies or even whole industries. And, by congressional custom, the most powerful single individual in shaping a committee's decisions is its chairman.

In short, at the time these campaign contributions were made,* Glenn Anderson was an extraordinarily powerful member of Congress.

That may explain why contributions to his 1988 and 1990 re-election campaign came from an engineering firm in Corvallis, Oregon; from a Morristown, New Jersey company that, among other things, makes seat belts; and the Lamar Corporation of Baton Rouge, which happens to be a major billboard company. But the average citizen reading the report on Congressman Anderson's

---

* In 1991, Anderson's fellow committee members, in a highly unusual move, deposed him as their chairman. However, he remains the second highest ranking Democrat on the committee. As such, Anderson continues to be a powerful member of Congress.

campaign finances would have difficulty perceiving those connections.

As with Robert Dole, there are several ways to gain the favorable attention of Representative Glenn Anderson.

There is, however, one important difference. Dole, as the Senate Republican leader, is a potent force across the spectrum of legislative issues. His sympathetic attention is equally important to virtually every industry, be it broadcasting, banking, oil, or insurance.

Anderson, by contrast, has no special sway over, say, broadcasting or banking legislation, so broadcasters' and bankers' PACs have no particular interest in contributing to his campaigns. But on legislation involving highways, trucking, air transport, billboard regulation, the construction of federal buildings, or the dredging of inland ports and waterways, Glenn Anderson, as chairman of the House Public Works and Transportation Committee, was, for a time, one of the most important members of the House. So from the viewpoint of gaining Congressman Anderson's sympathetic attention, those interest groups subject to his committee's jurisdiction—the truckers, the airlines, the billboard industry and the rest—*they*, and not the half-million residents and voters in Anderson's home district, are Congressman Anderson's "constituents."

Congressman Anderson has shown himself conspicuously receptive to campaign contributions from those outside economic "constituent" interest groups. Nearly four out of every five dollars of his 1988 and 1990 campaign funds came from people who are not even allowed to cast a ballot in the Thirty-second District of California on election day. Only one dollar in five came from his own *voting* constituents.

For starters, $524,566—more than half his 1988 and 1990 campaign receipts—came from special-interest political action committees which, being headquartered outside his district, may properly be regarded as outsiders.

Did he really need to accept over a half a million dollars from special-interest PACs?

Hardly. On average, since 1980, Congressman Anderson has won reelection by two to one margins, and, since his first election to Congress in 1968, he has never experienced a close election race (his victory margin has never been less than eight percent). In 1990, he outspent his Republican challenger 61 to 1, and raised $257,766 from PACs, while his opponent raised no PAC contributions.

In any event, in the 1988 and 1990 elections, Glenn Anderson accepted more than half a million dollars from special-interest PACs. Roughly $284,000 of that came from the PACs of groups with a stake—sometimes an immense stake—in actions of the committee which Anderson chairs, including the following:

- $56,250 from airline companies, unions and trade associations.
- $76,350 from trucking interests.
- $24,650 from bus companies and unions.
- $85,616 from construction firms, unions and trade associations, who have an interest in the public works projects an federal buildings.
- $64,350 from individual donors who could be identified, from Federal Election Commission records, as associated with companies having a stake in the Public Work's Committee's decisions.*

As noted earlier, it would be unthinkable for a judge to accept so much as a dollar from a defendant or a plaintiff, or *anyone* with an interest in a case before that judge. The acceptance of such a gift would lead to uncertainty about the fairness or objectivity of that judge's decision. But the election laws permitted Glenn Anderson to accept over $348,350 in campaign contributions

---

* This $64,350 figure does not include gifts from individual contributors whose occupations are *not* listed on the reports Congressman Anderson submitted to the FEC, notwithstanding a legal requirement that candidates make every effort to report their donors' occupations. Presumably some are associated with firms with an interest in his committee's actions.

from individuals and groups with immense stakes in his official decisions (see Appendix A).

Case Study 3: James J. Howard

As indicated throughout this book, campaign contributions are but one way in which "interested" parties confer favors on key members of Congress.

The quintessential illustration of this was Glenn Anderson's predecessor, the late Congressman James J. Howard, of New Jersey, who enjoyed a seven-year tenure as the Chairman of the powerful House Public Works and Transportation Committee prior to his death in 1988.

Several interests that had a particular stake in the decisions of his committee went to special lengths to develop a close personal relationship with Chairman Howard. None exceeded the billboard industry, whose hospitable treatment of Congressman and Mrs. Howard already has been described (Chapter 3). Over the years, Chairman Howard and often his wife were the guests of the Outdoor Advertising Association of America, the billboard industry's official trade association which, by happenstance, held its annual convention in Palm Springs, California in January or February of each year. At the OAAA conventions, Chairman (and, often, Mrs.) Howard enjoyed the hospitality of the OAAA for several days at a posh Palm Springs resort. This had a reciprocal advantage. For the Howards, this meant escaping Washington chilly climes for the balmy sunshine of Palm Springs. For billboard industry executives, it meant the opportunity to chat, in a relaxed, first-name atmosphere, with Chairman Howard and, if need be, to set forth the problems their industry was facing. After such an experience, Chairman Howard would be much less likely to turn down a telephone call from his golfing pal, "Jim" or "Bob," when billboard legislation was at the forefront of the congressional agenda and "Jim" or "Bob" needed Howards attention.

For Howard, the OAAA conventions had offered an additional emolument: the opportunity to pick up $2,000 speaking fees (which he could pocket) not only from the OAAA, but from the Tobacco Institute, which by coincidence (a) is one of the biggest users of billboards and (b) happens to hold its convention in Palm Springs at the same time as the OAAA, and frequently used to double up with the OAAA in dispensing speaking fees.

And then there is the American Busing Association—the ABA—which had an equal interest in the decisions of Howard and his committee on two scores: the level of Federal highway building and maintenance and Federal regulation of bus safety. Over the years, the ABA was strikingly open-handed with Howard. In addition to the $21,500 the association's PAC contributed to Howard's campaigns over the course of three elections, the ABA hosted Howard (often with his wife) on three all-expenses-paid trips to Puerto Rico during the ABA's annual conventions. Like the OAAA, the ABA had the good sense to hold its annual convention during December, a chilly month on the New Jersey coast, and the Howards' Puerto Rico jaunts lasted as long as five days.

Others of Howard's interest group "constituents" that were particularly generous to the Chairman in the period 1981–86 were:

Name	Total PAC Contribs	Total Honoraria	Special Trips
American Trucking Associations	$19,000	$4,000	Denver, CO Key Largo, FL
American Road & Transportation Builders	$ 6,500	$9,000	Houston, TX Tampa, FL Phoenix, AZ Kissimee, FL Hershey, PA
Associated General Contractors of America	$11,250	$4,000	San Fran., CA Honolulu, HI

If these interest-group favors merely amounted to a few gratis days in the sun for Congressman Howard and his wife, that would be disturbing enough. From the public's viewpoint, more troubling still was Howard's regular attendance at the annual meetings of the very groups over which he had regulatory responsibilities.

In theory, Congressman Howard and his committee colleagues were supposed to be the public's watchdogs over the various industries regulated by their committee. Citizens were (and are) entitled to feel that Howard and the members of his committee were (and are) free of special-interest influence in dealing with bus and airline safety and protecting against undue visual pollution of the countryside by billboards. Even if Howard had been scrupulous about paying his own expenses and had turned aside all honoraria, he still, over the years, turned up at the billboard industry's annual meetings as faithfully as if he were a member (and, probably, more regularly than many members). Every year he spent several days and evenings eating, drinking, and relaxing with billboard-company owners and industry lobbyists, presumably forming first-name friendships which could hardly, thereafter, be considered arms-length relationships.

Even with the new disclosure laws and the computerized reports of the Federal Election Commission, to identify the interested contributors to lawmakers such as James Howard and Glenn Anderson is a task worthy of a Sherlock Holmes.

Take, for example, the FEC's computer printout of Congressman Anderson's 1988 and 1990 PAC contributions—405 of them—covering thirty-three closely printed pages. That printout lists $5,600 in contributions from the PACs of the Lamar Corporation and of the Ralph M. Parsons company. What do those firms make or sell? Where are they located? The FEC reports contain no clue that Lamar is a billboard company in Baton Rouge, Louisiana and that Parsons is an engineering firm that consults on highways and bridges—information that was obtained for this book only by telephone calls to the firms themselves.

Identifying *individual* givers is even trickier. In the 1986 election, Congressman Howard received nearly $44,000 in contributions from individuals connected with the billboard industry. Either they were lawyers representing billboard interests, or employees of billboard companies or trade associations *or, in some cases, their spouses*. The detective work comes into play in those frequent instances when James Howard, and many of his fellow candidates, do not report the occupation or profession of all the over-$200 contributors. Who, other than someone who follows the billboard industry full-time* would ever guess that Eric Rubin—listed only as an "attorney"—is a lawyer for the OAAA, the billboard industry's trade association? Or that Barbara White of Crown Point, Indiana—a $1,000 contributor listed in FEC reports as "homemaker"—is the wife of Dean White, executive of a billboard company, Whiteco Metrocom?

Neither Barbara White nor her husband, Dean (who gave $575 to Representative Howard's 1986 campaign), could cast a ballot for Howard on election day, because they don't live in his district. The same is true of attorney Eric Rubin. In fact, those who gave nearly 90 percent of the money that Howard received in over-$200 contributions in 1986, resided outside his district.

Some lawmakers, such as Colorado's Pat Schroeder or Wisconsin's Les Aspin, are sufficiently known nationally as to be natural drawing cards for out-of-state contributors. But James Howard of New Jersey had no such national renown. Therefore, the people of the Third District of New Jersey (and, indeed, the people of the United States) were entitled to wonder:

- Why did $200-and-over contributors from Florida give nearly twice as much and those from Massachusetts two-and-a-half times as much to Congressman Howard as people who lived in his own district?
- Why did comparable contributors who lived in and around Washington, D.C.—who, of course, include lawyers and lobbyists doing business with the House Public Works and Transportation Committee—contribute *three times* as much to Congressman Howard as did his own constituents?

---

* Such as Edward McMahon, executive director of Scenic America, who spotted these donors' connections with the billboard industry. But McMahon was able to do so only because of his close familiarity with the industry.

- Why, for that matter, did large donors in California contribute more than Congressman Howard's own constituents? Did people 3,000 miles away from the Atlantic Ocean really have the interests of the Third District of New Jersey—or even the nation's interest—in mind when they made their $200-plus gifts?

Adding the contributions from out-of-district *individual* donors to the 57 percent of Howard's 1986 campaign funds he received from outside special-interest PACs, reveals this disturbing fact:

Only one dollar out of every six of Rep. Howard's 1986 campaign money came from his own constituents. The other five came from individuals or groups not qualified to vote in his district on election day.

When a congressman such as Howard is indebted for five-sixths of his campaign money to people and groups outside his district, whom does he *really* represent? His constituents? Or those outsiders? Is this the kind of representative democracy the Founding Fathers contemplated?

 *Chapter Five*

PRESENT AND FORMER MEMBERS OF CONGRESS SPEAK

WHAT IS THE effect on members of Congress of the skyrocketing need for campaign funds and the resulting never-ending scramble for money? What is the impact on the legislative process? How has campaigning been affected?

To find out, I interviewed several current and former members of Congress.

Here is what they told me:

1. Former Congressman Michael Barnes of Maryland

Mike Barnes came to national attention when, as the beneficiary of a liberal revolt on the House Foreign Affairs Committee, he became the Chairman of the Western Hemisphere Subcommittee and a principal spokesman against the Reagan Administration's policies in Central America.

From 1978 to 1986, Barnes represented Montgomery County, Maryland, a bedroom suburb of Washington, D.C. In 1986, he ran unsuccessfully for the U. S. Senate. Barnes has a mild-mannered bespectacled mien ("I'm criticized by my friends for not being more flamboyant," he once said). But he displays great passion, especially when speaking about the urgent need for campaign finance reform. His convictions on this subject were solidified by his 1986 experience as a senatorial candidate, during which money-raising was a constant preoccupation. ("There was never a waking moment that I was not either raising money or feeling guilty that I was not.")

Barnes practices law in Washington.

As I spoke to political consultants, they all said I should not even consider running for the Senate if I weren't prepared to spend 80 or 90 percent of my time raising money. It turned out that they were absolutely correct. That's an absolute outrage because the candidates should be talking about the issues and meeting with constituents and voters and working on policy questions.

As a congressman, I had plenty of phone calls from political directors of PACs in which the conversation went something like this:

"Mike, we're getting ready to make our next round of checks out, and I just want to let you know that you're right up there at the top. We really think we can help you with a nice contribution."

"Gee, that's great. Really appreciate it. Grateful to have your help."

"Oh, by the way, Mike, have you been following that bill in Ways and Means that's going to be coming to the floor next week? It's got an item in there we're concerned about—the amendment by Congressman Schwartz. You know, we'll be supporting that and we hope you'll be with us on that one. Hope you'll take a good look at it, and if you need any information about it, we'll send that up to you."

That conversation is perfectly legal under the current laws of the United States, and it probably takes place daily in Washington, D.C. It is an absolute outrage!

You know, if that conversation took place with someone in the executive branch, someone would go to jail.

I regard it as really demeaning to both people—the guy who gets the phone call and the guy who has to make it. It's just a terrible, terrible blight on our political process.

I remember standing on the floor of the House one night when we were voting on the issue of regulations affecting the funeral industry that were, in my view, eminently reasonable. The funeral industry was opposed to this regulation. I remember the evening it was voted on, a rumor swept across the floor of the House that anybody who voted against the regulation would get $5,000 from the industry PAC for his or her upcoming campaign. I don't know if that rumor was true or not, but it flew around the place. Everybody was sort of laughing about this. There's not a doubt in my mind that that rumor had an effect on votes. I was standing next to a guy who, as he put his card in the machine [that registers representatives' votes in the House], said, "You know, I was going to vote against the industry on this thing, but what the hell, I can use the $5,000."

During the months preceding an election, I would say that more than half the conversations between congressmen relate to fundraising. "How are you doing with your fundraising? Will you stop by my fundraiser? God, I'm having a tough time getting money out of X—do you know anybody over there that could help? Do you have access to a rock group or a movie star that could help me with my fundraising?"

More often than not the question is not "Who's your opponent?" or "What are the issues in your race?" It's "How much money have you raised?" Money permeates the whole place.

You have to make a choice. Who are you going to let in the door first? You get back from lunch. You got fourteen phone messages on your desk. Thirteen of them are from constituents you've never heard of, and one of them is from a guy who doesn't live in your district, and is therefore not a constituent, but who just came to your fundraiser two weeks earlier and gave you $2,000. Which phone call are you going to return first?

Money just warps the democratic process in ways that are very sad for the country. You have otherwise responsible, dedicated public servants grubbing for money and having to spend inordinate amounts of their time raising money rather than addressing the issues that they came to Washington to deal with. And you have people trying to present their cases on the merits feeling they have no choice but to buy access to the people who will make the decisions. It demeans both sides in ways that are very sad. You've got good people on both sides, a lot of dedicated lobbyists in Washington who are trying in a responsible way to present their points of view and get forced into becoming fundraisers and contributors in a way that's really outrageous.

2. Former Congressman Toby Moffett of Connecticut

Toby Moffett was thirty years old when, as a former Naderite (he was the first director of the Connecticut Citizen Action Group, one of Ralph Nader's early grass-roots organizations), he was elected to Congress as a member of the post-Watergate class of 1974.

He soon won a seat on the House Energy and Commerce Committee, one of the PAC hot-spots, handling legislation regulating the oil, chemical, broadcasting, and health industries.

An unalloyed liberal (he might prefer the term "progressive") with prodigious energy, he initially chafed at the need, in Congress, for compromise and accommodation. As a new congressman, he observed, "After you stay in the House for a while, all the square edges get rounded off, and you get to look like all the other congressmen." Later, though, he took pleasure in the legislative skills he developed, in "working the system."

In 1982, 1984 and 1990, he ran unsuccessfully for, respectively, U.S. Senate, governor and U.S. representative.

There was always pressure to raise more and spend more, and build up your margin. If you win by 58 percent, it's one of a heck of a big difference from winning by 52 percent—in terms of what you have to face next time. So the goal is always to try and get yourself up over 60 or 62 and then 64 percent, and then, in many states, if you get up over 70 or 75, maybe you'll be unopposed. That's the dream, to be unopposed. So as a result, you go to where you have to go to get the money to build up that margin.

I remember during the Carter years, right in the middle of the hospital-cost-control vote*—the hospitals and the AMA were just throwing money at the [House Commerce] Committee [which was handling the bill] as fast as they could. It was coming in wheelbarrows.

Our committee was a prime target, because the Commerce Committee had clean-air legislation, we had all the health bills, we had all the energy stuff—you know, natural gas pricing and that sort of stuff. We had all the communications stuff. So there was a lot of PAC money aimed at neutralizing the Committee. The PACs took those ten or fifteen [swing] votes, and they really went to work on 'em. It was just no secret. Everybody in the room knew it.

You're sitting next to a guy on the Committee and you're trying to get his vote on a clean-air amendment, and you suddenly realize that the night before he had a fundraiser, and all the people who were lobbying against the bill were at the fundraiser. Ways and Means members used to boast about the timing of their fundraisers. What kind of system is that?

In my 1982 Senate race, we had some fundraising people, the kinds of people that you bring on when you've got to raise a lot of money—I mean, very cold-blooded. You know, never mind the issues, let's get the money in. And I remember very, very well their telling me in, maybe, September, that we had to come up with $25,000 immediately for a down payment on a television buy. And I remember sitting down with a member of the House from the farm states, and he said, "How's it going?" I said, "Horrible, I've got to come up with $25,000." He said, "How about some dairy money?" And I said, "Oh, no! I can't do that." Remember, in the seventies, dairy money had a pretty bad name.†

He said, "Well, I can get you ten or fifteen thousand." I said, "Really?" He said, "Yeah. You know, your record has been pretty good on those issues. I think I can do it." Well, I went back to him the next day and said, "Let's do it."

---

* See Chapter 7.

† Because of the dairy lobby's offer of $2 million to the 1972 Nixon campaign in exchange for a higher government dairy subsidy.

By the time I got to the last month of the campaign, I was telling my wife and my close friends that here I was, somebody who took less PAC money, I think, than anybody running that year, but I felt strongly that I wasn't going to be the kind of senator that I had planned on being when I started out. I felt like they were taking a piece out of me and a piece out of my propensity to be progressive and aggressive on issues. I felt like, little by little, the process was eating away at me. One day it was insurance money, the next day it was dairy money.

3. Former Senator Charles McC. Mathias of Maryland

To say that "Mac" Mathias was not a mainstream Republican is the height of understatement. An illustration: in the Senate "club," where the ordinary rule is politeness and accommodation, Mathias' fellow Republicans prodded South Carolina's Strom Thurmond to give up his senior position on the Armed Services Committee solely to elbow Mathias out of the spot of ranking Republican on the Judiciary Committee. Later, when the Republicans won control of the Senate, Thurmond abolished the important Antitrust Subcommittee, which Mathias was in line to head, and instead gave him the unglamourous Subcommittee on Patents.

He was almost as unwelcome among many conservative Republican party officials in his home state. In 1984, he barely eked out a place on the Maryland delegation to the 1984 Republican national convention. Asked why he fared so badly, one Baltimore member of the party's central committee answered, "Because he's a liberal swine."

On the other hand, his moderate stances made him popular among Maryland Democrats, and helped him win three successive Senate terms, beginning in 1968.

Mathias' seniority made him the chairman of the Senate Rules Committee, which handles campaign finance reform legislation. So it was significant that in 1985, he was the prime sponsor of a bill providing government financing of Senate general elections. At the time, public financing was widely considered an impossible dream. But in the following Congress, his basic ideas were adopted by

Senate Majority Leader Robert Byrd of West Virginia, and put the
prime campaign finance reform bill on the Senate's agenda.

In 1986, Mathias chose not to seek reelection. A factor in that
decision was what he called the "daunting" prospect of having to
raise millions in campaign funds.

In all honesty, money was not the crucial factor in my decision not
to run again. But the thought of going out to raise $4 million, or
anything like $4 million, was too much. In 1980, my campaign cost
$1 million, which was a substantial effort. The thought of doubling
that, let alone quadrupling, was a daunting prospect.

The need to raise money has now gotten so serious that the
practice has grown up in the last several years of providing "windows" in the Senate schedule. A window is a period of time in
which it is understood that there will be no roll-call votes. Senators
are assured that they won't be embarrassed by being absent for a
recorded vote. Windows usually occur between six and eight in the
evening, which is the normal time for holding fundraising cocktail
parties. The Senate Majority Leader says, "There will be a window
between six and eight"—or between seven and nine, or whatever.
That is a euphemism for saying that's the period in which you can
go out and raise money while the Senate's in session [conducting the
Nation's business]. You're giving senators time off to raise the
money. It seems to me that the public should be shocked into
action.

I think the Supreme Court was wrong in the *Valeo* case [a 1976
ruling holding that in politics, money is a form of speech protected
by the First Amendment]. Instead of *protecting* freedom of expression, I think they have provided a means of *suppressing* freedom of
expression. As it is, the big contributor can just drown out the little
contributor by creating these enormous disparities. If I'm only able
to give $100 to the candidate of my choice and someone else can
give thousands, that's just going to submerge my voice completely.

I did one of those TV debates for the U.S. Chamber of Commerce. I was shocked because one of the Chamber's people in the
course of this discussion, said, "You can't do away with campaign

contributions because no public official would do anything for you. How would you ever get anything done?" In some circles that is really the naked truth—that is, this is an outright lever that you can *buy* to get governmental action. And this person said so right on the air.

I don't think that the majority of the members of Congress are venal. But there are degrees of temptation. If someone came in and said, "I contributed $1,000, or am about to contribute $1,000 to your campaign and I expect you to vote No," I think most members would, if not kick 'em out of the office, at least make an outraged statement. But, a contributor calls you up on a busy day when your inclination is not to take any calls, and if that person says, "I must speak to you urgently," the chances are you will take that call when you wouldn't have taken any other calls. So to that extent I think money does impact.

4. Former Senator Barry Goldwater of Arizona

First elected to the Senate in 1952 from a seat on the Phoenix City Council, Barry Goldwater quickly rose, in 1964, to be his party's presidential standard-bearer, and the champion of the conservatives within the GOP.

To do that, he had to give up his seat in the Senate, but he returned four years later, and remained (despite one narrow escape at the polls in 1980) until his retirement in 1986.

In 1985, disturbed by the effects of the ever-mounting costs of campaigns and the demands this placed on candidates, he joined Democratic Senator David Boren of Oklahoma in leading the fight for campaign finance reform. The Boren-Goldwater measure to limit the amount of political action committee money a congressional candidate could receive passed the Senate by a top-heavy 69–30 margin in 1986, but went no further before Goldwater's retirement at the end of that term.

My first election in 1952 cost $45,000. We used to have $50 dinners. $25 dinners. I don't think I saw a $100 dinner until maybe 1955, '56, along there. If I had run again last year, I would have had to raise at least $3 million. When I ran the first time, the state [population] was about 800,000 and now it's about, coming up 3 million. So say two and a half times. So theoretically, if I lived on the same dollar basis, I would have spent $3 million. But that's not the way it's going. Up, up, up, up.

Today, the congressmen are more interested in being reelected than in their country. The day after they're elected, literally, they want to have a fundraising dinner for the next campaign. I don't know how many letters I've had from sitting senators and sitting congressmen wanting me to either raise money, come to dinner, or put my name down as the chairman of a fundraising committee. I don't like the attitude that I have to be reelected and that's the prime thing I'm going to work on in the coming two or six years.

There's many subtle things they [the interest groups] can do. They can take your wife and you on a trip to Florida, or California, or Honolulu, or the Bahamas. A very social event. Not just the two of you, but your entire—you go as a group. And you can travel on the company airplane. So it doesn't cost you a cent.

There's no question that the Senate has changed in its performance. The Senates of today can't compare with the Senates of thirty, thirty-five, forty years ago. Those great men that we had never worried about money; they just ran on their record. And they weren't faced with the initial job of raising millions of dollars. When I first came to the Senate, nobody that I knew was immediately thinking of next time. I didn't begin worrying about my reelection until about two years before. But, as I say, today, it's the next day! Will you raise some money for me?

5. Former Senator Thomas Eagleton of Missouri

By the time Tom Eagleton vaulted into the national spotlight as George McGovern's 1972 running mate, Missourians had long known him as a liberal boy wonder. Elected city attorney in St. Louis three years out of law school, Eagleton celebrated his thirty-fifth birthday in 1964 by winning a two-to-one victory as lieutenant governor. He moved on to the U.S. Senate four years later.

Eagleton consistently opposed U.S. involvement in Vietnam, and in general had a solid liberal-labor voting record.

But he was no rubber-stamp liberal. For example, he favored a constitutional amendment reversing the Supreme Court ruling that sanctioned abortion.

A chain-smoker, he also crusaded against the tobacco subsidy and favored a cigarette label, "WARNING! Cigarette smoking causes CANCER, EMPHYSEMA, HEART DISEASE, may complicate PREGNANCY, and is ADDICTIVE." He was only persuaded to drop the words, "and may cause DEATH" on the ground it was redundant.

Shortly after his reelection in 1980, Eagleton and his wife decided he would not seek another term in 1986, largely because he was disgusted by what he called "tin-cupping" to raise campaign funds. But the Eagletons kept the decision to themselves for two years.

Senator Eagleton now practices law and teaches in St. Louis.

There were about three compelling reasons not to seek re-election and the money-raising factor was very high on the list. I just did not want to go through what I called the tin- cup routine— that is, begging for money, literally, from Maine to Hawaii. Psychologically, I didn't want to do it. It was just making me view the whole process of seeking reelection in a very negative way. My wife and I knew in '80 that that was the last one I was going to go through. After raising $1.3 million, I just said I'm just not going to do the tin-cupping again.

So the question of where the money was going to come from wasn't a problem for me for the final six years. When Mr. X came in to see me on behalf of, or opposed to, a certain amendment, I didn't have to put money on the scale and say, "How does this factor out in fundraising?"—as might be the case if I were running for reelection. If I'd been thinking of running again, I'd have said, "That's a good potential fundraising source. Those people are some big bucks."

When I ran for the Senate in 1968, I had a hotly contested primary. I think I spent about a half a million dollars. In the general election, I think we spent about $300,000. In 1974, I think I spent, total, about $600,000. In 1980, my final Senate race, I spent $1.4

million, my opponent $1.2 million. Now get this. In 1986, the Democratic nominee for my seat, Harriet Woods, spent $4.3 million. And the winner, Christopher Bond, spent about $5.4 million. So from '80 to '86, the cost of a Senate race in Missouri on the Democratic side, went up three and a half times. Thus, for the last two years [or his or her term], a senator is personally spending 60 or 70 percent of his time either thinking about, planning, or implementing fundraising strategy. And the other 30 percent, he is spending being a senator.

There's really not the need to spend all that money except your opponent may be spending huge sums, and thus, psychologically, you don't want to be outspent three and four to one. You don't want to see your opponent every time you turn on the television in prime time. You do it to keep up with the Joneses.

An enforceable legal ceiling on the amount candidates could spend would be hallelujah. It would be a benefit to the candidates. It would be a benefit to the public. Part of the reason we have low voter turnout, in my opinion, is political oversaturation: people, between September and November, buffeted with never-ending blasts of political ads. One of the ways they protest about it is by not voting at all.

It just stands to common sense reason that if the backbone of political financing is the $5,000 PACs and the $1,000 individuals, then a candidate, wittingly or *un*wittingly, tends to be more predisposed to those contributors. I read the other day that over 40 percent of the funds of House members who sought reelection came from PACs. Used to be 26 percent. That means that for that candidate, those House winners, those PACs get priority attention and access into his office, his staff, him personally, and to what I call his witting or unwitting predisposition.

We would get some calls from Missouri from Joe Citizen—just worried about an issue. Some of them had a beef because of a vote—but it's a Missouri call, OK? I don't know him, but he's a guy out there in St. Louis. I never took one of those calls. Some staffer took all of them. That's just the way, from a pragmatic view, that it was. I didn't have enough time in the day to answer them all. If I got a letter from J.P. Morgan and he was a big contributor, I would answer it personally. "Dear J.P., good to hear from you." But what about answering Joe Citizen? Well, staffer, send Joe Citizen a nice answer. What did Jimmy Carter say? "Life ain't fair."

Every PAC has its special interest or special interests. If I take X thousands of dollars from a dairy PAC, I know what it is the dairy boys are interested in. If I take X thousands of dollars from a tobacco or a trucking PAC, I know what is it those fellows are interested in, because I've been around 'em. So, the minute you accept their money, you are tacitly acknowledging that you are part of their philosophical orientation.

I had any number of senators come up to me and say, "Some day I guess I'll make the decision to retire. I know how you feel about the money-raising thing. God, I feel the same as you do . . . except I just want to serve one more term." You could talk privately to a hundred members of the Senate—ninety of them would deplore the present fundraising system. But not all ninety of them would vote to change it.

6. Senator Kent Conrad of North Dakota

The narrow election of Kent Conrad to the U.S. Senate in 1986 resulted from a grass-roots farm revolt among farmers and residents of small towns hurt by a steadily declining farm economy.

As state tax commissioner since 1981, Conrad had won popularity by closely auditing out-of-state corporations such as, for example, the Burlington Northern railroad, for its abandonment of North Dakota rail lines used by farmers.

The 1986 senatorial campaign in North Dakota was extraordinarily expensive for that state (total spending was about six times what it had been six years earlier). Both Conrad and his opponent, Republican incumbent Mark Andrews, relied to an unusual extent on PACs (each got half his money from PACs, far above the average in a senatorial contest). And both traveled to distant states in search of contributions from wealthy individuals.

Yet in the end, Conrad's election, as well as other 1986 senatorial contests, demonstrated that financial superiority has diminishing returns, for Conrad won despite being outspent more than two to one (just over $900,000 for Conrad versus over $2.2 million for Republican Andrews).

You ask if I've already started raising money for the next time. The answer is absolutely.

Those who want to represent the broad public interest find themselves in a terrible dilemma. If you're going to run successfully in the country today, you have to have sufficient funds to do so. Take my own state. I spent about $900,000 in my campaign, my opponent probably three times as much. There's no way you can raise that kind of money in a state like North Dakota. So you're going to California to raise money for a race in North Dakota. You're going to New York to raise money for a race in North Dakota. It just doesn't make any sense. It's in the national interest to put a cap on spending.

I had tremendous trouble raising PAC money as a challenger. I even had trouble getting the PACs to return my phone calls. This current system puts such weight on incumbency. It is very difficult for a challenger to win. Very difficult for them to mount a respectable campaign.

7. Former Congresswoman Claudine Schneider of Rhode Island

Claudine Schneider, a person who exudes electric energy, was a political anomaly: a Republican officeholder—and an apparently invincible one—in the solidly Democratic state of Rhode Island.

When she first ran for Congress in 1978, the conventional wisdom did not hold out a prayer for her. That year, she raised a total of $56,000—almost all through bake sales, art auctions and the like. PACs that year gave her a grand total of $1,700. Yet even spending just $54,000, she received 48 percent of the vote.

So when she ran again in 1980, her cause was no longer regarded as hopeless and the PACs came through with nearly $105,000. She won comfortably that year, with 55 percent of the vote. In ensuing years, her popularity has increased (she won, successively, 56%, 68% and, in 1986 and 1988, 72% of the vote).

And as her popularity with the voters increased, so did the money she received from PACs. In 1988, even though she did not sit on any of the lucrative "PAC heaven" committees (she sat on the Merchant Marine Committee and the Science and Technology Committee) she received $193,656 from PACs, nearly half her total campaign receipts.

In 1990, Rep. Schneider made an unsuccessful bid for the U.S. Senate.

When I went to the PACs for money in 1978, they said, "You've got to be kidding. Rhode Island is a hard-core Democratic state. They haven't had a Republican since 1938. Not a chance." Secondly, the comments were, "Wait a minute, that's a very ethnic state." We have a lot of Italians in my district, and I had many older Italian men and women say to me, "You know, you ought to be home making spaghetti and having babies." And that was very frustrating. And the PACs basically anticipated that. "The likelihood of them [the voters] selecting a woman is pretty slim. So I'm afraid we can't help you on two counts." So it was [my being] both a woman and a Republican that were the deterrents to many to make contributions.

I don't spend much time raising PAC money at all, now. It didn't require a whole lot of effort to go and raise that $163,000 of PAC money I got in 1986. But the fact was that it was coming in; I wasn't about to say, "Hold off, boys." My feeling is whenever I can raise money, even though I got 68 percent of the vote, or whatever, is that what I raise today, I won't have to raise tomorrow. I spend more time strategizing and trying to figure out who would I like to get money from that I haven't yet. I'm on the Science and Technology Committee. So what am I doing that would be of interest to, for example, the high-tech community?

I don't feel a conflict of interest being on the Merchant Marine Committee and getting contributions from interested maritime PACs. I think a more direct way to put that question is, "Do I feel like I am compromising my decision-making by soliciting funds from those groups? Am I encouraging them to buy my vote?" And my answer there is no.* When I first ran, people were taking a chance on me, PACs were taking a chance on how I would vote. I was an unknown entity. Then once I started voting, and they saw my philosophy, which direction I might be going, a number of PACs pulled out and don't support me anymore. Other PACs joined on the bandwagon. Those contributions are usually made after I have performed something, not because they have come to me and said, we want you to do X, Y and Z.

I think that one of the unfortunate situations is the return of so many incumbents. And I think that a lot of that has to do with contributions made to people who are in very powerful positions. Obviously, someone who is on the Ways and Means Committee raises infinitely more money than someone on Merchant Marine and Fisheries. And a challenger who is attempting to unseat an incumbent on one of those more powerful committees has a very tough time trying to get elected.

8. Congressman Mike Synar of Oklahoma

Since he came to the U.S. House in 1978 at age twenty-eight, Mike Synar has been anything but a typical congressman. He thinks in national terms.

He set himself apart in a *New York Times* profile, early in his career, when he said, "I want to be a U.S. congressman from Oklahoma, not an Oklahoma congressman."

That determination found expression in 1985 when Mike Synar voted against the Gramm-Rudman-Hollings deficit reduction act, at a time when most legislators, even many liberals, rushed to embrace it. Synar also joined with other lawmakers in a lawsuit challenging the constitutionality of a pivotal section of the law (calling for automatic budget cuts to meet deficit targets). Synar said that "If members (of Congress) can't make hard choices, they ought to seek other employment." That lawsuit prevailed in the U.S. Supreme Court, 7–2.

Synar is one of the few members of Congress who refuses to accept

---

* See Baseball Scenario on page xix.

campaign contributions from PACs. He says he raises all he needs from two mammoth barbecues a year—one in his home district and one in Washington. Those are unusually successful events, for in the 1984 and 1986 elections, he took in $335,000 and $271,000, respectively.

Synar is a passionate advocate of campaign finance reform in general and government aid to election campaigns in particular.

In 1978 when I ran for office, a winning person spent about $52,000 to get elected. Today that number is over $400,000. What that means is that someone like Mike Synar, if he were sitting in Muskogee, Oklahoma today, could not run for the United States Congress.

The second problem is the amount of time that a member of Congress has to spend raising money. When you figure that an average race costs $400,000 to win, and you figure that there's only twenty-four months in a campaign cycle, and you divide those out, you're talking about having to raise somewhere in the neighborhood of $20,000 a month. Think of the amount of time that you have to focus to do that. That is time taken away from the duties of your office, which is representing people.

With more and more demands on elected officials' time, they try to seek the path of least resistance, and the path of least resistance is large globs of money from political action committees. So PACs have a disproportionate role in the process. Individual contributors aren't competitive with PACs.

How bad is it? Well, I'll tell you how bad it is. If you're a Republican from Oklahoma and you want to run against Mike Synar today, you could fly here to Washington, D.C., and based upon my liberal voting record, walk around this town for two days and raise $250,000 and become a legitimate candidate for my office without ever having raised a penny in my home district. I think there's something wrong when you can become a legitimate candidate without showing any sense of support financially or organizationally within your own district.

There's only two things in politics now—money and media. The day of the grass-roots organization is a thing of the past. In Oklahoma in 1986, we had a Senate campaign and a governor's campaign where the last thing you would see is the candidates out in the rural areas campaigning. It's a waste of their time. All they really did was raise money and go on TV. The hands-on type of approach is a thing of the past. It's all money and media.

9. Congressman Jim Leach of Iowa

Congressman Leach is one of a handful of House members who refuse to take campaign money from PACs, and is at the forefront of the campaign-reform movement in the House. In 1985 and 1986, he joined with Democratic Representative Mike Synar of Oklahoma in sponsoring a bill to limit the amount of PAC money any House candidate could receive in an election.

Although listed as a Republican, Jim Leach sides with the Democrats in the House on issues such as arms control, the cessation of chemical-warfare weapons production, sanctions against South Africa and denying funds for the Contra forces in Central America.

I argue that what you have in a campaign contribution is an implicit contract with the person who gave. If you listen carefully to that group's concerns, and abide by them, there is an implicit promise of another contribution for the next election.

What you've done is turn upside-down the American premise of government, which is the idea that people are elected to represent people. Officeholders should be indebted to the individuals that cast the ballots. Today candidates are becoming increasingly indebted to the people that *influence* the people who cast the ballots. It's a one-step removal. And so we're having an indirect, secondary kind of democracy—one that is increasingly group oriented and financially influenced.

If I had my way, I would eliminate all group giving to campaigns. Prohibit group giving, period. I'd make all contributions individual. I would also prohibit giving from outside the state. That is, why allow a Iowan to influence a Nebraskan or a New Yorker to influence a Californian? That's why in my own campaigns I don't accept PACs and I also don't accept out-of-state gifts.

We have $10 or $20 receptions throughout the district. We have hog roasts, we have barbecues in which we seek small contributions. But it's very time-consuming and difficult as contrasted with the people around Washington. Every night of the week, here, there's a reception at the Capitol Hill Club for candidates, and they can raise $10,000 to $150,000. That takes me three weeks. Twenty events. But on the other hand, my way gets more people involved in the process. And I think it makes them feel a little bit more part of it. For example, how much a part of a campaign is someone going to feel if they give $10 to a candidate who just got $10,000 from ten different unions? Or ten different businesses?

There's always an argument that PACs get more people involved. I've never seen it. I think it's exactly the reverse. Not having PACs forces candidates to go to the voters. I don't raise near as much as other candidates. But I raise over $100,000 and sometimes $150,000. That should be adequate to run a campaign in a state like Iowa. The fact that others in our state spend two to four to five times as much is an indication of how sick the system has become. In part, one side raises all that money because the other side does. It amounts to an arms race. What you need is a domestic SALT agreement.

10. Former Congressman Bob Edgar of Pennsylvania

Bob Edgar, a Methodist minister with a serious, almost prim, aspect was elected by a lopsidedly Republican congressional district in the Philadelphia suburbs in the post-Watergate year, 1974. Thereafter, for six successive elections, the Republicans resolved to unseat this Democrat with a solidly liberal-labor voting record. Six times they failed—but never by much. Not once did Edgar win by more than 55 percent of the vote.

A member of the House Public Works and Transportation Committee, where mutually congenial back-scratching on water and other public-works projects is the order of the day, Edgar was an unpopular loner, opposing what he considered pork-barrel enterprises dear to his colleagues. But his anti-pork-barrel stance only served to win him Republican votes in his home district.

As chairman of the Northeast-Midwest Coalition, a group of congressmen defending their regions against the Sunbelt, Edgar, far from a loner, proved to be a legislator of such skill that before he left Congress, a Sunbelt coalition had sprung up in response.

When first elected, Edgar announced he would serve six terms in the House and no more. True to his word, in 1986, he left the House and made an unsuccessful run for the U.S. Senate.

A hundred days before the November 1986 election for the Senate, I realized that I had to raise $2.5 million. That's $25,000 a day, every day, from that hundredth day down to zero. Anyone who has ever raised money knows that if you're a really good fundraiser, you can probably raise $25,000 in one event. Think about raising that today and waking up tomorrow morning knowing you had to raise it tomorrow, the next day, the following day, to raise enough money to continue to keep your message on the air.

Eighty percent of my time, 80 percent of my staff's time, 80 percent of my events and meetings were fundraisers.

It has a terrible impact on you, when you start making choices in your schedule. Rather than going to a senior center, I would go to a party where I could raise $3,000 or $4,000. I started to go to fundraising events—three, four, five a day.

That whole fundraising fever has a dramatic impact on a campaign that wants to talk peace-and-justice issues, women's rights, senior-citizen rights, environmental issues. It really gets you warped at the way in which you make those choices.

In the 1986 election in Pennsylvania, the major candidates for governor and the U.S. Senate spent a total of about $21 million, $18 million of which was spent on television. You know, it's just an obscenity to have that kind of an investment in time, energy and resources flow into a media message where the candidate who gets the cleverest commercial or the nastiest commercial can shape his image and his message, and prevail over the candidate who might be the most thoughtful, the most insightful in terms of the future problems that we face.

So, in addition to some form of public-private financing of campaigns, I'm very much for opening up the airwaves so that people can get access so their candidates without the candidates having to spend a bundle. They're public airways.

I don't think that we ought to assume that lobbyists and lobbying is bad. If you have an eight-hundred-page health-care bill and three paragraphs deal with the dentists, it is very helpful to have a dental lobby in Washington and in the district teaching their people the impact of those three paragraphs on dentists. If you have a technical amendment on electroplating in an environmental bill, it's very helpful to hear from the electroplaters who are going to be impacted by that. It's where they get involved in hosting a fundraising event and get twenty-five different businesses to give a $5,000 contribution that you begin to see the buying of influence.

11. Governor and Former Senator Lawton Chiles of Florida

In 1970, an unknown state senator running for the U.S. Senate pulled on a pair of khaki trousers and hiking boots and spent ninety-two days hiking across Florida. His thousand-mile trek transformed his long-shot candidacy into a seat in the U.S. Senate.

One of his trademarks in the Senate became "sunshine government"—conducting the processes of government out in the open rather than behind closed doors, and subjecting officeholders' personal financial statements and the activities of lobbyists to public disclosure requirements.

In his next campaign, in 1976, Senator Chiles limited contributions to $10 and refused to accept contributions from out-of-state donors. In 1982, when the Republican Party promised to underwrite his opponent heavily, he apologetically raised the donor ceiling to $100, but added a new restriction: he would not accept contributions from political action committees. Much to the frustration of his fundraisers, he retained all of those limits for his would-be 1988 re-election campaign

In late 1987, Chiles announced he would not seek a fourth Senate term in 1988. But he returned to politics in 1990, winning the governorship after a hard-fought campaign in which he once again limited contributions to $100 and refused to accept out-of-state contributions.

Today, PACs are running in packs, where segments of industry or segments of labor, or segments of this group, get together with multiple PACs and decide how they are going to contribute. Sometimes you're talking about $250,000 for a campaign. Overall I think they're distorting the electoral system and what I sense is, very strong, that your John Q. Public is saying, "I don't count any more. My vote doesn't count, I can't contribute enough money to count. No one is going to listen to me."

I'm looking at congressmen 50 percent of whom, I don't know exactly, but around half that get half of their money or more by PACs. They don't even have to come home. Their money is raised at [Washington] cocktail parties.

At the same time, when I sit down with my fellow senators, they say, "The bane of our existence is fund-raising. We're having to do it over six years and we're having to go to Chicago, Los Angeles, New York, Florida. A lot of us spend a lot of time there. But that's what I have to do at night. That's what I have to do on weekends. And, of course, for these big, big PACs, I have to be pretty careful about what my voting record is going to be."

I think if out-of-state contributions were prohibited, you'd have a better chance of those people in your state making the decision based on the merit of the candidate. I think if one candidate, who usually would be an incumbent, can go raise all kinds of out-of-state money, I think he can [distort] his record very much.

A lot of people seem to think that somebody gives you a PAC contribution, then they come in and say, "I expect you to vote for this." It never happens that way. All that person wants you to do is to take and take and take, and then when he comes in, he never says, "I expect." It's always on the basis of, "This is a big one for me, and maybe my job's on the line." He doesn't need to say anything more than that because the hook is already in you and if you've taken it, you know it, and you *know* you know it.

12. Former Congressman Tom Railsback of Illinois

Television viewers over forty will remember Tom Railsback from the televised impeachment proceedings against President Nixon before the House Judiciary Committee in the Spring in early 1974. Railsback was considered a "swing" vote among the Republicans as he wrestled with the question of whether to vote to impeach a president of his own party. Railsback's public agonizing remains vividly in the minds of many who followed those hearings. Ultimately, he voted for impeachment on two of the counts presented.

In the House, where he represented a southeastern Illinois district from 1966 to 1982, Railsback's name was prominently associated with the cause of campaign finance reform. Along with his Democratic colleague, Dave Obey of Wisconsin, he authored the Obey-Railsback bill, to limit the amount of money any congressional candidate could receive from PACs.

In 1982, Railsback was defeated in the primary by a conservative Republican. He now practices law in Washington, D. C.

I'm inclined to think that campaign finance reform may have been influenced by the PACs. In other words, I think a lot of people wanted to vote for reforms of the campaign financing laws and the political action committees, but they backed off when they saw it was going to affect their ability to raise money from PACs.

I favor trying to even the playing field and give challengers a better opportunity to present their views. I say that as a Republican. That was my argument during the seventies and I could never persuade my Republican brethren why they would stand to benefit if there was a more even playing field. I kept pointing out that labor PACs were giving 95 percent of their money to Democrats and the business PACs were giving anywhere from 55 to 60 percent to Republicans. Incumbents were getting a lot more money and Republicans were in the minority in the House. But I think we were able to get only 24 percent of the Republicans in the House to vote for the original campaign finance reform bill.

 *Chapter Six*

THE PAC MANAGERS
SPEAK

How do the people who manage the political action committees view what they do? How do they see the role of their PACs in the political process? How do they decide how to distribute their PAC's largess? Do they think their money buys influence—or if not outright influence, do they believe their dollars gain them access to lawmakers' ears?

Here are the answers to those questions offered by four PAC managers, one from each of four major categories of PACs (labor, corporate, ideological, and a cooperative): Bill Holayter, legislative and political director of the Machinists' Union; Elliott Hall, Vice President of Washington Affairs in the Ford Motor Company's Washington office; John Isaacs, legislative director of the Council for a Livable World, a major national peace organization; and Frank Vacca, Vice President for governmental relations of Mid-America Dairymen, one of the three major dairy farmers' cooperatives.

1. Bill Holayter of the Machinists' Union

Ebullient Bill Holayter of the International Association of Machinists and Aerospace Workers is a long-time union man with a pun-

151

gent tongue and a full, graying beard. He is a man much to be cultivated by congressional candidates, for he is the person most responsible for dispensing the $1,456,595 the Machinists' PAC handed out in the 1990 elections. That sum made his the twelfth largest PAC.

The Machinists' PAC collects its money in annual gifts of $10 or more from roughly seventeen thousand of its members nationwide. According to Holayter, a "standard" contribution is about a dollar a month. Payroll deduction plans, provided in some union contracts, yield the PAC around $400,000 a year.

Operating out of a Machinist-owned building in Washington, Holayter divides his time between directing the union's political activities and its lobbying (assisted by a full-time lobbyist). Thus, he stays in touch with senators' and representatives' voting records and gathers political intelligence on upcoming House and Senate contests from union political operatives in the various states.

The final who-gets-what decisions are made by a committee of three top union officers. But they act largely on the basis of Holayter's recommendations.

The decision-making process of the Machinists' PAC contains one democratic element unusual to political action committees: no candidate receives a dollar without the endorsement of the local or state branch of the union. But there is a limit to the say the PAC contributors have about where their money goes. Earmarking of contributions to a particular candidate, for example, is strictly forbidden: Holayter declares, "We don't want anybody telling us what to do with the money they send us. Once you start earmarking, you'll get back to the situation of too much money going to the wrong people. A person that gives to the union PAC has to put some trust in the judgment of the leadership."

The Machinists' selection criteria differ in one critical respect from those of other PACs, whose decision-making begins with the question: Which congressmen and senators can help or hurt our group the most? PACs that start with that question tend, in their giving, to favor incumbents—especially members of those committees that handle legislation most vital to the group—whether or not those particular lawmakers face tight contests and need the PAC's help.

By contrast, Holayter says that in selecting candidates to receive Machinist money, his PAC's analysis starts with a deliberate survey of the probable "marginal" House and Senate contests in the forthcoming election—the contests that are up for grabs, where a contribution could affect the outcome. To identify the marginal contests, Holayter collects political intelligence from Machinist leaders in the various states and from other union political operatives in Washington. Half the Machinists' PAC money goes into those marginal races.

On occasion, the Machinists' PAC does stray from the marginal-district criterion and, like the PACs of Ford, Mid-America and the others, it gives to candidates surely headed for easy reelection—for example, 1990 cycle gifts totaling $5,500 to Michigan Democrat John Conyers even though he averaged ninety-two percent of the vote in his Detroit district throughout the 1980s. Why give even a dollar of union members' money to a sure-fire winner like Conyers? "Because," Holayter says, "he still has to run a campaign, or feels he does." But Holayter insists, however, that you'll never see the Machinists giving $10,000—the legal maximum—to an easy winner, nor a contribution to a candidate who doesn't agree with the Machinists' viewpoint. "You can't compare the bankers with us. You'll find the American Bankers Association giving all over the place, whether a person's a friend or not."

Holayter draws a sharp distinction between "people PACs" such as his, and "PACs that represent money interests," such as General Electric's or the American Bankers Association PAC. Those are "special interest PACs"; they "don't represent people."

But how does Holayter distinguish between his PAC and those others? After all, the Machinists' PAC is looking out for the machinists just as the bankers' PAC is looking out for the bankers.

"Because we're not parochial like they are. We're broad-based. Where most of your corporate PACs—take General Dynamics: all they give a shit about is what happens on the Armed Services Committee and where the Pentagon contracts go. We're interested in a hell of a lot more than that. Safety laws, consumer laws, you can go on and on about the interests we have, because we figure what's good for a Machinist Union member is good for the whole popula-tion, and vice versa."

How does that differ from what GM President Charlie Wilson said in the fifties—"What's good for General Motors is good for the country"?

"Because the Machinists' Union member is no different than any other person that's a worker in this country. They just happen to be a machinist."

Holayter entertains no doubt that his PAC magnifies the political power of individual Machinists' Union members. "If you walk up to a candidate and give them ten dollars—which is about all some of our members can afford—it doesn't mean a goddamn thing. But if we as an organization walk up to a candidate and give him or her $10,000, it means a whole lot more. Also, our union is big and strong in some places and we have hardly any members in others. By pooling the money, we can put New York members' money into Wyoming or New Hampshire, where a senator's vote is just as important to us."

Holayter declares emphatically that his PAC *never* gives to op-posing candidates in a given election contest, as many PACs do. In one instance when the union local wanted to contribute to both candidates in a primary election in California, "I said 'Bullshit. You've got to pick one or the other, or nobody's going to get money.' "

Does the PAC money get Holayter greater access to lawmakers' ears?

"Oh, I don't think there's any question that it makes it easy for me to pick up the phone and get a call back. I'm not just Bill Holayter, *who*? I'm Bill Holayter of the Machinists, the people who gave you a good chunk of dough. We don't get a vote from 'em all the time, but we sure have the access."

What does Holayter expect from the lawmakers who get Machin-ist money? "We expect them to vote right, by our standards."

Isn't that me-first politics?

"Of course it is. That's what we're in business for. Even if you didn't have a PAC, you'd be in business for that. A PAC is just incidental. It's just a money-flowing vehicle."

Bill Holayter stands apart from most of his fellow PAC managers in his distaste for the whole PAC system. "I would like to get out of the business of going around begging for money from our members, because we spend an awful lot of time doing that."

Holayter's personal view is consistent with that of his union which, as far back as 1972, has plumped for government financing of congressional campaigns. That remains the union's position today.

2. Elliott Hall of the Ford Motor Company

From his well-furnished office overlooking Franklin Park in downtown Washington, Elliott Hall, a trim, well-spoken man, oversees the Washington legislative operations of the Ford Motor Company and its staff of twelve full-time lobbyists. They meet twice a month and send their recommendations to the Ford PAC committee in Detroit. That committee, in turn, decides on how Ford should distribute its contributions ($231,000 in 1990) to members of Congress and to state and local public officials.

The PAC committee, which sits in Detroit, consists of five top-level vice presidents, named by the chairman of the company. Contributors to the PAC have little or no say at all about the composition of the PAC committee. While employees are allowed to earmark their contributions to particular candidates, Hall says that less than one percent do, in fact, earmark. Hall says he is "pleased" by the low level of earmarking, because "it means we must be doing our job." He says that the only times employees raise questions about Ford's PAC donations is when "we contribute more than once within an election cycle—which calls for an explanation of what that public official is doing for the company." Questions such as that are raised and answered in the periodic solicitation "pitches" Ford makes to its employees.

The PAC committee receives its recommendations from two

sources: for state and local officials, from six regional managers throughout the country; and, for members of Congress, from Elliott Hall and his groups of lobbyists.

Ford has made little or no effort to solicit contributions from what Hall calls "the lower echelon" employees of the company, believing that the company should not ask the rank and file to contribute until close to one-hundred percent of top management contribute. Presently the figure is about eighty percent—not high enough, in the minds of Ford officials, to justify asking the rank and file to contribute.

Ford's legislative interests before the U.S. Congress fall into two principal categories: financial and automotive. Why financial? Because Ford owns what Hall describes as the third largest savings and loan in the country (the San Francisco based First Nationwide Bank); U.S. Leasing, also headquartered in San Francisco, that leases heavy equipment; Ford Motor Credit Corporation, which finances the bulk of the cars Ford sells to its dealers; and a Dallas-based finance company.

Two full-time Ford lobbyists are on what Hall calls the "banking beat." They concentrate on the members of the House and Senate Banking Committees. Two other lobbyists handle trade-related matters; and the other seven deal with automotive issues—such issues as the Clean Air Act, fuel efficiency standards, and safety-related issues.

Hall says the company targets its contributions to specific committees that specialize in handling legislation of concern to the company: the banking committees, energy committees and tax-writing committees of both houses.

How much influence does Hall find a Ford PAC contribution has with a given legislator?

"It's hard to tell, sometime. But I think generally they have had a positive effect. You know, you can only tell by a vote. If he votes with us, that's the clearest indication that he's been helpful to us."

Does a Ford contribution help gain access?

"Oh, of course."

Hall says that the company has recently initiated a PAC newsletter for its employees, of which, as of December, 1991, there had only been one issue. It is notable about what Ford chooses to tell and not to tell its employees about its PACs practices. For example, it fails to tell them of the $52,125 that its PAC gave to incumbents who were "shoo-ins" for re-election, having won re-election by at least seventy-five percent of the vote over the last two cycles. Nor does it mention the PAC's overwhelming favoritism for incumbents over challengers (96% to incumbents, only 4% to challengers).

How would Elliott Hall respond to any criticism that Ford's incumbent favoritism is perpetuating a "permanent Congress," whereby incumbents vastly outspend challengers and manage, as a consequence to enjoy a phenomenal success rate at the polls?

Hall's response: "We only support incumbents who are doing a good job for business and who seem to merit the approval of their local constituents. We do not support 'trash.' "

Moreover, the company apparently has few compunctions about giving to "shoo-in" lawmakers—legislators who have received an overwhelming share of the electoral vote in recent elections; and it even, on occasion gives to candidates who have *no* opponent whatever.

Exhibit A of the "shoo-in" is Democratic Congressman John Dingell, of Michigan, the powerful chairman of the House Energy and Commerce Committee, which handles many of the key issues of interest to Ford Motor Company. Dingell has not won by less than than a two-to-one margin since 1964, and received, on average, eighty percent of the vote in his most recent three elections. Nonetheless, in the 1990 election, when Dingell's two opponents raised less than a total of $4,000, the Ford PAC gave Dingell a $5,000 contribution—more than the *total* receipts of Dingell's two opponents combined.

Why? "Well, there's a simple way of answering that. Dingell sends an invitation to a fund-raiser. We can turn him down, and say, 'No, you don't need the money. Sorry, John.' But we choose not to do that. He is the strongest advocate of the automobile industry in the Congress. When he sends an invitation, we want to give it serious consideration. And we do. For all the help he's given us over a long period of time—we're going to give him a hand. And we do it without any shame, because he's been our friend. Now, he, of course, hasn't had any serious opposition in a long time. But John Dingell has been very, very helpful to us on a lot of things. Now, he doesn't agree with us on everything. For instance, on the banking issues, he was on the opposite side on a lot of the issues [. . .] but we have never gone to John on any issue, the most miniscule issue, when he hasn't been helpful [so] to the extent under the law we can help him, that he requests that help, we're going to do it . . . He's sixty-two years old now, and I don't know what we're going to do when he's not around. All I know is that when John Dingell's not there, the auto industry is going to be in trouble. And in the eighty-five years that this business has been operating in this country, we've had only one man who has been Chairman of the Energy and Commerce Committee of the House of Representatives that has helped with this business. $5,000 I have no apologies for, because I don't think it's going to happen again for a long, long time."

And Ford gives him that $5,000 even though, politically speaking, he doesn't need it? Hall's answer: "Well, he may not need it. But who knows? He may have a tough race next year [due to redistricting]. You never know."

And what about candidates who have *no* opposition—such as Republican Joseph McDade, of Pennsylvania, who received $1,000 from Ford in 1990? Hall: "McDade. Have we given to him? OK. Let me answer it this way. We have never taken the position that we're going to make a judgment about whether a candidate is opposed or unopposed . . . We have never gone back to a representative in Congress and said, 'Listen, thanks for helping us. We got your invitation to your fund-raiser. You don't need the money. We're not going to give it to you.' When we walk in there next time, what do you think our reception is going to be? This is how this crazy system operates . . . and until it changes . . . we want to get the business of Ford Motor Company accomplished."

3. John Isaacs of the Council For a Livable World

John Isaacs, a small, intense, bearded man runs one of the "ideological" PACs: that of the Council for a Livable World, one of the nation's major national peace organizations.

The Council, which concentrates on arms-control issues, is one of the nation's oldest nonlabor PACs. It dates back to 1962, the same year the American Medical Association's PAC was formed.

But the Council's PAC operates differently from conventional PACs. In his cluttered Capitol Hill office, Isaacs explains the distinction: "Most PACs want to maintain control over the money that's sent to them. They want to decide who gets the money and who doesn't. They are the ones who play God. But we let our supporters make that decision."

The Council achieves that by mailing letters to its supporters on behalf of one or another specific candidate the Council's board of directors endorses. The letter asks those who wish to contribute to that particular candidate to send their checks directly to the Council in Washington, pledging that the entire amount of the contribution will go to the candidate and that none will go to support the Council.

Isaacs says that has been an extraordinarily effective fundraising mechanism. In the 1990 election, the Council raised $826,952 and gave $83,893 to congressional candidates.

The difference between the Council's PAC and others goes beyond the sheer logistics of soliciting and collecting the money. It steers clear of candidates headed for easy victories, concentrating instead on marginal races. It also diverges sharply from most PACs in the proportion of its help goes to challengers versus incumbents. In contrast to the Ford PAC, 96 percent of whose 1990 beneficiaries were incumbents, Isaacs says that in Senate races "the overwhelming majority of the money we raise is for challengers. In the House, it is probably a little less. It might be more half and half." Isaacs acknowledges that "we will stay with an incumbent who is a friend as opposed to a challenger who may promise to have a good voting record, and we stay with our friends if they are running for reelection. [Republican] Senator Mark Hatfield in Oregon had a very good opponent the last time he ran. But Hatfield had been an important leader in arms control, and we weren't going to abandon him for some challenger."

"We prefer small states where our money can make a difference. We'd rather get involved in South Dakota and Nevada than California or New York, because the money goes further."

Unlike most conventional PACs, the council does not concentrate on the members of any particular committee. "Our preference is for leaders, not committees," Isaacs says. Democratic Senator Dale Bumpers of Arkansas, for example, "is an important leader in arms control. He's not on Armed Services or Foreign Relations. But he's a leader in this arms control field, and someone we'd help."

Like the Machinists' Bill Holayter, John Isaacs himself detests the current PAC system and strongly favors abolishing all PACs, including his own. "I think the current campaign finance system is a disgrace. I think the amount of time people have to spend raising funds is terribly destructive to our whole democratic system."

"But," he quickly continues, "as long as the system's there that way, we'll continue to try to operate with that system, even if we'd like to see it changed."

So despite the things that set Isaacs' PAC apart from all the rest, a basic similarity connects his with the others: what he wants from the candidates he and his PAC help.

"We hope, in general that they'll vote in the direction we'd like to see. And if they're not sure of the position we hold, at least we hope that they'll give us a hearing. Clearly the money helps us to get that hearing."

4. Frank Vacca of Mid-America Dairymen

Frank Vacca's dairy PAC has it made. It has the perfect mechanism for collecting money from the dairy farmers of the marketing cooperative, Mid-America Dairymen, it represents: the co-op deducts farmers' PAC contributions from their monthly milk checks. That is, once a farmer signs up for that plan, the monthly deductions become automatic and relatively painless.

In the early seventies, the dairy PACs suggested to their members making monthly PAC contributions of $8.25, a total of $99 a year. That figure barely squeaked under the new disclosure law, which required gifts of over $100 or more to be separately listed. Later, when the disclosure threshold was raised to cover gifts greater than $200, the dairy groups doubled the recommended monthly contribution to slide under the new disclosure requirement—"for their privacy," Frank Vacca explains.

Vacca, Mid-America's strikingly handsome vice-president for government relations, sits in his Capitol Hill townhouse that doubles for office and home, relating with pride about how, since he went to work for "Mid-Am" in 1976, the proportion of the Mid-America farmer-members contributing to the PAC has risen from 28 percent to over 46 percent. Result: with roughly 5,000 farmers contributing, the Mid-Am PAC amassed $484,450 to toss into the 1990 congressional elections.

For Mid-America and the PACs of the other two giant dairy co-ops, the system of deducting PAC contributions from the monthly milk checks has become a money machine, generating huge sums to throw into the campaigns of friendly representatives and senators. Dairymen, Inc., gave away $119,501 in 1990. Associated Milk Producers, Inc., or AMPI, the giant of the three, dispensed $769,800, making it the thirty-second largest PAC. The three dairy PACs thus were able to contribute over $1,370,000 to 1990 House and Senate candidates.

With such immense PAC treasuries, all three can easily afford to—and do—spread their largess across the congressional spectrum, including to big-city congressmen in whose districts nary a cow roams, as we saw in Chapter 3. In 1990, the three dairy PACs contributed, on average, to 220 House and Senate candidates, most of them incumbents.

Before the dairy PACs were formed, Vacca explains, the National Milk Producers Federation had "been around for seventy-five years as a lobby—not political, not involved in campaigns. Just up here on Capitol Hill." Then dairy leaders "realized that a way to be more involved in the political process was to establish a PAC" as another step in becoming "better known to the elected officials."

The three dairy co-ops formed their PACs unusually early—in the late sixties, long before the 1974 law laid the framework for the PAC explosion. The biggest of them—AMPI—got a black eye when it was revealed that its pledge of $2 million to Richard Nixon's 1972 reelection campaign was a quid pro quo for Nixon's raising the federal dairy price-support level.

Frank Vacca, a veteran of sundry Democratic congressional and presidential campaigns (including that of Robert Kennedy in 1968), is Mid-Am's sole operative on Capitol Hill. He says he also spends a great deal of his time extolling Mid-Am's PAC to the organization's hundred field workers, who in turn sell it to the farmer-members.

Vacca freely acknowledges the need for his PAC to sell a majority of the Congress on the problems of the declining number of dairy farmers who are concentrated in a few congressional districts. How many dairy farmers *are* there nationwide? "Less than 200,000," Vacca says. "Probably about 180,000. Twenty years ago, there were over a million of them. It's a dying breed. They're projecting that by, oh, 1995, there will be probably around 135,000, somewhere around there."

"You've got to look at it this way," Vacca says. "Today, there are about 50 congressional districts that produce over half the milk. There are about 138 districts that don't produce one ounce of milk. So in roughly 250 districts, the congressmen don't look at the dairy farmers' issues unless someone brings it to their attention. So these PACs were started, not to buy votes—that wasn't their intention at all—but as just another way to get the ear of the congressman so the dairy farmers could present their story."

That reasoning underlies the shift in Mid-Am's giving pattern since Vacca took over its political relations operation in 1976. Before Vacca's arrival, Mid-Am's political action committee followed the traditional PAC pattern of concentrating its contributions in the committees that most affected dairy farmers, primarily the agriculture committees. But after surviving the various committee hurdles, farm legislation must finally come before the full 435-member House of Representatives. "Then the magic number is 218," Vacca explains. "What are you going to do concentrating on the 17 or so on the Agriculture Committee? You've got to get 218 votes. You need a shotgun approach—spread it out all over the place."

"You know, there's some guys from the urban-suburban areas that know nothing about dairy. But they've got to vote on the dairy issue. They should know something about it. Who the hell is going to educate them?"

Mid-America occasionally does contribute to coast-in candidates, even congressmen who have no opponent. In the 1990 election cycle, Mid-America gave to 39 incumbents who had won by an average of at least three to one in the previous three elections, 20 recipients were unopposed. ("Every candidate needs a little maintenance money to carry on. I mean, a candidate has to get his name before the public, even if he's unopposed.") And Vacca has "no problem" with a postelection switch, with Mid-Am giving to the winner after backing the other candidate before the votes were counted. In some such cases, lawmakers "hold it against you" for having backed their opponent. "When you visit their offices, it'll take you an hour or two before you get in to see them. Things like that. That's happened." Others, though, "are broad minded and they understand it's a professional thing. Not personal."

How does Vacca view the role of PACs in the political system?

"With congressmen and congresswomen representing half a million people, they cannot run around on a horse and bag of oats like they could when the country was rural and they represented about 35,000 people. And with the disappearance of the parties and the city clubs and the ward parties, there is still a need for the candidates to get their message across. The PACs act as another vehicle—to do what ward clubs and city clubs used to do. I see nothing wrong with that at all."

Do Mid-Am's PAC contributions win influence with lawmakers?

"I'd be a fool to say no. But what is influence?" Vacca goes on to explain that some Mid-Am beneficiaries "say, 'Thank you very much,' and go right on their way." Others pay more attention.

Does Mid-Am money gain Vacca favored access to congressmen and senators?

"It can. It should. That's what we said it would. Sure. Because you're a friend. You've helped them out at a time when they needed it."

Does Vacca ever feel extorted by lawmakers' requests for money? Are those requests more heavy-handed than they used to be?

"It's not heavy-handed. It's getting to the point where the candidates feel that the PACs are a natural source of contributions"—especially the PACs that have Washington representatives like Vacca, who "are somewhat easier to get to. It's becoming more onerous for us PAC contributors."

Vacca makes a mental calculation. "There are about 100 days a year for congressmen to hold Washington fundraisers. Now you take those 100 nights and divide it into 435, you're going to come up with four or five a night. Some nights I'll go to ten or twelve. How can we handle that? And that doesn't include the fundraising steering committees that congressmen ask me to serve on."

"Really," says Frank Vacca, "It's getting out of hand."

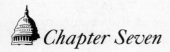 *Chapter Seven*

THE TRUE COSTS OF THE PRESENT CAMPAIGN FINANCE SYSTEM

ONE MAJOR ALTERNATIVE to having PACs and private individuals pay for congressional election campaigns is for those campaigns to be publicly financed by the federal government, just as presidential campaigns have been paid for since 1976.

But mention that idea to that proverbial man or woman on the street and you're liable to be greeted with a protesting roar. "What—*me* pay my hard-earned dough for those crummy political campaigns?"

The truth is that the average man or woman on the street—in fact *all* the men and women on the street—are paying for "those crummy political campaigns" *right now*. They pay every time they buy a pound of sugar or a quart of milk at the supermarket. And they pay every April 15, when they write their checks to the Internal Revenue Service.

That probably comes as a surprise to many citizens, who may well have assumed that because the present system of financing congressional campaigns involves no direct *government* outlays, it

165

entails no cost. Not so. The present system is immensely costly to all citizens, either as consumers or as taxpayers, or both.

The dairy subsidy offers the ideal illustration. In September, 1985, the interests of 200,000 dairy farmers, located in a limited number of congressional districts, were pitted against those of the rest of the population in a vote in the House of Representatives on whether to maintain the dairy subsidy at a higher level (as desired by the dairy farmers) or at a lower level (as desired by a coalition of consumer and labor groups). On that vote, the 200,000 dairy farmers prevailed, 244 to 166, with the result that millions of taxpayers were not only obliged to lay out $1 billion extra a year but, more serious still, consumers of dairy products were obliged to pay up to 60 cents a gallon more for milk by 1990. That is, 200,000 dairy farmers won out over tens of millions of consumers and taxpayers—a result that directly contravenes a strict one-person one-vote political calculation.

Why would ordinarily self-interested politicians oppose the wishes of most voters? The answer, in part at least, is to be found in money—millions of dollars in political contributions that the dairy lobby—principally three huge dairy cooperatives—collected and showered upon members of Congress, including representatives who do not have a dairy cow in their districts.

The raw statistics suggesting that these contributions had an impact follow:

Of those receiving this amount from the dairy lobby in 1979 through 1986 . . .	. . . This percent voted for higher dairy subsidies in 1985
More than $30,000	100%
$20,000 to $30,000	97%
$10,000 to $20,000	81%
$2,500 to $10,000	60%
$1 to $2,500	33%
Zero	23%

Some political analysts argue that such statistical presentations are one-dimensional and over-simplistic—that many factors besides political contributions (party affiliations and pressures, constituent interest, personal philosophy, etc.) also play a part. But, given statistics such as those presented in the table above, would such analysts maintain that money was *no* factor?

The sugar subsidies offer another dramatic illustration. That subsidy is estimated by the U.S. Department of Commerce to cost consumers $3 billion a year in higher sugar prices. It pits the interests of the sugar industry, confined to just sixteen states and fifty congressional districts, against the interests of tens of millions of consumers and taxpayers scattered throughout the country. For the sugar growers to prevail, they must win the support of senators and representatives from the thirty-four states and 385 congressional districts in which not a granule of sugar is grown.

There are, of course, two sides to the sugar and dairy subsidy debates. But it is a matter of fact that those debates take place after of millions of dollars in campaign contributions have been showered upon the Congress.

So to whatever extent political money supported sugar and dairy subsidies, part of the cost to consumers and taxpayers may fairly be attributed to the current system of financing congressional campaigns.

Similar statistics, presented in this chapter, suggest that auto industry contributions were a factor in defeating stricter auto fuel efficiency standards, thus adding tens of billions of dollars to drivers' gasoline purchase costs; that tobacco company political largess helped preserve a tobacco subsidy that will cost U.S. taxpayers as much as $900 million; and that the American Medical Association's multi-million-dollar generosity to hundreds of lawmakers played a part in Congress' defeat of President Carter's plan to curb the incessant rise in hospital costs. Thus, some portion of the billions that plan could have saved hospital bill payers is also part of the price tag attached to the existing campaign finance system.

To indicate the magnitude of that price tag, this chapter presents five examples of congressional actions in which there is evidence of influence by campaign contributions, resulting in a discernible cost to taxpayers or consumers or both.

* * *

1. The Sugar Subsidy

Annual cost to consumers: $3 billion.

On September 26, 1985, the House of Representatives cast a vote that departed from strict one-person-one-vote politics in a mystifying manner.

On the sugar vote, the House was deciding whether to continue a federal sugar subsidy that annually benefits roughly 12,000 American sugar growers by an average of a quarter of a million dollars *each*. As against those 12,000 growers, the potential losers numbered in the tens of millions—namely, every American family, forced to pay among the highest sugar prices in the world. At the time that vote took place, a quantity of sugar that cost 85 cents in Washington, D.C. cost just half as much a few hundred miles away, in Ottawa, Canada, and only 31 cents in Mexico.

For growers, the subsidy is enormously lucrative: at the time of the 1985 vote, sugar beets in Minnesota were nearly four times as profitable as corn; in Louisiana, cane sugar yielded $458 per acre, compared with just $69 for soybeans.

As noted above, sugar is grown in only 16 of the 50 states and 50 of the 435 congressional districts. Why would the representatives and senators in the other districts and states vote to give massive help to people who can't cast a vote for them, while injuring every family in their own constituencies? To find the answer, let's look at the sugar subsidy through two ends of a telescope: the consumers' end and the growers' end.

The sugar subsidy makes an estimated $3 billion difference. From the consumer's viewpoint, that three billion costs the average household $41 a year, or about 80 cents a week. More relevant to the political tug-of-war, consumers have no way of making common cause to protest high prices. And they certainly lack the means of organizing a political action committee.

From the growers' point of view, however, that $3 billion looks quite different. If all those 12,000 growers were equal, the three billion would come out to $250,000 each. But of course all growers are *not* equal. In Hawaii, for example, 95 percent of the sugar is grown by five companies. In Florida, three companies produce half the crop. There, to take but one example, the American sugar subsidy has made the four Fanjul brothers rich. The Fanjuls fled Cuba when Castro came to power, and operated seven sugar companies, owned 120,000 acres of sugar land in Florida, branched into real estate and Caribbean resorts, and, for $200 million, bought from Gulf & Western three resort hotels and 240,000 acres of prime sugar land in the Dominican Republic. The Fanjul family have been generous political givers: in 1989 and 1990 alone, they gave $84,000 to various congressional campaigns.

With the stakes in the billions, the sugar growers are intensely well organized, able to make large political contributions and have a huge incentive to do so as well as an efficient mechanism—seventeen PACs—to dispense their gifts. In just four years (1980 to 1984), the major sugar PACs alone expanded in number from ten to seventeen, and their contributions to congressional candidates doubled. Between 1985 and 1990, those seventeen sugar PACs showered a total of $2,600,000 on congressional lawmakers.

The propped-up price of American sugar paved the way for a boom in corn sweeteners, a sugar substitute, whose manufacturers can make extraordinarily high profits merely by undercutting the price of sugar by a few cents and selling their product to, say, the soft drink makers. The corn sweetener firms have become potent allies in pushing for high sugar subsidies, and they are heavy hitters. In 1984, just three corn-sweetener firms—Cargill, Staley and Archer-Daniels-Midland—had total sales of nearly $40 billion. Moreover, they and the sugar growers are generous political givers. Because they are few in number and highly concentrated, the sugar growers and their allies have successfully formed political action committees. In the 1980s the corn-sweetener industry joined forces with the sugar forces, and by 1984, they had built up an impressive pool of money to throw into congressional campaigns. According to *Common Cause* magazine, the sugar PACs put about $640,000 into the 1984 campaigns. The three largest corn companies sweetened the pot with an added $260,000, bringing the total to $900,000. On top of that, a single individual—Dwayne Andreas, largest stockholder in Archer-Daniels-Midland—and his family contrived to contribute a grand total of $152,100 to congressional candidates, notwithstanding the $1,000 ceiling on individual gifts in the election laws.

Grand total: over $1 million—enough to shower money on a very large number of congressmen and senators. In fact, in the 1984 elections, the sugar-corn-sweetener alliance contributed to the campaigns of more than 450 congressional candidates.

In 1985 alone, over half a million dollars of sugar money flowed to members of Congress, even though 1985 was a *non*-election year. The reason: that year, Congress was scheduled to cast one of its quadrennial votes on cutting back the sugar subsidy.

On September 26, 1985, here was the array of forces as the House prepared to vote on the sugar subsidy: *For* retaining the subsidy at a high level: the sugar growers' associations; the corn-sweetener companies and other agricultural groups that receive generous subsidies. Against them and in favor of a mild cutback of the subsidy: A variety of consumer, labor and sugar-using industries (candy, ice cream, bakeries, etc.)—*plus the Reagan Administration.*

When the dust had cleared, the consumer-labor-administration forces had lost by a substantial margin, 142 to 263.

Had the sugar money played any part in this result? Here is the evidence that it had had at least some effect:

Of those receiving this amount from the sugar lobby in 1983 through 1986 . . .	. . . This percent voted for for sugar subsidies in 1985
More than $5,000	100%
$2,500 to $5,000	97%
$1,000 to $2,500	68%
$1 to $1,000	45%
Zero	20%

Five years went by. The year was 1990. That year, the average world market price for sugar was seventeen cents per pound; in the United States the price was twenty-three cents per pound, and another congressional effort was made to trim the sugar price support program. The result was the same as 1985. Despite broad support from a coalition of consumer groups, food processors, retailers, sugar refiners—*and the Bush Administration*, the 1990 cutback efforts were defeated by a vote of 150 to 271 in the House and 44–54 in the Senate. Once again, the effect of sugar money on the vote is suggested by the following statistics:

SENATE

Of those receiving this amount from the sugar lobby from 1985 through 1990 . . .	. . . this percent voted for for sugar subsidies in 1990
More than $15,000	85%
$10,001 – $15,000	71%
$5,001 – $10,000	60%
$1 – $5,000	20%
$0	0%

HOUSE

Of those receiving this amount from the sugar lobby from 1985 through 1990 . . .	. . . this percent voted for for sugar subsidies in 1990
More than $15,000	100%
$5,001 – $15,000	92%
$1 – $5,000	53%
$0	12%

2. The Dairy Subsidy

Additional cost to taxpayers: $2.77 billion over a five year period.

Cost to consumers: $11.5 billion over five years.

On the same afternoon as the 1985 vote on the sugar subsidy, the House was called on to choose between two alternative programs for subsidizing the nation's dairy industry. The choice was between continuing to increase dairy price supports while paying farmers to take cows out of production, as proposed by the House Agriculture Committee, and a gradual lowering of the dairy supports, as proposed by Democratic Congressman Jim Olin of Virginia and the House Republican Leader, Bob Michel of Illinois.

The Department of Agriculture and the Congressional Budget Office estimated that, over the years 1985–1990, the Agriculture

Committee bill would cost taxpayers $2.77 billion more than the Olin-Michel bill in direct supports. In addition, the Milk Industry Foundation estimated that the higher subsidy would, over those same years, cost consumers an added $11.52 billion in higher prices for dairy products at the check-out counters.

Like the sugar subsidy, this vote on the dairy subsidy is a vivid illustration of the distortion of the one-person-one-vote principle. On the one hand stood just 200,000 dairy farmers—a tiny sliver of the entire population, whose milk production was confined to a limited number of congressional districts—yet highly and efficiently organized into three giant dairy milk-marketing cooperatives. Each of those, in turn, was armed with a political action committee, funded with one of the most efficient money-collecting instruments ever developed: a check-off mechanism, whereby the co-op would automatically withhold each farmer's PAC dues from his or her milk-marketing payments. No muss, no fuss, no monthly invoices.

As a result, the three milk-marketing coops managed to collect $3.3 million for 1984 election contributions many of which went to *big-city members who have, at most, a scant number of dairy cows in their districts.* *

That September day, the higher subsidy contained in the committee bill and favored by the three giant dairy political action committees prevailed in the House by a vote of 244 to 166. And campaign contributions by those dairy PACs had an impact on the 1985 House vote. (See table on page 166.)

3. Auto Fuel Efficiency Standard

Annual cost to consumers: $38 billion.

On the face of it, the United States has a powerful interest in oil use and oil conservation. America went to war in the Persian Gulf

---

* For example, the fifteenth highest recipient of dairy money during the years 1979 to 1986 was Texas Congressman Martin Frost, whose Dallas district contained, at most, three dairy farmers.

ostensibly for the partial purpose of preventing Saddam Hussein from gaining undue control of world oil supplies and production.

According to the Energy Information Administration, an arm of the Department of Energy, the U.S. imported 290 million barrels of oil annually from Iraq and Kuwait at the onset of the Gulf crisis. According to calculations based on official government figures by the Safe Energy Communication Council, a public interest group concerned with energy policy, that much oil could be saved by raising automobile fuel efficiency standards by a mere 2.75 miles per gallon—just a ten percent increase above the current legal mandate of 27.5 miles per gallon for all passenger cars.

Notwithstanding, federal law governing domestic and foreign auto efficiency has remained unchanged since 1975, when the so-called CAFE—Corporate Average Fuel Economy standard—was set at a maximum rate of 27.5 miles per gallon.

In 1990, Nevada Democratic Senator Richard Bryan introduced a bill that would require automakers to increase fuel efficiency by twenty percent by 1995 and forty percent by the year 2001. Bryan's bill was originally part of the Clean Air package, but was dropped therefrom in the spring of 1990 in exchange for a promise for separate Senate consideration of the bill later that year.

But in September, auto industry proponents mounted two successive filibusters to prevent the Senate from coming to an up-or-down vote on the fuel efficiency question.

A high drama began to unfold. The Senate voted to end the first filibuster, and won comfortably with eight votes to spare, 68 to 28 (it takes 60 votes to end a filibuster). The bill was again scheduled for debate. But a business coalition, led by the auto industry, strongly backed by the Bush Administration—only intensified its efforts. Auto industry forces in the Senate mounted a second filibuster, and this time, an anti-filibuster vote fell just three votes short, 57–42, thus killing the legislation. (A similar bill never made it out of House committee.)

Amazingly enough, in the few short days between those two anti-filibuster votes, eleven senators switched their votes and, instead of voting against the auto industry position, changed their votes to side *with* the industry.

Here is the money-vs.-votes on that second anti-filibuster vote:

Those who received this amount from the auto industry, 1985–1990 . . .	This percent voted with the auto industry
$20,000 or more	64%
$12,000 to $19,999	42%
$0 to $11,999	15%

Based on figures from the Energy Information Administration, the annual savings to consumers at the gas pump had the Bryan Bill passed would have come to $38 billion (not to mention the environmental benefits of diminished carbon dioxide emissions).

4. The Tobacco Price Support Program

Ultimate Cost to taxpayers: between $660 million and $900 million.

In the early 1930s, the Agriculture Adjustment Act designated tobacco as a basic commodity and authorized payments to growers who restricted production. These growing quotas, still in place today, restrict tobacco growth and thereby artificially raise the price received by growers.

Defenders of the tobacco price-support program contend that it will entail no cost to taxpayers or consumers, owing to a 1982 "no net cost" provision, requiring manufacturers and growers to contribute to a government fund. However, recent figures from the Congressional Research Service and the U.S. Department of Agriculture show that eventual cost to the taxpayer will be between $660 million and $900 million, excluding the $35.4 million it costs the Agriculture Department to administer the program.

In 1985, Wisconsin Representative Thomas Petri introduced an amendment to the farm bill that would have done away with the tobacco price support program altogether. The Petri amendment was defeated. Now as a result, the tobacco price support is permanently embedded in the nation's farm program, not even requiring periodic reauthorization, as many other farm price support programs do.

The following are the money-vote comparisons on the Petri amendment.

For those receiving this amount from the tobacco industry from 1981–86 . . .	. . . this percent voted with the tobacco industry
more than $5,000	90%
$2,500 to $4,999	70%
$1 to $2,499	51%
$0	26%

From 1981 to 1986 the industry contributed an average of $2,944 to those House members siding with it on the Petri amendment, compared with only $1,241 to those members opposing the industry position.

5. The Hospital-Cost Containment Bill

Annual Cost to Consumers: $10 billion.

In 1977, President Carter proposed to Congress a bill to curb soaring hospital costs, which had quintupled in the preceding decade. His program was aimed at holding the future rise of hospital costs to 9 percent a year. The Department of Health, Education and Welfare estimated that this could save consumers about $27 billion through 1982.

The Carter program was strenuously opposed by the American Medical Association because, the AMA said, it would be a regulatory nightmare; it would unfairly single out the hospital industry for price controls; and was unnecessary because the industry's Voluntary Effort campaign was already bringing down the rate of hospital-cost inflation. The AMA's PAC was and is one of the largest (in 1990, second-highest in contributions to congressional candidates) and most active in the United States.

On July 18, 1978, the House Commerce Committee defeated the Carter proposal by a single vote, 21–22, and the bill went no farther in the Congress that ended that year. When President Carter submitted a new plan to Congress in 1979, he estimated that savings to consumers and to federal, state and local governments would amount to $53 billion over the ensuing five years, or about $10 billion a year.

On November 15, 1979 the new measure was defeated by a vote of 166 to 234 in the House of Representatives. Did AMA campaign contributions affect that vote? Again, the figures suggest that they did.

Of those receiving this amount from the American Medical Association in 1977 through 1980 . . .	. . . this percent voted against containing hospital costs in 1979
More than $15,000	100%
$10,000 to $15,000	95%
$5,000 to $10,000	82%
$2,500 to $5,000	80%
$100 to $2,500	38%

The Total Costs

Recapping the estimated annual cost to consumers and taxpayers of the four measures described above:

The votes on these measures . . .	. . . may cost the public this much every year
Sugar subsidy	$3 billion
Fuel efficiency standards	$38 billion
Dairy subsidy	$.55 billion (taxpayers)
	$2.3 billion (consumers)
Hospital cost containment	$10 billion
TOTAL	$53.85 billion*

Calculating how much of that $54 billion may be fairly attributed to the existing campaign finance system is a tricky and imprecise business. For example, how much of the $10 billion annual cost of the defeat of the Carter hospital cost-containment plan may fairly

---

* This total omits the $660–900 million tobacco subsidy, which is a one-time, rather than an annual figure.

be assigned to campaign contributions by the AMA's PAC? All of it? Surely that would be a hard claim to support, for that would require proving that a Congress uninfluenced by AMA money would have passed the Carter plan wholly unchanged. Such an event is too rare, with or without special-interest money, to be credible.

On the other hand, to argue that *none* of the $10 billion is due to the millions of AMA contributions is to say those campaign contributions had no impact whatever—an equally implausible proposition.*

So the answer as to how much of the cost to attribute to the current campaign finance system lies somewhere between zero and 100 percent. Those who put little credence in this whole line of reasoning might put it at, say, 10 percent, which would be a $5 billion annual cost for the legislative measures covered in this chapter. Others might prefer to place 50 percent of the burden on the PAC system, for an annual cost of $27 billion.

Whichever one chooses, the cost of the way we now finance congressional campaigns—even if $5 billion is a more accurate figure—is prodigious, and exceeds by many times the cost of even the most expensive program of public financing of congressional campaigns in primary as well as general elections—estimated at most at $400 million a year. (And the examples cited here by no means represent the totality of costs.)

The point is: it is difficult to conceive a plan for government financing of congressional campaigns that would be more costly to taxpayers and consumers than the current special-interest dominated system of paying for those elections—if we face up to the *true* costs of the present system.

---

* Even the most skeptical will have difficulty failing to lay at the feet of the present finance system the $1.3 billion cost of delaying the shutdown and government takeover of Lincoln Savings and Loan, whose principal stockholder was Charles Keating. The $1.3 billion figure is generally acknowledged to be the cost of delaying the action of federal regulators, who wanted to shut down and effect a government takeover of Lincoln Savings and Loan, but were persuaded not to do so by the active intervention of five U.S. senators who had received political contributions from Charles Keating totaling $324,000. The $1.3 billion, therefore, can, almost indisputably, be counted as a cost to the taxpayers of the present campaign finance system.

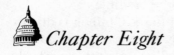 *Chapter Eight*

CAMPAIGN CONTRIBUTION OR BRIBE? "A HAIRLINE'S DIFFERENCE"

"The distinction between a large campaign contribution and a bribe is almost a hairline's difference."

—SENATOR RUSSELL B. LONG (D-LA)

THE DISTINCTION BETWEEN a campaign contribution and a bribe can indeed be thin—so thin, in fact, that the U.S. Court of Appeals ordered a new trial in the 1972 bribery conviction of Maryland Senator Daniel B. Brewster because the trial judge had failed to make that distinction clear to the jury.

Presented below are the facts about the official behavior of certain U.S. senators and representatives either shortly before or shortly after they received campaign contributions from various interest groups. Considering all the facts, were those campaign contributions? Or were they bribes?

In posing that question, I am not asking readers to sit as jurors in a court of law and render a verdict on whether these legislators

178

should be sent to jail. Nor am I suggesting official laxity in failure to prosecute these cases. On the contrary, so sophisticated is the minuet performed by givers and receivers that evidence of an explicit *quid pro quo* is extremely difficult to come by. Indeed, such are the subtleties that not even the lawmakers themselves know for certain which side of the line they are on.

My point is to illustrate the difficulty of distinguishing a campaign contribution from a bribe, and to demonstrate that our election laws tolerate official behavior that comes far closer to bribery than most of us would feel comfortable with.

As background, here are the critical phrases of the federal bribery statute, which subjects to criminal prosecution any—

> public official [who],
> directly or indirectly,
> corruptly demands, seeks, receives, accepts, or agrees to receive or accept
> anything of value personally or for any other person or entity in return for being influenced in the performance of any official act . . .

Against that backdrop, here are the facts concerning six congressional actions.

On April 1, 1987, the Oshkosh Truck Company hosted a breakfast meeting attended by seven members of the House Armed Services Committee. The company paid each of the seven an honorarium or speaking fee, then permitted under House rules (but since forbidden). Oshkosh paid each of the seven $2,000, the maximum per-appearance honorarium then allowed by congressional rules.*

Just *hours* after the breakfast meeting, that committee met and

---

* Unlike campaign contributions, which can only be placed in candidates' campaign treasuries, these so-called "honoraria" (subsequently outlawed by House rules) could be directly pocketed by the lawmakers themselves, and thus could be said to resemble a bribe.

voted to force the Army to buy five hundred *more* of the company's heavy-duty trucks *than the Army wanted to buy!*

The trucks cost $130,000 each. "It looks kind of funny, doesn't it?" said "Pres" Grove, Oshkosh's Vice President for Government Affairs, when asked why the ninety-minute breakfast was held the same day as the vote. "But it really was a sheer coincidence," Grove told the *Dallas Morning News*. Grove said that efforts to schedule the breakfast earlier had failed.

Grove also told the *News* that honoraria are just "sort of the way business is done" in Washington. "We are living at the government trough,* so to speak, and we feel we have got to contribute back to it."

Prime mover among members of Congress in arranging the April breakfast meeting was former Texas Democratic Congressman Marvin Leath, who had led a lengthy legislative fight to make the Army keep buying Oshkosh trucks. According to the *Dallas Morning News*, Oshkosh had paid Leath an additional $2,000 honorarium in 1986 and Oshkosh campaign executives had contributed another $2,000 to the Congressman's campaign that year. Leath also acknowledged that a key consultant to Oshkosh, W. Leonard Killgore, Jr., was a "special friend."

However, Leath insisted to the *News* that neither his friendship with Killgore nor the funds he had received from Oshkosh affected his stance on the Army-Oshkosh truck contract.†

On March 22, 1990, the *Aleutian Enterprise*, one of a twenty-nine-ship fishing fleet owned by the Arctic Alaska Company, was returning to port from a fishing expedition in the Bering Sea, heavily loaded with a huge haul of cod and pollock. Suddenly, an on-deck net broke, spewing tons of flopping fish onto the deck, and causing the vessel to list noticeably to port. Water rushed in through uncovered openings in the side of the hull. A few minutes later the

---

* Securities and Exchange Commission records show that in 1986 and 1987, government contracts constituted eighty-three percent of Oshkosh's sales.

† See Baseball Scenario, page xix.

Aleutian Enterprise capsized and sank. Nine crew members perished.

Coast Guard investigators insist that the accident would not have happened had a safety law known as the "load line" law been observed and enforced. A "load line" is a line—actually a series of lines—on the hull of a vessel indicating how low in the water it can safely float; and ordinarily that "load line" is accompanied by a Coast Guard inspection to assure that all safety systems aboard the vessel are in proper operation. In the case of the *Aleutian Enterprise*, investigators found that an alarm failed to sound, that crew members had trouble getting survival suits and that escape routes were partly blocked. Moreover, had the ship been forced to pass a competent load line inspection, the openings in the hull would have been closed, and water probably wouldn't have been able to shoot so ferociously into the lower portions of the vessel.

But in fact, that law had not been enforced against Arctic Alaska and the ships in its fleet, due principally to the personal intervention of Washington Republican Congressman John Miller.

According to *The Wall Street Journal*, a major reason for Congressman Miller's "concerted campaign" against enforcement of the load line law against Arctic Alaska's fleet: the "thousands of dollars" contributed to Miller's campaigns by Arctic Alaska employees. *The Wall Street Journal* tabulated contributions from Arctic Alaska executives totaling $10,000 to Miller's 1988 and 1990 campaigns. In addition, the company's political action committee contributed $3,400 to his campaign in 1989 and '90, making him its largest single beneficiary.

Congressman Miller, as is usual in cases such as this, denies any connection between the campaign gifts and his actions.* Nonetheless, he and his staff cooperated closely with Arctic Alaska officials: his fisheries aide says he relied on a thick memorandum from company lawyers to draft a letter to a Coast Guard admiral, which Congressman Miller signed and sent, arguing that Arctic Alaska's fleet was exempt from the load line law.

Evidently the letter carried great weight with the Coast Guard,

---

* See Baseball Scenario, page xix.

which replied in a letter of its own that although the Coast Guard thought Miller was "misinformed about the vessel [in question] and the law . . . *because of your concerns*" the Coast Guard would defer further enforcement action. Miller's special influence may well have been his membership on the House Merchant Marine and Fisheries Committee, which oversees the Coast Guard; so Arctic Alaska evidently chose well in bestowing its political largess on Representative Miller.

More important (from the point of view of this chapter), in noting (and speculating about) the effect of Arctic Alaska's campaign contributions on Congressman Miller's active interest in this matter, it should be noted that, according to the *The Wall Street Journal*, Congressman Miller "has been known as a champion of fishing-ship safety legislation."

Understandably, relatives of the victims of the *Aleutian Enterprise* accident were angry about Congressman Miller's intervention. At a meeting with Ann C. Williams, whose brother, John Dieterich, perished in the sinking, the Congressman defended his actions by saying he was "helping a constituent."

Mrs. Williams' reply: "Our brother was one of your constituents, too, and he's dead now."

Very late one June night in 1984, members of the Senate and House strove to reconcile the differences between their respective versions of a tax bill.

Suddenly, and without warning, Illinois Democratic Congressman Dan Rostenkowski, leader of the House negotiators, brought up a proposal to solve a pressing tax problem faced by some 333 wealthy commodity traders, most of them from Rostenkowski's home city of Chicago.

According to an account of the incident in *Common Cause* magazine, Kansas Republican Senator Robert Dole, who was heading the Senate negotiating team, quickly agreed to Rostenkowski's proposal. Within a matter of minutes, the commodity traders had secured a provision worth at least $300 million—an average of $866,000 per trader.

Senator Dole had not always been so sympathetic to the traders' tax problem. Indeed, three years earlier in 1985, he had been instrumental in blocking a proposal to single out the traders for preferred treatment involving the very same provision of the tax law. The 1981 plan that Dole blocked had been spearheaded by Democrats to whom the traders had been politically generous, and on the Senate floor, Dole had chided the Democrats. The commodity traders, he said, are "nice fellows . . . and they are great contributors. They haven't missed a fundraiser. If you [Democrats] do not pay any taxes, you can afford to go to all the fundraisers."

But Dole's efforts to thwart the traders' tax avoidance had gone beyond a mere Senate floor speech. When the traders claimed that the compromise provision enacted in 1981 gave them amnesty for their past tax avoidance maneuvers, *Common Cause* magazine reports that Dole took the trouble to write the Internal Revenue Service saying the IRS was free to go after traders who in earlier years had unlawfully abused the tax law. The IRS did just that and soon, several thousand cases were pending in the Tax Court involving several hundred million dollars in disputed taxes.

Enter now Representative Rostenkowski and Senator Dole with their late-night rescue—a provision one senator claimed would "virtually preclude" the IRS from pursuing tax cases.

During the period when Dole was reversing field, the commodity industry and individual traders had been most generous about contributing to Dole's own PAC, Campaign America. Through Campaign America, Dole had spent $300,000 helping the campaigns of forty-seven of fifty-three Republican senators—surely no hindrance in his election in 1984 as Senate Republican leader.

A *Common Cause* magazine scrutiny of official records disclosed that—

- in 1983–84, individuals and PACs from the commodity industry gave Campaign America $70,500—six times what they had given in 1981–82.
- in the three months prior to Senator Dole's turnabout approval of the late-night amnesty provision, they had given $10,500 to Campaign America.

- in the three *weeks* preceding the Dole-Rostenkowski rescue, individual traders had contributed $3,600 to a fundraiser co-hosted by Campaign America.

Political contributions? Or bribes?

As recounted in Chapter 3, on February 3, 1987, the Senate voted on a provision to vastly reduce the cost to the taxpayers of removing billboards that violate the Highway Beautification Act.

The provision, offered by Vermont's Republican Senator Robert T. Stafford, would have revived the procedure the states and localities had historically used to compensate billboard owners for signs torn down pursuant to local laws. That traditional method granted billboard owners a grace period before having to remove a sign, with the revenues the owners collected during that interval considered proper compensation. But in the '60s and '70s, Congress required that billboard owners be paid in cash for signs they were obliged to take down.

Among the senators voting against reviving the grace-period method of compensation was Brock Adams, the newly-elected Democratic senator from the state of Washington. He told his colleagues in the Senate that while "the government may have the right to take property, it also has an obligation to provide direct compensation for it."

That had not always been Adams' position. Nine years earlier, as Secretary of Transportation in the Carter administration, Adams had vigorously protested the very cash-only compensation formula he now defended. On August 17, 1978, Secretary Adams had written to Pennsylvania's Democratic Representative Peter H. Kostmayer that to require cash payments and strip localities of their historic ability to use the grace-period method of compensation "would represent an unprecedented intrusion by the federal government into the prerogatives of localities to control land uses within their jurisdiction."

But, in 1987, what had been, for *Secretary* Adams, a government "intrusion" had, for *Senator* Adams, been transformed into a government "obligation." (Senator Adams explained to the *Washington Post* that he had assumed his 1978 stance to conform with the policies of the Carter Administration.)

In the intervening period, Brock Adams had conducted a successful senatorial campaign, in the course of which he had received campaign contributions totaling $12,200 from the billboard industry, principally from individuals connected with the industry. Many of those resided outside the state of Washington.

The fast-rising millions the leading defense contractors poured into lawmakers' pockets (via honoraria) and their reelection campaigns (via political contributions) inevitably raise questions about the crossing of the slender bribery line. Three illustrations:

Illustration No. 1: In late 1985, Congress enacted a measure aimed at reducing the price of military equipment by obliging Pentagon contractors to report on how well they control their labor costs.

The Wall Street Journal reported that a few months later, a group of Pentagon lobbyists met to decide what could be done to repair the damage. The result: a concerted congressional effort to repeal the 1985 provision outright. According to the *Journal*, leading the Senate repeal effort was Indiana Republican Senator (now Vice President) Dan Quayle, the chairman of the military procurement subcommittee that had cleared the labor cost-control measure only a few months earlier. Senator Quayle faced reelection in November, 1986. The *Journal* reported that between January, 1983 and June, 1986, Quayle received $92,000 in campaign contributions from defense contractors' PACs. In addition, in 1984 and 1985, defense firms gave the senator $7,500 in honoraria, which he could legally put in his pocket.

Quayle's office said it was "outrageous" to infer a connection between those $92,000 of defense contractor campaign contributions and the senator's flip-flop on the cost-reporting measure.* Other backers of the repeal favored by Quayle pointed out that the

---

* See Baseball Scenario, page xix.

original cost-reporting law had been passed in 1985 without any hearings and was poorly written. But the heavily taxed public might wonder why the solution to those problems didn't lie in holding hearings and perfecting the 1985 law, rather than repealing it. (Ultimately, a compromise version was passed.)

Illustration No. 2: In 1983, the Dravo Corporation of Pittsburgh was low bidder to build a $103 million steam plant for the Navy in Portsmouth, Virginia. Later, though, Dravo found that it had to redesign the plant, and faced a $25 million overrun on the project. According to *Time*, rather than "waste time trying to persuade unsympathetic Navy brass to renegotiate," in September, 1986, Dravo lobbyist Martin Hamberger went to Pennsylvania Republican Senator Arlen Specter, to whose 1986 reelection campaign the Dravo PAC had already contributed $4,000. Hamberger presented to Specter a draft of what Dravo wanted inserted in the defense appropriation bill: a provision instructing the Navy to reimburse Dravo for its cost overrun. Without telling the Navy what he was doing, Specter inserted the brief provision within a thick ninety-seven page bill. After Hamberger's September visit, the Dravo PAC gave Specter an added contribution of $2,500.

Senator Specter declined to comment on the matter, but a member of his staff said he "did nothing for Dravo that he doesn't do regularly for Pennsylvania companies, many of whom are not contributors." But former Republican Congressman Robert Badham of California saw the Dravo incident as far more than a constituent-service matter. "It was an extremely dangerous precedent," said Badham. "It gives a whole new dimension to bidding and contracting. If all else fails, go to the Congress."

Did Dravo's $6,500 campaign contributions have any connection with Senator Specter's assistance to Dravo that set that "dangerous precedent"? The public cannot be sure. But both are fixed on the public record: the Dravo contributions and the Specter rescue.

Illustration No. 3: In December, 1982, the late Congressman Joseph Addabbo, a Democrat from Queens, and chairman of the House Appropriations Subcommittee on defense spending was reported to be a "prime mover" in an action to end the monopoly theretofore enjoyed by the Avco Corporation in making engines for the Army's M–1 tank. Addabbo and his colleagues had ample reason to allow competitive bidding on the engine contract: Avco's engines cost more than targeted, were delivered later than promised, were often defective, and they consumed five gallons per mile (not five miles per gallon; five gallons *per mile*).

But on July 20 of the following year, Congressman Addabbo reversed himself, and voted to continue the Avco monopoly, even though in the meantime the Army had received a bid from a competing firm that could have saved the taxpayers $300 million.

In the interval, Representative Addabbo (now deceased) received two $2,500 campaign contributions from Avco, one on April 13 and one on May 10.

Those facts are all contained in easily available public documents. When the facts were published in *The Wall Street Journal* in October, 1983, no one in an official position apparently thought to inquire whether Avco's gifts crossed the line between bribe and legal political contribution.

In May, 1985, at Chasen's restaurant in Beverly Hills, California, New York Republican Senator Alfonse D'Amato was guest of honor at a $1,000-per-plate fundraising dinner for his reelection campaign. The dinner was arranged by the investment banking firm Drexel Burnham Lambert, Inc., since celebrated for its role in the S&L debacle. Drexel was the nation's leading (and pioneering) underwriter of so-called "junk bonds," high-risk bonds typically used to finance corporate mergers and takeovers.

Senator D'Amato was Chairman of the Senate Subcommittee on Securities, and during the week following the Chasen's dinner, D'Amato's subcommittee was scheduled to hold a hearing on legislation to regulate the sale of junk bonds. D'Amato's committee had two proposals before it: one, to curb the use of junk bonds in corporate takeovers, and the other to limit the purchase of those bonds by federally insured savings banks. Either proposal would have put a major crimp in Drexel Burnham's business.

Of the $33,000 raised at the dinner, $23,000 came from the twenty-three Drexel Burnham executives who each contributed

$1,000 to Senator D'Amato's campaign. Another $4,000 came from two executives of Columbia Savings & Loan Association, a prime customer of the Drexel firm. At the time, Columbia already owned far more junk bonds than would be permitted under legislation to be considered at the D'Amato hearing.

According to a story by Brooks Jackson in *The Wall Street Journal*, when D'Amato finally introduced his bill regulating corporate take-overs later that year, "the provision [regulating junk bonds] so dreaded by Drexel was missing."

Five days after the D'Amato shoe dropped, Jackson reported, Drexel's chief executive officer and thirty-five other Drexel executives from New York donated $500 to each senator. D'Amato's campaign. D'Amato called the timing "absolutely coincidental." *

In 1975, Texas billionaire H. Ross Perot faced a peculiar tax problem. On November 4, of that year, by a 20–14 vote, the House Ways and Means Committee approved an amendment carefully tailored to solve Perot's problem. The amendment stood to save Perot $15 million in taxes.

An examination of Federal campaign reports later disclosed that in the 1974 elections, Perot had favored various congressional candidates with twenty-six campaign contributions totaling $75,900. All but two of the gifts were made *after* the election.

Twelve members of the Ways and Means Committee received Perot gifts. Of the twelve, ten supported the specially-tailored provision to confer a $15 million tax saving on the their Texas benefactor.

Two Ways and Means members, Democrats Joe Waggoner of Louisiana and Omar Burleson of Texas, each received $5,000 from Perot just after the election. Perot made the campaign gifts, and Waggoner and Burleson accepted them, even though both congressmen had been unopposed in the 1974 primary and general elections. Both supported the "Perot Amendment" in committee.

---

* See Baseball Scenario, page xix.

Later, after the exposure of the Perot campaign gifts in *The Wall Street Journal* set off a storm of controversy, the special Perot provision was overwhelmingly defeated on the House floor, by a vote of 379–27. Waggoner and Burleson cast two of the 27 pro-Perot votes.

In any of the above examples, did anyone step over the slender, the narrow line between contribution and bribe?

Perhaps, perhaps not. We don't know for certain. We aren't privy to what was said by giver or receiver.

But, even if we had been, we might not be certain whether the line had been crossed. Recall what former Democratic Congressman Mike Barnes reported hearing frequently with PAC managers during the eight years he served in the House (see Chapter 5): "Mike, we're getting ready to make our next round of checks out . . . We really think we can help you . . . By the way, Mike, have you been following that bill in Ways and Means . . . ? It's got an item we're concerned about . . . and we hope you'll be with us on that one."

Even if a representative on the receiving end of such a call believes there is a bribe embedded in that interchange, there's no way to be sure. Is the would-be recipient (in the case Congressman Barnes) to affront an ally (not to mention a potential large contributor) by accusing them of so grave an act?

Most disturbing of all, not only will the public remain unsure whether the bribery line has been crossed—*the recipient of the contribution may also be unsure.* That is, once the knowledge of a large contributor's interest in the amendment or bill is planted in an officeholder's mind, can even the most honest of lawmakers wholly banish that thought when considering the measure—especially when caught up in a hard-fought and expensive campaign for political survival? If not, can the lawmakers themselves be positive they have not violated the bribery statute by accepting something of value "in return for being influenced in the performance of any official act"?

As the U. S. Court of Appeals said in sending the bribery conviction of Senator Brewster back for retrial:

"No politician who knows the identity and business interests of his campaign contributors is ever completely devoid of knowledge as to the inspiration behind the donation."

In 1986, the House Agriculture Committee considered a proposal by the Reagan Administration to levy a fee on commodity traders to finance the federal agency overseeing that trading. When Agriculture Committee members were showered with campaign contributions from traders opposing the fee, the *New York Times* said, "[It all] sounds very much like legal bribery."

Was the *Times* far wrong?

 *Chapter Nine*

JUNKETS, ETC.

Up until recently, interest groups lined the pockets of politicians. And, believe it or not, it was entirely legal.

The pocket-lining could take place in a variety of ways:

First alternative: Interest Group A would invite Lawmaker B (who happened, not by coincidence, to be a key member of a committee handling legislation of vital interest to Group A) to address A's annual convention. B would prepare a full speech, which he would deliver to A's convention. Group A would pay B up to $2,000 for his or her effort.

Second alternative: Lawmaker B would neither prepare nor deliver any speech at all, but would merely visit or tour one of A's facilities—perhaps a defense plant or a commodity exchange. Clearly, this scenario represented far less effort on B's behalf. Nonetheless, A would still give B a cash payment.

A third alternative: Lawmaker B, en route to his or her Capitol Hill office, would drop by the Washington headquarters of Interest Group A and spend an hour or so with A's lobbying staff, briefing them on the status of legislation of particular interest to Group A. Having done so, B would proceed on to resume his or her day's business schedule. If Group A paid B, say, $2,000 for this one-hour appearance, the result, in effect, would be a fee to B of $2,000 an hour—dwarfing even the most fabled hourly fee earned by a top Wall Street lawyer or the highest paid lobbyist in Washington.

In any one of these three scenarios, no matter how little or great Lawmaker B's effort, Interest Group A paid B a so-called "speaking fee" (even though no speech may have been involved) for as high as $2,000 per event. These fees were typically referred to as honoraria.

These honoraria involved the direct lining of the politicians pockets in that, unlike campaign contributions, which could only go into legislators' campaign treasuries, honoraria could, and typically did, go directly into politicians' bank accounts. Thus, from both the point of view of interest groups and lawmakers, these honoraria tended to be far more attention-getting and efficacious than campaign contributions.

The bottom-line about these honoraria: they represented cash flowing from interest groups directly into the pockets and bank accounts of lawmakers. Critics found this unseemly at best and, at the worst, unethical.

In 1989, in exchange for a substantial pay raise, the House put an end to the practice of honoraria for its own members, beginning in January 1991. In 1991, the Senate sought to follow suit.*

So Congress has cleaned up the honoraria blemish on its ethical escutcheon, right?

Wrong. At least, not quite.

There remains a gaping loophole: interest groups are still free to give, and lawmakers to accept, all-expense-paid trips (often including members of their families) to exotic resorts.

This opens up many of the same evils embodied in the now-outlawed honoraria. Principal among these: an opportunity for in-

---

* At this writing (January 1992) the fate of the Senate action is uncertain. Its effectiveness depends on the final enactment and signing into law of the campaign finance reform bill enacted by both Houses, which President Bush has vowed to veto if it contains either spending limits or public financing of congressional elections. The 1991 reform legislation contains both.

terest groups to ingratiate themselves to legislators in a manner unavailable to, and largely unseen by, the voters.*

Moreover, like honoraria (and, for that matter, campaign contributions), these junkets lend themselves to flagrant conflicts of interest. Example: of the fifty trips paid for by businesses or business trade associations on behalf of Texas Democratic Congressman Charles Stenholm, thirty-seven came from agricultural interests over which he has legislative jurisdiction as a senior member of the House Agriculture Committee.

Like campaign contributions, these interest groups tend to focus their favors on members of legislative committees with jurisdiction over the interest group's particular economic concerns. Agriculture groups "target" the members of the Agriculture Committee; defense contractors members of the defense related committees, and so forth.

In two respects, however, these trips are worse than honoraria. First, there is no limit to the number or value of such junkets.

Second, and more serious (from the public's viewpoint), they offer an opportunity for interest groups' lobbyists to get to know lawmakers on a first-name basis, and to meet with them free of the pressure of legislators' tightly packed Washington schedules. Said Tom Lauria of the Tobacco Institute: "A fifteen minute meeting in a Washington office isn't the same as sitting down over a long lunch [at a] resort. That fifteen minute interval [usually the limit of a Washington, D.C. appointment] isn't hanging over your head. Often at an informal setting like a resort, you can communicate more effectively."

Interest groups make no bones about making these junkets as comfortable and alluring as possible. For example, a spokesperson for the U.S. Telephone Association, which sponsors a number of congressional trips to resort locations, made it clear how eager

---

* Lawmakers are not obliged to report these junkets to the Federal Election Commission; they merely have to disclose them once a year in personal disclosure reports of a widely varying degree of specificity submitted to the Secretary of the Senate and the Clerk of the House. Indeed, they are not required to list the actual *value* of each trip. They must simply list any trip valued at $250 or more.

corporate sponsors are to please lawmakers: "We hold meetings at resorts and let the members play golf, or tennis or anything they want to do . . ." Tobacco Institute spokesperson Tom Lauria, openly acknowledged that if members of Congress "have a choice of meeting in Minnesota and Palm Springs, they'll choose Palm Springs. We make it as comfortable as we can."

In this spirit, frequently recreation, rather than business, is the watchword. For example, meetings sponsored by the Electronic Industries Association at Florida's Captiva Island were limited to the mornings, so that lawmakers would have the rest of the afternoon free to enjoy golf, tennis and swimming. The American Medical Association similarly limited its Phoenix seminar sessions to the morning, reserving the balance of the day for recreation. An AMA spokesperson conceded that the free transport, accommodations and entertainment were the main reasons the lawmakers attended the conference.

Not surprisingly, the peak months for giving and accepting these junkets were during Washington winters. Moreover, two states—California and Florida—were, by far, the most popular destinations for traveling lawmakers. In fact, those two states alone accounted for a quarter of the trips taken during 1989 and 1990.

Lest any reader get the notion that the above examples are exceptional or anecdotal, they are not. In September, 1991, Public Citizen's Congress Watch, an offshoot of an organization started by Ralph Nader some twenty years ago, issued a study ("They Love To Fly . . . And It Shows!") analyzing the privately financed trips taken by House members taken during a two-year period (1989 and 1990). The total came to just under 4,000 (3,984 to be precise). Two-thirds of these were sponsored by corporations, corporate-sponsored trade associations or general business associations. By contrast, labor unions sponsored only two percent of the trips.

Among the top groups sponsoring such junkets in 1989 and 1990 were:

• The Chicago Mercantile Exchange and Chicago Board of Trade (118 trips between them): Legislative interests include a variety of tax issues affecting the futures industry and opposition to stricter regulation by the Securities and Exchange Commission.

- National Cable Television Association (75 trips): 56 of the trips went to members of the Energy and Commerce Committee, which was developing legislation to re-regulate the cable industry.
- The American Medical Association: 49 trips to such locations as Naples and Miami, Florida and Phoenix, Arizona. The Association's seminar sessions held in Phoenix were limited to the morning, with golf, tennis and swimming consuming the rest of the day.

In addition to the ethical difficulties of the privately-sponsored junkets, there is the question of their fairness and their role in the democratic process. As the 1991 Public Citizen report, from which the facts in this chapter were taken, observes, "The practice of allowing Congress to accept free travel and entertainment provides special interests with the unique opportunity to meet privately with powerful lawmakers *in a manner not typically enjoyed by the average constituent.*" (Emphasis added.)

Urging Congress to "act immediately to stop [this] practice," the Public Citizen report concludes, "If a trip is deemed to be in the interest of the general public and, therefore, worth taking, it should be funded by the government."

 *Chapter Ten*

THE MANY WAYS
OF SKIRTING THE
"REFORM" LAWS

In the early 1970s, the Watergate investigation laid bare a host of under-the-table abuses in political giving. Among other things that investigation revealed that—

- The International Telephone & Telegraph Corporation had pledged $400,000 to the Republican National Committee, and had received a favorable antitrust ruling from the Justice Department.
- The milk producers had pledged $2 million to the reelection of President Richard Nixon; and that, soon thereafter, Nixon raised dairy price supports, overriding the initial recommendations of key cabinet members.
- Illegal contributions from Gulf Oil, American Airlines and other corporations, some "laundered" through foreign countries, had found their way, in cash, into the Nixon campaign.

At the same time, super-rich individuals made enormous personal contributions to presidential candidates in both parties.

Herbert Kalmbach, Nixon's later-indicted-and-convicted personal "bag man," scouted the country, picking up, among others, personal pledges totaling $3 million from Chicago insurance magnate W. Clement Stone and John Mulcahy, president of a subsidiary of the Pfizer pharmaceutical firm. Richard Mellon Scaife, heir to the Mellon fortune, pledged $1 million.

On the Democratic side, Stewart Mott, a General Motors heir, contributed $400,000 to the McGovern cause.

Then, largely as a result of those revelations, Congress enacted two reform laws. In 1972 disclosure requirements came into effect—to eliminate, or at least reduce, the secrecy. And in 1974, as noted in Chapter 2, stringent ceilings were imposed on personal contributions. Under the new law, a W. Clement Stone could only give $1,000 per election to any candidate's campaign, with an annual ceiling of $25,000 in gifts to all federal candidates. Under that same reform law, the federal government, rather than the Stones and the Scaifes, would pay for presidential general elections.

With those reform laws in place, most citizens stopped worrying about Watergate, confident that public disclosure of and ceilings on contributions would prevent renewed abuses.

Then, in 1976, the Supreme Court opened gaping (some said limitless) loopholes with its interpretation of the new reform laws. Subsequently, Congress eroded those laws through "technical" amendments that turned out not to be so technical after all, and ingenious politicians and their lawyers sought and found ways to skirt the new restrictions.

Viewing all this in 1984, a decade after Watergate, *Wall Street Journal* reporter Brooks Jackson observed that "the 'new' system of financing congressional and presidential campaigns is starting to bear a startling resemblance to those pre-Watergate days."

Brooks Jackson's view may be overly bleak. After all, the reform statues outlawed huge and secret contributions by companies, labor unions and the very rich. But are such gifts really barred today? The answer is no. They not only take place; but they are entirely legal. These new, over-sized gifts—the standard size for which has become $100,000—fall in the category of something called "soft money," donations to the national and state parties. There is not only no ceiling on such gifts; they were, until recently, free of the usual disclosure requirements placed on ordinary political gifts.

In the 1988 presidential elections, both parties raised "soft money" in gargantuan proportions—typically in units of $100,000.

Reviewing a 1991 list of corporate, union and rich individual givers of "soft money," campaign finance attorney Kenneth A. Gross commented, "It's like reading the papers one hundred years ago." He was referring to the early 1900s, when corporate interests including the Standard Oil trust, railroad barons and J.P. Morgan's bank gave $100,000 donations to Theodore Roosevelt's presidential race—equivalent to $1.5 million in inflation-adjusted dollars. In those days, the money was given in secret, and the exposure of clandestine contributions led to a major investigation. Congress proceeded to ban direct corporate donations to federal candidates in 1907. Later, in 1943, Congress likewise prohibited contributions to federal candidates from union treasuries.

But by the time of the 1988 elections, you would never have known that those respective prohibitions had ever existed. During the 1988 Presidential campaigns, fund raisers for both national parties succeeded in raising prodigious amounts of "soft money" contributions from corporations and unions as well as from the super rich. All told, they raised $45 million in soft money to support the 1988 Presidential campaigns—nearly half as much as the $92 million in public funds that the U.S. Treasury was furnishing those very campaigns. Thus, clearly, soft money had already begun to erode the 1974 law that provided total funding of Presidential general elections. The supposed purpose of that law was to cleanse those post-primary Presidential contests of "interested" money. But what had started out as a purely public element in the political process was now threatened with contamination, if not domination, by gifts from interested "fat cats," corporations and unions in colossal amounts.

New laws required the disclosure of soft money contributions to national parties starting in 1991. Although the first required disclosures (in the first six months of 1991) preceded the 1992 presidential elections by nearly eighteen months, there were already conspicuous gifts from entities with a large and definite stake in governmental policy. For example, the agri-business conglomerate, Archer-Daniels-Midland, whose interest in the federal sugar and gasahol subsidies is recounted on pages 114 and 117, gave $370,000 to the Republicans, and $46,500 to the Democrats. (In addition, ADM's chairman Dwayne Andreas, personally give $100,000 to the Republicans.)

A similar corporate/cum-personal giving pattern was exhibited in a $200,000 gift to the Republican National Committee by Edgar M. Bronfman, chairman of Joseph E. Seagram & Sons, the liquor company. In addition to Bronfman's personal gift, the Seagram Company, which belongs to an industry that is heavily taxed and regulated by the federal government, contributed $30,000 to the Republican National Committee out of its corporate coffers. Immense as the Bronfman gift was, it was far overshadowed by the astounding check for $1 million the Democratic National Committee received in 1987 from Joan Kroc, widow of Ray Kroc who built McDonald's into a mammoth fast food chain.

By now, $100,000 had almost become the standard soft money gift. Republican fund-seekers established a "Team 100" effort, made up of $100,000 donors in 1988. As of September, 1991, Team 100 boasted 275 members!

The labor unions gave massive sums to the Democrats in the first half of 1991: the United Steel Workers donated $117,000 to the Democratic National Committee; the National Education Association donated $112,500, also to the Democrats.

It is instructive to review the differences between the restrictions in current campaign election law governing ordinary contributions versus the absence of such restrictions applicable to soft money. Here is the comparison:

Type of Donor	Regular Statute	Soft Money
Individual giver	$1,000 per election	unlimited
Funds from corporate and union treasuries	prohibited	permitted
Public disclosure of all contributions	required	required for donations to national parties only

It is widely—and incorrectly—believed that "soft money" originated in amendments to the basic campaign law enacted by Congress in 1979. But former *Wall Street Journal* reporter Brooks Jackson disagrees. He observes that it originated in a 1978 Federal Election Commission ruling giving a state party permission to use corporate and union funds (legal under that state's law) in a voter registration drive to benefit both state *and* federal candidates. Jackson observes that the FEC "was interpreting the law in ways that gutted its [the law's] central intent—restraint of big money in federal elections." Thereafter, he notes "little by little through a growing body of lenient enforcement actions, advisory opinions and regulations, it allowed unrestricted, secret donations to be used indirectly in federal campaigns . . ."

It is true that in 1979, Congress amended the law to allow state parties to spend unlimited amounts of money in a presidential campaign for bumper stickers, pins, and other such volunteer materials and for voter drives. But Jackson notes that these amendments only relaxed the *spending* requirements while preserving the prohibitions against donations by corporations, unions and oversized gifts from wealthy individuals.

Whatever its origins, critics of the soft money provision say that the premise that soft money gifts to parties can be insulated from federal contests is a sham. For example, after Minneapolis department store heir Mark Dayton's $100,000 contribution to the Democratic National Committee came to light during the 1984 presidential campaign, Dayton said publicly that the real purpose of his large gift was to help his Minnesota political mentor, Walter Mondale.

Occasionally, the recipients of soft money funds are equally candid. In 1984, for example, the executive director of the Florida GOP deliberately used a *state* charter to form VIVA '84 (a group intended to help reelect President Reagan by mobilizing Hispanic voters), because as a state-chartered group, "we can take a check for $1 million. We can take corporate checks." Likewise, the New Jersey Republican Party's budget of $680,000 that year was unusually high, considering that, as a party leader told a reporter, no state or local candidates were on the ballot, so all the "party-building" funds could be elevated to the Reagan reelection effort.

Another suspicious "party-building" contribution was the intriguing interest in the Illinois State Republican Party displayed in 1980 by two large California farming corporations (the Sayler Land Company and the J. G. Boswell Corporation) and by the Marriott Corporation of Bethesda, Maryland. The explanation: their gifts were part of a multi-million dollar soft-money fund called the Victory Fund '80, dispensed at the direction of Robert Perkins from an office at the Republican National Committee. Perkins told *The New Yorker*'s Elizabeth Drew, "We picked out the states that needed the money, identified money from major contributors, and funneled it into those states."

Even in the absence of such suspect circumstances, there remains the basic truism that money is fungible—that a dollar is a dollar is a dollar, no matter where it comes from. Thus, even when soft money *is* spent purely for non-federal purposes, it frees up money for other uses that *can* affect the outcome in federal contests. As veteran Republican practitioner (and Reagan friend) Lyn Nofziger puts it, "If I give $50,000 in corporate funds in California, [where corporate donations are permitted], that frees the campaign to spend $50,000 for whatever it wants."

Both political parties recognize that their soft-money practices skirt the spirit, if not the letter, of the 1974 campaign finance reform laws and, on occasion, seem to treat those laws with unabashed disdain.

When the Center for Responsive Politics interviewed guests at the 1984 Democratic National Convention in San Francisco, one guest said a party official told him not to worry about the federal limit in the 1974 law—all he needed to "decide was how much he wanted to give and someone would instruct him how to make out the checks."

Republican fundraiser Paul Dietrich told of how the law can be interpreted so as to hide the source of funds for party-financed TV commercials in a closely-contested House election. "It is perfectly legal," said Dietrich, "or within the *letter* of the law." (Emphasis supplied.) "So we have a little dance in which we dance around the law in a way that never breaks the letter but breaks the spirit of the law, but we don't agree with the law anyway."

But it isn't even necessary to do a "little dance around the law" in order to shake off all the legal spending limits. In 1976, the U.S. Supreme Court ruled that the First Amendment grants people or groups the right to spend unlimited amounts for or against a candidate, provided the spending is undertaken *independently*—that is, without coordination or consultation with the candidate.

To illustrate: in the mid–1980s, two Democratic representatives, Fortney H. (Pete) Stark of California and Andrew Jacobs of Indiana, drew the opposition of the American Medical Association by advocating ceilings on Medicare fees to physicians. Jacobs had the temerity to urge his House colleagues to "vote with the canes, not the stethoscopes," and Stark infuriated the AMA leadership by referring to doctors as "greedy troglodytes."

If the AMA had chosen to be bound by the regular election law, the expression of its outrage would have been limited to contributions of $10,000 each to Stark's and Jacobs' opponents—not enough to make a decisive difference in their election outcomes, nor even enough to teach these congressional upstarts a good lesson. But instead, in the 1986 election, the AMA and its political action committee, AMPAC, charged through the loophole the

Supreme Court had opened. AMPAC dumped $252,000 of "independent expenditures" on behalf of Stark's opponent, and $315,000 to defeat Congressman Jacobs—enormous amounts to inject into House campaigns. Both efforts failed miserably; the two congressmen garnered, respectively, 70 percent and 58 percent of the vote. But the AMA seemed undismayed: "I hope it sends a message to everyone in Congress who won by 51 percent," said AMPAC chairman Dr. Thomas Berglund. AMPAC executive director Peter Lauer told a seminar on campaign financing that his PAC was telling Stark and Jacobs, "That is it, you have reached that level [of AMA annoyance] and you damn well better understand that we're coming after you and we're going to make life damned miserable."

More likely to impress (and frighten) other lawmakers and candidates is the decisive impact the AMA's $100,000 of "independent" money is thought to have had in helping Democrat David Skaggs to a surprise 1986 win in Colorado's Second District, in the Denver-Boulder area. Two years earlier, the AMA had supported Skaggs' opponent, but it switched in 1986 because Skaggs favored the AMA position in a state legislature fight to cap malpractice awards against doctors. Skaggs was certainly impressed by his come-from-behind victory: "When you win with 51.5 percent of the vote and the AMA spent . . . $100,000 [to] my $500,000, you can draw your own conclusions," he said. Colorado Republicans were disturbed enough by the AMA's pro-Democratic intervention that they had the state's Republican Senator, William Armstrong, call the AMA to complain.

In 1976, when the Supreme Court struck down the independent-spending ceiling, there was, as yet, no experience to disprove the Court's finding that uncoordinated expenditures do "not presently appear to pose dangers of real or apparent corruption comparable with those identified with large [direct] contributions." Subsequent events have proven the Court's supposition naive. Independent spending enjoyed its first widespread use in 1980, when the National Conservative Political Action Committee (NCPAC) launched a barrage of TV ads against liberal senators in six states, attacking them, long before their opponents had been chosen, as "too liberal" for their respective states. NCPAC's stratagem was monumentally successful. Liberals such as George McGovern in South Dakota, John Culver in Iowa, Frank Church in Idaho, and Birch Bayh in Indiana all fell. Rightly or wrongly, the NCPAC ads were credited with major roles in those contests.

In 1982, the same NCPAC tactic was portrayed as "carpetbagging," and NCPAC had far less influence on the election. But in 1984, the conventional PACs began to adopt the independent-spending device. The National Rifle Association, for example, spent $328,000 helping elect Texas Republican Senator Phil Gramm.

Two years later, the traditional PACs pulled out the stops. AMPAC tripled its independent spending; the Realtors' PAC spent $1,700,000. A new entrant, the Auto Dealers and Drivers for Free Trade, representing the sellers of Japanese automobiles, became a major player. In all, independent outlays in congressional elections rose sharply, from $2.8 million in the 1980 election, to $8.8 million six years later.

Independent spending is open to individuals as well as groups, although only a few have the means to spend on a large scale. One such, however, is Michael Goland, a wealthy California real-estate magnate from Los Angeles and an ardent pro-Israel activist. Beginning in 1981, Goland's ire was aroused by the conduct of Illinois Republican Senator Charles Percy, at the time chairman of the Senate Foreign Relations Committee. In particular, Percy angered Goland by his key role in engineering the sale of AWACS planes to Saudi Arabia. According to Kathy Lydon, Percy's former press secretary, Goland "warned that [Percy] wouldn't know what hit him in the next election" if he failed to alter his position. True to his word, when Percy came up for re-election in 1984, Goland threw $1.1 million of his own money into seeking Percy's defeat. (Goland got his wish. Percy lost to then-Congressman Paul Simon.)

Independent spending poses many dangers for the republic, beginning with the absence of any ceiling or other government regulation. The Supreme Court assumed that the spending would *truly* be uncoordinated with any candidate, a questionable assumption in the practical world of politics. An "independent" spender can easily tap into the close-knit network of political consultants and pollsters and glean an authoritative view of the tactics a candidate and his campaign staff want to follow. At times, the coordination is straightforward and acknowledged, as in the case of Republican James Abdnor, who was persuaded to run against Senator George McGovern in South Dakota in 1980 after talking with NCPAC's then-chairman, the late Terry Dolan and pollster Arthur Finkelstein. NCPAC ultimately spent $178,000 on Abdnor's behalf, and Terry Dolan acknowledged his effort to recruit the candidate. "I know we did it," Dolan said. "We admit it. He admits it. We just led him up to the nomination." But the burden of proving that there was coordination rests with the aggrieved party, and when McGovern's attorney brought a complaint before the Federal Election Commission, the FEC found no collusion, despite Dolan's candid statement.

In 1988, the Auto Dealers and Drivers for Free Trade, representing the Japanese car dealers, openly hired the same political consultant and the same media buyer as the Florida senatorial candidate Congressman Connie Mack that they were trying to help. Again a complaint filed with the FEC fell on deaf ears.

Even in the rare case where the FEC and the courts do find collaboration, as in the New York senatorial race of 1982, where NCPAC spent $75,000 trying to defeat Democrat Daniel Patrick Moynihan, the penalty—imposed long after the votes had been counted—is ridiculously painless. In the Moynihan case, the FEC recommended a $5,000 fine against NCPAC, which the court later increased to $10,000.

As it happens, Senator Moynihan won that race handily. But what if he had *lost* by a handful of votes and there was strong evidence (say, from exit polling) that the ads paid for by NCPAC's illegal spending had tipped the balance? Of what use would that paltry after-the-election fine have been?

Many object to "independent" spending on the ground that it exacerbates the extent to which modern campaigns (especially Senate campaigns) are paid for by "carpetbagging" dollars. Candidate reliance on outside PACs for their campaign money is bad enough. At least conventional PACs are restricted to contributing $5,000 per candidate per election. By contrast, the "independent" money is unlimited, and its carpetbagging nature is illustrated by the plans laid by the Auto Dealers and Drivers for Free Trade to launch a $400,000 TV blitz for Republican Senator Paula Hawkins in the 1986 Florida Senate race, only to discover that the dealers' state chapter had endorsed the Democratic candidate, Governor Bob Graham. The embarrassed Auto Dealers canceled the ad campaign. When Graham won, just to show there had been nothing personal, they gave him a post-election gift of $5,000.

The independent spenders are not only unregulated in the amounts they can spend but unaccountable in what they say. NCPAC's Terry Dolan once said, "A group like ours could lie through its teeth, and the candidate it helps stays clean." Republican strategist Lyn Nofziger has observed that, as an independent spender, he "could go on the attack in a way the [candidate's] campaign might not be comfortable doing." Former Washington Republican Senator Dan Evans, himself the beneficiary of questionably "independent" expenditures in his first Senatorial election, has said, "I think unquestionably . . . that independent expenditures on campaigns are probably the highest sleaze factor in campaigns today."

Senator Evans' view finds support in the 1986 TV ads aired by NCPAC against what it termed the "Ortega 33"—the principal congressional opponents of continued aid to the Nicaraguan Contras. One such ad, targeting Michigan Democratic Congressman Howard Wolpe, portrayed soldiers running through the jungle, while a voice, thick with a Spanish accent said, "One day we're going to take five to ten million Mexicans, and they're going to have one thing on their mind—cross the border into Dallas, El Paso, Houston, New Mexico, San Diego, and each one has embedded in his mind the idea of killing ten Americans." Cut to photo of Congressman Wolpe. Another voice: "Even so, Congressman Wolpe voted against President Reagan and aid to the freedom fighters in Nicaragua. Help President Reagan defeat Congressman Wolpe." The ad failed to defeat Congressman Wolpe.

For whatever reason, independent expenditures declined between 1988 and 1990. This was particularly true regarding the groups that previously had been most active in independent spending. For example, the imported auto dealers cut their independent spending in half and the American Medical Association virtually eliminated the tactic from its political activities, dropping its independent spending from nearly $837,000 in 1988 to a mere $6,700 in 1990. Overall, however, total independent spending dropped only slightly between 1988 and 1990, so it is probably too early to predict future trends in the use of this tool. The crucial thing to remember, however, is that should individual groups choose to go to the lists on a so-called "independent" basis, as NCPAC did on a widespread scale in 1980, the United States Supreme Court has decreed that there is no way of blocking it.

Bundling, n. the custom of unmarried couples occupying the same bed without undressing, practiced chiefly in earlier days, esp. during courtship in some British and American communities.

That's the dictionary definition of "bundling." But to modern American political practitioners and interest groups, bundling has a new and different meaning. To them bundling is a way of getting around the limits in the election laws—especially the $5,000 per-election ceiling on PAC contributions to congressional candidates.

PAC defenders often insist that, with congressional campaign budgets in the hundreds of thousands or millions of dollars, it's ridiculous to imagine that a paltry $5,000 PAC contribution ($10,000 if there's a primary as well) can buy a representative's or a senator's vote.

But what about a gift of $168,000? That would at least get a legislator's attention, and it would probably win a donor a *most* sympathetic hearing.

Such a prodigious, attention-getting gift—more than thirty-three times the usual legal ceiling for a PAC—was achieved by bundling, modern-style, and was presented to Oregon Republican Senator Robert Packwood, chairman of the tax-writing Senate Finance Committee, to assist his 1986 re-election bid. The $168,000 was collected by a group called Alignpac from insurance agents around the country, who made their checks payable to the Packwood campaign. Persuading the insurance agents to pony up was presumably no great chore, because all of them needed the support of Packwood, the ranking Republican on the Senate tax-writing committee, in fending off a Reagan Administration effort to repeal one of the long-standing tax loopholes enjoyed by the insurance industry—the one allowing the gains in the value of life-insurance policies to be untaxed to the policyholder. As one of Alignpac's donors, Denver insurance agent Lyle Blessman, put it, the repeal of that loophole "would dry up the life-insurance product."

Taken separately, the agents' contributions would have had little impact on a campaign like Packwood's, which ended up collecting $6.7 million. The trick was to have the agents send their checks to the PAC, which bundled them together and presented them, periodically, in unforgettable packages to the Packwood campaign. So much for the $5,000 ceiling on PAC contributions.

Evidently, bundled contributions contain significant advantages both for givers and receivers, principally in that they offer significantly greater cosmetic advantages, over and above the giving and receiving of funds from political action committees. Thus, for example, gifts in the form of bundled contributions from company executives enables such lawmakers as Massachusetts Senator John Kerry and Congressman Edward J. Markey to publicly eschew PAC funds, while receiving (and even soliciting) individual large gifts from the executives of companies over which their committees may exert regulatory control.

A dramatic illustration of this is the recent soaring of gifts by executives (as distinct from the PACs) of four major movie studios—Disney, Warner, Paramount and MCA/Universal. According to an enterprising piece of journalism by Sara Fritz and Dwight Morris, of the *Los Angeles Times*, the figures are most striking in the case of Disney, whose executives' giving to congressional candidates rose between 1982 and 1990 from $2,500 to $141,365. (The Disney PAC giving rose from zero to just under $37,000.)

The greatest "star attraction" for movie executives is, without doubt, New Jersey Democratic Senator Bill Bradley, the former basketball star, thanks to his friendship with Disney chief executive officer, Michael D. Eisner. The *Los Angeles Times* reported that among Eisner's fundraising events for Bradley was a $1,000-a-plate dinner he co-hosted in 1989 with Michael Ovitz, head of Creative Artists Agency. The gala netted Senator Bradley about $600,000—the largest haul ever recorded for any Democrat in California, according to Eisner.

As set forth in Chapter 6, the Council for a Livable World, a major national peace organization, has long employed, and staunchly defends, bundling of a slightly different variety. John Isaacs, the Council's highly articulate Washington director, says that since 1962, the Council has been raising substantial amounts of money from its members through the mail. The Council's letters appeal for help for one or two particular congressional candidates that the Council believes need and merit help. Members mail their checks to the Council, which then forwards them to the candidate. The total sent to a candidate usually exceeds the $5,000-per-candidate-per-election limit on PAC contributions.

"If a company gets twenty-five or thirty executives in a room and gets them to give $1,000 each to Candidate X, that exceeds the $5,000 PAC limit, but that's considered perfectly legal," says Isaacs. "And it could be a hundred or a hundred and fifty people, and it would be legal. What's the difference between that and what we do?"

"If you want to illegalize *all* group solicitation, that's all right with us," Isaacs continues. "And if you want to do away with all PACs, that's OK too. But we think it's unfair to single out our method of fundraising and do away with it, and leave the other two methods—the PACs and the groups-of-executives-in-a-room—untouched."

EMILY's List (EMILY being an acronym for "Early Money Is Like Yeast") engages in fundraising and bundling practices almost identical to the Council for a Livable World, and contributes the proceeds to female candidates. Ellen Malcolm, who founded and manages EMILY's List, shares John Isaacs' distaste for the current campaign finance system, but until she is advised that EMILY's bundling practices are illegal, she intends to continue this effective method of fundraising to make up for the discrepancy she finds in the ability of women to raise campaign funds.

* * *

The National Republican Senatorial Committee—the NRSC—used quite another version of "bundling" to skirt the legal ceilings on the aid the NRSC could give to individual Republican senatorial candidates in 1986.

This is the way that particular bundling scheme worked:

In 1986, the NRSC sent out a mail appeal, mentioning, in each letter, four Republican senate candidates who particularly needed help. When donors sent their checks, payable to the NRSC, the Committee exercised its own judgment about how to apportion the funds. But in its reports to the Federal Election Commission, the NRSC attributed donations to particular givers, and thus claimed the gifts were exempt from the committee's own giving ceiling.

Apparently though, the NRSC failed to consult its donors, for an October 22, 1986 article in the *Atlanta Journal* quotes Mr. E. W. Dixon of Tulsa, Oklahoma—who the NRSC listed as giving to the campaign of Georgia Senator Mack Mattingly—as saying "I don't know Mattingly from Adam's old fox." Ms. Katherine Eberhard of Grand Rapids, Michigan, listed as having contributed to Louisiana senatorial candidate Henson Moore, said, "I live in Michigan . . . No way I would have sent money to Louisiana to Senator Moore or whoever he is."

The Wall Street Journal reported in October, 1986, that the excess gifts to GOP Senate candidates by the NRSC had already reached $6.6 million, and that the committee expected the total to reach $13 million by election day. Most of the funds were concentrated in small tightly contested states where TV budgets were small and money exercised great leverage. For example, the the NRSC gave the reelection campaign of South Dakota Senator James Abdnor some $931,554—nine times the legal ceiling for party donations and expenditures in that state. James Santini, the Republican senatorial candidate in Nevada, received $738,504; Ken Kramer in Colorado, $508,910. (The FEC recommended the maximum allowable fine of $4.6 million. But Federal Judge Gerhard Gesell reduced that to only $24,000 on the grounds the NRSC "did not deliberately violate the law.")

Apparently, the Republicans felt they had discovered a potent new idea, because, in the 1990 congressional elections, they formed a supposedly independent group, called the "Inner Circle," to exceed the $17,500 legal limit on party contributions to senatorial candidates. All told, the Inner Circle distributed a total of $11 million in bundled funds to Senate candidates. "This is industrial strength fundraising taken to the next plateau," said William Canfield, a lawyer for the NRSC. Canfield's notion was echoed by University of Virginia Professor Larry Sabato, a campaign finance expert who termed bundling the "hot new idea." "That's where the real influence is," he said, "It's with the gatherers—the people who collect $100,000 at a shot."

If you are a super-rich person and want to be sure to get an important officeholder's attention with a contribution of, say, $100,000, there may be yet another way to go about it, even though a campaign contribution of that size would exceed your legal giving ceiling fifty to a hundred times over. If you are, say, the principal stockholder in a company, and want your sure-to-be-noticed $100,000 gift to be made by your corporation, that, too, can be achieved, even though corporate contributions to federal candidates have been forbidden since 1907.

The way around all those legal obstacles is simple if the officeholder has formed a charitable foundation. In such a case, attention-getting gifts of unlimited size are not only feasible, but entirely legal. Mr. and Mrs. William Keck II of Los Angeles chose precisely that route to make a $100,000 contribution ($50,000 each) to a foundation established by Republican Senator Robert Dole of Kansas. Mr. Keck is President of the Coalinga Corporation, an oil and gas investing company.

The Keck mode of giving offers a significant advantage to the donor. Gifts to such charitable foundations are tax-deductible, which means that the donors shift much of the burden to the shoulders of other taxpayers. As noted earlier, AT&T made contributions totaling $100,000 to the Dole Foundation. Because that gift was tax-deductible, it reduced AT&T's taxes by $46,000, a burden other taxpayers had to pay.

The tax law requires charitable organizations to be strictly nonpolitical. But sometimes, when a foundation has close connections with a political personage, the dividing line gets very thin. Take, for example, the Fund for the American Renaissance, the foundation established by former New York Republican Congressman, and now, Secretary of Housing and Urban Development, Jack Kemp. In March, 1986, *The Wall Street Journal* reported that Kemp's foundation had recently laid out about $20,000 to finance a fact-finding trip to Europe by the congressman and a few aides; that the foundation planned to publish a book by Mr. Kemp about that trip and his foreign policy ideas; and that the foundation's executive director, James Roberts, who formerly headed Congressman Kemp's political action committee, "also is personally producing a Kemp-narrated TV documentary promoting Rep. Kemp's pet domestic projects." Jack Kemp was a prominent candidate for the Republican presidential nomination in 1988.

According to Douglas Turner, writing in the *Buffalo News*, not only did the Kemp foundation and Kemp's personal PAC share an office building; at one point they actually shared office space and telephone expenses. More significantly, the foundation's board of directors once consisted of Kemp and three of his key political advisors, and its staff director had been Kemp's fundraiser. After the *News*'s revelations, the board of directors was rearranged and Kemp became "honorary chairman," eventually resigning even that post in December of 1986.

Unlike Senator Dole, Congressman Kemp was persistent about guarding the secrecy of his foundation's contributor list. He repeatedly refused to give the donor list to reporter Turner and others until, in late summer 1986 he ultimately gave Turner the list. *The Wall Street Journal* reported that some of the contributors included Chase Manhattan Bank, Dow Chemical, W.R. Grace, and Pepsico. Apparently, Representative Kemp did not tell the *Journal* to what financial extent those companies ingratiated themselves with him, although a spokesman said the fund has accepted gifts as large as $50,000. By February, 1987, the Kemp foundation had ceased operating. David Hoope, a former board member, explained that this was due to the Congressman's "total concentration on politics" and a desire to avoid confusing the fund's activities with Kemp's political aspirations.

Kemp and Dole are by no means the only prominent political figures to form charitable foundations. Before his withdrawal from the Democratic presidential race, former Colorado Senator Gary Hart had a foundation which sent a mail appeal to fifty thousand 1984 presidential contributors asking for donations to help Hart "set the agenda for an American renewal." Former Governor Bruce Babbitt of Arizona had both a PAC and a foundation (American Horizons). Among non-presidential aspirants, Senator Edward M. Kennedy has established the Social Awareness Fund, which paid for a widely publicized Kennedy trip to Africa. Senator Bill Bradley of New Jersey formed a Fair Tax Foundation. A 1987 study by the the Center for Responsive Politics, a Washington research group, found, "There has been a significant increase in the 1980s" in the number of public charities "affiliated with federal elected officials or federal aspirants."

But a politician does not have to set up a charitable foundation to steer tax-deductible dollars to political ends. The ever-inventive Democratic Senator Alan Cranston, for example, found a way to persuade donors to stir hundreds of thousands of such dollars into tax-exempt entities devoted to the laudable object of getting people registered and to the polls. *The Wall Street Journal* reported that in 1986, for example, Senator Cranston thanked donors for $4 million of such contributions, including one of $400,000, while promising anonymity to the donors—who included executives with interests before the Senate Banking Committee, of which the Senator was a senior member.

Lest it be thought that the Cranston operation was exclusively Democratic activity, the *Journal* discovered that the Cranston operation was modeled in part on Republican efforts in 1984 to use tax-exempt groups to register evangelical Christians and to get overseas military personnel to vote by absentee ballots.

Internal Revenue Service regulations allow the use of tax-deductible money to sign up voters, so long as canvassers don't ask in advance which party or candidate potential voters favor. But only the politically naive would suppose that partisan politicians would be impartial about the areas and populations they would choose to concentrate their efforts on.

In all, seventy-five donors gave a total of $4.1 million to Cranston-connected voter registration organizations for the 1986 elections, according to memos by organizers. According to *The Wall Street Journal*, Senator Cranston solicited several million more in donations two years later.

Still later, these gifts of tax-deductible funds—most prominently to Senator Cranston—broke into the headlines during the so-called Keating scandals when it was revealed that savings and loan magnate Charles Keating, Jr., had given $850,000 to three voter-registration groups in which Senator Cranston was involved.

To make things worse, in contrast to the strict disclosure rules governing ordinary political donations, Senator Cranston promised—and honored—anonymity to the contributors to his Democratically-tilted get-out-the-vote enterprises.

Clearly, there are loopholes and abuses aplenty, enough to occupy three or four watchdog agencies, not just the one—the Federal Election Commission—established under the post-Watergate reform laws and envisaged by the Watergate investigating committee as a tougher enforcer of the law, to "win the confidence of the public."

But as a *Wall Street Journal* headline put it in a 1987 article, the watchdog has turned into a pussycat. For example, notwithstanding the $25,000 legal ceiling on all federal contributions in any one election by a single individual, the FEC turned a blind eye toward Harold Simmons' contributions of nearly $60,000—more than twice the legal limit—to federal candidates. Another corporate buy-out specialist, Henry Kravis, donated $56,711 directly to candidates and PACs in 1988 and his brother, Raymond, also exceeded the limit by giving $34,500. A *Los Angeles Times* search of FEC records shows no penalties for exceeding the limit on individual contributions in excess of $250 (an FEC spokesman told the *Times* the FEC has "no legal authority to fine anyone.")

In an earlier open and shut case in 1984, Democratic Senator Alan Cranston, then seeking the presidency, admitted to a $45,000 illegal contribution by Beverly Hills commodity trader Mark Weinberg (who would later turn out to be in trouble with federal authorities because of his underworld clients). Weinberg never disputed his guilt but five years later the Commission still hadn't collected a penny in penalties from him.

A major reason the FEC fails to catch big fish like Weinberg, Kravis and Simmons is that it has no field investigators. Instead, such investigators as it has are desk-bound in Washington, and must content themselves to written interrogatories to suspects, each question having to be approved by a majority of an evenly-divided Commission—hardly the ideal prescription for tracking down suspected violators. Perhaps that explains why the only time the Commission has sent a case to the Department of Justice for prosecution was an attempt by Pennsylvania Governor Milton Shapp to extract $300,000 in questionable federal subsidies to his 1976 Presidential campaign. At the time, the FEC *did* have investigators; but its reaction to the Shapp case was to rid itself of its investigators!

While missing the big fish, the Commission is capable of pursuing—and catching—tiny minnows, especially where the infraction affects an incumbent member of Congress. Example: in 1986, the FEC pursued a formal months-long investigation of a late disclosure filing by the Republican opponent of Congressman Claude Pepper, Tom Brodie. In some cases, late filings can be consequential if they hide large amounts of money for too long to inform voters and sway an election; but the sin in this case involved only $1,425 in donations and Representative Pepper, spending $1.4 million (vs. $16,000 by his opponent) had crushed his opponent in the polls, winning 74 percent of the vote. Nonetheless, the FEC ultimately insisted Pepper's opponent pay a $250 fine.

Contrast the Pepper case with the FEC's three year delay in penalizing the illegal arrangements under which Republican Webb Franklin, of Mississippi, was first elected to the House in 1982, with the illegal help of $60,000 in loans from a friendly local bank. Franklin won that election by just two percent of the vote; and the illegal money might have been a good issue for his opponent Robert Clark, when he ran against Franklin again two years later. But the FEC took *three* years to settle the case with a minor fine—by which time Franklin had won by an even closer margin (1.8 percent of the vote).

The Pepper case also stands in stark contrast with a *Wall Street Journal* revelation in 1986 of illegal contributions to the campaign of New York Republican Senator Alfonse D'Amato, concerning contributions to D'Amato in the names of persons who had not, in fact, made them—a patent illegality. So far as is known, the FEC never investigated those.

Other deficiencies and inconsistencies in the performance by the FEC include:

- When random audits of candidates' reports disclosed minor but embarrassing inaccuracies in the reports of some candidates, Congress responded in 1979, by stripping the FEC of *all* its power to conduct random audits, placing Congress, in effect, on an honor system.
- Republican Senator Phil Gramm, of Texas, was able to frustrate an FEC probe of seeming irregularities in his 1984 election campaign (during which he accepted excessive donations totaling nearly $691,000). The FEC's failure to act resulted in part from Gramm's delaying tactics, but also in part from the FEC's inability to afford the expense of sending auditors to Texas to review Gramm headquarters' records. Ironically, the FEC's fiscal restraints were due principally to the Gramm-Rudman-Hollings deficit-reduction legislation, in which Gramm, himself was a major sponsor.
- These budget cuts have crippled the FEC's enforcement capabilities: between 1979 and 1982, the audit staff shrank from thirty-five to sixteen while the number of PACs and overall election spending both roughly doubled.

But all these are, essentially, details compared with the inherent structural deficiencies of the Commission and the fact that the FEC is, essentially, dominated by the politicians it is *supposed* to regulate—the classic case of the fox guarding the chicken coops. Among the structural weaknesses:

- The Commission has an even number of members (six). Even more serious, it is, by law, evenly divided between Republicans and Democrats.
- No significant action can proceed without the affirmative action of *four* members—a perfect prescription for *in*action, since an even partisan split can block the probe of a complaint—even one favored by the Commission staff.* The only other government agency with an even split of that sort is the International Trade Commission, but there, three votes produce, rather than block action.
- The chairmanship of the FEC is uniquely weak, compared with other government agencies: The FEC's chairmanship rotates annually and is largely ceremonial.
- The FEC is to a large extent unprotected from budget cuts made by the very people it is supposed to regulate. (This stands in contrast to a comparable regulatory commission in California, the California Fair Political Practices Commission, whose budget is guaranteed automatic cost of living increases.)
- There has a been a tendency to fill the Commission and its key regulatory positions with people sympathetic to the practices and proclivities of elected officials, rather than to man those positions with persons disposed to strict regulation. More significant, however, is the pattern of appointees to Commissionerships. Example: in 1977, President Jimmy Carter wanted to appoint Susan King, who not only had a deep background in campaign finance matters, but had the backing of

---

* For example, Congressman Pete Stark brought a complaint about the American Medical Association's $258,000 "independent expenditure" against him. The FEC staff felt a probe was justified. But all three Republican Commissioners opposed it, and the probe ended there, since four votes are required to pursue any investigation. Stark was especially angry at the negative vote cast by Commissioner Lee Ann Elliott, who for eighteen years worked for the AMA and continued to draw an $18,831 pension, and hence appeared to be burdened with a patent conflict of interest.

Common Cause and the United Auto Workers. But Carter was forced to back down when House Speaker O'Neill objected, reportedly calling her a "do-good Common Cause type." Instead, Carter appointed an O'Neill protégé, John McGarry, who, in the eyes of the Commissioner he was replacing, Neil Staebler, was O'Neill's effort to "keep a thumb on the FEC." Another more flagrant example: President Reagan's reappointment of Lee Ann Elliott, despite her open connections with the American Medical Association PAC. By contrast, the Administration refused to reappoint two enforcement-minded commissioners, Democrat Thomas Harris and Republican Frank Reiche.

• Moreover, the Clerk of the House and the Secretary of the Senate sit, as non-voting ex-officio members of the Commission and, as such, are privy to the Commission's most sensitive discussions which they are free to report back to their Capitol Hill employers.

At one juncture, the GOP members thwarted an effort to probe a suspected spending violation by the National Republican Congressional Committee. But this time the Commission was slapped down by a Federal judge who ruled the FEC had acted "contrary to law." The FEC, rather than acquiesce, appealed the case.

The Commissioners also refused, then were sluggish, in permitting a rewriting of the loophole-ridden rules on soft money, as recommended by the FEC staff. Ultimately, however, the FEC required disclosure of soft money contributions to national parties starting in 1991. In addition, *The Wall Street Journal* reported, without investigators, the FEC "seldom uses its subpoena power and only rarely takes sworn testimony from witnesses."

All this encourages lawyers and politicians to be scofflaws with campaign funds. As already noted, the penalties for being caught are painless. Campaign finance expert Herbert Alexander told the *Journal*, "The price of operatives doing what they want to do is to pay a fine. They just consider it part of campaigning. If they catch up with you, you pay a couple of thousand dollars and you go scot-free."

Journal reporter Jackson also comments that the FEC "seems more intent on pinching off disclosure of campaign money abuses than investigating them." For example, an investigative-journalism project founded by the author of this book helped finance a newspaper's investigation of Idaho Republican Congressman George Hansen's financial activities. When Hansen complained to the FEC, the FEC responded by trying to subpoena *all* the story proposals submitted to the project. The FEC is also vigorously seeking to prosecute two organizations seeking to disseminate data drawn from FEC candidate reports.

Ronald Brownstein of the *National Journal* summed up the multiple ways of circumventing the post-Watergate reform law with this observation:

> Campaign finance reforms tend to succumb to the same immutable law that keeps the Neiman-Marcus catalogue [with its chocolate Monopoly boards] flourishing: People with money always find new ways to spend it.

To which *The Wall Street Journal*'s Brooks Jackson adds:

> Post-Watergate reforms are so eroded that secret contributions from corporations and labor unions are once again flowing, and the era of $1 million fat-cat contributions has returned.

Jackson, in a 1990 report for the Twentieth Century Fund on the failure of the FEC, observes (with perhaps excessive sanguinity) that "Congress now seems more likely to act on campaign finance legislation than at any time in the past decade. But," he asks, "who would enforce such new limits?" Jackson adds that "without proper enforcement, any new reforms will be nothing but a sham, and the faith of citizens in their system of representative democracy will continue to be eroded."

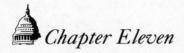 *Chapter Eleven*

HOW DO WE GET OUT OF THE MESS WE'RE IN?

Free and untrammeled representation of the public is possible only when men and women in high office are not indebted to special interests for financial donations.

—FROM THE FIRST BILL PROPOSING
PUBLIC FINANCING OF ELECTIONS, 1956

WHAT ARE THE necessary ingredients for reforming the present campaign finance system?

Sensible physicians, before prescribing, lay out and consider all the elements of the ailment. When it comes to America's current system of paying for congressional campaigns, what are those elements?

As presented in this book, the existing method of financing congressional campaigns has afflicted the American political system in the following respects:

- It has undermined representative democracy by placing money-power over people-power and by thwarting the one-person-one-vote principle.
- It has instilled in politicians an over-weening preoccupation

220

with money, which has often overridden considerations of what is good for the country.

- It has given incumbents an overwhelming financial edge over challengers, thereby destroying competition in congressional elections and creating, in effect, a "permanent Congress."
- It has, by and large, limited congressional candidacy to the rich, or to those who can raise money from the rich, thereby barring from candidacy the "average" citizen.
- It has paved the way for the wholesale corruption of Congress by constantly creating potential—or, more often, real conflicts of interest.
- It has encouraged politicians to derive substantial portions of campaign funds from sources outside their states or districts—that is, from people or entities who are not even allowed to vote for them on election day—thereby lessening their accountability to their own *voting* constituents.
- It has led to an "arms race" in campaign spending, which in itself has contributed to the escalation of campaign expenditures, to politicians' never-ending, often desperate preoccupation with fundraising, and to the overwhelming financial advantage of incumbents over challengers.
- It has tended to deprive voters of true choices as both major political parties and their nominees for federal office receive their funds from essentially the same sources.
- It has diminished the voters' confidence that government serves *their* interest rather than those of special monied interests. Thus it may have contributed to the decline in voter participation in congressional elections.
- It has created the temptation for actual, or borderline, bribery on the part of both givers and receivers of campaign contributions and other favors.
- It has created an artificial new kind of "constituency" (financial and economic) that has wholly or partially supplanted the local *voter* constituencies envisioned by the Framers of the Constitution.
- It has opened the way for lawmakers to extort campaign contributions from lobbyists and others seeking their favors.

- It has paved the way for tiny special-interest groups to impose huge costs on the majority of the population in the form of subsidies of uncertain, and uncontrollable, size.
- It has created an artificial definition of "serious" candidates— limited to those with access to *money* regardless of their backgrounds, qualifications or, most important, how seriously they address the issues.

Only fundamental and sweeping reform will solve that broad array of problems.

In my view, nothing short of a total elimination of *all* private money from congressional campaigns and a substitution of total government funding (I prefer to call it "citizen funding") of those elections will suffice. Under such a plan, in contests for the U.S. House and Senate, contributions from individual citizens as well as PACs would be prohibited.*

That proposal, which for brevity's sake, I will call the "100 percent solution," may sound radical. In fact, it is not. It is now the law of the land for presidential *general* elections, and has been since 1974.† I am merely suggesting broadening that existing law to cover congressional elections.

As a test of this "100 percent solution," I entreat readers to apply it to each of the problems set forth above. Would it solve each problem?

More important, would any *lesser* solution solve each?

The "100 percent solution" embodies two over-arching goals. The first is to lessen the role and influence of "interested" money, given by people and groups who hope to benefit financially from their contributions. America needs a system whereby campaigns are paid for as much as possible by "*dis*interested money."

---

* Except those pre-primary contributions that may be required, under any new law, to make a candidate eligible for citizen funding of his or her campaign, as discussed more fully below.

† I refer here to the original 1974 law, before it became corrupted by the soft-money loophole, described in Chapter 10.

In a democracy, the quintessence of disinterested money is money that comes from *all* citizens equally, through their government. When campaign funds thus come from all the citizens, candidates and officeholders cannot identify the money as coming from any particular person or group.

The second principle—a corollary of the first—is the need to liberate House and Senate candidates from their obligations to special-interest contributors by enabling them to pay for their campaigns with funds for which they feel no special obligation.

Total citizen funding of federal elections is both court-tested (it has been specifically approved by the U.S. Supreme Court for presidential elections) and time-tested.* It has worked on the presidential level. Since Congress enacted that plan, no presidential contest has been marred by the illegal corporate contributions and the "laundering" of money that characterized the 1972 election of Richard Nixon. Thus, the plan offers comfort to those concerned that an untested campaign finance reform might have unintended consequences (as did the 1974 "reform" law which gave rise to the PACs).

The "100 percent solution" has many advantages. It is simple. It draws a clear distinction between what is legal (citizens' funding) and what is not legal (private contributions, whether by individual citizens or by political action committees). Mind you, I am not naive enough to suppose that this will prevent ingenious (and well-paid) legal minds from making crevasses out of cracks in the law. The stakes in influencing governmental policy are simply too high for that. But the very simplicity and clarity of the "100 percent solution" will, I argue, minimize the flow of special interest money into the congressional system.

If it succeeded in doing that, it would, in a single action, come close to solving each one of the problems set forth at the outset of this chapter.

On the other hand, proposals for *partial* citizen funding would leave each of those problems largely *un*solved, and would, more-

---

* Once again, I refer to the original 1974 public-financing plan, prior to the advent of the gaping "soft-money" loophole.

over, give lawyers countless opportunities to find ways of wiggling through the system.

America provides far less in the way of systematic government help in election campaigns than comparable democracies. Such governmental aid as we give to candidates was, until the 1970s, piecemeal, and we still only subsidize a tiny portion of our electoral system.

A key issue in any "100 percent solution"—probably *the* key issue—is how candidates would become eligible for citizen financing.

There are, of course, an infinite number of answers to this question, depending on how difficult or easy one wishes to make the eligibility requirements. This involves walking a tight wire between, on the one hand, earning public confidence that the keys to the Treasury would be accorded only to non-frivolous candidates who enjoy a respectable degree of public support, and, on the other hand, that candidacy would not be unduly restricted.

As one suggestion, I propose that in order to become eligible for citizen financing in a primary election, a candidate would have to raise X number of contributions of less than Y dollars each from residents of the candidate's district or state. For example, a candidate who wanted to enter a primary race for the House of Representatives might be required to raise, say, a thousand contributions of not more than $25 each from persons eligible to vote in that district.

Those requirements could, of course, be adjusted up or down, but I personally feel strongly about two principles.

First, that the ceiling on qualifying gifts be kept as low as possible—preferably a maximum of twenty-five dollars (certainly no more than fifty dollars), for two reasons: it should be an amount that anyone can afford to contribute; and second, that a single contributor cannot buy undue influence.

Second, I also feel very strongly that qualifying gifts *must* come from persons entitled to vote for the candidate on election day (i.e., residents of the given state or congressional district) in order to maintain candidates' accountability to their voting constituencies and to minimize the "carpetbagging" that has been reintroduced into American politics.

Some may find it anomalous to predicate a supposedly "all-public-money" funding plan on the initial raising of funds from private citizens and may question the appropriateness of labeling my plan a "100 percent solution," rather than, say, a "99 percent solution."

My own view is that, provided the two principles I have enunciated are adhered to, the difference between a "99 percent" and a "100 percent" plan is inconsequential.

Primary candidates who meet this eligibility requirement would each be entitled to a uniform amount of citizen funding, provided they meet the following conditions: to forswear raising and receiving *any* private funds (including their own) in excess of the citizens' grant (this in order to assure the principle of maintaining a financially level playing field in the contest*); and to participate in a given number of public debates.

As a further means of assuring "level playing fields" so that no candidate need fear being grossly out-spent by, say, a multi-millionaire, I propose that every dollar raised by privately funded candidates over and above the amount to be granted to citizen-funded candidates trigger an additional dollar of citizen funding to the latter. For example, if, by "opting in" to the citizen financing system, Candidate A becomes entitled to, say, $500,000 and if A's opponent, Candidate B, elects to "opt out" of the citizen financing system, if B raises and spends, say, $600,000, that would entitle A to receive an additional $100,000.

Maintaining a level financial playing field is a far more democratic way of achieving the result sought by arbitrary term limits which

---

* I emphasize *"financially* level playing field" in full recognition of the limitations of that term. For example, I don't pretend that it can eliminate the many non-financial advantages enjoyed by incumbents, such as free media time, taxpayer-supported staff, constituent services, etc. But at least the granting of equal public dollars to all candidates smoothes out the inequalities insofar as the *financing* of campaigns is capable of doing so.

deprive the voters of the ability to reelect a lawmaker of which they approve.

It would be essential to craft any "100 percent solution" plan in such a way as not to freeze out minor or new parties and to provide citizen funding in such a way as to be generous to both. I will not, here, present any formula for doing so; I merely bring up the point in order to register my strong view that it is important, if not essential, to provide citizen funding in such a way as to encourage the formation and preservation of new and/or minor parties.

Most recent reform proposals provide for *partial* citizen financing—that is, they would provide that a certain percent of a candidate's expenditures come from citizen funds, but they fail to go as far as the "100 percent solution."

Presumably, these partial citizen funding proposals are predicated on the premise that some citizen funding is better than the existing system. I disagree. To me, any partial citizen funding plan that requires candidates to raise a significant portion of their campaign funds from private sources leaves untouched (or only marginally improves) all of the major deficiencies in the existing system, as set forth at the outset of this chapter. In particular, partial citizen funding proposals fall short in that they:

- fail to set ceilings on campaign expenditures, and thus do not address the problem of candidates' appetites for more and more money;
- fail to liberate candidates from their dependence on special-interest campaign contributions;
- fail to diminish the pervasive corruption of Congress via conflicts of interest;
- fail to significantly arrest the "arms race" that now accounts for spiraling campaign expenditures and costs; and
- fail to open up candidacy to *all* citizens, regardless of their own wealth or their access to wealthy contributors.

* * *

Few industries are more profitable than broadcasting. Before the current recession, which has hit the television industry with special force, many TV stations in the larger markets used to garner returns on equity ranging from twenty-five to fifty-seven percent, compared with ten to twelve percent on manufacturing industries. That translated into sale prices for broadcast stations in the hundreds of millions. Before the recession, a network-affiliated TV station in Boston sold for $450 million and an *independent* station in Los Angeles went for over $500 million. The physical assets of those stations were worth about $50 million at most. The rest represented the value of the piece of paper issued, at virtually no charge, by the people of the United States: namely, a federal license to use the *public's* airwaves. Bluntly put, a VHF-TV license in the top fifty markets represents a license to print money.

Meanwhile, television has become *the* indispensable medium for selling politicians, and TV has become—especially for political candidates—a seller's market. So, although Congress has passed a law that supposedly requires stations to sell time to political candidates at a discount, in practice it frequently works out the opposite way. That's because the crucial period for reaching voters is of limited duration (the last two or three weeks of the campaign being choicest), and during that period, candidates often find themselves paying premium rates to bump commercial advertisers from the best evening spot announcement times. While corrective legislation has been introduced in Congress, at this writing (January, 1992) it has not been finally enacted. So for the moment, at least, the result is that political candidates must obligate themselves to special-interest contributors in large part to add to local broadcasters' already stupendous profits. The broadcasters, of course, apoplectically oppose any laws to compel them to donate even the smallest particle of their broadcast time to political candidates. The whole spectacle is obscene.

Granted, there are myriad complexities to any proposal to provide political candidates with free or reduced-rate broadcast time. But that is not a reason for total inaction—that is, for leaving the obscenity wholly untouched.

As a first-cut suggestion:

Citizen-financed candidates desiring to buy political broadcast time would be permitted to purchase it—on radio as well as TV and commercial cable systems—at a fraction (say, one-half) of the lowest rate charged by a given station at *any time during its broadcast day.**

Under this plan, stations would be required to sell time to citizen-financed House and Senate candidates on a first-come, first-served basis, up to a given percent of that station's available for-sale time.

To be eligible for this plan, candidates must:

- have opted into the citizen-financing plan;
- appear in person for at least X percent (say, for example, half) of each program purchased under this plan. That would assure candidate responsibility for a program's contents without regulating those contents;
- buy time in units of no less than X minutes (say, one minute or, preferably, two or five minutes) in length;† and
- agree to participate in a minimum number of public debates‡ against their opponents.

This requirement to sell reduced-rate time would be separate and apart from requirements on broadcast stations and networks to grant *free* time for candidate debates.

Would this plan impose an undue burden on broadcasters? Clearly not. In all probability, candidates would only avail them-

---

* Presumably, that cheapest rate would be for preemptible time—that is, for time that could be bought at a premium rate by another sponsor—but under this plan, as soon as a citizen-financed congressional candidate buys the time, the time would become non-preemptible.

† Eliminating the 30-second spot should elevate the level of political discourse by decreasing the manipulative quality of existing political TV commercials. Increasing the minimum required length to two or five minutes would encourage *substantive* discussion of the issues, especially if coupled with a requirement that the candidate appear in person on a given proportion of each broadcast.

‡ I don't want to oversimplify the problem of mandating public debates, for such debates present numerous complications and questions. For example, what should be the rules governing those debates? And how does one obtain agreement among the candidates as to those rules?

selves of it for a maximum of four weeks prior to the primary election and four weeks prior to the general election—a total of two months out of each twenty-four month period—roughly eight percent of the total two years of each election cycle. That would leave broadcasters with use of the other ninety-two percent of their for-sale time. That hardly seems an excessive price to ask them to pay for their highly profitable—and free—use of the *public's* airwaves that belong to all citizens.

Several other problems remain to be addressed.

• *"Soft money":* Clearly, the most important is "soft money." The clearest and simplest solution is: outlaw it. Soft money serves little or no beneficial public purpose and simply restores—and legalizes—"fat cat" contributions. Worse still, "soft money" legalizes direct contributions from corporate and labor union treasuries, which have been outlawed for decades.

• *Independent expenditures:* Expenditures by outside parties that are uncoordinated with a candidate's campaign were found constitutional by the Supreme Court in 1976, so presumably they cannot be done away with entirely. Two alternative solutions appeal to me. The first is "fresh air": requiring all ads financed by so-called independent expenditures to be prominently—and continuously—identified in the course of any TV commercial paid for by an independent financer.

The second alternative would be to allow any citizen-financed "target" of an independent expenditure to receive added citizen funding, dollar for dollar, for the amount provided by the independent spender. Thus, for example, if an independent financer elected to inject $50,000 against citizen-financed candidate A, that would make A eligible for an added $50,000 of citizen-financing. Such a plan would, presumably, create a disencentive for the independent spender to throw dollars against the campaigns of citizen-financed candidates.

• *"Bundling":* One of the prime advantages of the "100 percent solution" is that it solves, in one fell swoop, a myriad of problems with the existing system of financing congressional elections. One of those is the problem of "bundling." The "100 percent solution" would eliminate this problem in that it would prohibit *all* private contributions in congressional elections. That is, if private contributions are prohibited, it follows that they cannot be "bundled."

Many Americans will doubtless find it anathema to think of their tax dollars being used to support the campaign of a candidate they find highly distasteful (e.g., former Klansman David Duke, right-wing candidate Lyndon LaRouche or, say, a candidate of the Communist Party).

While those feelings are entirely understandable, they are subject to a number of rebuttals. First, direct government funding of presidential elections is already the law of the land (respecting presidential general elections), and so we have already crossed the David Duke bridge. Moreover, candidates—especially incumbent lawmakers—presently use public funds in indirect ways (the use of free mailing privileges and of their government-paid staffs) to promote themselves among the voting public. If David Duke, or someone like him, were a member of Congress, there would be nothing to prevent him from taking advantage of those same taxpayer-funded "perks."

But the fundamental counter-argument is that *someone* has to pay for election campaigns. So the question is: Who pays for those campaigns: special-interest groups (such as General Motors, the United Auto Workers and the American Medical Association) or all the citizens, through their government (as in most other industrial democracies)?

To me, that question may be usefully thought of in the following manner: would any reader accept the notion of, say, official voter registration, or the supervision and counting of voting on election day being *privately* financed, say, by General Motors, or the UAW, or the AMA? And if not, why not? Presumably because no one wants those processes to be skewed in favor of one interest group or another. Likewise, no one, I think, wants politics to be skewed in favor of one or other interest group.

Thought of in this light, the purpose of spending public funds for voter registration, or election-day supervision—or political campaigns is *not* to help any particular candidate, but to assure a fair and unbiased election result.

It comes down to a simple proposition. Citizen funding of election campaigns is part of the price of being a democracy.*

What would be the price tag for a "100 percent solution" for all federal elections (presidential as well as congressional; primary and well as general elections)? Can we afford it?

Bear in mind, at the outset, that we are only talking about the cost of such a plan from the public treasury. Just as there is "no such thing as a free lunch," there is no such thing as a cost-free election. That was the central point of Chapter 7, which set forth multi-billion-dollar subsidies and other costs arguably growing out of the present system of financing congressional campaigns.

Nonetheless, there is no dodging the fact that any "100 percent solution" citizen funding plan will entail taking tax dollars from the public treasury. It is, of course, difficult to estimate or predict that figure with precision. Particularly crucial is the *amount* of funding to be granted in each presidential, Senate and House contest. Even then, the total cost hinges on the number of candidates who will qualify for citizen funding.

One calculation—the most carefully worked out I have seen, prepared by Randy Kehler who heads the Working Group on Electoral Democracy, a non-profit campaign reform organization—puts the yearly cost of a "100 percent solution" plan for primary and general elections for president, the senate and the house (plus $25

---

* For this reason, I strongly favor paying for congressional and presidential elections directly out of the U.S. Treasury, rather than through some device, such as the present elective taxpayer earmarking procedure, whereby each taxpayer decides, by checking a "yes" or "no" box on his or her tax return whether to earmark a dollar of his/her taxes for a special presidential campaign fund.

million for annual operating and convention costs to the national parties) at slightly over $400 million.*

Even if the annual cost of a "100 percent solution" were *twice* the $400 million estimated above, that would still be substantially less than the $1 billion annual cost to taxpayers of the dairy subsidy— arguably just one consequence of the present system of financing congressional campaigns.

Is $400 million—or even $800 million—too high a price to pay for the assurance that elections will not be unduly controlled by any particular special interest? Or for the assurance that our public officials will make their decisions based on the proposal's merits rather than on campaign contributions and obligations? Or to pay for a Congress free of the temptations of conflicts of interest? Or to assure the rights of *all* citizens to run for office, even though they are not themselves wealthy or do not have access to the wealth of the rich?

Consider all these questions in light of America's current willingness to spend nearly $200 million a year on military bands!

As I write, I can almost hear the voices of skeptical readers (and reviewers) reading my suggestion for a "100 percent solution," smiling, figuratively patting me on the head and saying, "All very-well-meaning and idealistic; but where has this fellow Stern been? Does he really live in the United States in the 1990s? There's not a prayer of such a program being enacted."

Don't worry. I *have* been living in America. I am all too painfully aware of the difficulty of getting Congress to agree on far more modest political reforms. The Republicans differ with the Demo-

---

* This is based on giving House candidates $200,000 ($50,000 for the primary and $150,000 for the general elections) and Senate candidates an amount roughly based on the voting age population of their respective states. While these amounts may *seem* insufficient at first glance, that appearance stems mainly from thinking in terms of *current* campaign costs. But under the plan proposed here, candidates would no longer have to lay out substantial funds for broadcast expenses (which currently eat up the lion's share of campaign outlays, and which would, henceforth, be either free or heavily subsidized). Nor would candidates incur the heavy expenses now devoted merely to raising funds—through direct-mail and other means.

crats; and the political "haves" clash with the "have-nots," because their oxen are differently gored by any given reform. The difficulties are compounded by the fact that even people of *identical* philosophies often disagree on what is the "best" solution.

However, I put forward the "100 percent solution" deliberately, without regard for the momentary conventional wisdom as to what is politically enactable. I do so for two reasons. First and foremost, I consider my plan indispensable—the minimum required—to solve many political problems. No self-respecting physician would dream of prescribing half-way measures knowing—or believing—that they would not cure the patient.

Second, who can say what will "never" be passed? What is "politically enactable" is subject to change from year to year. After all, Congress *did* manage to overcome all the obstacles and agree on a reform law in 1974. Citizen financing of congressional elections, which most regard as an impossible dream, *did* pass the Senate twice in the early seventies and nearly passed the House.

Moreover, present and former lawmakers of the most conservative stripe—people who would ordinarily be considered die-hard foes of any forms of government financing of elections have changed their minds. A conspicuous example is former Nevada Senator Paul Laxalt, the former chairman of Ronald Reagan's presidential campaigns. As recently as January, 1991, he said, "There's far too much emphasis on money and far too much time spent collecting it. It's the most corrupting thing I see on the congressional scene."

"The problem is so bad," he continued, "*we ought to start thinking about federal financing*" of House and Senate campaigns. (Emphasis added.) "It was an anathema to me, but in my experience with the [Reagan] presidential campaign, it worked, and it was like a breath of fresh air . . . A lot of us who retired [from Congress] did so because we just didn't have the stomach to go out and hustle for money the way you have to do now."

When a senator as conservative as Laxalt backs citizen financing, who can say what is impossible?

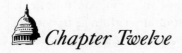 *Chapter Twelve*

CONCLUSION

I END THIS book as I began it: with statements by two veteran politicians about the campaign finance crisis facing this country:

> It is not "we, the people" but political action committees and moneyed interests who are setting the nation's political agenda and are influencing the position of candidates on the important issues of the day.

> The flood of money now polluting our campaign system is like drug to the addicts. The longer we go without admitting we have the problem of addiction, the more ingrained the addiction becomes and the harder it will be to ever break the habit.

The first statement is by a conservative Republican, former Arizona Senator Barry Goldwater; the second is by a moderate Democrat, Oklahoma Senator David Boren. Clearly there is bipartisan agreement that an emergency is upon us.

From the point of view of the recipients of campaign contributions—the United States Congress—that emergency may be summarized in two facts:

Fact No. 1: With the average cost of a winning 1990 Senate campaign at $3,870,621, U.S. senators must, on average, raise about $12,405 every week, *week in and week out, during their entire six-year terms.*

234

Fact No. 2: Based on the average cost of a winning campaign for the U. S. House of Representatives in 1990 ($407,556), in order to be assured victory, representatives must, on average, raise about $17,000 *a month*, every month, during their entire two-year terms.

Those two facts mean that campaign fund-raising is an ever-present preoccupation with nearly every member of Congress.

But those facts portray only half the campaign finance crisis, half of the equation: the viewpoint of the *sellers* of influence (potential and actual), the members of the U.S. Congress.

From the viewpoint of the American public, however, the other side of the equation is the more troubling one, the one that threatens to disenfranchise ordinary unmonied citizens: the seemingly infinite willingness and capacity of the *buyers* of influence— the special-interest groups, their political action committees, and affiliated wealthy individual contributors to muster whatever money senators and representatives need.

The influence-buyers' money-raising capacity is no speculative matter. Here are the amounts actually raised by the leading PACs (i.e., those that raised over $100,000) in each major category, in the first six months of 1989, compared with the comparable period six years earlier:

FUNDS RAISED IN THE 1ST 6 MONTHS OF —

	1983	1989	Percent Increase
By leading *corporate* PACs	$1,709,743	$ 8,406,791	491%
By leading *labor* PACs	$6,612,946	$16,358,546	247%
By leading *trade ass'n* PACs	$3,046,586	$ 7,492,578	246%
By leading *professional* PACs	$3,410,098	$ 6,476,174	190%

In his recent book on the Reagan years, *Sleepwalking Through History*, Haynes Johnson observes:

Midland, Texas, entrepreneurs in the nation's oil production capital, gathered in the Holiday Inn to celebrate Reagan's inaugural. On a buffet table . . . they placed a cutout of the Capitol dome in Washington. On it was one word: *"Ours."* (Emphasis added.)

What kind of political system could lead any single group in the population to think of the United States Capitol as "theirs?"

It is the same system that led the Kettering Foundation, in its 1991 report, *Citizens and Politics*, to reach the following conclusions:

> . . . Many Americans do not believe that they are living in a democracy now. They don't believe 'we the people' actually rule . . . [they] describe the political system as impervious to public direction, a system run by a a professional political class and *controlled by money*, not votes. (Emphasis mine.)
>
> The people talk as though our political system had been taken over by alien beings . . . They feel as though they have been locked out of their own homes, and they react the way people do when they have been evicted from their own property.
>
> Citizens now believe that individual Americans simply do not count in politics . . . Their ability to affect politics is overshadowed—rather, overwhelmed—by a 'political system,' a leviathan made up of media that seems to promote controversy over substance, expensive and negative campaigns, etc. . . . The American peoples' concerns about political campaigns are no secret: too much money and mud-slinging, too few good people involved.

The Kettering Foundation report concludes that, "Americans have [not] 'turned their backs' on politics, they do not want to participate . . . Americans are abstaining from politics . . . until they believe they can make a difference."

Apparently, the political system still works for those who provide the vast bulk of the campaign cash: the top one percent of income earners. They have seen their median after-tax income skyrocket between 1977 and 1990 (from $190,000 to just under $300,000).

* * *

Unhappily, those statements in the Kettering Report are more than mere assertions. They are backed up by survey research data, emanating from the Michigan Institute for Social Research at the University of Michigan.

After the 1988 election sixty-three percent of voters questioned by the Institute agreed with the following statement: "The government is pretty much run by a few big interests looking out for themselves." Only thirty-one percent thought government "is run for the benefit of all the people." A considerable number weren't sure.

This represented a deterioration of the public's confidence. Four years earlier, fifty-five percent had thought big interests were running government, and thirty-nine percent thought it was run for all.

During the course of the Senate Ethics Committee's consideration of the conduct of the so-called "Keating Five," South Carolina Democratic Senator Ernest F. Hollings submitted an affidavit on behalf of his colleague, Dennis DeConcini of Arizona. In the course of the affidavit, he touched on the other four senators as well. "Knowing [them], I know none of them are corrupt," he said. *"What is corrupt is the system,"* he continued. (Emphasis added.) "There is too darn much money required to seek and hold office."

In mid–1987, when the U. S. Senate debated a measure to provide citizen financing of Senate general elections, senator after senator—especially the freshly-elected ones—rose to express dismay at the enormous proportion of their time they had been obliged to spend, as candidates, appealing for money. Democratic Senator Harry Reid of Nevada, who had scoffed when a friend had predicted he would spend 70 to 80 percent of his time raising money, had found the prediction to be true. His fellow Democrat, Senator Brock Adams of Washington said, "I do not think a candidate for the U.S. Senate should have to sit in a motel room in Goldendale,

Washington at six in the morning and spend three hours on the phone talking to political action committees [on the east coast] . . . to the folks who make a living figuring out the odds on each race and betting the percentages. I wish I had been able to win by debating the issues with my opponent rather than debating my political prospects with political banks."

Members of Congress from both parties, when they speak privately, claim that most of their colleagues are disgusted with the system. But few of them will say so publicly. Nor has a majority of them been willing to vote for sweeping reforms.

In the Antwerp zoo, the birds are confined within walls of light, rather than cages. They *could* get out, but they don't *believe* they can. So they stay in.

Have members of Congress built their own wall of light? There is no doubt that they *could*, with a new law providing citizen financing of their campaigns, liberate themselves from the incessant quest for money, from the constant and demeaning need to "tin cup" it, from their dependence on "interested" contributors.

Yet they choose to remain in their prison.

Some contend that truly meaningful campaign finance reform is unattainable, arguing that, given the necessities of politics, the enormous role of government, the correspondingly huge stakes in governmental policies, and the ever-fretful, ever-ambitious nature of politicians, "interested" money will somehow find its way into the political system no matter how many prohibitions and ceilings Congress might enact.

But even if that's the case, given the array and gravity of problems caused by the current campaign finance system (set forth at the outset of Chapter 11), the elusiveness of perfection surely doesn't justify a failure to make an all-out effort to enact the "100 percent solution" of citizen financing of federal campaigns at all levels. By enacting such a plan, Congress could, at the least, drastically dilute the influence of that "interested money," and enable independent-minded, public-spirited candidates to enter the political lists—*and* retain their independence once in office.

That possibility was suggested by Walter Mondale's observation about how he felt when, as his party's nominee in 1984, he received the public funds that would finance his general election campaign: "After I was nominated for President, and received the some $40 million in direct federal support and was totally relieved from fund-raising," he once told me, "I was finally my own man, able to concentrate solely on the issues and the campaign. I no longer had to give first priority to fundraising and I could avoid the inevitable efforts to pressure my position on the issues."*

However much political cynics or Mondale detractors wish to discount that statement, imagine the effect of broadening citizen funding beyond presidential elections to include congressional elections, so that House and Senate candidates could experience Mondale's feeling of liberation. In every House and Senate election, candidates (especially, major-party nominees)—as many as 870 in the House and 66 or 68 in the Senate—would be *assured* of enough money to mount a respectable campaign. And if the guarantee of a "level playing field" were also written into the new laws, candidates would also be assured they would not be grossly outspent. Thus they could feel what Walter Mondale said he felt: liberated, free to speak their minds without worrying who was going to give or withhold money.

I do not suggest that if the proposed "100 percent solution" were enacted tomorrow, the House and Senate would instantly be peopled by public-spirited men and women. No law could guarantee that. But such a law could *make possible* something virtually ruled out by the present campaign finance system: independent-minded candidates and officeholders free of the influence of interested money.

---

* These Mondale words foreshadowed Senator Laxalt's 1991 comment that the Federal funds that assisted Ronald Reagan's 1980 presidential campaign were "like a breath of fresh air."

That would be a night-and-day improvement over the current system. It is very much worth fighting for.

The present campaign finance laws were not handed down from a mountain top. They are not engraved in marble. Congress made those laws, and Congress can change them.

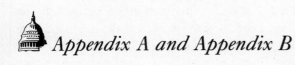

Appendix A and Appendix B

MEMBER-BY-MEMBER STATISTICS FOR THE U.S. HOUSE AND THE U.S. SENATE

THE FOLLOWING TABLES contain data for all current members of the U.S. Congress, designed to indicate (a) each member's need for campaign funds and (b) the extent to which that lawmaker raised money from special interest PACs.

Relevant to a lawmaker's *need* for funds are—

(a) the percentage of the electoral vote that a lawmaker has received in previous elections; and

(b) the amount of leftover cash in that member's campaign treasury at the end of the preceding campaign. This appears in the column headed "Leftover Cash."

As to the funds a member has raised from special interest PACs, two columns of figures list the amount the member has raised, both in absolute terms and in the percentage that these PAC funds comprise of the member's total campaign receipts. In the case of U.S. senators, the figures are for the election cycle immediately prior to that senator's most recent election.

The far right hand column on each page lists each member's "conflict of interest" receipts, meaning contributions given to, and accepted by, that lawmaker from groups having a particular interest

241

in the decisions of the legislative committee on which that law-maker sits (e.g., gifts by the PACs of military contractors to members of the House Armed Services Committee or gifts by bank and other financial PACs to members of the House Banking Committee). This figure represents those contributions accepted by a member of Congress since 1985. For those lawmakers elected in 1986 or 1988, the total is calculated from year of election.

These "conflict" figures have been arrived at by comparing the description of each committee's official jurisdiction with the major legislative interests of each contributing PAC. For this purpose, the PACs have been divided into interest group categories according to a system designed by the Center for Responsive Politics, a non-partisan Washington research group.

Readers will note that not every member has been assigned a "conflict" receipts figure. This is because not every member sits on a legislative committee that matches up readily with PACs of particular industries or interest groups (e.g., the Committee on Post Office and Civil Service). Therefore, in an effort to err on the side of caution, the author has refrained from assigning a "conflict receipts" figure to those members.

Members elected in 1990 also lack a conflict figure inasmuch as they had not been in office an entire election cycle when these figures were calculated. An asterisk (*) indicates a special election.

A note on the source of these statistics: No single source of statistics is wholly satisfactory. For example, statistics emanating from the Federal Election Commission are based on reports submitted by the PACs. In certain cases (e.g., when a member, as a matter of policy, declines PAC contributions), these FEC statistics may be defective, in that they fail to reflect the PAC contributions returned by members to the PACs.

Accordingly, the statistics in this table are, by and large, taken from *Politics in America*, a publication of Congressional Quarterly, which is based on figures furnished by the members themselves in their individual reports. The two exceptions are the figures for cash surpluses, which are taken from reports issued by the FEC, and the "conflict of interest" totals, which were calculated directly from FEC computer tapes by the National Library on Money & Politics.

HOUSE OF REPRESENTATIVES

Dist. No.	Name	Election %	PAC Receipts	PAC %	Leftover Cash	Conflict of Interest Receipts (1985–1990)
ALABAMA						
1	**Callahan (R)**					
	1990	100%	$169,350	53%	$ 236,511	$ 168,470
	1988	59%	$253,301	42%	$ 101,741	
	1986	100%	$114,197	39%	$ 156,236	
	1984	51%	$197,068	35%	$ 3,945	
2	**Dickinson (R)**					
	1990	51%	$218,921	52%	$ 250,325	$ 227,090
	1988	94%	$168,639	55%	$ 421,368	
	1986	67%	$180,581	47%	$ 351,585	
	1984	60%	$214,815	50%	$ 215,773	
3	**Browder (D)**					
	1990	74%	$547,750	63%	$ 119,913	$ 13,700
	*1989	65%	$354,100	60%	$ 16,226	
4	**Bevill (D)**					
	1990	100%	$106,550	48%	$ 566,499	n/a
	1988	96%	$ 94,850	46%	$ 513,647	
	1986	78%	$107,471	47%	$ 437,485	
	1984	100%	$102,668	38%	$ 358,023	
5	**Cramer (D)**					
	1990	67%	$246,932	37%	$ 20,771	n/a
6	**Erdreich (D)**					
	1990	93%	$172,819	73%	$ 364,025	$ 186,906
	1988	66%	$173,850	69%	$ 239,472	
	1986	73%	$214,440	63%	$ 146,955	
	1984	60%	$318,500	55%	$ 20,598	
7	**Harris (D)**					
	1990	71%	$151,307	64%	$ 77,742	$ 61,532
	1988	68%	$257,205	63%	$ 78,631	
	1986	60%	$182,800	38%	$ 1,501	
ALASKA						
AT LARGE	**Young (R)**					
	1990	52%	$277,725	50%	$ 5,543	$ 206,225
	1988	62%	$296,950	48%	$ 9,394	
	1986	57%	$250,133	51%	$ 12,010	
	1984	55%	$186,253	38%	$ 3,842	

HOUSE OF REPRESENTATIVES

Dist. No.	Name	Election %	PAC Receipts	PAC %	Leftover Cash	Conflict of Interest Receipts (1985–1990)

ARIZONA

1 Rhodes (R)

	1990	100%	$170,339	52%	$ 9,621	$ 38,714
	1988	72%	$135,419	46%	$ 6,309	
	1986	71%	$112,065	23%	$ 5,226	

2 Pastor (D)

1991 Election						n/a

3 Stump (R)

	1990	57%	$132,850	57%	$ 113,651	$ 70,050
	1988	69%	$115,046	45%	$ 107,674	
	1986	100%	$ 97,050	42%	$ 170,179	
	1984	72%	$109,965	42%	$ 72,127	

4 Kyl (R)

	1990	61%	$171,389	29%	$ 335,702	$ 50,350
	1988	87%	$178,114	36%	$ 189,890	
	1986	65%	$239,561	24%	$ 9,053	

5 Kolbe (R)

	1990	65%	$133,605	41%	$ 81,087	$ 45,600
	1988	68%	$158,738	38%	$ 6,272	
	1986	65%	$183,487	29%	$ 21,725	
	1984	51%	$245,901	34%	$ 11,448	

ARKANSAS

1 Alexander (D)

	1990	64%	$405,150	52%	$ 4,763	n/a
	1988	100%	$321,524	48%	$ 17,381	
	1986	64%	$303,900	48%	$ 8,540	
	1984	97%	$138,553	45%	$ 81,689	

2 Thornton (D)

	1990	60%	$242,900	35%	$ 18,638	n/a

3 Hammerschmidt (R)

	1990	71%	$166,500	62%	$ 500,684	$ 114,950
	1988	75%	$166,700	50%	$ 339,600	
	1986	80%	$ 83,950	53%	$ 168,435	
	1984	100%	$ 61,176	64%	$ 72,537	

HOUSE OF REPRESENTATIVES

Dist. No.	Name	Election %	PAC Receipts	PAC %	Leftover Cash	Conflict of Interest Receipts (1985–1990)
ARKANSAS (continued						
4	**Anthony (D)**					
	1990	72%	$374,300	71%	$ 364,662	$1,012,769
	1988	69%	$353,042	65%	$ 314,855	
	1986	78%	$276,757	71%	$ 337,764	
	1984	98%	$145,300	66%	$ 126,236	
CALIFORNIA						
1	**Riggs (R)**					
	1990	43%	$ 8,000	3%	$ 6,677	n/a
2	**Herger (R)**					
	1990	64%	$212,749	35%	$ 114,862	$ 166,464
	1988	59%	$258,675	37%	$ 13,809	
	1986	58%	$197,641	31%	$ 18,589	
3	**Matsui (D)**					
	1990	60%	$582,964	48%	$1,128,637	$1,314,387
	1988	71%	$475,366	52%	$ 654,798	
	1986	76%	$300,634	46%	$ 376,464	
	1984	100%	$176,518	51%	$ 277,820	
4	**Fazio (D)**					
	1990	55%	$451,245	53%	$ 194,935	n/a
	1988	99%	$378,783	50%	$ 378,618	
	1986	70%	$324,157	51%	$ 285,596	
	1984	61%	$210,864	49%	$ 36,397	
5	**Pelosi (D)**					
	1990	77%	$262,900	57%	$ 97,689	$ 107,050
	1988	76%	$548,815	29%	$ 72,852	
	*1987	63%	$215,090	20%	$ 0	
6	**Boxer (D)**					
	1990	68%	$337,124	37%	$ 449,349	$ 600
	1988	73%	$185,330	41%	$ 233,086	
	1986	74%	$164,611	46%	$ 134,467	
	1984	68%	$191,140	37%	$ 56,180	

HOUSE OF REPRESENTATIVES

Dist. No.	Name	Election %	PAC Receipts	PAC %	Leftover Cash	Conflict of Interest Receipts (1985–1990)
CALIFORNIA (continued)						
7	**Miller (D)**					
	1990	61%	$262,657	56%	$ 438,229	$ 141,014
	1988	68%	$179,984	42%	$ 416,855	
	1986	67%	$152,243	39%	$ 257,437	
	1984	66%	$102,107	37%	$ 178,602	
8	**Dellums (D)**					
	1990	61%	$ 71,935	9%	$ 82,629	$ 8,400
	1988	67%	$ 87,299	8%	$ 132,270	
	1986	60%	$ 93,123	7%	$ 153,259	
	1984	60%	$ 77,002	8%	$ 5,930	
9	**Stark (D)**					
	1990	58%	$270,170	51%	$ 362,004	$ 963,365
	1988	73%	$325,428	64%	$ 131,730	
	1986	70%	$355,263	63%	$ 37,565	
	1984	70%	$200,185	35%	$ 4,136	
10	**Edwards (D)**					
	1990	63%	$171,050	76%	$ 55,464	$ 1,300
	1988	86%	$117,256	70%	$ 39,708	
	1986	71%	$112,625	60%	$ 46,556	
	1984	62%	$ 88,827	58%	$ 14,802	
11	**Lantos (D)**					
	1990	66%	$120,550	15%	$ 637,734	$ 11,750
	1988	71%	$111,267	29%	$ 470,219	
	1986	74%	$ 58,850	20%	$ 353,277	
	1984	70%	$ 92,283	15%	$ 379,480	
12	**Campbell (R)**					
	1990	61%	$249,581	19%	$ 633,197	$ 17,650
	1988	52%	$239,382	17%	$ 5,132	
13	**Mineta (D)**					
	1990	58%	$361,274	54%	$ 342,701	$ 198,959
	1988	67%	$277,450	48%	$ 320,749	
	1986	70%	$231,921	42%	$ 265,258	
	1984	65%	$166,292	33%	$ 162,868	
14	**Doolittle (R)**					
	1990	52%	$234,764	44%	$ 12,142	n/a

HOUSE OF REPRESENTATIVES

Dist. No.	Name	Election %	PAC Receipts	PAC %	Leftover Cash	Conflict of Interest Receipts (1985–1990)
CALIFORNIA (continued)						
15	**Condit (D)**					
	1990	66%	$ 74,970	32%	$ 21,991	$ 104,095
	*1989	57%	$247,767	41%	$ 12,186	
16	**Panetta (D)**					
	1990	74%	$133,750	45%	$ 204,599	$ 84,950
	1988	79%	$112,600	35%	$ 181,908	
	1986	78%	$ 78,875	47%	$ 116,169	
	1984	71%	$ 87,718	39%	$ 64,824	
17	**Dooley (D)**					
	1990	55%	$171,185	31%	$ 9,409	n/a
18	**Lehman (D)**					
	1990	100%	$201,780	67%	$ 96,145	$ 168,131
	1988	70%	$131,276	47%	$ 93,399	
	1986	71%	$ 61,770	24%	$ 7,099	
	1984	67%	$122,522	52%	$ 43,934	
19	**Lagomarsino (R)**					
	1990	55%	$145,517	23%	$ 13,120	$ 62,703
	1988	50%	$338,996	28%	$ 28,043	
	1986	72%	$ 63,636	19%	$ 272,488	
	1984	67%	$ 90,078	19%	$ 264,453	
20	**Thomas (R)**					
	1990	60%	$235,447	55%	$ 157,392	$ 637,634
	1988	71%	$215,150	64%	$ 200,913	
	1986	73%	$165,617	64%	$ 220,486	
	1984	71%	$148,321	50%	$ 215,057	
21	**Gallegly (R)**					
	1990	58%	$156,861	26%	$ 231,271	$ 26,830
	1988	69%	$163,825	32%	$ 81,485	
	1986	68%	$143,573	23%	$ 40,407	
22	**Moorhead (R)**					
	1990	60%	$231,350	52%	$ 666,684	$ 276,250
	1988	70%	$215,165	54%	$ 622,634	
	1986	74%	$154,766	49%	$ 460,138	
	1984	85%	$ 98,275	49%	$ 288,907	

HOUSE OF REPRESENTATIVES

Dist. No.	Name	Election %	PAC Receipts	PAC %	Leftover Cash	Conflict of Interest Receipts (1985–1990)
CALIFORNIA (continued)						
23	**Beilenson (D)**					
	1990	62%	$ 0	0%	$ 45,449	n/a
	1988	64%	$ 0	0%	$ 15,467	
	1986	66%	$ 0	0%	$ 5,678	
	1984	62%	$ 4,213	2%	$ 25,588	
24	**Waxman (D)**					
	1990	69%	$315,400	63%	$ 468,893	$ 344,988
	1988	72%	$257,841	75%	$ 255,551	
	1986	88%	$105,900	72%	$ 101,881	
	1984	63%	$143,246	82%	$ 91,942	
25	**Roybal (D)**					
	1990	70%	$ 79,877	55%	$ 196,852	n/a
	1988	85%	$ 46,800	54%	$ 243,294	
	1986	76%	$ 40,400	41%	$ 224,527	
	1984	72%	$ 65,221	43%	$ 189,604	
26	**Berman (D)**					
	1990	61%	$181,500	36%	$ 200,471	$ 8,500
	1988	70%	$209,317	40%	$ 140,335	
	1986	65%	$118,827	43%	$ 21,273	
	1984	63%	$ 99,738	45%	$ 16,541	
27	**Levine (D)**					
	1990	58%	$239,207	16%	$1,714,807	$ 52,425
	1988	68%	$153,500	17%	$ 805,977	
	1986	64%	$121,524	17%	$ 310,765	
	1984	55%	$ 68,333	20%	$ 98,474	
28	**Dixon (D)**					
	1990	73%	$124,145	77%	$ 136,981	$ 10,200
	1988	76%	$ 70,980	59%	$ 86,741	
	1986	76%	$ 89,005	60%	$ 80,527	
	1984	76%	$ 79,553	68%	$ 35,590	
29	**Waters (D)**					
	1990	79%	$211,172	29%	$ 27,717	n/a

HOUSE OF REPRESENTATIVES

Dist. No.	Name	Election %	PAC Receipts	PAC %	Leftover Cash	Conflict of Interest Receipts (1985–1990)

CALIFORNIA (continued)

30	**Martinez (D)**					
	1990	58%	$ 93,803	45%	$ 43,205	$ 263,051
	1988	60%	$226,400	52%	$ 19,677	
	1986	63%	$119,525.	72%	$ 42,524	
	1984	52%	$127,680	65%	$ 12,741	
31	**Dymally (D)**					
	1990	67%	$173,316	40%	$ 25,795	$ 86,200
	1988	72%	$156,449	32%	$ 9,886	
	1986	70%	$ 71,358	19%	$ 3,788	
	1984	71%	$ 88,858	26%	$ 1,360	
32	**Anderson (D)**					
	1990	62%	$257,766	63%	$ 31,783	$ 190,986
	1988	67%	$276,785	56%	$ 82,442	
	1986	69%	$218,627	48%	$ 46,556	
	1984	61%	$214,733	53%	$ 6,143	
33	**Dreier (R)**					
	1990	64%	$100,276	17%	$1,669,915	$ 152,550
	1988	69%	$101,850	21%	$1,251,053	
	1986	72%	$106,800	22%	$ 949,829	
	1984	71%	$132,200	25%	$ 606,484	
34	**Torres (D)**					
	1990	61%	$ 87,788	36%	$ 148,388	$ 95,925
	1988	63%	$108,280	48%	$ 124,561	
	1986	60%	$ 93,259	51%	$ 124,694	
	1984	60%	$120,995	54%	$ 42,876	
35	**Lewis (R)**					
	1990	61%	$292,014	65%	$ 338,797	n/a
	1988	70%	$156,400	73%	$ 98,359	
	1986	77%	$105,103	75%	$ 223,268	
	1984	85%	$ 85,705	44%	$ 173,482	
36	**Brown (D)**					
	1990	53%	$454,935	56%	$ 4,345	$ 88,600
	1988	54%	$276,543	55%	$ 8,852	
	1986	57%	$227,867	42%	$ 37,388	
	1984	57%	$226,262	37%	$ 1,392	

HOUSE OF REPRESENTATIVES

Dist. No.	Name	Election %	PAC Receipts	PAC %	Leftover Cash	Conflict of Interest Receipts (1985–1990)
CALIFORNIA (continued)						
37	**McCandless (R)**					
	1990	50%	$179,600	33%	$ 5,600	$ 108,750
	1988	64%	$ 75,500	58%	$ 58,257	
	1986	64%	$ 65,500	43%	$ 51,783	
	1984	64%	$ 50,403	41%	$ 28,142	
38	**Dornan (R)**					
	1990	58%	$ 35,234	2%	$ 185,200	$ 11,100
	1988	60%	$ 83,231	5%	$ 15,497	
	1986	55%	$163,273	14%	$ 39,508	
	1984	53%	$157,110	15%	$ 23,908	
39	**Dannemeyer (R)**					
	1990	65%	$129,250	22%	$ 97,744	$ 182,400
	1988	74%	$144,472	48%	$ 130,893	
	1986	75%	$132,750	50%	$ 80,989	
	1984	76%	$131,897	45%	$ 76,961	
40	**Cox (R)**					
	1990	67%	$179,516	26%	$ 5,113	$ 33,500
	1988	67%	$198,786	18%	$ 5,940	
41	**Lowery (R)**					
	1990	49%	$205,165	42%	$ 28,497	n/a
	1988	66%	$182,415	40%	$ 118,172	
	1986	68%	$138,149	36%	$ 71,707	
	1984	63%	$182,647	38%	$ 84,415	
42	**Rohrabacher (R)**					
	1990	59%	$119,075	28%	$ 50,016	$ 2,050
	1988	64%	$186,427	36%	$ 27,177	
43	**Packard (R)**					
	1990	68%	$ 99,716	60%	$ 174,589	$ 64,525
	1988	72%	$114,538	53%	$ 154,821	
	1986	73%	$ 87,700	49%	$ 99,131	
	1984	74%	$119,275	29%	$ 52,503	
44	**Cunningham (R)**					
	1990	46%	$214,547	40%	$ 5,553	n/a

HOUSE OF REPRESENTATIVES

Dist. No.	Name	Election %	PAC Receipts	PAC %	Leftover Cash	Conflict of Interest Receipts (1985–1990)

CALIFORNIA (continued)

45 Hunter (R)

	1990	73%	$110,465	30%	$ 6,229	$ 79,250
	1988	74%	$150,718	38%	$ 14,078	
	1986	77%	$136,710	34%	$ 122,032	
	1984	75%	$139,465	36%	$ 121,569	

COLORADO

1 Schroeder (D)

	1990	64%	$113,588	26%	$ 182,156	$ 13,300
	1988	70%	$131,785	48%	$ 262,049	
	1986	68%	$105,815	44%	$ 203,758	
	1984	62%	$ 82,297	31%	$ 116,612	

2 Skaggs (D)

	1990	61%	$242,070	58%	$ 31,628	$ 49,775
	1988	63%	$452,772	62%	$ 12,411	
	1986	51%	$225,257	44%	$ 3,068	

3 Campbell (D)

	1990	70%	$215,980	70%	$ 13,513	$ 100,075
	1988	78%	$302,590	58%	$ 39,099	
	1986	52%	$204,968	52%	$ 11,062	

4 Allard (R)

	1990	54%	$174,550	48%	$ 3,428	n/a

5 Hefley (R)

	1990	66%	$114,981	85%	$ 85,219	$ 25,750
	1988	75%	$112,827	49%	$ 60,949	
	1986	70%	$113,206	38%	$ 15,282	

6 Schaefer (R)

	1990	65%	$229,103	61%	$ 122,410	$ 256,784
	1988	63%	$335,747	54%	$ 26,832	
	1986	65%	$ 99,833	69%	$ 44,428	
	1984	89%	$ 67,873	42%	$ 25,536	

HOUSE OF REPRESENTATIVES

Dist. No.	Name	Election %	PAC Receipts	PAC %	Leftover Cash	Conflict of Interest Receipts (1985–1990)
CONNECTICUT						
1	**Kennelly (D)**					
	1990	71%	$297,700	62%	$ 176,983	$ 785,211
	1988	77%	$269,603	60%	$ 100,078	
	1986	74%	$254,783	56%	$ 123,599	
	1984	62%	$174,983	48%	$ 54,590	
2	**Gejdenson (D)**					
	1990	60%	$185,950	41%	$ 4,658	$ 90,500
	1988	64%	$208,800	29%	$ 10,177	
	1986	67%	$294,448	30%	$ 6,586	
	1984	54%	$117,704	22%	$ 17,969	
3	**DeLauro (D)**					
	1990	52%	$401,805	41%	$ 15,642	n/a
4	**Shays (R)**					
	1990	77%	$ 58,000	13%	$ 74,546	$ 0
	1988	72%	$151,617	22%	$ 23,361	
	*1987	57%	$ 13,100	11%	$ 0	
5	**Franks (R)**					
	1990	52%	$177,927	30%	$ 5,430	n/a
6	**Johnson (R)**					
	1990	74%	$252,737	49%	$ 117,662	$ 249,326
	1988	66%	$135,322	26%	$ 156,660	
	1986	64%	$135,074	32%	$ 28,865	
	1984	64%	$200,247	38%	$ 25,653	
DELAWARE						
AT LARGE	**Carper (D)**					
	1990	67%	$204,220	37%	$ 53,814	$ 231,808
	1988	68%	$161,235	44%	$ 26,468	
	1986	66%	$151,669	46%	$ 32,784	
	1984	59%	$227,805	62%	$ 13,291	

HOUSE OF REPRESENTATIVES

Dist. No.	Name	Election %	PAC Receipts	PAC %	Leftover Cash	Conflict of Interest Receipts (1985–1990)
FLORIDA						
1	**Hutto (D)**					
	1990	52%	$ 95,307	52%	$ 109,103	$ 65,150
	1988	67%	$109,186	51%	$ 89,841	
	1986	64%	$ 29,545	35%	$ 53,805	
	1984	100%	$ 40,020	48%	$ 103,085	
2	**Peterson (D)**					
	1990	57%	$133,170	43%	$ 323	n/a
3	**Bennett (D)**					
	1990	73%	$ 30,450	35%	$ 280,990	$ 37,800
	1988	100%	$ 53,861	52%	$ 302,363	
	1986	100%	$ 76,441	61%	$ 217,345	
	1984	100%	$ 38,550	65%	$ 111,157	
4	**James (R)**					
	1990	56%	$211,951	33%	$ 11,526	$ 1,300
	1988	50%	$ 7,295	2%	$ 2,838	
5	**McCollum (R)**					
	1990	60%	$148,050	35%	$ 101,264	$ 113,400
	1988	100%	$117,835	37%	$ 239,063	
	1986	100%	$ 79,700	48%	$ 22,209	
	1984	100%	$ 75,110	43%	$ 177,095	
6	**Stearns (R)**					
	1990	59%	$200,346	40%	$ 47,634	$ 60,669
	1988	53%	$ 52,270	12%	$ 12,885	
7	**Gibbons (D)**					
	1990	68%	$316,125	64%	$ 278,960	$1,183,982
	1988	100%	$345,387	57%	$ 612,241	
	1986	100%	$560,270	62%	$ 390,559	
	1984	59%	$149,275	62%	$ 50,584	
8	**Young (R)**					
	1990	100%	$132,900	57%	$ 341,773	$ 110,224
	1988	73%	$109,600	51%	$ 311,561	
	1986	100%	$ 91,945	43%	$ 306,907	
	1984	80%	$ 74,383	44%	$ 188,362	

HOUSE OF REPRESENTATIVES

Dist. No.	Name	Election %	PAC Receipts	PAC %	Leftover Cash	Conflict of Interest Receipts (1985–1990)
FLORIDA (continued)						
9	**Bilirakis (R)**					
	1990	58%	$234,430	39%	$ 2,617	$ 249,280
	1988	100%	$149,975	38%	$ 217,312	
	1986	71%	$151,898	32%	$ 12,063	
	1984	79%	$123,718	35%	$ 49,771	
10	**Ireland (R)**					
	1990	100%	$169,683	41%	$ 98,267	$ 43,875
	1988	73%	$164,389	41%	$ 72,351	
	1986	71%	$167,178	36%	$ 127,819	
	1984	62%	$198,592	34%	$ 59,338	
11	**Bacchus (D)**					
	1990	52%	$412,573	47%	$ 2,112	n/a
12	**Lewis (R)**					
	1990	100%	$ 80,425	24%	$ 121,358	$ 59,025
	1988	100%	$ 64,465	22%	$ 186,252	
	1986	99%	$ 90,238	29%	$ 150,369	
	1984	100%	$ 78,144	24%	$ 126,132	
13	**Goss (R)**					
	1990	100%	$122,125	40%	$ 100,030	$ 9,450
	1988	71%	$141,976	16%	$ 42,215	
14	**Johnston (D)**					
	1990	66%	$253,169	50%	$ 42,284	$ 15,200
	1988	55%	$296,636	30%	$ 2,860	
15	**Shaw (R)**					
	1990	98%	$245,760	59%	$ 306,224	$ 395,554
	1988	66%	$153,750	44%	$ 13,467	
	1986	100%	$ 83,075	41%	$ 120,811	
	1984	66%	$107,620	28%	$ 19,717	
16	**Smith (D)**					
	1990	100%	$246,935	47%	$ 413,843	$ 113,867
	1988	69%	$280,493	40%	$ 161,721	
	1986	70%	$308,283	40%	$ 57,030	
	1984	56%	$306,320	47%	$ 87,131	

HOUSE OF REPRESENTATIVES

Dist. No.	Name	Election %	PAC Receipts	PAC %	Leftover Cash	Conflict of Interest Receipts (1985–1990)
FLORIDA (continued)						
17 Lehman (D)						
	1990	78%	$216,350	51%	$ 275,781	n/a
	1988	100%	$132,250	41%	$ 220,429	
	1986	100%	$ 97,700	45%	$ 153,854	
	1984	100%	$ 82,887	41%	$ 111,370	
18 Ros-Lehtinen (R)						
	1990	60%	$168,784	29%	$ 14,387	n/a
	*1989	53%	$222,757	22%	$ 16,173	
19 Fascell (D)						
	1990	62%	$164,116	36%	$ 546,593	$ 65,365
	1988	72%	$176,935	36%	$ 586,920	
	1986	69%	$144,550	31%	$ 42,693	
	1984	64%	$162,720	35%	$ 246,140	
GEORGIA						
1 Thomas (D)						
	1990	71%	$167,765	44%	$ 67,690	$ 39,150
	1988	67%	$149,969	44%	$ 88,518	
	1986	100%	$132,350	54%	$ 85,580	
	1984	82%	$115,477	42%	$ 42,784	
2 Hatcher (D)						
	1990	73%	$211,150	64%	$ 38,709	$ 149,020
	1988	62%	$200,458	58%	$ 6,673	
	1986	100%	$ 55,950	34%	$ 29,786	
	1984	100%	$ 85,550	52%	$ 5,162	
3 Ray (D)						
	1990	63%	$155,950	42%	$ 180,654	$ 98,367
	1988	100%	$131,117	47%	$ 190,165	
	1986	100%	$120,812	41%	$ 165,621	
	1984	81%	$152,239	30%	$ 24,727	
4 Jones (D)						
	1990	52%	$416,333	59%	$ 1,959	$ 14,350
	1988	60%	$265,606	51%	$ 5,937	

HOUSE OF REPRESENTATIVES

Dist. No.	Name	Election %	PAC Receipts	PAC %	Leftover Cash	Conflict of Interest Receipts (1985–1990)
GEORGIA (continued)						
5	**Lewis (D)**					
	1990	76%	$175,510	65%	$ 260,822	$ 19,200
	1988	78%	$142,915	74%	$ 92,401	
	1986	75%	$157,994	41%	$ 358	
6	**Gingrich (R)**					
	1990	50%	$433,421	28%	$ 24,739	$ 81,700
	1988	59%	$262,976	31%	$ 24,858	
	1986	60%	$200,726	27%	$ 11,731	
	1984	69%	$129,044	36%	$ 20,556	
7	**Darden (D)**					
	1990	60%	$238,006	51%	$ 100,737	$ 129,150
	1988	65%	$241,375	54%	$ 115,951	
	1986	66%	$252,920	48%	$ 49,834	
	1984	55%	$137,881	48%	$ 51,746	
8	**Rowland (D)**					
	1990	69%	$228,050	62%	$ 210,642	$ 131,400
	1988	100%	$129,637	50%	$ 207,955	
	1986	86%	$ 90,125	39%	$ 142,306	
	1984	100%	$ 67,625	36%	$ 59,178	
9	**Jenkins (D)**					
	1990	56%	$186,000	62%	$ 448,273	$ 694,087
	1988	63%	$310,897	69%	$ 464,486	
	1986	100%	$212,473	64%	$ 416,351	
	1984	67%	$178,090	64%	$ 230,312	
10	**Barnard (D)**					
	1990	55%	$264,551	34%	$ 359,869	$ 341,701
	1988	64%	$148,371	52%	$ 519,193	
	1986	67%	$183,071	53%	$ 427,257	
	1984	100%	$114,125	61%	$ 290,556	
HAWAII						
1	**Abercrombie (D)**					
	1990	60%	$143,600	30%	$ 34,017	n/a

HOUSE OF REPRESENTATIVES

Dist. No.	Name	Election %	PAC Receipts	PAC %	Leftover Cash	Conflict of Interest Receipts (1985–1990)
HAWAII (continued)						
2	**Mink (D)**					
	*1990	66%	$147,784	23%	$ 288	n/a
IDAHO						
1	**LaRocco (D)**					
	1990	53%	$238,753	53%	$ 1,522	n/a
2	**Stallings (D)**					
	1990	63%	$266,702	66%	$ 583	$ 131,330
	1988	63%	$266,739	53%	$ 1,687	
	1986	54%	$271,815	57%	$ 4,773	
	1984	50%	$182,407	57%	$ 229	
ILLINOIS						
1	**Hayes (D)**					
	1990	94%	$ 85,250	77%	$ 25,702	$ 226,359
	1988	96%	$115,634	71%	$ 40,554	
	1986	96%	$ 83,475	57%	$ 35,507	
	1984	96%	$ 62,518	34%	$ 1,686	
2	**Savage (D)**					
	1990	78%	$ 57,800	29%	$ 5,941	$ 4,068
	1988	83%	$116,218	48%	$ 702	
	1986	84%	$ 81,500	53%	$ 2,452	
	1984	83%	$ 46,058	38%	$ 90	
3	**Russo (D)**					
	1990	71%	$382,966	70%	$ 7,789	$ 980,659
	1988	62%	$357,996	64%	$ 2,289	
	1986	66%	$281,755	59%	$ 2,105	
	1984	64%	$165,806	54%	$ 6,855	
4	**Sangmeister (D)**					
	1990	59%	$356,393	75%	$ 23,142	$ 9,745
	1988	50%	$144,294	38%	$ 18,349	

* Mink stood for election in both September and November 1990.

HOUSE OF REPRESENTATIVES

Dist. No.	Name	Election %	PAC Receipts	PAC %	Leftover Cash	Conflict of Interest Receipts (1985–1990)
ILLINOIS (continued)						
5	**Lipinski (D)**					
	1990	66%	$137,317	75%	$ 19,110	$ 30,350
	1988	61%	$ 96,464	62%	$ 7,646	
	1986	70%	$ 64,925	43%	$ 18,225	
	1984	64%	$ 49,075	46%	$ 20,505	
6	**Hyde (R)**					
	1990	67%	$130,648	43%	$ 187,768	$ 0
	1988	74%	$121,453	40%	$ 155,663	
	1986	75%	$ 93,337	39%	$ 133,497	
	1984	75%	$ 88,732	37%	$ 121,438	
7	**Collins (D)**					
	1990	80%	$229,648	82%	$ 90,094	$ 180,069
	1988	100%	$199,043	85%	$ 211,451	
	1986	80%	$230,570	76%	$ 103,880	
	1984	78%	$171,051	83%	$ 32,723	
8	**Rostenkowski (D)**					
	1990	79%	$197,700	52%	$1,114,068	$ 869,933
	1988	75%	$444,698	51%	$1,034,438	
	1986	79%	$199,124	82%	$ 596,703	
	1984	71%	$325,131	69%	$ 592,935	
9	**Yates (D)**					
	1990	71%	$267,746	34%	$ 53,828	n/a
	1988	66%	$ 25,250	20%	$ 113,811	
	1986	72%	$ 16,401	11%	$ 110,010	
	1984	68%	$ 25,417	17%	$ 58,347	
10	**Porter (R)**					
	1990	68%	$110,025	43%	$ 71,996	n/a
	1988	72%	$115,321	47%	$ 129,521	
	1986	75%	$ 77,041	41%	$ 96,786	
	1984	73%	$ 89,967	40%	$ 84,674	
11	**Annunzio (D)**					
	1990	54%	$478,891	66%	$ 35,719	$ 177,700
	1988	65%	$158,200	61%	$ 168,512	
	1986	71%	$130,832	58%	$ 147,155	
	1984	63%	$ 91,123	44%	$ 92,826	

HOUSE OF REPRESENTATIVES

Dist. No.	Name	Election %	PAC Receipts	PAC %	Leftover Cash	Conflict of Interest Receipts (1985–1990)
ILLINOIS (continued)						
12	**Crane (R)**					
	1990	82%	$ 0	0%	$ 115,919	$ 0
	1988	75%	$ 0	0%	$ 115,804	
	1986	78%	$ 1,000	.3%	$ 129,371	
	1984	78%	$ 7,967	2%	$ 156,251	
13	**Fawell (R)**					
	1990	66%	$119,570	36%	$ 103,808	$ 12,445
	1988	70%	$ 98,171	34%	$ 38,935	
	1986	73%	$ 71,028	36%	$ 35,230	
	1984	67%	$ 67,612	32%	$ 34,226	
14	**Hastert (R)**					
	1990	67%	$181,074	39%	$ 191,061	$ 33,370
	1988	74%	$148,608	40%	$ 42,612	
	1986	52%	$138,737	41%	$ 15,521	
15	**Ewing (R)**					
	1990	66%	$152,117	47%	$ 51,103	n/a
16	**Cox (D)**					
	1990	55%	$191,666	51%	$ 6,306	n/a
17	**Evans (D)**					
	1990	67%	$228,998	55%	$ 30,911	$ 42,650
	1988	65%	$211,218	46%	$ 3,686	
	1986	56%	$334,136	53%	$ 14,307	
	1984	57%	$277,919	60%	$ 2,095	
18	**Michel (R)**					
	1990	98%	$519,161	74%	$ 241,996	n/a
	1988	55%	$555,417	64%	$ 115,375	
	1986	63%	$456,371	66%	$ 100,315	
	1984	61%	$390,646	57%	$ 50,231	
19	**Bruce (D)**					
	1990	66%	$306,491	65%	$ 574,423	$ 395,512
	1988	64%	$276,182	60%	$ 360,770	
	1986	66%	$221,790	60%	$ 96,020	
	1984	52%	$182,816	60%	$ 2,708	

HOUSE OF REPRESENTATIVES

Dist. No.	Name	Election %	PAC Receipts	PAC %	Leftover Cash	Conflict of Interest Receipts (1985–1990)
ILLINOIS (continued)						
20	**Durbin (D)**					
	1990	66%	$207,978	62%	$ 307,371	$ 63,661
	1988	69%	$220,605	60%	$ 178,667	
	1986	68%	$168,774	49%	$ 62,833	
	1984	61%	$232,382	49%	$ 8,519	
21	**Costello (D)**					
	1990	66%	$231,550	35%	$ 273,831	$ 18,200
	*1988	53%	$329,661	30%	$ 260	
	1988	51%	$ 85,775	32%	$ 109,169	
22	**Poshard (D)**					
	1990	84%	$ 5,150	8%	$ 2,136	$ 100
	1988	65%	$248,970	58%	$ 37,457	
INDIANA						
1	**Visclosky (D)**					
	1990	66%	$168,020	68%	$ 43,701	$ 106,884
	1988	77%	$157,250	71%	$ 95,066	
	1986	73%	$ 97,067	61%	$ 14,301	
	1984	71%	$ 50,682	26%	$ 19,056	
2	**Sharp (D)**					
	1990	59%	$498,599	70%	$ 29,944	$ 396,153
	1988	53%	$311,581	67%	$ 88,631	
	1986	62%	$264,410	65%	$ 67,639	
	1984	53%	$246,069	57%	$ 47,929	
3	**Roemer (D)**					
	1990	51%	$269,313	53%	$ 31,826	n/a
4	**Long (D)**					
	1990	61%	$448,381	59%	$ 1,363	$ 62,784
	*1989	51%	$182,763	56%	$ 12,736	
5	**Jontz (D)**					
	1990	53%	$405,145	65%	$ 1,746	$ 526,267
	1988	56%	$471,725	65%	$ 33,315	
	1986	51%	$292,749	63%	$ 762	

* April 1988

HOUSE OF REPRESENTATIVES

Dist. No.	Name	Election %	PAC Receipts	PAC %	Leftover Cash	Conflict of Interest Receipts (1985–1990)
INDIANA (continued)						
6 Burton (R)						
	1990	63%	$203,426	39%	$ 400,894	$ 44,650
	1988	73%	$141,170	37%	$ 186,172	
	1986	68%	$143,292	44%	$ 148,379	
	1984	73%	$102,222	40%	$ 39,506	
7 Myers (R)						
	1990	58%	$ 98,870	50%	$ 102,885	$ 35,600
	1988	62%	$ 96,500	56%	$ 132,552	
	1986	67%	$ 79,000	44%	$ 125,521	
	1984	67%	$ 78,092	39%	$ 107,915	
8 McCloskey (D)						
	1990	55%	$322,320	69%	$ 23,382	$ 49,100
	1988	62%	$342,058	62%	$ 1,441	
	1986	53%	$337,686	54%	$ 3,832	
	1984	50%	$279,903	58%	$ 2,652	
9 Hamilton (D)						
	1990	69%	$188,824	47%	$ 58,592	$ 59,050
	1988	71%	$152,066	41%	$ 51,442	
	1986	72%	$124,400	43%	$ 15,851	
	1984	65%	$104,157	43%	$ 35,422	
10 Jacobs (D)						
	1990	66%	$ 0	0%	$ 32,188	$ 0
	1988	61%	$ 0	0%	$ 18,293	
	1986	58%	$ 0	0%	$ 18,346	
	1984	59%	$ 82	.2%	$ 6,920	
IOWA						
1 Leach (R)						
	1990	100%	$ 0	0%	$ 46,917	$ 0
	1988	61%	$ 0	0%	$ 19,354	
	1986	66%	$ 0	0%	$ 31,443	
	1984	67%	$ 999	.4%	$ 33,773	
2 Nussle (R)						
	1990	50%	$146,558	31%	$ 3,673	n/a

HOUSE OF REPRESENTATIVES

Dist. No.	Name	Election %	PAC Receipts	PAC %	Leftover Cash	Conflict of Interest Receipts (1985–1990)
IOWA (continued)						
3	**Nagle (D)**					
	1990	100%	$264,001	73%	$ 30,045	$ 91,675
	1988	63%	$406,018	67%	$ 14,930	
	1986	55%	$171,017	59%	$ 1,618	
4	**Smith (D)**					
	1990	98%	$116,970	70%	$ 376,309	$ 35,700
	1988	72%	$162,585	79%	$ 264,580	
	1986	68%	$109,400	71%	$ 143,017	
	1984	61%	$122,061	74%	$ 90,014	
5	**Lightfoot (R)**					
	1990	68%	$146,243	29%	$ 140,810	$ 100,764
	1988	64%	$166,077	35%	$ 61,580	
	1986	59%	$207,047	45%	$ 3,467	
	1984	51%	$200,952	48%	$ 13,530	
6	**Grandy (R)**					
	1990	72%	$251,675	62%	$ 85,951	$ 149,650
	1988	64%	$294,944	56%	−$ 554	
	1986	51%	$231,472	34%	$ 3,109	
KANSAS						
1	**Roberts (R)**					
	1990	63%	$132,250	59%	$ 400,824	$ 102,752
	1988	100%	$ 99,600	52%	$ 330,315	
	1986	77%	$101,606	56%	$ 219,871	
	1984	76%	$ 65,445	42%	$ 125,309	
2	**Slattery (D)**					
	1990	63%	$327,550	70%	$ 52,999	$ 311,033
	1988	73%	$266,122	59%	$ 90,853	
	1986	71%	$240,455	63%	$ 25,888	
	1984	60%	$167,674	54%	$ 6,345	
3	**Meyers (R)**					
	1990	60%	$110,641	52%	$ 2,081	$ 10,381
	1988	74%	$110,395	55%	$ 561	
	1986	100%	$108,612	63%	$ 33,914	
	1984	55%	$217,389	49%	$ 1,348	

HOUSE OF REPRESENTATIVES

Dist. No.	Name	Election %	PAC Receipts	PAC %	Leftover Cash	Conflict of Interest Receipts (1985–1990)
KANSAS (continued)						
4 Glickman (D)						
	1990	71%	$294,865	57%	$ 192,262	$ 144,480
	1988	64%	$280,540	50%	$ 26,900	
	1986	65%	$180,225	39%	$ 10,391	
	1984	74%	$ 57,089	29%	$ 77,510	
5 Nichols (R)						
	1990	59%	$100,125	17%	$ 7,776	n/a
KENTUCKY						
1 Hubbard (D)						
	1990	87%	$271,327	77%	$ 335,477	$ 244,127
	1988	95%	$356,663	69%	$ 223,129	
	1986	100%	$196,775	68%	$ 251,699	
	1984	100%	$166,450	70%	$ 200,155	
2 Natcher (D)						
	1990	66%	$ 0	0%	$ 0	$ 0
	1988	61%	$ 0	0%	$ 0	
	1986	100%	$ 0	0%	$ 0	
	1984	62%	$ 0	0%	$ 0	
3 Mazzoli (D)						
	1990	61%	$ 0	0%	–$ 1,484	$ 3,150
	1988	70%	$196,650	52%	$ 30,687	
	1986	73%	$ 79,700	54%	$ 23,680	
	1984	68%	$ 81,959	52%	$ 2,463	
4 Bunning (R)						
	1990	69%	$225,900	42%	$ 97,018	$ 122,450
	1988	74%	$236,184	40%	$ 127,653	
	1986	55%	$250,865	28%	$ 2,937	
5 Rogers (R)						
	1990	100%	$ 71,025	39%	$ 270,493	$ 11,250
	1988	100%	$ 69,566	39%	$ 193,172	
	1986	100%	$ 63,962	25%	$ 135,552	
	1984	76%	$ 79,792	36%	$ 79,999	

HOUSE OF REPRESENTATIVES

Dist. No.	Name	Election %	PAC Receipts	PAC %	Leftover Cash	Conflict of Interest Receipts (1985–1990)
KENTUCKY (continued)						
6	**Hopkins (R)**					
	1990	100%	$ 92,200	45%	$ 691,433	$ 147,250
	1988	74%	$134,335	38%	$ 608,792	
	1986	74%	$129,428	32%	$ 547,846	
	1984	71%	$142,067	40%	$ 299,238	
7	**Perkins (D)**					
	1990	51%	$267,575	79%	$ 3,640	$ 418,837
	1988	59%	$264,300	63%	$ 8,161	
	1986	80%	$144,200	66%	$ 1,114	
	1984	74%	$ 53,718	71%	$ 35,463	
LOUISIANA						
1	**Livingston (R)**					
	1990	84%	$140,878	50%	$ 282,513	$ 81,850
	1988	78%	$127,834	49%	$ 111,115	
	1986	100%	$ 46,995	20%	$ 403,766	
	1984	88%	$105,133	31%	$ 368,781	
2	**Jefferson (D)**					
	1990	53%	$104,950	23%	$ 1,355	n/a
3	**Tauzin (D)**					
	1990	88%	$243,922	53%	$ 48,411	$ 363,017
	1988	89%	$263,228	76%	$ 61,804	
	1986	100%	$150,975	40%	$ 421,002	
	1984	100%	$178,186	41%	$ 372,024	
4	**McCrery (R)**					
	1990	55%	$190,623	41%	$ 37,690	$ 21,300
	1988	69%	$287,341	36%	$ 49,429	
	*1988	51%	$ 63,221	22%	$ 1,350	
5	**Huckaby (D)**					
	1990	74%	$106,498	49%	$ 273,331	$ 165,261
	1988	68%	$131,650	49%	$ 295,390	
	1986	68%	$113,895	49%	$ 222,559	
	1984	100%	$ 77,109	37%	$ 314,483	

HOUSE OF REPRESENTATIVES

Dist. No.	Name	Election %	PAC Receipts	PAC %	Leftover Cash	Conflict of Interest Receipts (1985–1990)

LOUISIANA (continued)

6 Baker (R)

	1990	100%	$153,761	40%	$ 67,056	$ 72,369
	1988	100%	$124,525	43%	$ 17,341	
	1986	51%	$ 85,467	20%	$ 1,008	

7 Hayes (D)

	1990	58%	$164,850	52%	$ 48,849	$ 36,800
	1988	100%	$206,100	68%	$ 40,784	
	1986	57%	$ 46,550	5%	$ 3,987	

8 Holloway (R)

	1990	56%	$144,263	38%	$ 62,110	$ 76,030
	1988	57%	$315,886	46%	$ 64,285	
	1986	51%	$133,803	30%	$ 4,157	

MAINE

1 Andrews (D)

| | 1990 | 60% | $244,473 | 35% | $ 9,437 | n/a |

2 Snowe (R)

	1990	51%	$ 97,655	35%	$ 3,335	$ 10,750
	1988	66%	$ 72,300	31%	$ 31,404	
	1986	77%	$ 79,075	37%	$ 3,791	
	1984	76%	$ 86,150	36%	$ 3,050	

MARYLAND

1 Gilchrest (R)

| | 1990 | 57% | $ 60,074 | 23% | $ 2,856 | n/a |

2 Bentley (R)

	1990	74%	$214,305	27%	$ 131,837	$ 90,915
	1988	71%	$293,984	35%	$ 81,681	
	1986	59%	$361,985	34%	$ 13,577	
	1984	51%	$181,719	30%	$ 10,036	

3 Cardin (D)

	1990	70%	$200,790	38%	$ 250,724	$ 295,268
	1988	72%	$208,148	51%	$ 81,819	
	1986	79%	$143,977	28%	$ 30,731	

HOUSE OF REPRESENTATIVES

Dist. No.	Name	Election %	PAC Receipts	PAC %	Leftover Cash	Conflict of Interest Receipts (1985–1990)
MARYLAND (continued)						
4 McMillen (D)						
	1990	58%	$423,275	56%	$ 328,285	$ 194,758
	1988	68%	$392,892	54%	$ 132,049	
	1986	50%	$307,549	39%	$ 1,281	
5 Hoyer (D)						
	1990	81%	$417,235	58%	$ 321,405	n/a
	1988	79%	$239,828	49%	$ 312,458	
	1986	82%	$166,262	43%	$ 237,908	
	1984	72%	$125,388	42%	$ 153,823	
6 Byron (D)						
	1990	65%	$165,245	59%	$ 33,737	$ 143,100
	1988	75%	$142,722	65%	$ 77,397	
	1986	72%	$126,603	59%	$ 72,853	
	1984	65%	$108,715	53%	$ 65,815	
7 Mfume (D)						
	1990	85%	$128,000	57%	$ 84,387	$ 95,640
	1988	100%	$ 72,250	55%	$ 65,234	
	1986	87%	$ 61,523	41%	$ 45,331	
8 Morella (R)						
	1990	74%	$239,709	44%	$ 201,384	$ 13,600
	1988	62%	$305,374	37%	$ 11,454	
	1986	53%	$147,240	24%	$ 3,591	
MASSACHUSETTS						
1 Olver (D)						
	*1991	50%	$294,850	38%	$ 4,455	n/a
2 Neal (D)						
	1990	100%	$248,878	54%	$ 12,496	$ 43,200
	1988	80%	$ 87,000	25%	$ 84,169	
3 Early (D)						
	1990	100%	$ 86,348	31%	$ 111,190	n/a
	1988	100%	$ 93,250	42%	$ 111,500	
	1986	100%	$ 86,710	36%	$ 95,439	
	1984	67%	$ 38,688	19%	$ 38,724	

HOUSE OF REPRESENTATIVES

Dist. No.	Name	Election %	PAC Receipts	PAC %	Leftover Cash	Conflict of Interest Receipts (1985–1990)
MASSACHUSETTS (continued)						
4 Frank (D)						
	1990	66%	$220,517	34%	$ 53,329	$ 149,317
	1988	70%	$141,635	33%	$ 127,567	
	1986	89%	$ 68,975	33%	$ 37,478	
	1984	74%	$113,964	28%	$ 42,855	
5 Atkins (D)						
	1990	52%	$ 0	0%	$ 2,449	n/a
	1988	84%	$ 0	0%	$ 19,889	
	1986	100%	$ 5,127	1%	$ 5,359	
	1984	53%	$ 5,541	.6%	$ 4,683	
6 Mavroules (D)						
	1990	65%	$119,749	41%	$ 61,574	$ 31,425
	1988	69%	$107,360	31%	$ 105,693	
	1986	100%	$ 91,250	39%	$ 94,283	
	1984	70%	$107,568	38%	$ 43,010	
7 Markey (D)						
	1990	100%	$ 0	0%	$ 579,994	$ 0
	1988	100%	$ 0	0%	$ 451,058	
	1986	100%	$ 10,600	3%	$ 101,126	
	1984	71%	$ 37,802	6%	$ 3,379	
8 Kennedy (D)						
	1990	72%	$108,550	13%	$ 227,284	$ 44,220
	1988	80%	$272,840	16%	$ 253,264	
	1986	72%	$ 77,795	4%	$ 20,298	
9 Moakley (D)						
	1990	70%	$279,274	54%	$ 489,816	n/a
	1988	100%	$180,830	47%	$ 290,806	
	1986	84%	$171,485	42%	$ 178,641	
	1984	100%	$ 86,698	30%	$ 89,361	
10 Studds (D)						
	1990	53%	$221,581	37%	$ 21,912	$ 11,375
	1988	67%	$ 83,545	34%	$ 41,973	
	1986	65%	$ 83,820	22%	$ 34,826	
	1984	56%	$155,443	27%	$ 46,396	

HOUSE OF REPRESENTATIVES

Dist. No.	Name	Election %	PAC Receipts	PAC %	Leftover Cash	Conflict of Interest Receipts (1985–1990)
MASSACHUSETTS (continued)						
11	**Donnelly (D)**					
	1990	100%	$168,850	56%	$ 669,414	$ 459,050
	1988	80%	$131,300	50%	$ 469,693	
	1986	100%	$138,065	54%	$ 365,379	
	1984	100%	$ 65,393	45%	$ 157,757	.
MICHIGAN						
1	**Conyers (D)**					
	1990	89%	$178,360	59%	$ 38,192	$ 4,050
	1988	91%	$ 82,614	54%	$ 34,832	
	1986	89%	$ 66,845	51%	$ 8,352	
	1984	89%	$ 45,415	60%	$ 39,513	
2	**Pursell (R)**					n/a
	1990	64%	$ 96,415	34%	$ 240,044	
	1988	55%	$264,994	33%	$ 90,037	
	1986	59%	$ 67,445	29%	$ 155,432	
	1984	69%	$ 55,038	39%	$ 64,619	
3	**Wolpe (D)**					
	1990	58%	$414,976	52%	$ 59,327	$ 98,050
	1988	57%	$263,224	46%	$ 82,880	
	1986	60%	$252,649	29%	$ 107,429	
	1984	53%	$193,630	41%	$ 81,539	
4	**Upton (R)**					
	1990	58%	$152,654	34%	$ 42,144	$ 39,713
	1988	71%	$117,465	28%	$ 99,428	
	1986	62%	$ 42,685	11%	$ 377	
5	**Henry (R)**					
	1990	75%	$ 92,880	23%	$ 275,521	$ 18,400
	1988	73%	$ 97,425	25%	$ 118,046	
	1986	71%	$102,592	30%	$ 39,583	
	1984	62%	$132,989	30%	$ 128	
6	**Carr (D)**					
	1990	100%	$208,550	53%	$ 255,444	n/a
	1988	59%	$277,823	52%	$ 83,069	
	1986	57%	$448,672	61%	$ 52,534	
	1984	52%	$330,001	56%	$ 10,402	

HOUSE OF REPRESENTATIVES

Dist. No.	Name	Election %	PAC Receipts	PAC %	Leftover Cash	Conflict of Interest Receipts (1985–1990)
MICHIGAN (continued)						
7	**Kildee (D)**					
	1990	68%	$187,746	72%	$ 39,580	$ 240,956
	1988	75%	$103,770	68%	$ 2,634	
	1986	80%	$ 80,510	84%	$ 984	
	1984	93%	$ 48,467	81%	$ 6,439	
8	**Traxler (D)**					
	1990	69%	$186,860	63%	$ 358,806	$ 82,645
	1988	72%	$148,987	63%	$ 239,742	
	1986	73%	$ 90,112	60%	$ 130,143	
	1984	64%	$ 77,408	56%	$ 79,671	
9	**Vander Jagt (R)**					
	1990	55%	$270,171	60%	$ 104,106	$ 715,361
	1988	70%	$238,725	52%	$ 108,182	
	1986	64%	$217,830	51%	$ 102,356	
	1984	71%	$210,115	55%	$ 73,310	
10	**Camp (R)**					
	1990	65%	$175,075	26%	$ 10,483	n/a
11	**Davis (R)**					
	1990	61%	$242,224	71%	$ 114,637	$ 151,700
	1988	60%	$310,359	53%	$ 99,789	
	1986	63%	$164,190	41%	$ 197,990	
	1984	59%	$ 85,805	46%	$ 8,732	
12	**Bonior (D)**					
	1990	65%	$728,055	61%	$ 89,849	n/a
	1988	54%	$328,317	69%	$ 89,628	
	1986	66%	$203,455	65%	$ 48,366	
	1984	58%	$ 79,770	53%	$ 16,726	
13	**Collins (D)**					
	1990	80%	$ 68,620	20%	$ 61,044	n/a
14	**Hertel (D)**					
	1990	64%	$186,680	61%	$ 281,310	$ 56,750
	1988	63%	$154,565	62%	$ 162,005	
	1986	73%	$120,549	60%	$ 48,563	
	1984	59%	$ 86,179	54%	$ 21,433	

HOUSE OF REPRESENTATIVES

Dist. No.	Name	Election %	PAC Receipts	PAC %	Leftover Cash	Conflict of Interest Receipts (1985–1990)
MICHIGAN (continued)						
15	**Ford (D)**					
	1990	61%	$280,598	73%	$ 186,613	$ 433,023
	1988	64%	$267,901	80%	$ 158,221	
	1986	75%	$220,735	67%	$ 55,943	
	1984	60%	$186,143	66%	$ 31,117	
16	**Dingell (D)**					
	1990	67%	$625,727	74%	$ 490,871	$ 614,655
	1988	97%	$459,242	74%	$ 252,240	
	1986	78%	$375,177	76%	$ 100,677	
	1984	64%	$234,618	64%	$ 88,048	
17	**Levin (D)**					
	1990	70%	$241,525	68%	$ 255,205	$ 423,556
	1988	70%	$193,430	64%	$ 170,048	
	1986	76%	$121,903	55%	$ 102,814	
	1984	100%	$ 80,295	48%	$ 15,533	
18	**Broomfield (R)**					
	1990	66%	$ 56,200	23%	$ 754,678	$ 16,000
	1988	76%	$ 57,700	24%	$ 589,123	
	1986	74%	$ 33,520	19%	$ 430,594	
	1984	79%	$ 45,800	20%	$ 319,684	
MINNESOTA						
1	**Penny (D)**					
	1990	78%	$113,050	49%	$ 256,193	$ 114,300
	1988	70%	$125,377	44%	$ 223,595	
	1986	72%	$151,491	40%	$ 104,056	
	1984	57%	$226,637	47%	$ 62,914	
2	**Weber (R)**					
	1990	62%	$240,653	39%	$ 213,403	$ 97,400
	1988	57%	$232,704	32%	$ 270,539	
	1986	52%	$283,203	30%	$ 165,888	
	1984	63%	$136,085	30%	$ 134,260	
3	**Ramstad (R)**					
	1990	67%	$237,745	25%	$ 753	n/a

HOUSE OF REPRESENTATIVES

Dist. No.	Name	Election %	PAC Receipts	PAC %	Leftover Cash	Conflict of Interest Receipts (1985–1990)
MINNESOTA (continued)						
4	**Vento (D)**					
	1990	65%	$187,095	72%	$ 155,180	$ 105,204
	1988	72%	$189,759	71%	$ 162,421	
	1986	73%	$145,790	67%	$ 110,355	
	1984	74%	$113,071	64%	$ 89,049	
5	**Sabo (D)**					
	1990	73%	$226,950	64%	$ 216,221	$ 64,100
	1988	72%	$237,550	65%	$ 182,181	
	1986	73%	$ 86,681	36%	$ 99,669	
	1984	70%	$ 89,187	53%	$ 69,944	
6	**Sikorski (D)**					
	1990	65%	$335,487	76%	$ 306,294	$ 261,400
	1988	65%	$358,582	66%	$ 239,181	
	1986	66%	$310,155	61%	$ 16,421	
	1984	60%	$388,827	57%	$ 1,812	
7	**Peterson (D)**					
	1990	54%	$185,598	70%	$ 9,233	n/a
8	**Oberstar (D)**					
	1990	73%	$248,780	68%	$ 393,551	$ 120,809
	1988	75%	$206,320	73%	$ 258,235	
	1986	73%	$211,247	72%	$ 134,706	
	1984	67%	$208,215	80%	$ 1,451	
MISSISSIPPI						
1	**Whitten (D)**					
	1990	65%	$129,450	71%	$ 435,724	$ 120,050
	1988	78%	$135,400	77%	$ 348,365	
	1986	66%	$187,770	74%	$ 230,809	
	1984	88%	$115,050	83%	$ 147,823	
2	**Espy (D)**					
	1990	84%	$219,225	49%	$ 85,459	$ 106,070
	1988	65%	$480,490	55%	$ 3,060	
	1986	52%	$307,865	51%	$ 9,373	

HOUSE OF REPRESENTATIVES

Dist. No.	Name	Election %	PAC Receipts	PAC %	Leftover Cash	Conflict of Interest Receipts (1985–1990)
MISSISSIPPI (continued)						
3	**Montgomery (D)**					
	1990	100%	$ 55,250	49%	$ 171,908	$ 34,825
	1988	89%	$ 71,650	48%	$ 130,311	
	1986	100%	$ 31,799	63%	$ 98,995	
	1984	100%	$ 37,700	45%	$ 118,867	
4	**Parker (D)**					
	1990	81%	$286,473	54%	$ 48,162	$ 36,069
	1988	55%	$234,164	28%	$ 1,398	
5	**Taylor (D)**					
	1990	81%	$143,426	45%	$ 2,874	n/a
	*1989	65%	$104,160	31%	$ 8,873	
MISSOURI						
1	**Clay (D)**					
	1990	61%	$182,550	85%	$ 119,666	$ 344,275
	1988	72%	$141,830	69%	$ 102,620	
	1986	66%	$141,457	69%	$ 58,734	
	1984	68%	$140,925	79%	$ 45,417	
2	**Horn (D)**					
	1990	50%	$160,515	45%	$ 16,376	n/a
3	**Gephardt (D)**					
	1990	57%	$762,687	46%	$ 193,485	$ 740,453
	1988	63%	$183,196	36%	$ 1,866	
	1986	69%	$420,827	51%	$ 178	
	1984	100%	$241,885	56%	$ 50,824	
4	**Skelton (D)**					
	1990	62%	$242,050	62%	$ 311,648	$ 90,050
	1988	72%	$195,725	62%	$ 228,021	
	1986	100%	$150,050	50%	$ 187,017	
	1984	67%	$150,770	55%	$ 70,973	
5	**Wheat (D)**					
	1990	62%	$224,435	72%	$ 263,939	n/a
	1988	70%	$205,500	68%	$ 198,865	
	1986	71%	$188,627	70%	$ 136,934	
	1984	66%	$284,989	61%	$ 61,761	

HOUSE OF REPRESENTATIVES

Dist. No.	Name	Election %	PAC Receipts	PAC %	Leftover Cash	Conflict of Interest Receipts (1985–1990)
MISSOURI (continued)						
6	**Coleman (R)**					
	1990	52%	$184,870	66%	$ 33,407	$ 117,050
	1988	59%	$175,134	57%	$ 67,494	
	1986	57%	$126,269	52%	$ 102,879	
	1984	65%	$109,009	53%	$ 112,186	
7	**Hancock (R)**					
	1990	52%	$122,782	44%	$ 129,033	$ 18,600
	1988	53%	$ 79,913	21%	$ 35,308	
8	**Emerson (R)**					
	1990	57%	$326,541	52%	$ 7,761	$ 324,940
	1988	58%	$421,852	50%	$ 87,454	
	1986	53%	$298,571	50%	$ 5,548	
	1984	65%	$204,078	42%	$ 9,726	
9	**Volkmer (D)**					
	1990	58%	$218,715	71%	$ 159,821	$ 141,575
	1988	68%	$218,185	73%	$ 89,968	
	1986	57%	$249,736	67%	$ 462	
	1984	53%	$180,738	56%	$ 10,131	
MONTANA						
1	**Williams (D)**					
	1990	61%	$296,640	65%	$ 214,350	$ 383,988
	1988	61%	$185,656	47%	$ 104,412	
	1986	62%	$168,055	61%	$ 74,863	
	1984	66%	$ 91,357	59%	$ 26,425	
2	**Marlenee (R)**					
	1990	64%	$140,750	47%	$ 76,486	$ 164,025
	1988	56%	$171,992	41%	$ 86,742	
	1986	53%	$110,725	42%	$ 51,639	
	1984	66%	$138,022	39%	$ 36,902	
NEBRASKA						
1	**Bereuter (R)**					
	1990	65%	$147,250	58%	$ 54,730	$ 103,045
	1988	67%	$ 99,120	46%	$ 24,008	
	1986	64%	$101,757	51%	$ 24,091	
	1984	74%	$ 74,978	43%	$ 51,534	

HOUSE OF REPRESENTATIVES

Dist. No.	Name	Election %	PAC Receipts	PAC %	Leftover Cash	Conflict of Interest Receipts (1985–1990)
NEBRASKA (continued)						
2	**Hoagland (D)**					
	1990	58%	$615,587	66%	$ 11,720	$ 101,650
	1988	50%	$325,900	38%	$ 2,045	
3	**Barrett (R)**					
	1990	51%	$193,583	30%	$ 19,982	$ 53,250
NEVADA						
1	**Bilbray (D)**					
	1990	61%	$218,056	32%	$ 1,107	$ 35,900
	1988	64%	$300,116	45%	$ 20,136	
	1986	54%	$166,825	43%	$ 3,324	
2	**Vucanovich (R)**					
	1990	59%	$166,275	37%	$ 5,705	$ 61,650
	1988	57%	$201,719	33%	$ 1,315	
	1986	58%	$126,534	39%	$ 8,158	
	1984	71%	$162,018	38%	$ 62,809	
NEW HAMPSHIRE						
1	**Zeliff (R)**					
	1990	55%	$130,601	16%	$ 4,826	n/a
2	**Swett (D)**					
	1990	53%	$186,000	40%	$ 5,090	n/a
NEW JERSEY						
1	**Andrews (D)**					
	1990	54%	$236,190	44%	$ 574	n/a
2	**Hughes (D)**					
	1990	88%	$ 91,270	32%	$ 208,172	$ 10,526
	1988	66%	$112,150	40%	$ 137,215	
	1986	68%	$ 98,915	40%	$ 89,313	
	1984	63%	$ 93,452	44%	$ 83,749	
3	**Pallone (D)**					
	1990	49%	$394,464	62%	$ 761	$ 18,100
	1988	52%	$437,739	64%	$ 2,423	

HOUSE OF REPRESENTATIVES

Dist. No.	Name	Election %	PAC Receipts	PAC %	Leftover Cash	Conflict of Interest Receipts (1985–1990)
NEW JERSEY (continued)						
4	**Smith (R)**					
	1990	63%	$113,126	40%	$ 65,394	$ 22,250
	1988	66%	$124,781	38%	$ 77,641	
	1986	61%	$ 98,850	30%	$ 628	
	1984	61%	$137,871	45%	$ 14,140	
5	**Roukema (R)**					
	1990	76%	$219,068	49%	$ 98,290	$ 203,379
	1988	76%	$181,513	45%	$ 95,251	
	1986	75%	$156,837	44%	$ 89,326	
	1984	71%	$110,824	37%	$ 36,332	
6	**Dwyer (D)**					
	1990	51%	$125,747	86%	$ 70,432	n/a
	1988	61%	$113,000	83%	$ 71,449	
	1986	69%	$106,325	74%	$ 58,750	
	1984	56%	$ 88,941	69%	$ 29,381	
7	**Rinaldo (R)**					
	1990	75%	$240,920	38%	$ 967,326	$ 267,950
	1988	75%	$271,527	45%	$ 746,181	
	1986	79%	$230,823	37%	$ 508,842	
	1984	74%	$219,572	36%	$ 265,467	
8	**Roe (D)**					
	1990	77%	$329,910	51%	$ 577,940	$ 189,557
	1988	100%	$273,100	56%	$ 484,615	
	1986	63%	$204,483	56%	$ 261,339	
	1984	63%	$160,278	60%	$ 105,303	
9	**Torricelli (D)**					
	1990	57%	$236,389	29%	$ 846,461	$ 46,215
	1988	67%	$177,488	28%	$ 522,762	
	1986	69%	$170,048	29%	$ 256,355	
	1984	63%	$226,820	38%	$ 85,448	
10	**Payne (D)**					
	1990	81%	$185,642	66%	$ 251,949	$ 95,350
	1988	77%	$205,177	38%	$ 132,152	

HOUSE OF REPRESENTATIVES

Dist. No.	Name	Election %	PAC Receipts	PAC %	Leftover Cash	Conflict of Interest Receipts (1985–1990)
NEW JERSEY (continued)						
11	**Gallo (R)**					
	1990	65%	$189,245	29%	$ 71,891	$ 33,290
	1988	70%	$151,245	28%	$ 114,241	
	1986	68%	$178,936	25%	$ 73,445	
	1984	56%	$203,363	27%	$ 20,231	
12	**Zimmer (R)**					
	1990	64%	$204,983	17%	$ 3,115	n/a
13	**Saxton (R)**					
	1990	58%	$250,149	40%	$ 48,861	$ 101,475
	1988	69%	$195,430	40%	$ 151,707	
	1986	65%	$154,238	39%	$ 72,292	
	1984	61%	$145,026	28%	$ 2,514	
14	**Guarini (D)**					
	1990	66%	$299,833	65%	$ 344,190	$ 832,590
	1988	67%	$213,835	39%	$ 182,701	
	1986	71%	$293,078	78%	$ 0	
	1984	66%	$237,282	61%	$ 14,545	
NEW MEXICO						
1	**Schiff (R)**					
	1990	70%	$223,203	40%	$ 20,540	$ 5,050
	1988	51%	$158,911	28%	$ 4,292	
2	**Skeen (R)**					
	1990	100%	$109,210	55%	$ 196,902	$ 60,171
	1988	100%	$ 87,050	60%	$ 79,810	
	1986	63%	$119,602	42%	$ 3,593	
	1984	74%	$ 95,326	30%	$ 9,804	
3	**Richardson (D)**					
	1990	74%	$346,707	65%	$ 329,903	$ 367,931
	1988	73%	$297,898	65%	$ 219,713	
	1986	71%	$244,188	66%	$ 30,556	
	1984	61%	$258,235	59%	$ 15,075	

HOUSE OF REPRESENTATIVES

Dist. No.	Name	Election %	PAC Receipts	PAC %	Leftover Cash	Conflict of Interest Receipts (1985–1990)
NEW YORK						
1	**Hochbrueckner (D)**					
	1990	56%	$398,062	61%	$ 15,836	$ 60,950
	1988	51%	$417,961	57%	$ 2,835	
	1986	51%	$245,054	59%	$ 467	
2	**Downey (D)**					
	1990	56%	$330,762	54%	$ 486,556	$ 879,347
	1988	62%	$333,761	42%	$ 509,072	
	1986	64%	$251,005	30%	$ 239,970	
	1984	55%	$175,457	32%	$ 155,758	
3	**Mrazek (D)**					
	1990	53%	$193,185	32%	$ 351,185	n/a
	1988	57%	$176,931	40%	$ 207,331	
	1986	56%	$239,608	33%	$ 123,517	
	1984	51%	$304,676	41%	$ 43,315	
4	**Lent (R)**					
	1990	61%	$406,820	68%	$ 687,015	$ 471,710
	1988	70%	$358,299	61%	$ 489,416	
	1986	65%	$274,092	56%	$ 336,403	
	1984	69%	$166,199	44%	$ 181,101	
5	**McGrath (R)**					
	1990	55%	$225,358	42%	$ 245,216	$ 838,154
	1988	65%	$251,324	50%	$ 326,731	
	1986	65%	$242,669	55%	$ 162,017	
	1984	62%	$ 79,787	33%	$ 17,092	
6	**Flake (D)**					
	1990	73%	$122,440	51%	$ 48,396	$ 72,297
	1988	86%	$150,681	44%	$ 16,034	
	1986	68%	$ 23,350	6%	$ 41,879	
7	**Ackerman (D)**					
	1990	100%	$186,537	61%	$ 285,362	$ 30,150
	1988	100%	$196,120	70%	$ 252,498	
	1986	77%	$ 87,417	48%	$ 114,070	
	1984	69%	$ 76,585	41%	$ 49,796	

HOUSE OF REPRESENTATIVES

Dist. No.	Name	Election %	PAC Receipts	PAC %	Leftover Cash	Conflict of Interest Receipts (1985–1990)
NEW YORK (continued)						
8	**Scheuer (D)**					
	1990	72%	$ 94,800	24%	$ 7,002	$ 87,150
	1988	100%	$ 55,600	71%	$ 1,459	
	1986	90%	$ 45,300	56%	$ 22,526	
	1984	63%	$ 28,641	43%	$ 5,387	
9	**Manton (D)**					
	1990	64%	$452,323	73%	$ 478,772	$ 257,719
	1988	100%	$263,545	62%	$ 174,474	
	1986	69%	$246,776	59%	$ 6,924	
	1984	53%	$137,988	52%	$ 3,740	
10	**Schumer (D)**					
	1990	80%	$163,612	20%	$1,580,475	$ 77,175
	1988	78%	$137,325	31%	$ 854,385	
	1986	93%	$ 52,025	32%	$ 503,941	
	1984	72%	$ 56,595	35%	$ 436,752	
11	**Towns (D)**					
	1990	93%	$186,250	55%	$ 151,035	$ 78,450
	1988	89%	$129,291	39%	$ 88,047	
	1986	89%	$116,618	52%	$ 39,036	
	1984	85%	$100,371	48%	$ 396	
12	**Owens (D)**					
	1990	95%	$111,525	69%	$ 6,451	$ 235,917
	1988	93%	$125,085	81%	$ 9,107	
	1986	92%	$ 92,500	55%	$ 1,053	
	1984	91%	$ 85,742	48%	$ 50	
13	**Solarz (D)**					
	1990	80%	$ 57,674	4%	$1,859,603	$ 35,906
	1988	75%	$ 60,605	7%	$1,158,484	
	1986	82%	$ 40,370	7%	$ 812,706	
	1984	66%	$ 24,542	13%	$ 621,978	
14	**Molinari (R)**					
	*1990	60%	$ 71,788	46%	$ 16,012	n/a

* Molinari stood for both a special and general election in 1990.

HOUSE OF REPRESENTATIVES

Dist. No.	Name	Election %	PAC Receipts	PAC %	Leftover Cash	Conflict of Interest Receipts (1985–1990)
NEW YORK (continued)						
15	**Green (R)**					
	1990	59%	$162,996	23%	$ 310,107	n/a
	1988	61%	$154,233	24%	$ 63,211	
	1986	58%	$127,630	18%	$ 9,863	
	1984	56%	$170,333	15%	$ 23,043	
16	**Rangel (D)**					
	1990	97%	$353,900	65%	$ 304,007	$1,008,456
	1988	97%	$358,875	62%	$ 363,796	
	1986	96%	$305,749	64%	$ 259,760	
	1984	97%	$196,398	68%	$ 154,186	
17	**Weiss (D)**					
	1990	80%	$ 72,800	50%	$ 80,492	$ 1,050
	1988	84%	$ 64,890	38%	$ 48,308	
	1986	86%	$ 95,927	35%	$ 46,952	
	1984	82%	$ 40,002	29%	$ 9,879	
18	**Serrano (D)**					
	*1990	93%	$ 74,550	67%	$ 16,391	n/a
19	**Engel (D)**					
	1990	61%	$324,173	81%	$ 11,899	$ 68,900
	1988	56%	$ 99,600	53%	$ 1,935	
20	**Lowey (D)**					
	1990	63%	$448,797	37%	$ 339,552	$ 201,935
	1988	50%	$164,175	12%	$ 28,273	
21	**Fish (R)**					
	1990	71%	$204,990	59%	$ 134,830	$ 8,950
	1988	75%	$196,388	55%	$ 168,252	
	1986	77%	$140,224	57%	$ 88,093	
	1984	78%	$ 95,527	45%	$ 58,892	
22	**Gilman (R)**					
	1990	69%	$195,968	44%	$ 68,257	$ 26,975
	1988	71%	$166,797	39%	$ 120,143	
	1986	70%	$129,771	38%	$ 103,292	
	1984	69%	$100,609	29%	$ 63,238	

* Serrano stood for both a special and a general election in 1990.

HOUSE OF REPRESENTATIVES

Dist. No.	Name	Election %	PAC Receipts	PAC %	Leftover Cash	Conflict of Interest Receipts (1985–1990)
NEW YORK (continued)						
23	**McNulty (D)**					
	1990	64%	$149,179	62%	$ 100,394	$ 15,700
	1988	62%	$141,975	45%	$ 8,866	
24	**Solomon (R)**					
	1990	67%	$147,715	58%	$ 111,840	$ 0
	1988	72%	$ 79,150	38%	$ 97,676	
	1986	70%	$ 63,780	39%	$ 54,018	
	1984	73%	$ 73,154	44%	$ 45,428	
25	**Boehlert (R)**					
	1990	84%	$130,950	43%	$ 189,652	$ 23,800
	1988	100%	$ 90,173	38%	$ 158,439	
	1986	69%	$ 98,113	33%	$ 68,810	
	1984	73%	$ 72,635	40%	$ 43,585	
26	**Martin (R)**					
	1990	100%	$ 52,050	70%	$ 84,339	$ 38,200
	1988	75%	$ 84,316	63%	$ 68,561	
	1986	100%	$ 73,656	60%	$ 55,729	
	1984	71%	$ 68,250	55%	$ 8,283	
27	**Walsh (R)**					
	1990	63%	$140,186	38%	$ 40,952	$ 27,700
	1988	57%	$202,620	33%	$ 15,970	
28	**McHugh (D)**					
	1990	65%	$121,815	53%	$ 137,521	$ 26,930
	1988	93%	$129,633	47%	$ 109,852	
	1986	68%	$ 85,414	31%	$ 6,161	
	1984	57%	$134,221	34%	$ 14,007	
29	**Horton (R)**					
	1990	63%	$160,040	77%	$ 162,845	n/a
	1988	69%	$126,560	77%	$ 142,721	
	1986	71%	$101,850	76%	$ 109,567	
	1984	70%	$ 73,726	65%	$ 71,072	
30	**Slaughter (D)**					
	1990	59%	$282,817	63%	$ 129,299	$ 7,931
	1988	57%	$444,422	50%	$ 4,851	
	1986	51%	$292,984	50%	$ 28,792	

HOUSE OF REPRESENTATIVES

Dist. No.	Name	Election %	PAC Receipts	PAC %	Leftover Cash	Conflict of Interest Receipts (1985–1990)
NEW YORK (continued)						
31	**Paxon (R)**					
	1990	57%	$239,020	35%	$ 180,313	$ 73,117
	1988	53%	$242,558	35%	$ 95	
32	**LaFalce (D)**					
	1990	55%	$196,675	58%	$ 645,138	$ 192,698
	1988	73%	$141,022	58%	$ 450,300	
	1986	91%	$ 79,112	52%	$ 342,253	
	1984	69%	$ 72,268	41%	$ 298,710	
33	**Nowak (D)**					
	1990	78%	$ 98,908	66%	$ 238,450	$ 47,540
	1988	100%	$ 91,225	75%	$ 181,018	
	1986	85%	$ 34,050	31%	$ 152,256	
	1984	78%	$ 73,668	53%	$ 118,885	
34	**Houghton (R)**					
	1990	70%	$102,000	31%	$ 306,780	n/a
	1988	96%	$129,950	26%	$ 151,219	
	1986	60%	$149,388	21%	$ 1,989	
NORTH CAROLINA						
1	**Jones (D)**					
	1990	65%	$ 72,100	56%	$ 328,428	$ 72,700
	1988	65%	$ 96,550	68%	$ 312,342	
	1986	70%	$134,650	68%	$ 253,016	
	1984	67%	$127,964	66%	$ 143,372	
2	**Valentine (D)**					
	1990	75%	$159,202	61%	$ 20,314	$ 37,400
	1988	100%	$ 58,650	75%	$ 44,954	
	1986	75%	$109,755	62%	$ 51,098	
	1984	68%	$166,236	43%	$ 37,463	
3	**Lancaster (D)**					
	1990	59%	$204,450	49%	$ 20,581	$ 103,680
	1988	100%	$132,249	67%	$ 98,735	
	1986	64%	$140,004	32%	$ 1,702	

HOUSE OF REPRESENTATIVES

Dist. No.	Name	Election %	PAC Receipts	PAC %	Leftover Cash	Conflict of Interest Receipts (1985–1990)
NORTH CAROLINA (continued)						
4	**Price (D)**					
	1990	58%	$385,210	50%	$ 11,899	$ 203,600
	1988	58%	$489,658	47%	$ 33,568	
	1986	56%	$234,118	27%	$ 9,207	
5	**Neal (D)**					
	1990	59%	$398,879	59%	$ 27,665	$ 377,100
	1988	53%	$411,180	57%	$ 3,113	
	1986	54%	$294,413	60%	$ 43,650	
	1984	51%	$178,956	60%	$ 44,182	
6	**Coble (R)**					
	1990	67%	$223,860	39%	$ 15,846	$ 17,050
	1988	62%	$282,524	38%	$ 16,650	
	1986	50%	$253,161	43%	$ 18,486	
	1984	51%	$114,899	30%	$ 13,434	
7	**Rose (D)**					
	1990	66%	$196,654	60%	$ 540,833	$ 206,646
	1988	67%	$177,500	61%	$ 365,916	
	1986	64%	$211,845	52%	$ 257,769	
	1984	59%	$154,571	51%	$ 156,616	
8	**Hefner (D)**					
	1990	55%	$445,293	67%	$ 111,471	$ 165,800
	1988	51%	$272,625	63%	$ 107,543	
	1986	58%	$224,892	63%	$ 256,999	
	1984	51%	$189,668	60%	$ 58,238	
9	**McMillan (R)**					
	1990	62%	$278,085	70%	$ 103,331	$ 243,493
	1988	66%	$214,455	42%	$ 89,508	
	1986	51%	$319,809	36%	$ 20,068	
	1984	50%	$192,337	28%	$ 10,421	
10	**Ballenger (R)**					
	1990	62%	$183,749	62%	$ 21,544	$ 50,230
	1988	61%	$153,375	47%	$ 26,135	
	1986	57%	$116,416	25%	$ 5,447	
11	**Taylor (R)**					
	1990	51%	$111,689	21%	$ 543	n/a

HOUSE OF REPRESENTATIVES

Dist. No.	Name	Election %	PAC Receipts	PAC %	Leftover Cash	Conflict of Interest Receipts (1985–1990)
NORTH DAKOTA						
AT LARGE	**Dorgan (D)**					
	1990	65%	$449,050	75%	$ 237,008	$1,161,052
	1988	71%	$462,346	67%	$ 143,210	
	1986	76%	$314,486	69%	$ 203,570	
	1984	79%	$216,865	59%	$ 136,946	
OHIO						
1	**Luken (D)**					
	1990	51%	$369,725	54%	$ 29,243	n/a
2	**Gradison, Jr. (D)**					
	1990	64%	$ 0	0%	$ 442,751	$ 0
	1988	72%	$ 0	0%	$ 364,822	
	1986	71%	$ 0	0%	$ 292,762	
	1984	69%	$ 438	.2%	$ 163,379	
3	**Hall (D)**					
	1990	100%	$130,592	75%	$ 312,635	n/a
	1988	76%	$140,160	65%	$ 272,692	
	1986	74%	$119,510	66%	$ 239,470	
	1984	100%	$ 83,331	62%	$ 134,380	
4	**Oxley (R)**					
	1990	62%	$200,333	67%	$ 188,791	$ 255,980
	1988	100%	$170,850	68%	$ 220,485	
	1986	75%	$155,352	72%	$ 176,024	
	1984	78%	$144,455	62%	$ 145,126	
5	**Gillmor (R)**					
	1990	68%	$230,425	71%	$ 83,139	$ 58,325
	1988	61%	$319,120	38%	$ 12,984	
6	**McEwen (R)**					
	1990	71%	$144,630	49%	$ 118,666	$ 74,150
	1988	74%	$147,066	19%	$ 22,951	
	1986	70%	$147,897	41%	$ 120,602	
	1984	74%	$ 72,976	58%	$ 8,414	
7	**Hobson (R)**					
	1990	62%	$202,427	52%	$ 602	n/a
8	**Boehner (R)**					
	1990	61%	$219,526	30%	$ 4,674	n/a

HOUSE OF REPRESENTATIVES

Dist. No.	Name	Election %	PAC Receipts	PAC %	Leftover Cash	Conflict of Interest Receipts (1985–1990)
OHIO (continued)						
9 Kaptur (D)						
	1990	78%	$114,830	50%	$ 58,129	$ 49,600
	1988	81%	$201,740	73%	$ 35,833	
	1986	78%	$185,706	65%	$ 2,139	
	1984	55%	$191,106	53%	$ 35,949	
10 Miller (R)						
	1990	63%	$ 71,250	72%	$ 126,334	$ 44,550
	1988	72%	$ 99,436	77%	$ 102,113	
	1986	70%	$ 69,349	81%	$ 71,615	
	1984	73%	$ 69,080	74%	$ 52,790	
11 Eckart (D)						
	1990	66%	$371,536	73%	$ 159,440	$ 395,640
	1988	61%	$382,928	67%	$ 102,623	
	1986	72%	$221,653	55%	$ 94,056	
	1984	67%	$150,053	53%	$ 39,477	
12 Kasich (R)						
	1990	72%	$128,715	39%	$ 93,542	$ 33,700
	1988	79%	$130,686	35%	$ 43,897	
	1986	73%	$129,817	37%	$ 24,835	
	1984	70%	$201,179	40%	$ 101,513	
13 Pease (D)						
	1990	57%	$184,728	59%	$ 211,677	$ 597,352
	1988	69%	$189,677	65%	$ 257,811	
	1986	63%	$252,800	58%	$ 118,167	
	1984	66%	$ 81,018	52%	$ 95,378	
14 Sawyer (D)						
	1990	60%	$187,195	71%	$ 48,321	$ 259,600
	1988	75%	$314,754	70%	$ 50,303	
	1986	54%	$233,445	47%	$ 21,890	
15 Wylie (R)						
	1990	59%	$167,153	73%	$ 18,194	$ 182,578
	1988	75%	$158,415	69%	$ 32,910	
	1986	64%	$185,352	61%	$ 13,813	
	1984	72%	$120,503	59%	$ 46,289	

HOUSE OF REPRESENTATIVES

Dist. No.	Name	Election %	PAC Receipts	PAC %	Leftover Cash	Conflict of Interest Receipts (1985–1990)
OHIO (continued)						
16	**Regula (R)**					
	1990	59%	$ 0	0%	$ 52,654	n/a
	1988	79%	$ 0	0%	$ 98,528	
	1986	76%	$ 0	0%	$ 84,348	
	1984	72%	$ 888	.7%	$ 59,496	
17	**Traficant (D)**					
	1990	78%	$ 54,930	55%	$ 76,169	$ 6,320
	1988	77%	$ 54,500	54%	$ 55,682	
	1986	72%	$ 76,780	55%	$ 51,577	
	1984	53%	$ 19,400	19%	$ 3,155	
18	**Applegate (D)**					
	1990	74%	$ 78,205	62%	$ 161,523	$ 19,330
	1988	77%	$ 66,751	55%	$ 130,506	
	1986	100%	$ 57,825	55%	$ 96,185	
	1984	76%	$ 48,528	54%	$ 75,025	
19	**Feighan (D)**					
	1990	65%	$217,618	67%	$ 290,445	$ 67,303
	1988	71%	$205,414	53%	$ 196,227	
	1986	55%	$345,029	52%	$ 33,115	
	1984	55%	$255,854	48%	$ 3,467	
20	**Oakar (D)**					
	1990	73%	$283,859	84%	$ 57,025	$ 171,990
	1988	83%	$392,918	57%	$ 3,640	
	1986	85%	$231,759	57%	$ 95,567	
	1984	100%	$118,489	79%	$ 64,714	
21	**Stokes (D)**					
	1990	80%	$137,575	55%	$ 241,864	n/a
	1988	86%	$147,800	61%	$ 190,827	
	1986	82%	$103,440	48%	$ 122,718	
	1984	82%	$ 60,518	46%	$ 61,327	
OKLAHOMA						
1	**Inhofe (R)**					
	1990	56%	$306,071	50%	$ 1,120	$ 90,650
	1988	53%	$263,222	55%	$ 3,452	
	1986	55%	$142,731	34%	$ 5,486	

HOUSE OF REPRESENTATIVES

Dist. No.	Name	Election %	PAC Receipts	PAC %	Leftover Cash	Conflict of Interest Receipts (1985–1990)
OKLAHOMA (continued)						
2	**Synar (D)**					
	1990	61%	$ 0	0%	$ 24,882	$ 0
	1988	64%	$ 0	0%	$ 34,269	
	1986	73%	$ 0	0%	$ 82,108	
	1984	74%	$ 22,162	7%	$ 80,409	
3	**Brewster (D)**					
	1990	80%	$179,466	40%	$ 2,055	n/a
4	**McCurdy (D)**					
	1990	74%	$149,775	44%	$ 81,622	$ 147,150
	1988	100%	$142,272	52%	$ 96,779	
	1986	76%	$130,725	53%	$ 75,721	
	1984	64%	$ 99,600	39%	$ 3,660	
5	**Edwards (R)**					
	1990	70%	$147,525	45%	$ 13,371	n/a
	1988	72%	$122,430	34%	$ 60,504	
	1986	71%	$ 87,195	29%	$ 39,285	
	1984	76%	$ 60,680	21%	$ 27,137	
6	**English (D)**					
	1990	80%	$146,050	61%	$ 324,042	$ 127,380
	1988	73%	$183,408	48%	$ 243,316	
	1986	100%	$132,558	53%	$ 164,549	
	1984	59%	$103,650	53%	$ 66,090	
OREGON						
1	**AuCoin (D)**					
	1990	63%	$308,748	52%	$ 361,578	$ 96,650
	1988	70%	$340,550	47%	$ 207,624	
	1986	62%	$438,377	46%	$ 25,698	
	1984	53%	$399,733	47%	$ 14,441	
2	**Smith (R)**					
	1990	68%	$148,953	40%	$ 179,736	$ 114,175
	1988	63%	$153,366	40%	$ 90,322	
	1986	60%	$120,154	36%	$ 49,601	
	1984	57%	$137,460	30%	$ 38,836	

HOUSE OF REPRESENTATIVES

Dist. No.	Name	Election %	PAC Receipts	PAC %	Leftover Cash	Conflict of Interest Receipts (1985–1990)
OREGON (continued)						
3 Wyden (D)						
	1990	81%	$341,242	48%	$ 451,751	$ 285,364
	1988	99%	$316,772	53%	$ 437,007	
	1986	86%	$152,004	56%	$ 128,785	
	1984	72%	$170,449	50%	$ 102,124	
4 DeFazio (D)						
	1990	86%	$172,635	67%	$ 95,794	$ 32,827
	1988	72%	$235,589	71%	$ 55,774	
	1986	54%	$179,857	59%	$ 7,945	
5 Kopetski (D)						
	1990	55%	$399,283	47%	$ 9,449	n/a
PENNSYLVANIA						
1 Foglietta (D)						
	1990	79%	$226,918	49%	$ 366,322	$ 33,700
	1988	76%	$172,700	51%	$ 135,520	
	1986	75%	$204,445	48%	$ 36,332	
	1984	75%	$206,156	45%	$ 34,819	
2 Blackwell (D)						
	*1991	39%	$ 25,100	32%	$ 8,460	n/a
3 Borski (D)						
	1990	60%	$152,800	47%	$ 155,234	$ 40,815
	1988	63%	$189,654	56%	$ 107,024	
	1986	62%	$269,014	66%	$ 19,781	
	1984	64%	$187,896	62%	$ 1,959	
4 Kolter (D)						
	1990	56%	$162,520	81%	$ 215,765	$ 31,967
	1988	70%	$146,606	83%	$ 149,083	
	1986	60%	$215,132	77%	$ 63,815	
	1984	57%	$146,632	70%	$ 37,619	
5 Schulze (R)						
	1990	57%	$370,759	64%	$ 182,353	$ 814,104
	1988	78%	$258,420	60%	$ 282,895	
	1986	66%	$205,038	55%	$ 291,355	
	1984	73%	$167,399	52%	$ 235,038	

HOUSE OF REPRESENTATIVES

Dist. No.	Name	Election %	PAC Receipts	PAC %	Leftover Cash	Conflict of Interest Receipts (1985–1990)
PENNSYLVANIA (continued)						
6	**Yatron (D)**					
	1990	57%	$127,955	63%	$ 157,501	$ 25,500
	1988	63%	$109,700	75%	$ 135,923	
	1986	69%	$ 83,380	65%	$ 111,244	
	1984	100%	$ 57,650	52%	$ 79,962	
7	**Weldon (R)**					
	1990	65%	$207,805	41%	$ 135,364	$ 52,950
	1988	68%	$215,617	38%	$ 110,936	
	1986	61%	$172,576	27%	$ 54,187	
8	**Kostmayer (D)**					
	1990	57%	$295,528	34%	$ 10,140	$ 114,415
	1988	57%	$418,821	36%	$ 77,225	
	1986	55%	$339,213	49%	$ 18,151	
	1984	51%	$254,364	47%	$ 5,508	
9	**Shuster (R)**					
	1990	100%	$181,469	43%	$ 102,101	$ 157,620
	1988	100%	$153,665	38%	$ 114,385	
	1986	100%	$152,002	51%	$ 44,821	
	1984	67%	$183,284	41%	$ 21,374	
10	**McDade (R)**					
	1990	100%	$236,778	62%	$ 335,857	$ 202,250
	1988	73%	$271,620	61%	$ 326,216	
	1986	75%	$203,665	52%	$ 313,730	
	1984	77%	$150,365	56%	$ 211,347	
11	**Kanjorski (D)**					
	1990	100%	$224,185	73%	$ 94,480	$ 202,599
	1988	100%	$286,370	53%	$ 191,767	
	1986	71%	$417,690	54%	$ 72,470	
	1984	59%	$103,173	32%	$ 8,072	
12	**Murtha (D)**					
	1990	62%	$496,920	57%	$ 33,122	$ 251,000
	1988	100%	$310,815	70%	$ 251,340	
	1986	67%	$244,705	66%	$ 206,198	
	1984	69%	$176,568	64%	$ 107,328	

HOUSE OF REPRESENTATIVES

Dist. No.	Name	Election %	PAC Receipts	PAC %	Leftover Cash	Conflict of Interest Receipts (1985–1990)
PENNSYLVANIA (continued)						
13	**Coughlin (R)**					
	1990	60%	$163,969	44%	$ 356,517	n/a
	1988	67%	$150,851	38%	$ 219,081	
	1986	59%	$226,446	32%	$ 48,228	
	1984	56%	$158,877	33%	$ 45,803	
14	**Coyne (D)**					
	1990	72%	$141,600	90%	$ 229,457	$ 365,483
	1988	79%	$156,075	93%	$ 191,524	
	1986	90%	$101,100	92%	$ 103,535	
	1984	77%	$ 49,500	69%	$ 53,997	
15	**Ritter (R)**					
	1990	61%	$275,106	49%	$ 25,821	$ 297,840
	1988	57%	$293,454	39%	$ 42,883	
	1986	57%	$153,178	35%	$ 35,501	
	1984	58%	$266,299	46%	$ 13,141	
16	**Walker (R)**					
	1990	66%	$ 43,810	45%	$ 35,408	$ 7,150
	1988	74%	$ 44,375	42%	$ 36,953	
	1986	75%	$ 31,297	39%	$ 22,586	
	1984	78%	$ 32,503	47%	$ 18,618	
17	**Gekas (R)**					
	1990	100%	$ 53,410	42%	$ 141,544	$ 600
	1988	100%	$ 46,750	49%	$ 106,439	
	1986	74%	$ 50,014	34%	$ 108,171	
	1984	73%	$ 61,850	36%	$ 50,049	
18	**Santorum (R)**					
	1990	51%	$ 27,660	11%	$ 6,289	n/a
19	**Goodling (R)**					
	1990	100%	$ 0	0%	$ 6,251	$ 0
	1988	77%	$ 0	0%	$ 5,938	
	1986	73%	$ 0	0%	$ 9,007	
	1984	76%	$ 0	0%	$ 6,174	

HOUSE OF REPRESENTATIVES

Dist. No.	Name	Election %	PAC Receipts	PAC %	Leftover Cash	Conflict of Interest Receipts (1985–1990)
PENNSYLVANIA (continued)						
20	**Gaydos (D)**					
	1990	66%	$158,250	83%	$ 123,222	$ 204,275
	1988	98%	$143,850	78%	$ 90,358	
	1986	99%	$109,175	69%	$ 42,798	
	1984	76%	$ 86,775	65%	$ 2,962	
21	**Ridge (R)**					
	1990	100%	$246,265	54%	$ 226,719	$ 227,125
	1988	79%	$211,711	50%	$ 134,081	
	1986	81%	$138,235	46%	$ 84,931	
	1984	65%	$237,712	51%	$ 54,183	
22	**Murphy (D)**					
	1990	63%	$139,310	70%	$ 111,254	$ 169,015
	1988	72%	$128,218	74%	$ 103,193	
	1986	100%	$ 98,586	74%	$ 103,364	
	1984	79%	$ 78,664	64%	$ 86,200	
23	**Clinger (R)**					
	1990	59%	$190,302	55%	$ 84,577	$ 129,568
	1988	62%	$189,036	47%	$ 73,800	
	1986	55%	$287,361	41%	$ 58,080	
	1984	52%	$145,895	47%	$ 1,703	
RHODE ISLAND						
1	**Machtley (R)**					
	1990	55%	$333,189	39%	$ 10,355	$ 37,450
	1988	55%	$ 81,524	20%	$ 32,046	
2	**Reed (D)**					
	1990	59%	$302,216	33%	$ 6,152	n/a
SOUTH CAROLINA						
1	**Ravenel (R)**					
	1990	65%	$113,350	51%	$ 284,458	$ 17,550
	1988	64%	$141,080	52%	$ 162,109	
	1986	52%	$ 41,250	15%	$ 6,984	

HOUSE OF REPRESENTATIVES

Dist. No.	Name	Election %	PAC Receipts	PAC %	Leftover Cash	Conflict of Interest Receipts (1985–1990)
SOUTH CAROLINA (continued)						
2	**Spence (R)**					
	1990	89%	$106,533	56%	$ 62,190	$ 84,300
	1988	53%	$191,268	53%	$ 3,378	
	1986	54%	$144,996	52%	$ 9,912	
	1984	62%	$120,291	46%	$ 27,050	
3	**Derrick (D)**					
	1990	58%	$542,789	64%	$ 106,192	n/a
	1988	54%	$370,841	64%	$ 166,031	
	1986	68%	$167,750	59%	$ 227,992	
	1984	58%	$152,163	60%	$ 122,857	
4	**Patterson (D)**					
	1990	61%	$303,354	63%	$ 2,730	$ 186,807
	1988	52%	$412,855	37%	$ 2,453	
	1986	51%	$148,405	24%	$ 2,520	
5	**Spratt (D)**					
	1990	100%	$ 84,950	77%	$ 153,025	$ 30,500
	1988	70%	$140,970	69%	$ 216,023	
	1986	100%	$ 67,226	43%	$ 118,089	
	1984	92%	$ 66,374	81%	$ 28,977	
6	**Tallon (D)**					
	1990	100%	$145,550	63%	$ 350,780	$ 136,600
	1988	76%	$203,958	53%	$ 214,838	
	1986	76%	$126,650	37%	$ 76,934	
	1984	60%	$222,197	53%	$ 2,526	
SOUTH DAKOTA						
AT LARGE	**Johnson (D)**					
	1990	68%	$251,800	49%	$ 104,643	$ 89,250
	1988	72%	$329,446	49%	$ 51,452	
	1986	59%	$230,864	53%	$ 7,331	
TENNESSEE						
1	**Quillen (R)**					
	1990	100%	$360,350	60%	$1,044,255	n/a
	1988	80%	$413,800	67%	$ 711,012	
	1986	69%	$363,400	77%	$ 321,484	
	1984	100%	$227,500	77%	$ 308,341	

HOUSE OF REPRESENTATIVES

Dist. No.	Name	Election %	PAC Receipts	PAC %	Leftover Cash	Conflict of Interest Receipts (1985–1990)
TENNESSEE (continued)						
2	**Duncan (R)**					
	1990	81%	$165,501	51%	$ 137,716	$ 18,450
	1988	56%	$161,675	36%	$ 12,961	
3	**Lloyd (D)**					
	1990	53%	$233,750	56%	$ 184,618	$ 119,800
	1988	57%	$320,387	52%	$ 3,672	
	1986	54%	$323,624	51%	$ 305	
	1984	52%	$125,670	48%	$ 2,973	
4	**Cooper (D)**					
	1990	67%	$107,400	59%	$ 205,616	$ 149,903
	1988	100%	$244,977	84%	$ 79,044	
	1986	100%	$ 90,754	62%	$ 20,648	
	1984	75%	$ 80,090	90%	$ 899	
5	**Clement (D)**					
	1990	72%	$272,825	64%	$ 163,739	$ 47,850
	1988	100%	$360,500	28%	$ 37,164	
	*1988	62%	$ 12,950	3%	$ 3,446	
6	**Gordon (D)**					
	1990	67%	$355,275	57%	$ 535,072	$ 44,406
	1988	76%	$256,095	44%	$ 282,110	
	1986	77%	$191,237	48%	$ 151,944	
	1984	63%	$190,740	29%	$ 6,606	
7	**Sundquist (R)**					
	1990	62%	$351,985	54%	$ 471,904	$ 340,335
	1988	80%	$182,103	46%	$ 275,374	
	1986	72%	$139,739	34%	$ 189,861	
	1984	100%	$139,617	39%	$ 62,029	
8	**Tanner (D)**					
	1990	100%	$135,500	43%	$ 228,267	$ 8,700
	1988	62%	$283,961	30%	$ 68,113	
9	**Ford (D)**					
	1990	58%	$169,925	60%	−$ 373	$ 540,063
	1988	82%	$211,500	71%	$ 824	
	1986	83%	$225,275	69%	$ 68,059	
	1984	72%	$179,108	73%	$ 61,458	

* January 1988

HOUSE OF REPRESENTATIVES

Dist. No.	Name	Election %	PAC Receipts	PAC %	Leftover Cash	Conflict of Interest Receipts (1985–1990)
TEXAS						
1	**Chapman (D)**					
	1990	61%	$296,839	56%	$ 126,440	$ 38,020
	1988	62%	$270,430	46%	$ 55,829	
	1986	100%	$197,439	23%	$ 20,282	
2	**Wilson (D)**					
	1990	56%	$439,517	66%	$ 860	$ 236,850
	1988	88%	$254,350	75%	$ 77,702	
	1986	66%	$265,206	72%	$ 48,222	
	1984	59%	$285,156	47%	$ 21,023	
3	**Johnson (R)**					
	*1991	53%	$ 99,022	26%	$ 19,770	n/a
4	**Hall (D)**					
	1990	100%	$202,850	78%	$ 213,621	$ 335,353
	1988	66%	$242,743	69%	$ 162,091	
	1986	72%	$171,616	62%	$ 128,654	
	1984	58%	$128,447	54%	$ 122,094	
5	**Bryant (D)**					
	1990	60%	$458,721	49%	$ 257,837	$ 362,403
	1988	61%	$393,057	44%	$ 353,031	
	1986	59%	$365,500	36%	$ 109,738	
	1984	100%	$153,542	40%	$ 83,821	
6	**Barton (R)**					
	1990	66%	$253,403	33%	$ 412,069	$ 316,589
	1988	68%	$288,083	38%	$ 99,460	
	1986	56%	$344,210	34%	$ 11,660	
	1984	57%	$174,647	35%	$ 21,929	
7	**Archer (R)**					
	1990	100%	$ 0	0%	$ 670,901	$ 0
	1988	79%	$ 0	0%	$ 629,909	
	1986	87%	$ 0	0%	$ 540,472	
	1984	87%	$ 0	0%	$ 411,515	
8	**Fields (R)**					
	1990	100%	$269,275	70%	$ 34,447	$ 343,364
	1988	100%	$271,825	53%	$ 69,460	
	1986	68%	$265,683	45%	$ 42,055	
	1984	65%	$346,066	37%	$ 26,404	

HOUSE OF REPRESENTATIVES

Dist. No.	Name	Election %	PAC Receipts	PAC %	Leftover Cash	Conflict of Interest Receipts (1985–1990)
TEXAS (continued)						
9	**Brooks (D)**					
	1990	58%	$459,444	59%	$ 330,424	$ 14,850
	1988	100%	$276,562	65%	$ 440,347	
	1986	62%	$242,809	54%	$ 242,155	
	1984	59%	$230,926	53%	$ 195,082	
10	**Pickle (D)**					
	1990	65%	$247,900	50%	$ 66,442	$ 671,411
	1988	93%	$ 46,463	27%	$ 137,760	
	1986	72%	$424,667	37%	$ 137,936	
	1984	100%	$ 45,818	18%	$ 356,574	
11	**Edwards (D)**					
	1990	53%	$345,480	51%	$ 3,460	n/a
12	**Geren (D)**					
	1990	71%	$257,509	52%	$ 18,132	$ 46,204
	*1989	51%	$350,390	37%	$ 15,703	
13	**Sarpalius (D)**					
	1990	56%	$387,684	57%	$ 175,429	$ 68,341
	1988	52%	$233,950	60%	$ 2,454	
14	**Laughlin (D)**					
	1990	54%	$433,314	52%	$ 1,820	$ 41,950
	1988	53%	$240,699	39%	$ 23,964	
15	**de la Garza (D)**					
	1990	100%	$ 58,675	68%	$ 137,477	$ 144,675
	1988	94%	$127,452	48%	$ 172,103	
	1986	100%	$134,500	80%	$ 127,733	
	1984	100%	$ 92,710	53%	$ 100,706	
16	**Coleman (D)**					
	1990	96%	$162,285	58%	$ 9,538	n/a
	1988	100%	$175,670	54%	$ 16,498	
	1986	66%	$257,367	50%	$ 11,123	
	1984	57%	$200,860	47%	$ 2,996	
17	**Stenholm (D)**					
	1990	100%	$ 98,075	39%	$ 89,736	$ 94,375
	1988	100%	$111,716	39%	$ 146,938	
	1986	100%	$ 91,840	41%	$ 200,152	
	1984	100%	$ 93,727	37%	$ 192,484	

HOUSE OF REPRESENTATIVES

Dist. No.	Name	Election %	PAC Receipts	PAC %	Leftover Cash	Conflict of Interest Receipts (1985–1990)
TEXAS (continued)						
18	**Washington (D)**					
	1990	100%	$ 87,250	60%	$ 13,250	n/a
	*1989	57%	$166,116	27%	$ 25,858	
19	**Combest (R)**					
	1990	100%	$ 85,976	44%	$ 129,221	$ 91,007
	1988	68%	$119,800	44%	$ 34,187	
	1986	62%	$139,266	44%	$ 6,409	
	1984	58%	$148,276	34%	$ 5,430	
20	**Gonzalez (D)**					
	1990	100%	$ 80,800	57%	$ 35,482	$ 40,556
	1988	71%	$100,387	44%	$ 6,697	
	1986	100%	$ 28,750	20%	$ 11,329	
	1984	100%	$ 24,258	36%	$ 1,681	
21	**Smith (R)**					
	1990	75%	$130,230	19%	$ 363,182	$ 6,200
	1988	93%	$ 97,832	17%	$ 152,844	
	1986	61%	$122,076	12%	$ 4,379	
22	**DeLay (R)**					
	1990	71%	$168,475	52%	$ 76,314	$ 21,350
	1988	67%	$171,650	47%	$ 49,334	
	1986	72%	$157,949	50%	$ 45,652	
	1984	65%	$208,380	38%	$ 24,311	
23	**Bustamante (D)**					
	1990	63%	$192,725	52%	$ 294,345	$ 47,350
	1988	65%	$155,786	56%	$ 159,640	
	1986	91%	$ 89,500	35%	$ 66,457	
	1984	100%	$118,196	20%	$ 3,548	
24	**Frost (D)**					
	1990	100%	$411,405	61%	$ 316,106	n/a
	1988	93%	$298,373	50%	$ 233,591	
	1986	67%	$336,099	43%	$ 81,566	
	1984	59%	$239,154	37%	$ 16,161	

HOUSE OF REPRESENTATIVES

Dist. No.	Name	Election %	PAC Receipts	PAC %	Leftover Cash	Conflict of Interest Receipts (1985–1990)
TEXAS (continued)						
25	**Andrews (D)**					
	1990	100%	$344,883	64%	$ 811,150	$ 827,658
	1988	71%	$403,635	63%	$ 565,626	
	1986	100%	$134,054	45%	$ 246,561	
	1984	64%	$158,195	48%	$ 80,305	
26	**Armey (R)**					
	1990	70%	$162,306	37%	$ 362,311	$ 12,957
	1988	69%	$150,800	36%	$ 118,993	
	1986	68%	$192,410	35%	$ 13,267	
	1984	51%	$100,810	26%	$ 24,096	
27	**Ortiz (D)**					
	1990	100%	$100,790	43%	$ 245,251	$ 43,600
	1988	100%	$100,383	51%	$ 150,139	
	1986	100%	$105,296	58%	$ 94,577	
	1984	64%	$110,890	32%	$ 41,247	
UTAH						
1	**Jansen (R)**					
	1990	52%	$180,750	67%	$ 41,944	$ 153,038
	1988	60%	$258,859	63%	$ 8,144	
	1986	52%	$214,610	53%	$ 23,561	
	1984	71%	$ 79,832	48%	$ 37,731	
2	**Owens (D)**					
	1990	58%	$541,232	53%	$ 9,239	$ 106,794
	1988	57%	$455,310	62%	$ 83,684	
	1986	55%	$389,113	56%	$ 23,958	
3	**Orton (D)**					
	1990	58%	$ 32,000	37%	−$ 1,874	n/a
VIRGINIA						
1	**Bateman (R)**					
	1990	51%	$218,750	42%	$ 15,817	$ 148,600
	1988	73%	$162,640	55%	$ 39,534	
	1986	56%	$222,709	36%	$ 31,129	
	1984	59%	$213,438	42%	$ 11,782	

HOUSE OF REPRESENTATIVES

Dist. No.	Name	Election %	PAC Receipts	PAC %	Leftover Cash	Conflict of Interest Receipts (1985–1990)
VIRGINIA (continued)						
2	**Pickett (D)**					
	1990	75%	$135,500	56%	$ 185,854	$ 41,150
	1988	61%	$215,810	49%	$ 28,550	
	1986	49%	$163,949	27%	$ 5,125	
3	**Bliley (R)**					
	1990	65%	$398,462	63%	$ 30,293	$ 430,488
	1988	100%	$270,550	58%	$ 108,636	
	1986	67%	$288,468	37%	$ 8,007	
	1984	86%	$143,537	50%	$ 44,469	
4	**Sisisky (D)**					
	1990	78%	$158,200	66%	$ 281,644	$ 59,850
	1988	100%	$102,636	55%	$ 316,592	
	1986	100%	$ 90,910	55%	$ 224,269	
	1984	100%	$121,308	56%	$ 113,492	
5	**Payne (D)**					
	1990	99%	$187,650	59%	$ 9,594	$ 41,800
	1988	54%	$199,500	24%	$ 9,041	
	*1988	59%	$ 36,300	12%	$ 3,049	
6	**Olin (D)**					
	1990	83%	$153,700	60%	$ 63,273	$ 99,700
	1988	64%	$140,400	44%	$ 11,751	
	1986	70%	$128,807	35%	$ 12,206	
	1984	54%	$197,504	43%	$ 5,459	
7	**Allen (R)**					
	*1991	62%	$227,580	36%	$ 15,441	n/a
8	**Moran (D)**					
	1990	52%	$257,821	29%	$ 20	n/a
9	**Boucher (D)**					
	1990	97%	$366,584	70%	$ 401,838	$ 317,587
	1988	63%	$367,600	60%	$ 130,299	
	1986	99%	$179,037	51%	$ 119,898	
	1984	52%	$202,025	42%	$ 34,183	

* June 1988

HOUSE OF REPRESENTATIVES

Dist. No.	Name	Election %	PAC Receipts	PAC %	Leftover Cash	Conflict of Interest Receipts (1985–1990)
VIRGINIA (continued)						
10	**Wolf (R)**					
	1990	62%	$192,395	37%	$ 59,412	n/a
	1988	68%	$237,490	30%	$ 57,022	
	1986	60%	$310,833	28%	$ 8,914	
	1984	63%	$230,729	35%	$ 39,817	
VERMONT						
AT LARGE	**Sanders (I)**					
	1990	56%	$ 72,250	13%	$ 3,216	n/a
WASHINGTON						
1	**Miller (R)**					
	1990	52%	$265,457	29%	$ 11,196	$ 122,727
	1988	55%	$333,860	25%	$ 10,758	
	1986	51%	$156,174	26%	$ 2,800	
	1984	56%	$ 99,507	26%	$ 943	
2	**Swift (D)**					
	1990	51%	$272,542	54%	$ 168,462	$ 326,047
	1988	100%	$286,312	76%	$ 131,488	
	1986	72%	$167,575	63%	$ 56,527	
	1984	59%	$206,082	66%	$ 30,936	
3	**Unsoeld (D)**					
	1990	54%	$624,498	48%	$ 5,610	$ 283,326
	1988	50%	$282,082	41%	$ 8,530	
4	**Morrison (R)**					
	1990	71%	$ 42,200	38%	$ 218,433	$ 50,340
	1988	75%	$ 82,558	41%	$ 156,996	
	1986	72%	$ 70,244	39%	$ 148,864	
	1984	76%	$ 76,960	46%	$ 75,093	
5	**Foley (D)**					
	1990	69%	$326,337	70%	$ 596,708	$ 86,900
	1988	76%	$555,140	57%	$ 587,378	
	1986	75%	$392,701	73%	$ 282,642	
	1984	70%	$293,798	66%	$ 154,021	

HOUSE OF REPRESENTATIVES

Dist. No.	Name	Election %	PAC Receipts	PAC %	Leftover Cash	Conflict of Interest Receipts (1985–1990)
WASHINGTON (continued)						
6	**Dicks (D)**					
	1990	61%	$240,055	61%	$ 107,649	$ 103,275
	1988	68%	$213,239	58%	$ 277,497	
	1986	71%	$179,660	60%	$ 198,732	
	1984	66%	$164,397	67%	$ 126,520	
7	**McDermott (D)**					
	1990	72%	$196,253	85%	$ 45,399	$ 44,484
	1988	76%	$233,226	62%	$ 18,727	
8	**Chandler (R)**					
	1990	56%	$300,815	64%	$ 127,364	$ 483,292
	1988	71%	$191,478	57%	$ 106,227	
	1986	65%	$120,581	46%	$ 73,256	
	1984	62%	$125,374	41%	$ 24,309	
WEST VIRGINIA						
1	**Mollohan (D)**					
	1990	67%	$131,498	66%	$ 136,457	n/a
	1988	75%	$112,893	67%	$ 95,346	
	1986	100%	$135,583	56%	$ 30,284	
	1984	54%	$243,266	67%	$ 2,840	
2	**Staggers (D)**					
	1990	55%	$302,800	72%	$ 1,646	$ 73,400
	1988	100%	$131,953	90%	$ 81,923	
	1986	69%	$133,695	84%	$ 25,537	
	1984	56%	$200,788	66%	$ 5,021	
3	**Wise (D)**					
	1990	100%	$126,118	69%	$ 179,230	$ 74,184
	1988	74%	$122,952	71%	$ 49,454	
	1986	65%	$ 94,421	64%	$ 41,520	
	1984	68%	$162,842	77%	$ 32,853	
4	**Rahall (D)**					
	1990	52%	$287,250	54%	$ 353,763	$ 107,804
	1988	61%	$175,442	53%	$ 395,005	
	1986	71%	$124,079	58%	$ 214,118	
	1984	67%	$ 98,893	67%	$ 70,944	

HOUSE OF REPRESENTATIVES

Dist. No.	Name	Election %	PAC Receipts	PAC %	Leftover Cash	Conflict of Interest Receipts (1985–1990)
WISCONSIN						
1	**Aspin (D)**					
	1990	99%	$322,900	36%	$ 162,669	$ 197,875
	1988	76%	$265,249	43%	$ 66,324	
	1986	74%	$195,382	39%	$ 80,127	
	1984	56%	$201,055	54%	$ 74,362	
2	**Klug (R)**					
	1990	53%	$ 32,800	18%	$ 5,660	n/a
3	**Gunderson (R)**					
	1990	61%	$196,595	51%	$ 98,169	$ 159,532
	1988	68%	$133,235	33%	$ 51,317	
	1986	64%	$125,847	43%	$ 6,176	
	1984	68%	$ 98,181	37%	$ 26,875	
4	**Kleczka (D)**					
	1990	69%	$186,048	61%	$ 86,327	$ 94,850
	1988	100%	$129,383	60%	$ 175,450	
	1986	100%	$109,983	68%	$ 111,635	
	1984	67%	$ 91,981	66%	$ 43,118	
5	**Moody (D)**					
	1990	68%	$450,704	61%	$ 237,639	$ 913,387
	1988	64%	$524,503	41%	$ 17,588	
	1986	99%	$155,056	56%	$ 4,551	
	1984	98%	$104,331	63%	$ 27,917	
6	**Petri (R)**					
	1990	100%	$ 98,455	41%	$ 397,666	$ 74,065
	1988	74%	$120,980	47%	$ 288,323	
	1986	97%	$ 92,875	45%	$ 217,162	
	1984	76%	$ 90,240	42%	$ 118,818	
7	**Obey (D)**					
	1990	62%	$311,550	50%	$ 334,565	n/a
	1988	62%	$308,399	58%	$ 181,692	
	1986	62%	$261,906	55%	$ 102,022	
	1984	61%	$110,897	50%	$ 91,542	

HOUSE OF REPRESENTATIVES

Dist. No.	Name	Election %	PAC Receipts	PAC %	Leftover Cash	Conflict of Interest Receipts (1985–1990)
WISCONSIN (continued)						
8 **Roth (R)**						
	1990	54%	$203,083	52%	$ 93,841	$ 157,852
	1988	70%	$180,814	53%	$ 203,375	
	1986	67%	$140,097	47%	$ 91,347	
	1984	68%	$ 84,717	33%	$ 78,229	
9 **Sensenbrenner (R)**						
	1990	100%	$ 98,635	37%	$ 312,478	$ 11,935
	1988	75%	$109,839	35%	$ 144,801	
	1986	78%	$ 60,950	35%	$ 123,693	
	1984	73%	$ 91,079	39%	$ 126,484	
WYOMING						
AT LARGE **Thomas (R)**						
	1990	55%	$174,995	43%	$ 4,531	$ 74,500
	*1989	52%	$237,345	42%	$ 37,993	

SENATE

Name	Election %	PAC Receipts	PAC %	Leftover Cash	Conflict of Interest Receipts (1985–1990)
ALABAMA					
Heflin (D) 1990	61%	$1,320,755	39%	$1,036,023	$ 397,588
Shelby (D) 1986	50%	$ 882,686	37%	$ 141,319	$ 173,497
ALASKA					
Stevens (R) 1990	66%	$ 751,450	54%	$ 234,997	$ 333,435
Murkowski (R) 1986	54%	$ 587,608	41%	$ 53,848	$ 162,266
ARIZONA					
DeConcini (D) 1988	56%	$ 968,495	34%	$ 509,972	$ 82,000
McCain (R) 1986	61%	$ 773,152	31%	$ 287,216	$ 26,040
ARKANSAS					
Bumpers (D) 1986	62%	$ 507,419	29%	$ 124,978	$ 114,425
Pryor (D) 1990	100%	$ 485,067	39%	$1,005,464	$ 564,527
CALIFORNIA					
Cranston (D) 1986	49%	$1,366,173	13%	$ 16,593	$ 463,397
Seymour (R) 1990		Appointed to replace		Pete Wilson	n/a
COLORADO					
Brown (D) 1990	56%	$1,389,784	33%	$ 455,834	n/a

SENATE

Name	Election %	PAC Receipts	PAC %	Leftover Cash	Conflict of Interest Receipts (1985–1990)
COLORADO (continued)					
Wirth (D)					
1986	50%	$ 845,855	22%	$ 32,106	$ 111,743
CONNECTICUT					
Lieberman (D)					
1988	50%	$ 175,566	7%	$ 79,824	$ 5,754
Dodd (D)					
1986	65%	$ 624,446	26%	$ 266,781	$ 460,394
DELAWARE					
Biden (D)					
1990	63%	$ 690,816	36%	$ 190,151	$ 43,500
Roth (R)					
1988	62%	$ 794,191	42%	$ 89,031	$ 801,151
FLORIDA					
Mack (R)					
1988	50%	$1,018,745	20%	$ 42,420	$ 53,500
Graham (D)					
1986	55%	$ 887,337	14%	$ 42,247	$ 116,440
GEORGIA					
Nunn (D)					
1990	100%	$ 627,010	32%	$1,550,058	$ 72,489
Fowler (D)					
1986	51%	$ 600,086	21%	$ 133,342	$ 132,253
HAWAII					
Akaka (D)					
1990	54%	$ 854,107	48%	$ 161,134	n/a
Inouye (D)					
1986	74%	$ 540,455	46%	$ 598,388	$ 151,672

SENATE

Name	Election %	PAC Receipts	PAC %	Leftover Cash	Conflict of Interest Receipts (1985–1990)
IDAHO					
Craig (R) 1990	61%	$ 811,026	47%	$ 91,834	n/a
Symms (R) 1986	52%	$1,366,527	40%	$ 188,369	n/a
ILLINOIS					
Simon (D) 1990	65%	$1,480,221	17%	$ 843,731	$ 770,073
Dixon (D) 1986	65%	$ 984,408	44%	$ 498,427	$ 491,652
INDIANA					
Coats (R) 1990	54%	$1,113,664	27%	$ 363,900	n/a
Lugar (R) 1988	68%	$ 775,836	26%	$ 417,309	$149,320
IOWA					
Harkin (D) 1990	55%	$1,546,535	31%	$ 59,737	$ 713,849
Grassley (R) 1986	66%	$ 971,730	35%	$ 486,432	$ 883,660
KANSAS					
Dole (R) 1986	70%	$1,034,324	39%	$2,166,732	n/a
Kassebaum (R) 1990	74%	$ 187,858	39%	$ 217,135	$ 52,750
KENTUCKY					
Ford (D) 1986	74%	$ 843,282	55%	$ 360,775	$ 215,280

SENATE

Name	Election %	PAC Receipts	PAC %	Leftover Cash	Conflict of Interest Receipts (1985–1990)
KENTUCKY (continued)					
McConnell (R)					
1990	52%	$1,076,029	26%	$ 190,373	$ 519,385
LOUISIANA					
Johnston (D)					
1990	54%	$1,416,331	34%	$ 945,371	$ 498,700
Breaux (D)					
1986	53%	$ 898,173	30%	$ 48,130	$ 109,600
MAINE					
Cohen (R)					
1990	61%	$ 549,194	38%	$ 17,906	$ 61,050
Mitchell (D)					
1988	81%	$ 724,547	40%	$ 480,728	$ 662,323
MARYLAND					
Sarbanes (D)					
1988	62%	$ 604,799	41%	$ 11,394	$ 98,950
Mikulski (D)					
1986	61%	$ 660,260	31%	$ 103,596	$ 80,730
MASSACHUSETTS					
Kennedy (D)					
1988	65%	$ 322,972	10%	$ 735,350	$ 165,850
Kerry (D)					
1990	57%	$ 0	0%	$ 12,055	$ 0
MICHIGAN					
Levin (D)					
1990	57%	$1,392,502	20%	$ 201,966	$ 75,624
Riegle (D)					
1988	60%	$1,281,641	39%	$ 855,659	$1,140,783

SENATE

Name	Election %	PAC Receipts	PAC %	Leftover Cash	Conflict of Interest Receipts (1985–1990)
MINNESOTA					
Durenberger (R) 1988	56%	$1,499,382	30%	$ 32,051	$1,649,092
Wellstone (D) 1990	50%	$ 294,520	21%	$ 62,500	n/a
MISSISSIPPI					
Cochran (R) 1990	100%	$ 534,450	41%	$ 908,834	$ 291,500
Lott (R) 1988	54%	$1,118,111	31%	$ 197,239	$ 5,500
MISSOURI					
Danforth (R) 1988	68%	$1,149,207	28%	$ 645,784	$1,271,753
Bond (R) 1986	53%	$1,320,353	24%	$ 67,773	$ 145,200
MONTANA					
Baucus (D) 1990	68%	$1,377,663	52%	$ 505,883	$1,479,399
Burns (R) 1988	52%	$ 315,387	29%	$ 23,477	$ 24,436
NEBRASKA					
Exon (D) 1990	59%	$1,503,897	58%	$ 270,574	$ 382,807
Kerrey (D) 1988	57%	$ 799,279	23%	$ 24,580	$ 26,250
NEVADA					
Bryan (D) 1988	50%	$ 802,792	27%	$ 30,963	$ 39,500

SENATE

Name	Election %	PAC Receipts	PAC %	Leftover Cash	Conflict of Interest Receipts (1985–1990)
NEVADA (continued)					
Reid (D)					
1986	50%	$ 817,377	39%	$ 33,490	$ 11,500
NEW HAMPSHIRE					
Rudman (R)					
1986	63%	$ 5,200	1%	$ 57,085	$ 0
Smith (R)					
1990	65%	$ 663,400	44%	$ 89,118	n/a
NEW JERSEY					
Bradley (D)					
1990	50%	$1,062,309	13%	$ 775,770	$1,286,186
Lautenberg (D)					
1988	53%	$1,410,360	20%	$ 40,146	$ 106,353
NEW MEXICO					
Bingaman (D)					
1988	63%	$1,100,451	35%	$ 163,315	$ 209,010
Domenici (R)					
1990	73%	$ 773,374	37%	$ 218,513	$ 211,011
NEW YORK					
Moynihan (D)					
1988	67%	$ 892,773	21%	$ 460,075	$1,113,198
D'Amato (R)					
1986	57%	$ 855,518	13%	$ 456,293	$ 467,388
NORTH CAROLINA					
Helms (R)					
1990	53%	$ 835,104	6%	$ 12,326	$ 225,890
Sanford (D)					
1986	52%	$ 571,787	15%	$ 13,190	$ 299,450

SENATE

Name	Election %	PAC Receipts	PAC %	Leftover Cash	Conflict of Interest Receipts (1985–1990)
NORTH DAKOTA					
Burdick (D) 1988	59%	$1,059,524	60%	$ 25,228	$ 190,526
Conrad (D) 1986	50%	$ 453,440	46%	$ 85,667	$ 182,300
OHIO					
Glenn (D) 1986	62%	$ 637,186	31%	$ 818,910	$ 72,250
Metzenbaum (D) 1988	57%	$1,028,183	14%	$ 221,751	$ 456,835
OKLAHOMA					
Boren (D) 1990	83%	$ 0	0%	$ 158,133	$ 0
Nickles (R) 1986	55%	$ 886,841	30%	$ 375,674	$ 222,574
OREGON					
Hatfield (R) 1990	54%	$ 969,720	44%	$ 4,332	$ 167,400
Packwood (R) 1986	63%	$ 974,367	14%	$ 692,290	$ 891,689
PENNSYLVANIA					
Specter (R) 1986	56%	$1,256,626	23%	$ 64,461	$ 88,663
Wofford (D)		Appointed then	elected 1991.		n/a

SENATE

Name	Election %	PAC Receipts	PAC %	Leftover Cash	Conflict of Interest Receipts (1985–1990)
RHODE ISLAND					
Chafee (R)					
1988	55%	$1,045,319	43%	$ 50,360	$1,125,529
Pell (D)					
1990	62%	$ 885,678	41%	$ 216,256	$ 451,800
SOUTH CAROLINA					
Thurmond (R)					
1990	64%	$ 562,695	27%	$ 221,092	$ 153,830
Hollings (D)					
1986	63%	$ 950,882	40%	$ 197,854	$ 464,473
SOUTH DAKOTA					
Pressler (R)					
1990	52%	$ 861,339	43%	$ 556,585	$ 384,784
Daschle (D)					
1986	52%	$1,153,906	33%	$ 40,245	$ 476,258
TENNESSEE					
Gore (D)					
1990	68%	$ 931,438	42%	$ 708,043	$ 254,580
Sasser (D)					
1988	65%	$1,379,817	43%	$ 328,990	$ 439,389
TEXAS					
Bentsen (D)					
1988	59%	$2,438,041	29%	$ 86,737	$2,368,100
Gramm (R)					
1990	60%	$1,426,839	12%	$4,147,378	$ 306,457
UTAH					
Garn (R)					
1986	72%	$ 576,114	57%	$ 285,275	$ 315,506

SENATE

Name	Election %	PAC Receipts	PAC %	Leftover Cash	Conflict of Interest Receipts (1985–1990)
UTAH (continued)					
Hatch (R) 1988	67%	$1,173,764	28%	$ 443,171	$ 186,494
VERMONT					
Jeffords (R) 1988	68%	$ 650,393	67%	$ 312,249	$ 1,000
Leahy (D) 1986	63%	$ 822,931	43%	$ 327,768	$ 110,525
VIRGINIA					
Robb (D) 1988	71%	$ 914,763	29%	$ 316,962	$ 2,750
Warner (R) 1990	81%	$ 621,899	36%	$ 622,138	$ 162,669
WASHINGTON					
Adams (D) 1986	51%	$ 635,361	35%	$ 86,797	$ 134,706
Gorton (R) 1988	51%	$ 939,406	34%	$ 45,958	$ 473,849
WEST VIRGINIA					
Byrd (D) 1988	65%	$ 938,720	67%	$ 482,690	$ 64,950
Rockefeller (D) 1990	68%	$1,425,405	41%	$ 902,198	$1,342,190
WISCONSIN					
Kasten (R) 1986	51%	$1,095,726	34%	$ 125,579	$ 349,530
Kohl (D) 1988	52%	$ 0	0%	$ 84,938	$ 0

SENATE

Name	Election %	PAC Receipts	PAC %	Leftover Cash	Conflict of Interest Receipts (1985–1990)
WYOMING					
Simpson (R) †1					
1990	64%	$ 705,773	56%	$ 433,246	$ 52,000
Wallop (R)					
1988	50%	$ 872,664	58%	$ 166,344	$ 896,105

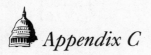 *Appendix C*

THE 100 LARGEST PACS
IN THE 1990 ELECTIONS

THE TABLE LISTS the 100 PACs that distributed the most money in 1989–90, ranked in order of their total contributions to federal candidates. For clarity's sake, the name of the PAC's sponsoring organization is listed, including, where not self-evident, a thumbnail description of the nature of the sponsoring group drawn from *The Almanac of Federal PACs, 1990,* by Edward Zuckerman, and published by Amward Press, Washington, D.C. The contribution figures are from the Federal Election Commission, as compiled by *PACs & Lobbies.*

	Total Contributions to Federal Candidates in 1990 Election Cycle
1. National Association of Realtors	$3,094,228
2. American Medical Association	2,375,992
3. International Brotherhood of Teamsters	2,349,575
4. National Education Association	2,320,155
5. United Auto Workers	1,790,912
6. National Association of Letter Carriers	1,731,050
7. American Federation of State, County & Municipal Employees	1,553,370

	Total Contributions to Federal Candidates in 1990 Election Cycle
8. National Association of Retired Federal Employees	1,533,000
9. Association of Trial Lawyers of America	1,526,600
10. United Brotherhood of Carpenters & Joiners	1,490,020
11. National Association of Life Underwriters	1,487,800
12. International Association of Machinists	1,458,595
13. American Telephone & Telegraph Company	1,457,325
14. National Association of Home Builders	1,364,150
15. American Bankers Association	1,323,659
16. National Automobile Dealers Association	1,301,400
17. International Brotherhood of Electrical Workers	1,214,410
18. Laborers' International Union	1,170,465
19. Air Line Pilots Association	1,167,797
20. American Institute of Certified Public Accountants	1,089,044
21. American Federation of Teachers	1,021,400
22. National PAC (pro-Israel)	973,500
23. American Postal Workers Union	966,828
24. American Academy of Opthalmology	960,411
25. United Food & Commercial Workers	954,322
26. Seafarers International Union	947,246
27. National Committee to Preserve Social Security and Medicare	913,802
28. United Steelworkers of America	897,675
29. AFL-CIO	837,927
30. American Dental Association	821,828
31. Communication Workers of America	781,037
32. Associated Milk Producers, Inc.	769,800
33. Federal Express Corporation	756,950
34. National Rifle Association	743,543
35. RJR Nabisco	720,500
36. United Transportation Union	717,300
37. Engineers Political Education Committee	697,750
38. American Council of Life Insurance	692,493
39. Independent Insurance Agents of America	676,335
40. Sheet Metal Workers International Association	664,858
41. United Parcel Service of America, Inc.	661,332

	Total Contributions to Federal Candidates in 1990 Election Cycle
42. Auto Dealers And Drivers for Free Trade (dealers of Japanese cars)	645,450
43. National Beer Wholesalers' Association	633,650
44. Associated General Contractors	615,594
45. United Association of Journeymen and Apprentices of the Plumbing Industry	614,134
46. District 2 Marine Engineers Beneficial Association	602,250
47. National Committee for an Effective Congress (supports liberal candidates)	598,675
48. National Rural Electric Cooperative Association	598,575
49. National Restaurant Association	575,142
50. Philip Morris, Inc.	573,410
51. National Cable Television Association	565,475
52. Aircraft Owners and Pilots Association	513,900
53. Union Pacific Corporation	512,614
54. Amalgamated Transit Union	511,880
55. American Hospital Association	502,189
56. Mid-America Dairymen, Inc.	491,150
57. Human Rights Campaign Fund	480,621
58. Credit Union National Association	475,493
59. Barnett Banks of Florida	462,050
60. Chicago Mercantile Exchange	459,500
61. National Rural Letter Carriers Association	430,875
62. American Family Corporation	430,250
63. Lockheed Corporation	425,159
64. Northrop Corporation	411,775
65. International Association of Ironworkers	410,349
66. Sierra Club	408,651
67. American Crystal Sugar Co.	407,625
68. Morgan Companies	403,525
69. Waste Management, Inc.	392,880
70. National Abortion Rights League	384,295
71. Citicorp	381,528
72. Martin Marietta Corporation	378,760
73. Chicago Board of Trade	377,311
74. Food Marketing Institute (trade association of supermarkets)	375,572
75. Textron Inc. (manufacturing, military products, financial services)	373,625

	Total Contributions to Federal Candidates in 1990 Election Cycle
76. Transportation Communication Union	373,401
77. GTE Corporation	370,930
78. General Dynamics Corporation	370,631
79. Rockwell International Corporation	365,085
80. General Electric Company	360,825
81. Marine Engineers Beneficial Association	357,850
82. U.S. West Inc.	334,657
83. KidsPAC (supports strong federal role in child development)	334,350
84. FMC Corporation (oil, chemical, and defense products)	333,740
85. National Utility Contractors Association	331,768
86. Transport Workers Union	330,665
87. American Optometric Association	329,600
88. American Sugar Beet Growers Association	327,057
89. Amoco Corporation	323,923
90. United Technologies Corporation	323,475
91. National Association of Postmasters	319,301
92. Continental Airlines Inc.	317,850
93. National Federation of Independent Business	316,710
94. United Mine Workers of America	313,415
95. Chevron Corporation	309,653
96. U.S. Tobacco Co.	306,900
97. Fluor Corporation	305,343
98. Atlantic Richfield Company	300,788
99. American Trucking Associations	300,040
100. Service Employees International Union	300,021

ABBREVIATIONS

BP Brooks Jackson, *Broken Promise: Why the Federal Election Commission Failed* (New York: Priority Press, 1990).

CA Citizen Action: a Washington D.C.-based research and advocacy organization.

CA Report *Hidden Power: Campaign Contributions of Large Individual Donors*, 1987–88 and 1989–90.

Campaign Practices *Campaign Practices Reports*: published bi-weekly by Congressional Quarterly.

CBO Congressional Budget Office.

CC Common Cause: A non-partisan citizen's group organization interested in, among other things, campaign finance reform.

CC Magazine Magazine published bi-monthly by Common Cause.

Cong. Rec. *Congressional Record.*

Congressional Yellow Book A complete listing of members of Congress, including committees and key staff members. Published at intervals, (Washington, D.C., Monitor Publishing Company).

CPI Center for Public Integrity: a Washington-based, non-profit investigative journalism group.

CPI Report, Short-changed by Jean Cobb. *Short-changed: How Congress and Special Interests Benefit at the Expense of the American People*, 1991.

CPI Report, Saving for a Rainy Day by Kevin Chafee. *Saving for a Rainy Day: How Congress Turns Leftover Campaign Cash Into "Golden Parachutes,"* 1991.

CQ Congressional Quarterly: a Washington publisher of reports on government agencies and affairs. Its publications include the *Weekly Report* and the *Almanac* (see below), and directories such as *PIA* (see below).

CQ Almanac Annual published by CQ summarizing congressional activities for the year covered.

CQ Weekly Report A report on the congressional activities of the week, published by CQ.

CRP Center for Responsive Politics: a non-profit, Washington D.C. research organization. Its reports deal primarily with congressional and political trends.

CRP Foundations Report *Public Policy and Foundations: The Role of Politicians in Public Charities*, 1987.

CRS Congressional Research Service, a department of the Library of Congress that does research and issues reports for members of Congress.

CRS 87–469 CRS Report No. 87–469, Joseph E. Cantor, *Campaign Financing in Federal Elections: A Guide to the Law and its Operation*, August 8, 1986, rev. July 20, 1987.

CRS 84–107 CRS Report No. 84–107 GOV, Joseph E. Cantor, *Public Financing of Congressional Elections: Legislative Proposals and Activity in the Twentieth Century*, August 15, 1984.

CTJ Study Robert McIntyre and Jeff Spinner, *130 Reasons Why We Need Tax Reform*, Citizens for Tax Justice, Washington, D.C., July 1986.

Dairy PACs The PACs of the three largest dairy co-ops: Associated Milk Producers, Inc.; Dairymen, Inc.; and Mid-America Dairymen, Inc.

Drew Elizabeth Drew, *Politics and Money: The New Road to Corruption* (New York: Macmillan, 1983).

FEC Federal Election Commission.

FEC Blue Books FEC *Reports on Financial Activity*, which provide complete campaign finance information on federal elections for each two-year election cycle. All cited are final reports with the exception of 1977–78. Unless otherwise specified, the Blue Books cited here are reports on U.S. Senate and House campaigns. Other Blue Books cited include (a) Vol. II: dealing with corporate and labor PACs, and (b) Vol. IV: containing data on other categories of PACs, such as those of trade associations and cooperatives discussed in Chapter 2.

FEC Indices The FEC produces several listings, most available on computer printout, including:

B Index All PACs extant on a given date.

D Index All contributions made to federal candidates by a given PAC in a two-year election cycle.

E Index All PAC contributions to a particular candidate in a two-year election cycle.

G Index Individual donors who give $500 or more in federal elections.

K Index Summaries of financial activities of PACs.

L Index Summaries of financial activities of candidates.

FEC disclosure reports The reports on receipts and disbursements required by law to be filed with the FEC by candidates at specified intervals.

Fumento Michael Fumento, "Some Dare Call Them Robber Barons," *National Review*, March 13, 1987.

GAO Government Accounting Office.

Graves and Norrgard Florence Graves and Lee Norrgard, "Money to Burn—How Chicago's Commodity Traders Get Their Way on Capitol Hill," *CC Magazine*, January/February 1985.

H.R. (followed by a number) Designates a bill introduced in the House of Representatives. H. Res.: stands for House Resolution, which only requires approval by the House to become effective; H. Con. Res.: stands for House Concurrent Resolution, which requires Senate concurrence but is not subject to presidential veto.

H. Rep. and H. Doc. House committee reports and House documents.

Library National Library on Money & Politics: An organization with a centralized database containing FEC data on givers and receivers in presidential, House and Senate elections.

Money Talks *How Money Talks in Congress—a Common Cause Study of the Impact of Money on Congressional Decision Making* (Common Cause, Washington, D.C., 1979).

NADA National Automobile Dealers Association.

OAAA Outdoor Advertising Association, the principal lobbying organization of the billboard industry.

Opp. Att. Gen. Opinions of the Attorney General; 33 Opp. Att. Gen. 275 refers to Volume 33 of the Opinions of the Attorney General, p. 275.

PAC Almanac Edward Zuckerman, *Almanac of Federal PACs* (Washington, D.C.: Amward, 1986, 1988, 1990).

PACs & Lobbies A bi-weekly newsletter on campaign finance issues, edited and published by Edward Zuckerman, 2000 National Press Building, Washington, D.C. 20045.

PIA *Politics in America* (see CQ above), a biennial almanac of biographical and statistical information about members of Congress (as well as governors) and about their states or districts.

POA Larry Makinson, *Price of Admission* (Washington, D.C.: Center for Responsive Politics, 1988 and 1990).

Sabato Larry J. Sabato, *PAC Power: Inside the World of Political Action Committees* (New York: W.W. Norton, 1985).

Stat The General Statutes of the United States.

Top Guns Philip J. Simon, *Top Guns: A Common Cause Guide to Defense Contractor Lobbying* (Washington, D.C.: Common Cause, 1987.)

USC United States Code: the continuously updated compilation of federal laws.

USDA United States Department of Agriculture.

WOL Washington On-Line: A now-defunct commercial database in Washington, D.C., which provided on-line access to computerized information drawn from FEC campaign finance disclosure reports.

NOTES ON SOURCES

Chapter 1

3 *Byrd statement:* Cong. Rec., January 6, 1987, p. S15.

3 *Goldwater statement:* U.S. Senate Committee on Rules and Administration. "Hearings on Campaign Finance Reform Proposals of 1983," p. 403, as quoted in *Annals, American Academy of Political and Social Sciences*, July 1986, p. 94.

4 *Goldwater favored repeal of public funding law:* S59, 99th Cong., 1st Session, introduced by Senator Goldwater on January 3, 1985.

4 *Incumbents outspent challengers 3.5 to 1:* calculated from FEC press release, February 22, 1991.

4 *House reelection percentage:* 1986 and 1988 averaged from 1988 POA; 1990 figures from CC, December 1990.

6 *Contributions of Mrs. Vernon Clark:* Library study.

6 *Madison on factionalism:* From *The Federalist, No. 10* (New York: Bantam, 1982), pp. 42–49, esp. 43.

6 *New contribution limits:* 88 Stat. 3 1263 (1974); Public Law 93–443.

7 *Increase in spending in South Dakota Races:* (a) *1978 figure:* FEC Blue Book, 1977–78, p. 298; (b) *1986 figure:* 1987 PIA, p. 1394.

7 *Cost of an average winning House campaign; Cost of a winning Senate campaign:* 1990 POA.

7 *Amount a senator must raise per week to pay for an average winning campaign:* calculated from 1990 POA.

7 *1976 Supreme Court ruling: Buckley v. Valeo*, 424 U.S. 1 (1976).

8 *House members receiving at least 50% from PACs:* calculated from 1992 PIA.

8 *Rep. Neal contributions from banking interests:* Library calculation.

9 *200,000 dairy farmers:* 1982 Census of Agriculture, U.S. Census Bureau, Table 11, p. 218.

9 *Dairy vote:* 166–244, recorded vote on the Olin-Michel amendment to

the 1985 farm bill. Roll call no. 319, Cong. Rec., September 26, 1985, p. H7857.

9 *Dairy cooperatives' $12 million collection:* (a) 1979–84: FEC Blue Books, Vol. IV. (b)1985–86: FEC K Index.

9 *Correlation of dairy contributions to pro-dairy votes:* Vote recorded in *Cong. Rec.*, September 26, 1985, p. H7857. *Dairy PAC contributions: FEC Combined D Indexes*, 1979–86, for principal dairy PACs.

9 *Frost ranked 15th in dairy contributions to House members from 1979–1986:* FEC D Indices for three principal dairy cooperative PACs, 1979–86.

9 *Frost's district:* (a) *Three dairy farmers:* Furnished by Mark Orrin in Representative Frost's Grand Prairie field office; the Texas Department of Agriculture, Milk Division; and the Dairy Herd Improvement Association. (b) *527,000 people; 210,000 below poverty line:* Bureau of the Census, *Congressional District Profiles, 98th Congress*, Publication PC 80-S1–11, Table 2, p. 27.

10 *Distribution of Capital Gains benefits:* Bob McIntyre, Director of Citizens for Tax Justice.

10 *Quote on tax cut: Washington Post*, October 30, 1989.

10 *Dole quote: Wall Street Journal*, July 1982, from CC compilation of Dole statements.

10 *One hundred thirty no-tax companies:* CTJ 1986 Study, pp. 15–16.

10 *Reduction of no-tax companies:* CTJ 1989 Study, pp. 1–3.

11 *Simon statement:* U.S. Senate Committee on Rules and Administration, hearing on S. 1787, November 5, 1985.

11 *Tribute to Rostenkowski: New Republic*, July 15–22, 1985.

12 *Rostenkowski's 1984 campaign surplus:* FEC Blue Book, 1983–84, p. 176.

12 *Rostenkowski's 1989 cash-on-hand:* Library calculation.

12 *Rostenkowski's 1990 honoraria and ranking: Washington Post*, June 15, 1991.

12 *LaFalce's 1990 honoraria and ranking: Washington Post*, June 15, 1991.

12 *House honoraria ban: Wall Street Journal*, May 31, 1990.

12 *Senate honoraria ban: Wall Street Journal*, May 22, 1991, p. A3.

13 *"Lobbyists say privately . . .": Wall Street Journal*, August 9, 1985.

13 *Gibbons' PAC receipts:* CC press release, August 11, 1985, "PACs Give Congressional Tax Writers Three Times More Money in 1985 than in 1983."

13 *AT&T taxes and rebates:* CTJ 1986 Study, p. 17.

13 *AT&T tax savings:* AT&T paid no taxes on profits made from 1982–85. If the $24.8 billion in profits had been subjected to the corporate tax

rate of 46%, AT&T would have paid as much as $11.4 billion in taxes. In addition, AT&T received $635 million in tax rebates, bringing its overall tax savings from 1982–85 to just over $12 billion. CTJ 1986 Study, p. 17.

13 *AT&T PAC contributions:* From 1979 through 1986, the PACs organized by AT&T contributed $1,394,761 to federal candidates. (a) *In 1979– 84*, these included contributions from AT&T Co. PAC (terminated in 1984), AT&T Communications Inc. PAC (terminated in 1985), AT&T Technologies Inc. PAC (terminated at end of 1984), and AT&T Inc. PAC (formed in 1984). Data from *PAC Almanac* (1986), p. 17. (b) *1985–86:* all contributions from AT&T Inc. PAC: FEC press release, May 21, 1987.

14 *Sears Roebuck and General Electric rates of return:* Sears' 1979–86 PAC outlays netted the company $2.3 billion in tax savings. GE's PAC contributions in the same period saved GE $4.7 billion in taxes. Figures from FEC Blue Books and CTJ 1986 Study.

14 *Large individual donations to candidates:* CA Report, May 1991, p. 9.

14 *Large individual contributions to candidates and PACs:* CA Report, May 1991, p. 9.

14–15 *Pro-Israel PAC contributions to 1990 candidates; Gun control opponent PAC contributions; Abortion issue PAC contributions; $3.5 million from pro-Israel individuals:* CRP press release, September 25, 1991.

15 *Tables of pro-Israel contributions to 1990 candidates:* CRP press release, September 25, 1991.

16 *Disclosure required by law; "worthless" disclosure:* CA Report, May 1991, p. 2.

16 *"Housewife" most frequently reported occupation:* CA Report, May 1991, p. 3.

16–17 *1990 contributions to candidates by "housewives"; $62 million in contributions with "worthless" or no disclosure:* CA Report, May 1991, p. 7.

17 *Information connecting Wirth and cable industry: Washington Post*, November, 6, 1990, p. A7.

18 *"Influence industry" contributions:* CA report, May 1991, p. 7.

18 *Percentages of voting age population accounting for total money raised by Senate and House candidates:* CA Report, May 1991, p. 1.

18 *Simmons' giving; no legal authority to impose fines: Los Angeles Times,* April 18, 1990.

19 *Table of Simmons family contributions: Los Angeles Times,* April 18, 1990.

19 *Keenan family trust contributions:* Library analysis.

19 *"Family" giving in 1990 elections:* CA Report, May 1991, p. 2.

19 *Gallo family contributions:* CA Report, May, 1991, p. 2.

19 *More out-of-state than in-state money in 1990:* CA Report, May 1991, p. 2.

20–21 *Los Angeles Times report on contributions of Simmons, Kravis and Perelman: Los Angeles Times*, April 18, 1990.

21 *Cameron donations:* Library study.

21 *Cameron represents Minnesota Mining and Manufacturing (3M) as well as the National Advertising Co.: Washington Representatives*, (Washington, D.C.: Columbia Books, 1990) p. 68.

22 *Barnes' statement:* Interview with author, March 27, 1987.

22 *Senate suspends voting:* Senator Charles McC. Mathias' interview with author, May 21, 1987.

23 *terHorst statement:* Interview with author, August 5, 1987.

24–27 *Story of Garvey's candidacy:* Ed Garvey, "It's Money That Matters," *The Progressive*, March 1989.

27 *Garvey-Kasten election and financial figures:* 1987 PIA, p. 1637.

27 *1986 and 1990 incumbent surplus figures: Washington Post*, November 7, 1991.

27 *Chuck Alston story: CQ Weekly*, May 25, 1991, pp. 1343–1350.

28 *92% of PAC contributions to incumbents; 8% to challengers in primary and general campaigns:* Calculated from FEC press release, February 22, 1991. Statistic is for races in which the incumbent sought reelection.

28–30 *Story of Steve Sovern: Washington Post*, August 25, 1991.

30 *Average cash on hand for incumbents and challengers:* calculated from FEC press release, November 2, 1990.

30 *Ninety percent of House races . . . .:* CC press release, December 1990.

31 *The Speaker's Club:* Letter from Tip O'Neill and Tony Coelho to Leopold Adler, October 29, 1984.

32 *Reich quote: New York Times*, October 12, 1989, A29.

34 *$12,405 per week:* calculated from 1990 POA.

34 *Fundraising of senators standing for reelection in 1994:* Library study.

Chapter 2

35 *Ceiling on contributions:* USC Title 2. Ch. 14, Sub. I, Sec. 441a (a) para. 3.

35–36 *PAC giving in 1990:* FEC Press Release, March 31, 1991.

36–37 *Statistics on Rangel:* (a) *vote percent:* 1991 PIA, p. 1036; (b) *increase in PAC receipts, 1980–84:* FEC Blue Books, 1979–80, p.344, and 1983–84, p. 257; (c) *1986 PAC receipts:* 1987 PIA, p. 1050.

36 *Rangel's ability to transfer cash surplus on retirement:* Sec. 493a of the

1976 amendments to the Federal Election Campaign Act (FECA) of 1971 (90 Stat. 475 [1976], Public Law 93–443) stated that excess campaign funds may be used . . . (c) "for any . . . lawful purpose." Pursuant to (c), it was deemed legally permissible for representatives to transfer campaign surpluses to their personal accounts when they left Congress. In 1979, under Public Law 96–187 (93 Stat. 1339) the FECA was amended to limit this privilege to members of the House elected after 1980. For those representatives holding office before January 8, 1980 (including Representative Rangel, who was elected in 1970), these surpluses still serve as a potential retirement fund, provided they leave Congress prior to January 3, 1993.

36 *Repeal of "grandfather" clause:* Ethics Reform Act of 1989: Section 504.

36 *Rangel's ranking on House Ways and Means:* Congressional Yellow Book, Summer 1991, p. IV–93.

37 *92% of PAC contributions to incumbents in 1990 primary and general elections:* Author's calculation from FEC press release, February 22, 1991. Statistic is for those elections in which the incumbent sought re-election.

37 *PACs gave 15% more to leading committee chairs in 1990:* Library calculation.

37 *PACs gave $13.2 million to unopposed House incumbents in 1990; less than half to 331 challengers:* cited in *Harper's*, August 1991, p. 11. Originally from CC.

37 *1990 PAC gifts to "shoo-in" House candidates:* calculated from FEC press release, February 22, 1991, and 1989 PIA.

39 *PAC giving to Chappell and James:* PIA, 1990 and 1992.

39 *PAC growth average:* (a) *For 1990:* FEC Press Release, February 22, 1991; (b) *For 1978–86:* FEC Press Release, May 21, 1987; (c) *For 1974–1976:* CRS 87–469, p. 36.

39–40 *Bentsen and Packwood breakfasts: Washington Post*, February 3, 1987, p. A1.

40 *American Trucking Association PAC statement:* Sabato, p. 136.

40 *Defense contributions and percentages:* Calculated from Library printout of April 4, 1991, House Financial Disclosure Reports for 1989, and Congressional Yellow Book, Fall 1990.

40 *PAC names:* FEC 933 Index (1989–1990).

40 *Pelican PAC and energy industry:* U.S. Public Interest Research Group report, *Abuse of Power: Energy Industry Money & the Johnston-Wallop Energy Package*, October 23, 1991.

41 *Monthly milk checkoff:* Michael McMenamin and Walter McNamara,

Milking the Public: Political Scandals of the Dairy Lobby from LBJ to Jimmy Carter (Chicago: Nelson-Hall, 1980), p. 45.

41 *(a) Dairy cooperatives 1984 PAC receipts:* FEC Blue Book, Vol. IV, 1983–84, pp. 410, 416. (b) *number of contributing members:* Information provided via phone interview with representatives of the three principal dairy cooperatives.

41–42 *Sabato findings; average gifts to corporate, trade, and labor PACs:* Sabato, p. 59.

42 *How PACs decide:* Sabato, p. 38.

42 *Lack of hard statistical data:* Letters from Herbert Alexander to author, February 8, 1991 and November 5, 1991.

42 *Sorauf quote:* Sorauf, "PACs in the American Political System," background paper, Twentieth Century Fund, Task Force on Political Action Committees, 1984, pp. 82–83.

42 *PAC gifts to incumbents increased by thirteen percent:* (a) *1983:* FEC press release, November 29, 1983. (b) *1990:* FEC press release February 22, 1991.

43 *Incumbent reelection rates since 1958:* POA, p. 13.

43 *1990 PAC contributions to banking committee members:* Library study.

43 *Business, corporate, labor and ideological PAC giving to incumbents in 1990:* calculated from FEC press release, March 31, 1991. *Rise since 1986:* FEC press release, May 21, 1987.

43–44 *Eagleton quote:* Interview with author, April 21, 1987.

45 *Table: Number of PACs* (a) *1974–1986:* FEC press release, July 10, 1987. (b) *1990:* FEC press release, March 31, 1991.

45 *Table: PAC gifts to candidates:* (a) *1974:* CRS 87–469, p. 36. (b) *1976–1986:* FEC release, May 21, 1987. (c) *1990:* FEC release, February 22, 1991.

45–46 *CRP survey data: New York Times,* December 30, 1987.

46 *Boschwitz and the CSMA: The Nation,* July 17, 1989, p. 84.

46 *Hatch and the HIMA: The Nation,* July 17, 1989, p. 85.

46–47 *Utilities industry and the Dorgan amendment: Wall Street Journal,* July 13, 1989.

48–49 *Details of the rise and fall of the product-liability bill: Wall Street Journal,* June 21, 1990, p. A16.

49 *Proxmire quote:* Senate debate on Boren-Goldwater amendment to establish aggregate limits on total PAC gifts which a candidate may accept, August 11, 1986.

49 *1990 Business v. labor PAC contributions:* calculated from FEC press release, March 31, 1991.

49–50 *Early history of PACs:* Sabato, pp. 3–10.

50 *Rostenkowski's first campaign: Wall Street Journal,* July 18, 1986.

50 *Insurance company contribution to Roosevelt:* Robert Mutch, *Campaigns, Congress, and Courts: The Making of Federal Campaign Finance Law* (New York: Praeger, 1988), pp. 2–3.

50 *Hemenway and Hackler statements:* Quoted in Sabato, p. 4.

51 *1988 PAC administrative costs:* Herbert Alexander and Monica Bauer, *Financing the 1988 Election* (Boulder, CO: Westview Press, 1991), p. 3.

51 *1974 amendments to FECA:* 88 Stat. 1263 (1974); Public Law 93–443.

51 *Cohen comments:* Interview with author.

51–52 *Business v. labor contributions:* (a) *1978:* CRS 87–469, p. 36. (b) *1990:* calculated from FEC press release, March 31, 1991.

52 *Growth in numbers of PACs and their contributions:* Number of PACs (a) *1974–1986:* FEC press release, July 10, 1987. (b) *1990:* FEC press release, March 31, 1991. *PAC gifts to candidates:* (a) *1974:* CRS 87–469, p. 36. (b) *1976–1986:* FEC release, May 21, 1987. (c) *1990:* FEC release, February 22, 1991.

52 *Decline in small contributions:* Richard P. Conlon, "The Declining Role of Individual Contributions in Financing Congressional Campaigns," *Journal of Law and Politics,* Winter 1987, p. 468.

52–53 *Percentage of House dependent on PACs for one-third of the receipts:* calculated from 1992 PIA.

53 *Table, average cost of a winning campaign for House and Senate:* (a) *1978–1986:* CRS 87–469, p. 53. (b) *1990:* 1990 POA.

53 *1990 dependency on PACs:* calculated from 1992 PIA.

53 *Table: House winners taking at least half their funds from PACs:* (a) *1978–1984:* CC release, April 7, 1987. (b) *1986:* calculated from 1987 PIA. (c) *1988:* Library study. (d) *1990:* calculated from 1992 PIA.

54 *House winners dependent on PACs for a least thirty percent:* (a) 1974–1982: CRP, *Money and Politics: Campaign Spending Out of Control,* 1985, p. 12. (b) 1986: calculated from 1987 PIA. (c) 1990: calculated from 1992 PIA.

Chapter 3

55–56 *GE giving to unopposed and sure winners:* calculated from 1990 FEC D-Index for GE PAC activity, FEC press release of February 22, 1991, and 1989 PIA.

56 *GE contributions compared to Chamber of Commerce approval ratings:*

calculated from 1990 FEC D-Index for GE PAC activity, and 1989 PIA, pp. 723 and 752.

56 *GE contributions to opposing candidates in Senate:* calculated from 1990 FEC D-Index for GE PAC activity, and FEC press release of February 22, 1991.

56–57 *Post-election switching in 1986:* CC press release, October 17, 1987.

56 *PACs gave $13.2 million to those without major-party opposition in 1990:* cited in *Harper's* magazine, August 1991, p. 11. Originally from CC.

56 *$26.4 million to incumbents who had won an average of 75 percent of the vote over the previous two elections:* calculated from FEC press release, February 22, 1991 and 1989 PIA.

57 *FEC post-election switches in North Dakota:* CC release, May 20, 1987.

57 *1988 post-election PAC contributions:* CC release, May 9, 1989.

57–58 *GE's incumbent favoritism in 1990 House elections:* calculated from FEC D index for 1990 GE PAC activity and FEC press release, February 22, 1991.

58 *GE's 1990 contributions to Senate candidates:* calculated from FEC D-index for 1990 GE PAC activity.

58 *One-third of all PACs gave at least 80 percent to incumbents in 1986:* CC release, September 4, 1987.

59–60 *Dingell's election percentages and 1990 PAC receipts:* 1992 PIA, p. 769.

60 *Increase in PAC favoritism of incumbents:* (a) *1978:* FEC press release, June 29, 1979; (b) *1982:* FEC press release, November 29, 1983; (c) *1986:* June 21, 1987; (d) *1990:* FEC press release February 22, 1991.

60 *Incumbent reelection figures:* (a) *1974–1986:* CQ Weekly Report, November 15, 1986, p. 2891. (b) *1990:* figures from CC, December 1990.

61 *"Congressman-for-Life" statement: Wall Street Journal,* December 4, 1986.

61 *Average campaign treasury balances:* Author's calculation from FEC press release, November 2, 1990.

62 *Goldwater statement: Washington Post,* November 4, 1986.

63 *United Technologies PAC solicitation:* Findings of Fact and Constitutional Questions for Certification under 2 USC S.437(h), finding 19, p. 14, *International Association of Machinists and Aerospace Workers v. FEC,* Civil Action No. 80–0354.

63 *General Dynamic's (GD) 1990 contributions to members of House committees regulating defense spending:* calculated from FEC D-index for GD's

PAC activity in 1990 cycle and 1989 and 1990 Congressional Yellow Books.

63 *Dickinson receipts from defense contractors:* Library calculation.

64 *Murtha's receipts from defense contractors:* Library calculation.

64 *Wall Street PACs and individual contributions to D'Amato: Wall Street Journal,* September 25, 1986.

64–65 *Paul Houston statement: Los Angeles Times,* August 7, 1984, p. 10.

65 *Dow, USX contributions to Dole:* (a) *From Dow and USX PACs:* Dole FEC E-index, 1985–86, (b) *From individuals connected to Dow and USX:* calculation based on FEC data on individual contributions to the "Dole for Senate" committee.

65 *1990 Gallo contributions:* CA study, 5/91.

65–66 *Facts on "Gallo Amendment": Wall Street Journal,* October 31, 1985, p. 81.

66 *1986 Gallo family contributions to Campaign America:* Campaign America FEC disclosure report, April 1986.

67 *Table on law firm PACs:* based on FEC D-Indices for firms in table, 1979–80 and 1989–90.

68 *Convington and Burling does not have PAC:* confirmed with telephone call to Jan Flack, staff member, January 27, 1992.

67–68 *Akin-Gump example:* Confidential interview with author.

70 *NADA PAC contributions:* (a) *For 1972 and 1976:* CC, Campaign Monitoring Project, "Federal Campaign Finances." (b) *For 1980:* 1980 FEC Blue Book, Vol. IV, p. D30.

70 *NADA's contributions to Edwards:* Edwards' FEC E-Indices for 1979–80 and 1981–82.

71 *Table matching NADA contributions to pro-NADA votes:* Based on vote recorded in *Cong. Rec.,* May 26, 1982, pp. H2882–83; and contributions recorded in FEC D-indices for NADA PAC, 1979–80 and 1981–82.

71 *Sabato on impact of NADA contributions:* Sabato, p. 134.

71 *Used-car vote:* (a) Senate: 1982 *CQ Almanac,* p. 24-S. (b) House: *Cong. Rec.,* May 26, 1982, pp. H2882–83.

72 *NADA rewarded its friends:* Sabato, p. 134.

72 *Congressman's statement on used-car vote:* Drew, p. 78.

73 *Billboards removed and erected:* GAO Report No. RCED–85–34, *The Outdoor Advertising Control Problem Needs to Be Reassessed,* January 3, 1985. (Data from 45 states.)

73 *Billboard industry income swelled: Reader's Digest,* June 1985, p. 4.

73 *Stafford statement: Cong. Rec.,* February 3, 1987, p. S1544.

73–74 *Background on billboard regulations:* GAO Report, January 3, 1985; also GAO Report No. CED–78–38, *Obstacles to Billboard Removal,* March 27, 1978. See also *Readers Digest,* June 1985; and Dept. of Transportation Report No. R4-FH–4–158, *Report on Highway Beautification Program Federal Highway Administration,* August 31, 1984.

74 *Changes to Highway Beautification Act, 1978:* Incorporated in 1985 highway bill (H.R. 11733, Public Law 95–599). See also House Public Works Committee Report (H. Rep. 95–1485).

74 *Additional costs of 1978 amendment:* GAO Report, January 3, 1985, p. 22.

74 *Billboard removal expenditures, 1984:* GAO Report, January 3, 1985, Appendix I.

74 *"Unzoned commercial zone" loophole:* Department of Transportation Report, August 31, 1984, p. 6, Exhibit A1, pp. 11, 14.

75 *Number of billboards erected:* GAO Report, January 3, 1985, p. 16.

75 *Billboard vs. used-car industry sales:* (a) *used-car sales:* Motor Vehicle Manufacturers Assoc., *Facts and Figures '87,* p. 60. (b) *billboard industry: National Journal,* Aug. 9, 1986, p. 1978.

75 *Billboard and auto-dealer PAC contributions:* (a) billboard industry PACs for 1990: Library analysis. (b) NADA PAC: FEC D-index, 1990.

76 *Billboard PAC contributions to Howard:* Howard's FEC E Indices for 1978–86.

76 *Contributions to Howard from individuals connected with billboard industry:* Drawn from Howard's FEC reports, for the 1985–86 election cycle.

76 *Clark family 1990 contributions:* Library analysis.

76 *Clark family contributions to Howard:* (a) *1982–1986:* WOL; (b) *1988:* Library analysis.

76–77 *1985 OAAA convention and honoraria: Washington Post,* 9/14/86; see also *CC Magazine,* Sheila Kaplan, September/October 1986.

77–00 *Congressional aides at OAAA convention: National Journal,* February 1, 1986, p. 274.

78 *Committee's approval of "sweeping change": Washington Post,* August 10, 1982.

78 *OAAA honoraria to Public Works Committee members; Howard Kurtz comment: Washington Post,* August 10, 1982.

78 *Billboard industry contributions to Shuster:* Library analysis.

78 *Billboard industry honoraria and junkets to Shuster:* Shuster's Financial Disclosure Reports, 1987, 1988 and 1989.

78–79 *Billboard Reform vote:* Roll call no. 15, *Cong. Rec.*, February 3, 1987, p. S1554.

79 *Graham turnaround:* (a) *staff reaction:* McMahon, interview with author. (b) *Senate floor vote: Cong. Rec.*, February 3, 1987, p. S1554.

79–80 *OAAA fundraising parties:* Report of Receipts and Disbursements, OAAA PAC. (a) *Mikulski:* quarterly report, April 15, 1987. (b) *Reid:* FEC report filed October 23, 1986.

80 *Brock Adams turnabout: Washington Post*, February 24, 1987, p. A19.

80 *Billboard industry contributions to Adams:* Adams' FEC E Index for 1985–86; data on individual contributions from WOL.

80 *Top industries in 1985 congressional honoraria:* Common Cause press release, June 25, 1986, p. 2.

80 *Defense and tobacco industry annual sales:* (a) *Defense contractors:* "100 Companies Receiving the Largest Dollar Volume of Prime Contract Awards, FY 1986." and "500 Contractors Receiving the Largest Dollar Volume of Prime Contract Awards for Research, Development, Test, and Evaluation, FY 1986," Dept. of Defense, Washington Headquarters Services, Directorate for Information Operations and Reports. (b) *Tobacco sales:* "Tobacco Industry Profile for 1986," Tobacco Institute, Washington, D.C.

80 *Roadside Business Association (RBA) appeal:* RBA memo, May 3, 1979, from William V. Reynolds to all RBA members.

81–82 *McMahon comments:* Interview with author, May 27, 1987.

Chapter 4

83 *Vacarro case:* 409 NYS 2d 1009 (1977).

84 *Energy and commerce interest PAC contributions to Dingell:* Library analysis.

84 *Defense contractor PAC contributions to Dickinson:* Library analysis.

79–80 *Statistics on Flippo:* (a) *PAC receipts:* For 1978: 1978 FEC Blue Book. For 1986: 1987 PIA, p. 27. For 1988: 1989 PIA, p. 27. (b) *Election percentages:* 1989 PIA, p. 27. (c) *Leftover cash:* 1978–84: FEC Blue Books from respective cycles. 1986: CC press release, April 7, 1987. 1988: CC press release, March 28, 1989.

87 *Retirement account transfers:* CPI Study, *Saving For A Rainy Day*, March, 1991.

87 *Swift quote: Atlantic* magazine, February 1992, p. 26.

87 *Campaign surpluses:* (a) *1990:* calculated from FEC press release, February 22, 1991. (b) *1986:* FEC press release, May 10, 1987.

89 *Table of surpluses greater than $100,000:* (a) *1976–84:* calculated from FEC Blue Books, 1976–84. (b) *1986:* calculated from CC press release, April 7, 1987. (c) *1988:* calculated from CC press release, March 28, 1989. (d) *1990:* calculated from FEC press release, February 22, 1991.

87–88 *Moore statistics:* (a) *Cash surplus from 1982 campaign:* Moore's FEC report, February 3, 1984. (b) *Statement on appropriateness of use of 1982 surplus for 1984 campaign:* Moore's televised comments in response to a Citizens Against PACs ad published in the *Baton Rouge Times-Advocate*, May 1, 1984. (c) *1984 surplus:* FEC press release, May 10, 1987.

88 *Gramm fundraiser: Washington Post*, September 26, 1990, p. A23.

88 *Gramm and Nunn's surpluses:* FEC press release, February 22, 1991.

88 *Gramm's 1996 reelection fund:* phone call to Gramm's Dallas office.

88–89 *Statistics on D'Amato:* (a) *Cash surpluses:* FEC year-end reports, for 1981–1985, committees including *D'Amato in 86* and *Friends of Senator D'Amato*; for 1985: *D'Amato for Senate*. (b) *History of 1980 race:* 1987 PIA.

89 *Holtzman declines to run: New York Times*, November 16, 1985.

89 *Dyson-Green contest: Wall Street Journal*, September 25, 1986.

90 *Contributions from Wall Street interests to D'Amato: Wall Street Journal*, September 25, 1986.

90 *Armstrong statement:* Interview on National Public Radio *Weekend Edition*, October 11, 1986.

90 *Abnor invitation: Washington Post*, November 31, 1985, p. A3.

91 *Aspin and defense contractors:* (a) *Statement on defense contractors: Racine Journal Times*, January 27, 1986. (b) *Defense PAC contributions:* 1979–84: FEC D Indices for defense industry PACs. During Aspin's first ten months as chairman: FEC E Index, *Friends of Les Aspin* committee, 1985–86.

92 *Cowtown Jamboree statistics:* Letter from Representative Wright to Whitney North Seymour, Jr., March 11, 1986.

92 *Contributions from Wright's PAC:* FEC D Index, *Majority Congress Committee*, 1985–86.

92–93 *Waxman's PAC: PAC Almanac*, p. 363.

92 *Waxman's reelection percentages:* 1992 PIA, p. 173.

93 *Simon's 1984 receipts:* 1983–84 FEC Blue Book, pp. 168–169.

93–94 *Statements on fundraising and on forming his PAC:* conversations with author.

93 *Percy's expenditures:* 1987 PIA, p. 414.

94–95 *Statistics on Bingaman:* (a) *personal loan:* Bingaman FEC year-end reports for 1981 and 1982. (b) *AMA contributions:* FEC D Index for AMA PAC 1981–82. (c) *Response to Citizens Against PACs:* Telephone conversation between Bingaman and Whitney North Seymour, Jr., co-chair, Citizens Against PACs., January 1984.

95 *Debts of incoming first-year representatives: CC Magazine,* March/April 1991, pp. 14–17.

95–97 (a) *Kuntz story of Sanford's loan;* (b) *Sanford's PAC receipts;* (c) *McConnell and Boren quotes: CQ Weekly,* July 6, 1991, pp. 1813–1818.

97 *Franks fundraising invitation: CC Magazine,* March/April 1991, p. 16.

98 *Kastenmeier subcommittee example:* Conversation with author.

98 *Matsui quote: CQ Weekly,* September 14, 1985, p. 1806.

98 *Hance's PAC receipts increase:* (a) *1980:* 1979–80 FEC Blue Book, p. 4343. (b) *1982:* 1981–1982 FEC Blue Book, p. 120.

99 *Anthony's PAC receipts increase:* (a) *1980:* 1979–80 FEC Blue Book, p. 164. (b) *1982:* 1981–1982 FEC Blue Book, p. 120.

99 *Statistics on Guarini:* (a) *1982 campaign funds:* 1981–82 FEC Blue Book, p. 246. (b) *Breakfast series: Los Angeles Times,* May 20, 1985. (c) *1984 PAC receipts:* 1984 FEC Blue Book, p. 249.

100–102 *Statistics on Flippo:* (a) *PAC contributions from interest groups:* Flippo's FEC E Index, 1985–86. (b) *Flippo amendment for banks: Washington Post,* October 16, 1985. (c) *Two-thirds of Flippo funds from PACs:* 1987 PIA. (d) *Out-of-district individual contributors:* Calculation by author based on WOL data.

103 *Percentage of Exon and Coyne's funds from PACs:* 1990 POA.

103 *ABA contributions to banking committee; Houston's observations: Los Angeles Times,* August 7, 1984.

103–104 *Statistics on Morrison:* (a) *History of 1982 election:* 1986 PIA, pp. 268–70. (b) *Telephone bill's beneficiaries; business PAC money in 1982 and mid–1984; statement on "standard practice": Los Angeles Times,* August 7, 1984. According to the *Times* article, J.C. Penney benefitted from a provision in the bill approved by the Banking Committee that allowed three companies, including J.C. Penney, to continue offering banking services for an additional six months beyond the cut-off date for other nonbank institutions. (c) *$21,000 by 1984 election:* Author's calculations based on FEC reports. (d) *1982 PAC receipts:* 1982 FEC Blue Book, p. 152. (e) *1984 campaign finances:* 1984 FEC Blue Book, pp. 152–153.

105 *Denardis' 1984 expenditures:* 1984 FEC Blue Book, p. 152.

106 *Statistics on Schneider:* (a) *1984 and 1986 PAC receipts:* 1987 PIA, p. 1362. (b) *Seeks interest group money:* Interview with author, October 29, 1987.

106 *Statistics on Boxer:* (a) *1984 and 1986 PAC receipts:* 1987 PIA, p. 108. (b) *Statements on war-chest and defense contractor money:* Interview with author, November 4, 1987.

107 *Dole statement on PAC expectations: Wall Street Journal,* July 1982, from CC compilation of Dole statements.

107 *Dole PAC receipts:* (a) *1972–86: New York Times,* August 10, 1987. (b) *1987–1990:* Library analysis.

107 *Dole 1986 PAC receipts and left-over cash:* FEC press release, May 10, 1987, pp. 15, 24.

107 *MacDonald's fundraising:* Guy MacDonald did not file any reports with the FEC on his 1986 campaign, which he could legally avoid only if he raised or spent less than $5,000 (2 USC Sec. 431[2]).

108 *Dole PAC contributions from interest groups:* Dole FEC E Index, 1985–86.

108–109 *Dole's 1986 individual and PAC receipts:* FEC press release, May 10, 1987, p. 24.

109 *Campaign America fundraising history:* (a) *1977–84:* FEC Blue Books for respective election cycles, Vol. IV. (b) *1985–86:* Campaign America FEC reports, January 31, 1986, and January 26, 1987.

109 *Gallo contributions:* (a) *1986:* Campaign America FEC monthly report, April, 1986. (b) *1989–90:* Library analysis.

110 *Contributions to Dole Foundation:* Dole Foundation 1985 tax form 990 (fiscal year July 1, 1985 to June 30, 1986).

110 *Kemp foundation refuses disclosure: Buffalo News,* June 15, 1986.

110 *Strange statement:* Letter to author from Jackie A. Strange, president and CEO of the Dole Foundation, August 11, 1987.

110 *Kemp foundation outlays:* CRP Foundations Report, p. 24.

111 *Dole Foundation financial data:* Dole Foundation 1985 tax form 990.

111 *RJR honorarium and jet ride for Dole:* Corn, p. 398.

111 *Top Honoraria recipient:* (a) *1981–1982:* CC press release, May 15, 1984. (b) *1983:* CC press release, May 18, 1984. (c) *1984:* CC press release, May 24, 1985. (d) *1985:* CC press release, May 20, 1986. (e) *1986:* CC press release, May 20, 1987.

111 *Dole honoraria:* (a) *1978–84: Kansas City Star,* August 20, 1985. (b) *1985–86:* Dole disclosure statements, 1985, 1986.

112 *Dole "multiple giver" table:* (a) *Dole Senate Reelection committee:* Dole FEC E Index, 1985–86. (b) *Campaign America:* FEC G Index, Cam-

paign America, 1985–86. (c) *Dole Foundation:* Dole Foundation 1985 tax form 990. (d) *Honoraria:* Dole disclosure statements, 1985, 1986.

113 *Dole's connections to ADM:* (a) Contributions by ADM PAC, Andreas, and Andreas' family: *Kansas City Star,* August 20, 1985. (b) *Donations to Dole foundation: Wall Street Journal,* September 28, 1990. (c) *Honoraria:* Dole disclosure reports, 1982, 1983. (d) *Corporate plane rides:* Dole disclosure report, 1983. (e) *Radio debates:* Cost of show shared equally by ADM and Mobil, each paying $500 per broadcast, $250 each to Dole and Kennedy. (f) *Bal Harbour apartment:* Martin Tolchin and Jeff Gerth, "The Contradictions of Bob Dole," *New York Times Magazine,* November 8, 1987.

113 *Dole's PAC receipts since 1972:* (a) *1972–86: New York Times,* August 10, 1987. (b) *1987–1990:* Library printout.

114 *Individual donations:* (a) *To Dole senatorial committee:* Dole FEC reports, January 31, 1986, January 28, 1987. (b) *To Campaign America:* Campaign America FEC reports, January 31, 1986, January 26, 1987.

114 *Total honoraria:* (a) *1978–1984: Kansas City Star,* August 20, 1985. (b) *1985–1986:* Dole disclosure statements, 1985, 1986.

114 *Dole Foundation receipts:* Dole 1985 tax form 990.

114–115 *Frenzel-Crane provision:* Sheila Kaplan, "A Sweet Deal," *CC Magazine,* May/June 1986, p. 29.

115 *Dole and tax loopholes: Wall Street Journal,* September 28, 1990.

115–116 *Facts on tobacco subsidy:* Corn, pp. 381–99.

116 *Tobacco contributions:* (a) *To Dole senatorial campaign:* Dole FEC E Index 1985–86. (b) *To Dole foundation:* Dole Foundation 1985 tax form 990. (c) *Dole honoraria:* Dole disclosure report, 1983. (d) *U.S. Tobacco jet: Newsday,* September 17, 1987.

117 *Commodity traders:* Graves and Norrgard, pp. 20–31.

117–118 *Subsidy for gasohol; Dole response to Michael Isikoff:* Fumento, pp. 32–38.

119 *Dole votes against PAC bill:* Roll call no. 209, *Cong. Rec.,* August 12, 1986, p. S11311.

119 *Dole statements, filibuster votes:* CC press release, December 2, 1987.

120–121 *Specific PAC contributions to Anderson:* Library analysis.

122 *Four out of five dollars from outside Anderson's district:* Author's calculation based on Library printout.

122 *1988 and 1990 PAC totals and PAC percent:* Library analysis.

123 *Election percentages and 1990 campaign spending:* 1992 PIA, p. 196.

123 *1988 and 1990 PAC conflict total and from specific industries:* Author's calculation based on Library analysis.

123 *1988 and 1990 contributions from interested individuals:* Author's calculation based on Library printout.

125 *American Bus Association contributions to Howard:* (a) *PAC money:* Howard FEC E Indices, 1981–86. (b) *Puerto Rico trips and honoraria:* Howard disclosure statements, 1981–86.

125 *Table on special interest contributions and trips:* (a) *Honoraria and trips:* Howard disclosure statements, 1981–86. (b) *PAC receipts:* Howard FEC E Indices, 1981–86.

126–127 *Billboard money to Howard from individuals:* Identified by Edward McMahon, executive director of Scenic America, based on Howard FEC reports 1985–86.

127–128 *Out-of-state contributions to Howard:* Author's calculations based on Howard FEC reports for 1985 and 1986.

Chapter 5

Introductions: Material for background introductions drawn largely from 1986 and 1987 PIA.

130–132 *Barnes comments:* Interview with author, March 27, 1987.

132–134 *Moffett comments:* Interview with author, August 8, 1987.

135–136 *Mathias comments:* Interview with author, May 21, 1987.

136 *Boren-Goldwater measure:* Amendment 2690 to S. 655, 99th Cong., 2nd Session, roll call no. 209, *Cong. Rec.*, August 12, 1986, p. S11311.

136–137 *Goldwater comments:* Interview with author, September 23, 1987.

138–140 *Eagleton comments:* Interview with author, April 21, 1987.

141 *Conrad comments:* Interview with author, April 21, 1987.

141–142 *Schneider's previous campaign finances and election percentages:* 1978: FEC Blue Book, 1900–78. 1980: FEC Blue Book, 1900–80. 1986: 1988 *PIA*. 1988: 1990 *PIA*.

142–143 *Schneider comments:* Interview with author, October 19, 1987.

144 *Synar previous campaign finances:* 1984: 1986 *PIA*. 1986: 1988 *PIA*.

144–145 *Synar comments:* Interview with author, July 1987.

145 *Synar-Leach campaign reform bill:* H.R. 3799, 99th Cong., 1st Session.

145–146 *Leach comments:* Interview with author, May 5, 1987.

147–148 *Edgar comments:* Interview with author, April 6, 1987.

149 *Chiles comments:* Interview with author, September 22, 1987.
150 *Railsback comments:* Interview with author, March 24, 1987.

Chapter 6

152 *Machinists 1990 PAC contributions:* FEC D Index, 1989–1990.
151–155 *Holayter interview:* Interview with author, July 30, 1987.
153 *Machinist PAC gift to Conyers:* Machinists FEC D Index, 1989–1990. *Conyer's average reelection percentage:* 1992 PIA.
155–159 *Hall interview:* Interview with author, November 5, 1991.
155 *1990 contributions by Ford to candidates:* Ford FEC D Index, 1989–90.
157 *Ford contributions to "shoo-ins" and incumbents v. challengers:* Author's calculation based on Ford FEC D Index, 1989–90.
157 *Ford contribution to John Dingell:* Ford FEC D Index, 1989–90.
157 *Dingell's election percentages:* 1992 PIA.
157 *Funds raised by Dingell's 1990 opponents:* FEC press release, February 22, 1991.
158 *Ford contributions to McDade:* Ford FEC D Index, 1989–90.
159–160 *Issacs interview:* Interview with author, August 12, 1987.
159 *Council for a Livable World 1990 receipts and contributions:* FEC press release, March 31, 1991; Council for a Livable World FEC D Index, 1989–90.
160–164 *Frank Vacca interview:* Interview with author, August 10, 1987.
161 *Dairy PACs: 1990 contributions; Number of candidates helped by dairy PACs:* FEC D Indexes, 1989–90, for principal dairy PACs.
161 *Dairymen, Inc. PAC participation rate:* Provided by James H. Sumner, Director of Corporate Communications, Dairymen, Inc.
163 *Mid-America contributions to easy winners:* Calculations by author based on Mid-America FEC D Index, 1989–1990.

Chapter 7

166 *Number of dairy farmers:* U.S. Census Bureau, 1982 Census of Agriculture, Table 11, p. 218.
166 *Dairy vote: Cong. Rec.*, September 26, 1985, p. H7857.
166 *Dairy cost estimates:* Provided in "Dear Colleague" letter, Representative Jim Olin (D-VA), September 18, 1985. See also letter from Rudolph G. Penner, director of CBO, to Representative Robert Michel, September 5, 1985; USDA, Office of Public Liaison, "USDA Backgrounders: 1985 Farm Bill," September 1985; and letter from

John W. Bode, assistant secretary for food and consumer services, USDA, to Representative E. (Kika) de la Garza, September 3, 1985.

166 *Table matching dairy money to pro-dairy votes:* House vote in *Cong. Rec.*, September 26, 1985, p. H7857; and dairy-cooperative contributions from FEC Combined D Indices for the three principal dairy PACs, 1979–86.

167 *Sugar subsidy cost of $3 billion annually:* "United States Sugar Policy: An Analysis," prepared by Ralph Ives and John Hurley, U.S. Department of Commerce, International Trade Administration, April, 1988, cited in CPI Report, *Short-changed*.

167 *Number of sugar-producing states and districts:* Based on information provided by the Economic Research Service, Sugar and Sweetener Division, USDA.

168 *12,000 sugar producers:* USDA, "Sugar," Agriculture Information Bulletin, No. 478, September 1984, pp. 4, 6. See also Economic Report of the President, February 1986, p. 138.

168 *Comparative sugar prices:* Statement of Nicholas Kominus, U.S. Cane Sugar Refiners' Association, before the Senate Committee on Agriculture, Nutrition and Forestry, April 2, 1985, citing USDA statistics. See also Rep. Gradison's statement, *Cong. Rec.*, September 26, 1985, p. H7820.

168 *Comparative commodity profit rates:* See statement of U.S. Cane Sugar Refiners' Association, before the Senate Committee on Agriculture, Nutrition and Forestry, April 2, 1985. See also *Cong. Rec.*, September 26, 1985, p. H7817.

168 *Cost of $41 per household per year:* See Allen R. Ferguson, "The Sugar Price Support Program," prepared for the U.S. Cane Sugar Refiners' Association, June 1985. Mr. Ferguson is with the Economists' Committee on Public Policy in Washington, D.C.

168–169 *Hawaii and Florida's sugar crop:* See Rep. Gradison's statement, Cong. Rec., September 26, 1985, p. H7826.

169 *History of Fanjul brothers:* Sheila Kaplan, "A Sweet Deal," *CC Magazine*, May/June 1986, p. 27.

169 *Fanjul family political contributions: Wall Street Journal*, July 29, 1991.

169 *Growth of number of sugar PACs and their contributions:* (a) *From 1980 to 1984: CC Magazine*, May/June, 1986. (b) *From 1985 to 1990:* July 1991 study by Public Voice (a non-profit research organization that examines food policy issues).

169 *Corn sweetener 1984 sales:* PAC Almanac, pp. 16, 35, 152.

169–170 *Sugar and corn-sweetener industry contributions to Congress in 1983–1985: CC Magazine*, May/June 1986.

170 *1985 Sugar subsidy vote:* Cong. Rec., September 26, 1985, p.H7829.

170 *Table matching sugar contributions with pro-sugar votes:* From House vote in Cong. Record, September 26, 1985, p. H7829, and FEC data on sugar industry PACs for January 1983-March 1986, as provided in Public Voice Report, "How Sweet It Is," September 1986.

170 *1990 market prices for sugar: Wall Street Journal*, July 29, 1991.

171 *1990 Sugar subsidy vote:* CPI Report, *Short-changed*, p. 5.

171 *Table matching sugar contributions with pro-sugar votes:* CPI Report, *Short-changed*, p. 6.

171–172 *Dairy subsidy costs:* Provided in "Dear Colleague" letter, Representative Jim Olin (D-VA), September 18, 1985. See also letter from Rudolph G. Penner, director of CBO, to Representative Robert Michel, September 5, 1985; USDA, Office of Public Liaison, "USDA Backgrounders: 1985 Farm Bill," September 1985; and letter from John Bode, Assistant Secretary for Food and Consumer services, USDA, to Representative E. (Kika) de la Garza, September 3, 1985.

172 *Number of dairy farmers:* U.S. Census Bureau, 1982 Census of Agriculture, Table 11, p. 218.

172 *Dairy PAC collection method:* Michael McMenamin and Walter McNamara, *Milking the Public: Political Scandals of the Dairy Lobby from LBJ to Jimmy Carter* (Chicago: Nelson-Hall, 1980), p. 45.

172 (a) *1984 dairy coops' combined kitty:* 1984 Blue Books, Vol. IV, pp. 409–15. (b) *Number of recipients:* FEC Combined D Index for dairy PACs.

172 *Number of dairy cows in Frost's district:* Furnished by Mark Orrin in Rep. Frost's Grand Prairie field office, the Texas Department of Agriculture, Milk Division; and the Dairy Herd Improvement Association.

172 *Dairy PAC contributions to Frost and other representatives:* FEC Combined D Indices for three principal dairy cooperative PACs, 1979–86.

172 *Dairy subsidy vote:* Cong. Rec., September 26, 1985, p. H7857.

172 *Potential fuel efficiency savings of $38 billion:* an estimate prepared by the Energy Information Administration (a division of the U.S. Department of Energy), as referenced in the congressional testimony of Marc Ledbetter of the American Council for an Energy-Efficient Economy, September 15, 1990.

172–174 *Details of the fuel efficiency standards debate, industry contributions and final vote:* CPI Report, *Short-changed*, pp. 8–9.

174 *Cost of tobacco subsidy:* Figures calculated by the Congressional Research Service and the U.S. Department of Agriculture as cited in *CC Magazine*, March/April 1991, p. 9.

174–175 *Details of tobacco subsidy debate, industry contributions and final vote:* CPI Report, *Short-changed*, pp. 20–21.

175 *1979 Hospital cost consumer savings estimate:* Hospital cost containment, presidential letter of transmittal, March 7, 1979, H. Doc. No. 96–68, p. III.

175–176 *Hospital cost containment debate: Money Talks*, p. 12; *AMA opposing arguments:* 1979 CQ Almanac, p. 513.

175 *1990 AMA PAC contributions:* FEC press release, March 31, 1991, p. 11.

175 *1978 Commerce committee vote:* June 18, 1978 vote, cited in *Money Talks*, p. 13.

176 *1979 Hospital cost containment vote:* 1979 CQ Almanac, p. 176-H.

176 *Table matching AMA money with pro-AMA votes:* From 1979 CQ Almanac, p. 176-H; and FEC D Indices for AMA PAC, 1977–80.

177 *Footnote on Keating:* CPI Report, *Short-changed*, pp. 16–19.

Chapter 8

178 *Russell Long statement: Money Talks*, p. 17.

178 *Brewster case:* 506 F.2d 62 (1974).

179 *Bribery statute:* 18 U.S.C.A. 201 (b)(2).

179–180 *Oshkosh truck example: The Dallas Morning News*, June 10, 1988, pp. 1, 5.

180–182 *Aleutian Enterprise and Rep. Miller story: Wall Street Journal*, April 10, 1991, p. A24.

182–184 *Dole/Rostenkowski deal:* Graves and Norrgard, pp. 20–31.

184 *Vote on Stafford amendment:* Motion to table Stafford Amendment No. 13 to Federal Highway Act of 1987, roll call 15, Cong. Rec., February 3, 1987, p. S1554.

184–185 *Brock Adams:* (a) *Statements on billboard compensation: Washington Post*, February 24, 1987, p. A–19. (b) *Billboard industry contributions:* PAC receipts from Adams' FEC E Index, 1985–86, and individual receipts from FEC data for 1985–86 provided by WOL.

185–186 *Facts on cost-disclosure law; defense contributions to Quayle: Wall Street Journal,* June 30, 1986, p. 48.

185 *Defense honoraria to Quayle:* Quayle disclosure statements, 1984 and 1985.

186 *Facts on Spector's relationship with Dravo Corporation:* (a) *Facts on Dravo:* "A Case of Rank v. Privilege: How a Senator Helped a Contractor Outflank the Navy," *Time,* September 14, 1987, p. 29. (b) *Dravo contributions:* Dravo-Spector FEC Combined D Index, 1985–86.

186–187 *Addabbo's relationship to Avco:* (a) *Addabbo as "prime mover"; tank's gas mileage: Cong. Rec.,* July 20, 1983, p. H5300. (b) *Inadequate engines, deficiencies:* Letter to Representative Norman Dicks from James Ambrose, undersecretary of the Army, June 13, 1983. (c) *Addabbo votes for Avco monopoly: Cong. Rec.,* June 20, 1983, p. H5308. (d)*Bid by competing firm:* Letter to Rep. Addabbo from J.D. Sculley, assistant secretary of the Army for research, development, and acquisition, August 10, 1983. (e)*Avco contributions to Addabbo:* Addabbo's FEC E Index, 1983–84. See also *Wall Street Journal,* October 13, 1983, which first brought the facts to the attention of the public.

187–188 *Drexel Burnham and D'Amato dinner: Wall Street Journal,* September 25, 1986.

188 *Facts on Perot Amendment: Money Talks,* p. 14.

188–189 *Perot Amendment vote: Cong. Rec.,* December 4, 1975, p. 38670.

189 *Wall Street Journal* exposes Perot: *Wall Street Journal,* November 7, 1975.

189 *Barnes statement:* Interview with author, March 27, 1987.

190 *U.S. Court of Appeals statement:* 506 F.2d 62 (1974), p. 81.

190 *New York Times statement:* Cited in Graves and Norrgard, p. 31.

Chapter 9

All facts and statements in Chapter 9 not previously cited were taken from a report published by Public Citizen's Congress Watch, "They Love to Fly . . . And It Shows," by Michael McCauley and Andrew Cohen, released in September 1991. The report analyzed the Financial Disclosure Reports filed by members of the House of Representatives in 1989 and 1990.

Chapter 10

196–197 *Watergate scandals:* J. Anthony Lukas, *Nightmare: the Underside of the Nixon Years* (New York: Viking, 1973), pp. 111–34.

197 *Mott contributions: New York Times*, December 5, 1972.

197 *1972 disclosure requirements:* FECA of 1971, 86 Stat. 3 (1971), Public Law 92–225.

197 *Reform laws:* Revenue Act of 1971 (Public Law 92–178) and Federal Election Campaign Act Amendments of 1974 (Public Law 93–443).

197 *1976 Supreme Court decision: Buckley v. Valeo*, 424 U.S. 1 (1976).

197 *Jackson on "startling resemblance": Wall Street Journal*, July 5, 1984.

198 *"Soft money" reporting requirements: The $43 Million Loophole*, CRP, 1991, p. 10.

198 *Gross comments and early 1900s donations: Washington Post*, September 30, 1991.

198 *Ban on corporate and union contributions: BP*, p. 41.

198 *$45 million in soft money:* "All the President's Donors," *CC Magazine*, March/April 1990, p. 23.

199 *1991 specific "soft money" contributions; 275 "Team 100" members in September 1991: Washington Post*, September 30, 1991.

200 *1978 FEC ruling: BP*, p. 43.

200 *Jackson quote "little by little": BP*, p. 44.

200 *Congressional soft money amendments: BP*, p. 7.

200–201 *Dayton statement: Minneapolis Star and Tribune*, January 17, 1985.

201 *Facts on VIVA '84, Victory Fund '80, and the New Jersey Republican Party:* CRP, *Money and Politics: Soft Money—A Loophole for the '80s*, 1985, pp. 9–10, 14.

201 *Nofziger and Perkins statements:* Drew, p. 106.

202 *Statements by convention guest and Paul Dietrich:* CRP, *Money and Politics: Soft Money—A Loophole for the '80s*, 1985, pp. 9–10, 14.

202 *Supreme Court ruling on independent expenditures: Buckley v. Valeo*, 424 U.S. 1 (1976), p. 79ff.

202 *Jacobs statement: Wall Street Journal*, September 9, 1986.

202 *Stark statement: Oakland Tribune*, October 24, 1986.

203 *AMA 1986 independent expenditures:* AMA FEC D Index, 1985–86.

203 *Stark and Jacobs 1986 election percentages:* 1992 *PIA*.

203 *Statements by Berglund, Lauer, and Skaggs; Armstrong's complaint; Supreme Court finding:* Viveca Novak and Jean Cobb, "The Kindness of Strangers," *CC Magazine*, September/October 1987, pp. 32–37.

203 *AMA independent expenditures in Colorado's 2nd district:* (a) *1984:* 1983–84 FEC Blue Book, Vol. IV, p. 250. (b) *1986:* AMA FEC D Index, 1985–86.

204 *NRA 1984 independent expenditures for Gramm: Wall Street Journal,* September 9, 1986.

204 *1986 independent expenditures by realtors and auto dealers associations:* FEC D Indexes, 1985–86.

204 *Total independent expenditures for 1980 and 1986 congressional elections:* CRS Report No. 87–649.

204–205 *Facts on Goland, NCPAC coordinated independent expenditures: CC Magazine,* September/October 1987, pp. 35–36.

204 *Dolan statement:* Sabato, p. 101.

205 *Auto Dealers and Drivers for Free Trade independent expenditures: CC Magazine,* September/October 1987, pp. 35–36.

206 *Dolan statement:* Sabato, p. 101.

206 *Nofziger statement:* Drew, p. 138.

206 *Evans statement; "Ortega 33" ads; CC Magazine,* September/October 1987, pp. 34–36.

207 *AMA independent expenditures 1988 and 1990:* 1987–88 and 1989–90 FEC D Indices.

207 *Total independent expenditures:* (a) *1988:* FEC press release, October 31, 1989, p. 3. (b) *1990:* FEC press release, March 31, 1991, p. 5.

207–208 *Bundled contributions to Packwood: Wall Street Journal,* October 10, 1985.

208 *Packwood's total 1986 receipts:* FEC press release, May 10, 1987, p. 27.

208–209 *Movie studio executives contributions to Bradley; Eisner fundraiser: Los Angeles Times,* July 30, 1990.

209 *Isaacs statement:* Interview with author, August 12, 1987.

210 *Malcolm statement:* Interview with author.

210 *NRSC bundling:* (a) *Mail appeal: Washington Post,* October 20, 1986, p. A8. (b) *Statements in Atlanta Journal: Atlanta Journal-Constitution,* October 22, 1986, cited in CC press release, "Common Cause Files Complaint with FEC," October 28, 1986, p. 2. (c) *Funds dispensed: Wall Street Journal,* October 24, 1986.

211 *Formation of "Inner Circle" and total 1990 contributions; Canfield statement: Wall Street Journal,* August 27, 1990.

211 *Sabato statement: Los Angeles Times,* July 30, 1990.

211 *Kecks' contribution:* Dole Foundation 1985 tax form 990.

212 *Kemp foundation:* (a) *Outlays on Kemp; limited donor identification: Wall Street Journal,* March 7, 1986. (b) *Ties to Kemp: Buffalo News,* June 15,

1986. (c) *Kemp as "honorary chairman":* CRP Foundations Report, p. 36.

212 *Kemp foundation terminated:* Ibid., p. 36.

213 *Gary Hart appeal: Wall Street Journal,* March 7, 1986.

213 *Babbit, Kennedy, and Bradley foundations:* CRP Foundations Report, pp. 52–53.

213 *CRP finding on increase in number of foundations:* Ibid., p. 3.

213–214 *Cranston and voter registration charities: Wall Street Journal,* March 1, 1990.

214 FEC a "pussy cat": *Wall Street Journal,* October 19, 1987.

214–215 *Cranston/Weinberg anecdote: BP,* p. 3.

215 *Lack of investigators; Shapp anecdote: BP,* pp. 7–8.

215 *FEC prosecution of Brodie: BP,* p. 13.

215–216 *Franklin example: BP,* p. 20–21.

216 *D'Amato contribution: BP,* p. 15.

216 *Gramm example: BP,* pp. 18–19.

216 *Random audits by FEC and their consequences: BP,* p. 30.

216 *Crippling budget cuts: BP,* p. 19.

217–218 *FEC's structural inadequacies: BP,* pp. 23–36.

217 *Stark and Elliott: Wall Street Journal,* June 24, 1987 and October 19, 1987.

218–219 *Inadequacy of FEC enforcement: Wall Street Journal,* October 19, 1987.

219 *Brownstein's statement: National Journal,* December 7, 1985, p. 2828.

219 *Jackson's statement on the erosion of enforcement: Wall Street Journal,* October 19, 1987.

219 *Jackson's Twentieth Century Fund statement: BP,* 72–73.

Chapter 11

220 *Public financing bill statement:* Sec. 1 of S.3242, Senator Richard Neuberger, introduced February 20, 1956.

222 *Presidential public financing:* The Revenue Act of 1971 (Public Law 92–178) provided for public financing of presidential general elections. The 1974 amendments to the FECA (Public Law 93–443) provided public matching grants in presidential primary elections, CRS Report No. 84–107, pp. 85–86, 114.

227 *Comparative returns on equity:* (a) *Broadcast industry: New York Times,* July 1, 1985. (b) *Manufacturing industry:* Economic Report of the President, transmitted to Congress, February 1986, Table B88, p. 355.

227 *TV station market values: New York Times,* July 1, 1985.

227 *1976 Supreme Court ruling: Buckley v. Valeo,* 424 U.S. 1 (1976).

231–232 *$400 million cost estimate:* calculated by Randy Keehler, of the Working Group on Electoral Democracy.

232 *$195.5 million spent on military bands in fiscal 1990: Newsday,* Martin Schram, November 22, 1990.

233 *Laxalt quote: Washington Post,* January 6, 1991, p. C1.

Conclusion

234 *Goldwater statement: Wall Street Journal,* July 18, 1986, p. 85.

234 *Boren statement: Cong. Rec.,* January 6, 1987, p. S109.

234–235 *Average cost of winning 1990 House and Senate campaigns:* 1990 POA.

234–235 *Average amount Representatives must raise per month; Senators must raise per week:* Calculated from 1990 POA.

235 *Funds raised in first six months of 1983 and 1989 by PAC category: PACs & Lobbies,* September 2, 1987; September 6, 1989.

236–237 *Citizens and Politics:* Kettering Foundation, 1991; as cited in *Washington Post,* June 5, 1991; and letter from Edmund (Jerry) Brown to author, September 6, 1991.

236 *Median after-tax income:* letter from Edmund (Jerry) Brown to author, September 6, 1991.

237 *1984 and 1988 survey information:* Research by the University of Michigan Institute for Social Research, as cited in BP, p. 40.

237 *Hollings quote:* Affidavit of Senator Ernest F. Hollings, sworn December 4, 1990.

237 *1987 public financing bill:* S.2, 100th Cong., 1st Session.

237–238 *Reid and Adams statements: Washington Post,* June 14, 1987.

238 *Antwerp zoo "light fence" for birds: Encyclopedia Britannica,* Vol. 19, p. 1162 (1975).

239 *Mondale quote:* letter to author, June 11, 1985.

INDEX